Air War in the Persian Gulf

by

Williamson Murray

The Nautical & Aviation Publishing Company of America
Baltimore, Maryland

Air War
—in·the—
Persian Gulf

Library of Congress Catalog Card Number: 94-34273

ISBN: 1-877853-36-4

Printed in the United States of America

Library of Congress Cataloging-in-Publication Data

Murray, Williamson.
Air War in Persian Gulf / by Williamson Murray.
p. cm
1. Persian Gulf War, 1991—Aerial operations, American.
2. United States. Air Force—History—Persian Gulf War, 1991.
I.Title.
DS79.724.U6M87 1994
956.704'4248—dc20
94-34273
CIP

Dedication

To Colonel Stan Pratt, USMC (Ret), who always gave a damn

and Wayne Woodrow Hayes, student, teacher, and patriot.

Contents

Maps

Acknowledgements

Innumerable people cooperated in the production of this report. Wayne Thompson and Gary Cox helped immeasurably in the research and writing of different sections. In particular, Dave Deptula gave unstintingly of his time to discuss his experiences in the war; Maj. Gens. Buster Glosson and Larry Henry were equally helpful. My colleagues in GWAPS, in particular, Barry Watts, Eliot Cohen, and Thomas Keaney provided support, encouragement, along with reading and honestly criticizing numerous drafts of this report. Lt. Col. Robert Eskridge of GWAPS and Maj. Mike Nichols of Checkmate were also very helpful in explaining crucial elements of the air campaign and its operations. Without the support of the Naval War College in giving me a Secretary of the Navy Fellowship for the 1991-92 academic year, I would not have been able to begin the initial research for this volume; therefore, Adm. Joseph Strasser, President of the College, and Professor William Fuller, Chairman of the Strategy Department deserve special thanks. Finally, I would be remiss if I did not thank Cecelia French and especially Peggy Kramer for the patience, fortitude, and good humor in bearing with my demands that everything be accomplished yesterday. Most of the credit for whatever success this report enjoys is due to those named above as well as others. Whatever errors or faults it contains are my responsibility alone.

Introduction

In some ways "Desert Storm" represented a watershed in the conduct of war. For much of the conflict, the fighting consisted of the application of air power to the economic and bureaucratic infrastructure of Iraq as well as its military forces, although the ways in which the Coalition applied air power differed in some important respects from previous conflicts. In the Gulf, Allied air forces used air power as both a rapier and as a bludgeon. Moreover, the technological changes in terms of stealth and the use of precision-guided munitions (pgms) represented significant additions to the capabilities that air forces possess. Before the ground war had even begun, the air campaign had, by itself, achieved considerable effects on the Iraqi military, its infrastructure, and its command and control systems. The rapid collapse of the Iraqi army before Coalition ground forces was in great part due to the collapse of its morale in the face of the massive bombing of its units in the Kuwaiti Theater of Operations (KTO).

And yet important questions still remain. How effective was the conduct of air operations in the war? What was the relationship between the expectations of airmen and their actual accomplishments? Were the armed forces of Iraq a significant challenge to the military capabilities developed by the Western allies to defend against an assault by a far more formidable opponent in Central Europe? How well did air commanders react to the challenges that the war posed? Was the war merely the final chapter in the Cold War, or did it suggest the direction that warfare in the 21st Century would take?

This volume represents a study of air operations in the Gulf War. It forms a part of the research undertaken at the behest of the Secretary of the Air Force, Donald Rice, when he established the Gulf War Air Power Survey to examine the preparations, planning, conduct, and impact of the air campaign against Iraq and its military forces. As such, the authors of both this volume and the other volumes in the study received general access to air force sources on the war. While time did not allow complete access to the records of the other U.S. services, we received considerable cooperation, including their after action reports.[1] Obviously, we were unable to gain

---

[1]It is worth noting that no other service put its conduct of operations under the kind of searching scrutiny that the *Gulf War Air Power Survey* volumes entail.

access to the records of the Iraqis. Thus, our work presents a picture mostly drawn from the side of the Coalition in general and the United States Air Force in particular. It is also important to note that in the writing and preparing of these volumes, Secretary Rice allowed the study group complete editorial independence.

Before one can examine the conduct of this air campaign, one must understand the conditions that war imposes on those who wage it. As the German military thinker Karl von Clausewitz concluded early in the 19th Century, war is an instrument of state policy aiming at political objectives, as well as a phenomenon involving the full range of human emotions and irrationalities. It possesses a dynamic of its own, created by the violence that lies at its core and which unleashes such incalculable emotions as anger, fear, desire for revenge, and hatred. Above all, war involves the effort to compel our opponent "to do our will."[2] Its fundamental essence is violence aimed at destroying the enemy's ability and willingness to continue the struggle. War creates a terrifying environment—one which peacetime conditions rarely duplicate. In addition, military professionals seldom perform their tasks in combat more than once or twice in a career, and then often under very different circumstances from those for which they had prepared.

A number of serious impediments exist to successful military operations; they lie at the heart of war. Clausewitz grouped such factors under the overarching concept of what he called "friction":

> Everything in war is very simple, but the simplest thing is difficult. The difficulties accumulate and end in producing a kind of friction that is inconceivable unless one has experienced war . . . Countless minor incidents—the kind you never foresee—combine to lower the general level of performance, so that one always falls short of the intended goal . . .[3]

The frictions of combat vary from chance encounters, to the difficulties involved in getting individuals to act with a common purpose, to unexpected patterns in weather. The Gulf War once again showed the profound influence that friction exercises over the conduct of military operations. From mid-January to the end of February, weather patterns produced one of the

---

[2]Karl von Clausewitz, *On War*, ed. and trans. Michael Howard and Peter Paret (Princeton, NJ: The Nautical & Aviation Publishing Company of America, Inc., 1976), 95.

[3]Ibid., 119.

longest sustained periods of bad weather in recent decades. Unfortunately, the arrival of bad weather coincided exactly with the course of combat in the war.

For Coalition air commanders and planners who had spent the previous five months in a hectic environment—one in which the sighting of small clouds was a major event—the sustained bad weather came as a nasty surprise. By the tenth day of the war, the weather had affected the air campaign to the extent that Coalition air forces were still on the fifth day of their intended tasks.

To the end of the war, the weather remained a serious impediment to the conduct of air operations. On the forty-first day, when commanders hoped to attack a number of crucial leadership and military support targets, a ferocious storm system forced the cancellation of all F-117 strikes scheduled for that night. The next evening the weather had scarcely improved, and the F-117s dropped only ten weapons—barely one-fifth of their average for the war.[4]

Perhaps the most serious friction is what historians refer to as the "fog of war," that pervasive atmosphere of ambiguity, breakdowns in communications, and the general uncertainties which permeate military organizations during the conduct of operations. Because military organizations confront human enemies who fight with unpredictable aims and objectives, it is difficult to estimate how any combat situation will evolve. Although we may calculate what our opponent *might* do, there are few certainties or absolutes in dealing with the enemy, and when military organizations calculate in certainties and absolutes, they flirt with disaster.

In war, commanders can place their strengths against an opponent's weaknesses, in effect maximizing the frictions with which the enemy will have to deal. The plan drawn up for "Desert Shield" in fact aimed at maximizing the frictions inherent in the Iraqi military system. By disrupting crucial centers in Iraq's air defense system, by attacking early warning and surface-to-air missile (SAM) radar sites, by disrupting electrical power for much of the country (thereby forcing many Iraqi military institutions to use back-up electrical power) and by bombing communications centers, planners hoped to cause maximum friction and confusion within Saddam

---

[4]Gulf War Air Power Survey (GWAPS) Mission Data Base.

Hussein's command structure.[5] The aim was not the destruction of one particular target or group of targets, but rather a synergistic degradation of the whole, in which confusion and uncertainty would combine to render the enemy's defenses generally ineffectual. The fact that Coalition air forces lost only a single F/A-18 the first night indicates the success of the air plan in imposing general disarray on the enemy's systems.

Thus, the same conditions that limit military operations on land and sea govern the conduct of war in the air. Nevertheless, war in the third dimension presents historians and analysts with intractable problems in determining a coherent picture of operations, or even in obtaining a grasp of the effects of such operations. In most respects the history of ground and naval actions in the twentieth century has been easier to evaluate than air actions. With its ebb and flow, ground war provides patterns from which to construct narratives. The key events announce themselves, victors and vanquished are generally obvious, and one can trace outcomes to specific events and trends that give rise to climactic or crucial moments on the battlefield. Similarly, the conduct of naval operations, with its clash of fleets, seemingly possesses clarity and simplicity.[6]

Air operations, however, possess considerably less clarity. The inherent chaos, the speed, and the lack of discernable landmarks in the sky make it difficult to reconstruct even the pattern of events. The real problem, however, is that most of the more important effects of air operations are indirect rather than direct. How, for example, does one calculate air power's impact on the enemy's capacity to conduct or even to manage his economy? Here, one is dealing with intangibles: what options might the enemy have exercised either militarily or economically had he not been under air attack? Did the air campaign lower his civilian or military morale and, if so, what impact did this fall in morale have on his capacity to fight or produce? What levels of production could enemy industry have reached but for the damage occasioned by air attacks? Such questions still pose intractable problems for historians of World War II fifty years after the event.

---

[5]Interview, Maj. Gen. Buster Glosson with GWAPS personnel (Williamson Murray, Barry Watts, and Thomas Keaney), 9 and 14 April 1992; interview, Lt. Col. David Deptula with GWAPS personnel (Williamson Murray, Barry Watts, and Thomas Keaney), 20 and 21 December 1991.

[6]Although the war between submarines and enemy commerce in both world wars does not lend itself to such easy analysis.

Not surprisingly, answers to such questions on air operations in the Gulf, especially without access to Iraqi records, will remain tentative far into the future. Fortunately for Allied air forces, Iraqi air power proved almost completely incapable of intervening against the aerial tide that swept into the Mesopotamian River Valley on 17 January and continued over succeeding weeks. But while the enemy was incapable of standing and fighting, the impact of the blows that he received remained unclear for much of the war. His air defenses were in tatters, his electrical system was badly damaged, his communications were in disarray, and his army lay exposed, pounded day and night; yet to the end of the war it remained unclear to the Coalition high command, particularly the ground commanders, how extensively the air campaign was damaging the Iraqi capacity to put up substantial resistance. Even if the documents concerning Iraq's conduct of the war were available, a number of crucial factors would probably remain uncertain: how much did the bombing of electrical and communication sites contribute to the collapse of the Iraqi air defense system? When did the morale of the Iraqi army into the KTO begin to crumble? Given the Iraqi political system, which often punished the bearer of bad news, did the high command in Baghdad ever recognize the extent of the damage? Could Coalition forces have moved earlier on the ground without suffering significantly higher casualties? For how long a period did air attacks set back Iraq's nuclear, chemical, and biological programs, in which Saddam's regime had invested so much of its capital?

This account of the air campaign against Iraq has broken its subject into chronologically ordered topics. The first chapter discusses the outbreak of the crisis, deployment of U.S. forces to the Persian Gulf, and the planning that established the framework within which Coalition air forces would fight. The next chapter turns to a net assessment of the opposing sides; here the emphasis will be on laying out the factors beyond "bean counts" to understand the complex balance of training, preparation, doctrine, and technological capabilities that factored into combat in the Gulf.

This work concentrates on the conduct of operations. Consequently, it emphasizes the first days of the air campaign, for it was in that critical period that Coalition air forces effectively gutted Iraq's capability to defend itself. Succeeding chapters will examine the remainder of the strategic air campaign against Iraq and the impact that frictions such as weather and SCUD missile attacks had on the campaign. Finally, the last chapter will examine the air campaign against Iraq's ground forces and its contribution to Coalition victory in the ground war.

Above all, this work aims to convey the ambiguities and difficulties that confronted air commanders and planners in the war against Iraq. It does not intend to provide simple answers, but rather to evaluate the difficult choices made at the time, more often than not on the basis of incomplete information. Moreover, this report relies on the incomplete information contained in the record of events, and the reader must remember that, in contrast to World War II, the Allied effort in this short, swift, and ferocious air offensive did not result in the collapse of the Iraqi regime. As a result assessments of the enemy, the damage to his systems, and the actions and reactions of Iraqi commanders can only be surmised. Nevertheless, this survey aims to provide an intelligent and useful account of air operations in the Persian Gulf War, given the limitations and constraints within which it was researched and written.

Security Review

The Gulf War Air Power Survey reports were submitted to the Department of Defense for policy and security review. In accordance with this review, certain information has been removed from the original text.

1

Desert Shield

In 1989, as the power of the Soviet Union drained away, U.S. Central Command began reassessing its mission. The Reagan administration had created the command in 1983 to block a possible Soviet drive through Iran to Persian Gulf oil. Since that threat no longer seemed credible, the new Chairman of the Joint Chiefs, Gen. Colin Powell, encouraged the command to turn its attention to Iraq.

The successful conclusion of its long war with Iran in 1988 had left Iraq with an enormous debt but also with one of the largest armies and air forces in the Middle East (with the possible exception of Israel). To the south, in apparently weaker countries, lay approximately half the world's proven oil reserves. By spring 1990, Central Command had drafted a revision of its Operations Plan 1002 to deal with an Iraqi invasion of Saudi Arabia through Kuwait. This draft plan, 1002-90, came none too soon.[1]

Central Command's first exercise of its new draft plan had just begun in Florida, when on 17 July 1990, Iraq's dictator, Saddam Hussein, publicly threatened Kuwait and the United Arab Emirates. In private, the Iraqis had repeatedly made known over the preceding six months a set of demands to their smaller neighbors: forgive Iraq's war debt, reduce oil production to raise the price of oil, and compensate Iraq both for its war against Iran and (in the case of Kuwait) for pumping oil from Iraq's portion of the Rumayla oil field. Within a week, credible intelligence reporting indicated the presence of two Iraqi armored divisions on Kuwait's northern border. Like most observers around the world, the

[1](S/NF) OPLAN, USCINCCENT 1002-90, 2d draft, 18 Jul 1990, GWAPS NA 41. See also 1st draft of outline plan, 16 Apr 1990, GWAPS, CHC 13. Gen H. Norman Schwarzkopf with Peter Petre, *It Doesn't Take a Hero* (New York: 1992) gives somewhat different version of the genesis of 1002-90 than the GWAPS Planning report. Schwarzkopf, who was then in charge of Central Command, says that he had the idea and sold it to Powell.

Kuwaitis believed that Saddam was bluffing. The United Arab Emirates, on the other hand, asked the United States for two KC-135 air refueling tankers to aid its Mirage fighters in maintaining an around-the-clock patrol over that country's offshore oil platforms. The KC-135s began operations in the United Arab Emirates on 24 July.[2]

Meanwhile, Central Command's command post exercise, Internal Look, had run its course. The exercise laid out basic conceptual problems in defending the region against Iraq. In particular, Internal Look examined military and operational problems involved in dealing with Iraq's military forces on the ground and in the air. Unfortunately, several problem areas emerged from the exercise, such as intelligence weaknesses that subsequent events would more than confirm. Nevertheless, given the focus of the American military over the previous forty years, the fact that considerable weaknesses existed in preparations to deal with a crisis in the Middle East should not be surprising. Whatever the defects of Internal Look, it represented an excellent primer for those who soon found themselves engaged in a full-blown Middle Eastern crisis.

Iraq's invasion of Kuwait began at 0100 hours on 2 August 1990; three of Saddam's elite Republican Guard divisions crossed the border on the ground, while a fourth launched a helicopter assault against the capital. Kuwait City fell by seven that morning. The Kuwaitis had failed to place their troops on alert and many fell into Iraqi hands at their normal duty posts rather than in forward prepared positions. The Kuwaitis did get six Mirages in the air early in the morning; those aircraft shot down a number of enemy helicopters before Iraqi fighters entered the battle and attacked all three Kuwaiti air bases at 0500. During the day, Iraqi tanks reached the airfields, and most of Kuwait's air force fled to Saudi Arabia; the Iraqis captured the airmen who remained and sent them on to Iraq.[3] It appeared possible that Saddam's forces would soon round up the

---

[2] (S/NF) msg, US Embassy Abu Dhabi to Secretary of State, subj: UAE Fears Iraqi Air attack, 212142Z Jul 90.

[3] Intvw, Kuwaiti Air Force officers captured in summer 1990 with GWAPS personnel, 14 Jul 1992.

American embassy staff and more than two thousand Americans working in Kuwait.[4]

The American Response

That same day, President George Bush met for the first time with Gen. H. Norman Schwarzkopf, commander of Central Command or "CENTCOM" [pronounced "Sent Com"] as most military people called it. The President warned Schwarzkopf that he should be prepared to fight if Iraq took the embassy staff hostage or extended its invasion into Saudi Arabia. Two days later at Camp David, Schwarzkopf and his air commander, Lt. Gen. Charles A. Horner, briefed the President on possible military responses. In peacetime, Horner commanded Ninth Air Force; in a Middle Eastern crisis that tactical command became Central Air Forces or CENTAF (pronounced "Sen Taf").[5]

By the time Schwarzkopf and Horner spoke to the President at Camp David, the Iraqis had moved approximately eleven divisions into or near Kuwait, nearly 200,000 men; some of these were already on Kuwait's border with Saudi Arabia. More than half a million Iraqi regulars and reservists remained at home, where that country's armed forces equaled approximately half the number of active duty U.S. forces worldwide. Few Americans, however, were in the Middle East. European Command had fourteen F-111Es and four F-16s in Turkey, but the U.S. did not know whether the Turks would allow air strikes against Iraq. Two aircraft carriers would reach the Red Sea and the Gulf of Oman in a few days, but this was all Schwarzkopf and Horner could offer unless Saudi Arabia or other Middle Eastern nations accepted American forces.[6]

Bush then sent Secretary of Defense Richard B. Cheney, Schwarzkopf, and Horner to Saudi Arabia to persuade King Fahd to allow implementation of CENTCOM's Operations Plan 1002-90. The plan called for deploying a quarter million U.S. troops to Saudi Arabia, where American ways–for example, American women in uniform–seemed likely to

---

[4]Intvw, GWAPS with Col Saber Al-Suwaidin, Acting Cmdr, Kuwait AF, 14 Jul 1992, GWAPS NA 377.

[5]Schwarzkopf, *Hero*, pp 297-302.

[6](S) Transcript, Lt Gen Horner's taped responses to written questions of CMSgt John Burton, CENTAF historian, Mar 1991, GWAPS CHP 13A; Schwarzkopf, *Hero*, pp 298-302.

upset traditional Muslims. But satellite photography underlined the threatening nature of Iraqi deployments on the Saudi frontier. On 6 August King Fahd invited the Americans to deploy their forces into his nation.[7]

The deployment that followed Fahd's decision was unprecedented in its combination of speed, size, and distance. The Americans called it Operation Desert Shield, to emphasize its defensive purpose. Most of the quarter million troops, the thousand aircraft, and the millions of tons of equipment and supplies ticketed by Operations Plan 1002-90 moved at least seven thousand miles from the continental United States during the next three months. While they arrived, the United States and Saudi Arabia moved their strategic conceptions beyond defense of Saudi Arabia toward Operation Desert Storm, the expulsion of Iraqi forces from Kuwait and the elimination of Iraq's capability to threaten its neighbors. For that strategic purpose another eight hundred U.S. aircraft eventually arrived in the theater along with another quarter million American troops–this time mostly from Europe, where the Soviet decline made their presence less necessary.[8]

Whether from the continental U.S. or Europe, a flight to Saudi Arabia took hours rather than the weeks required for ships to bring the cargo required to equip and sustain those forces. However, the Marines and the Air Force had stored munitions and other supplies in neighboring Oman as well as at the Indian Ocean island of Diego Garcia and the Pacific island of Guam; supply ships at Diego Garcia and Guam, already loaded with ammunition and supplies, moved when the deployment began. Luckily, the Saudis reduced U.S. logistic requirements considerably by providing gasoline and other petroleum needs to Coalition forces from their own refineries.

---

[7]Schwarzkopf, *Hero*, pp 302-08; OPLAN 1002-90 (July). In fact, the Iraqis may have only aimed at intimidating the Saudis, but by this time no one was particularly interested in taking chances with Saddam's regime.

[8]The GWAPS Logistics report treats the deployment. On the deployment's first phase, see also the (S/NF) monograph by William T. Y'Blood, "The Eagle and the Scorpion" (Washington

The burden of flying troops and urgently needed equipment fell on Military Airlift Command (MAC), which called on its long-range transports (C-5s and C-141s) as well as commercial air liners, especially Boeing 747s from American civilian carriers. MAC's C-5s were equally big and better suited for oversize cargo. Each C-5 could carry three times the lift-weight of C-141s, so that the fleet of approximately 120 active and reserve C-5s had a greater capacity than the 260 C-141s. However, commercial air liners carried almost two-thirds of the military passengers to the theater, as well as more than a fourth of the cargo delivered by air.[9]

Even with substantial commercial help, MAC's planes and crews worked to the breaking point. C-141s especially concerned MAC commanders, because of their age (more than two decades old) and the fact that they suffered from wing cracks. But an old C-5 was the only transport to crash; on 29 August taking off from Ramstein Air Base, Germany, with a load of medical supplies, the aircraft went down due to a mechanical problem and killed thirteen of seventeen on board. Although airlift crews were often as tired as their planes, the system provided some relief by establishing pools of pilots at European bases that served as halfway stops on the long flights between the United States and the principal aerial port at Dhahran.[10]

Navy carriers were first to arrive on station. They provided substantial strike capacity, while Air Force units were deploying from the continental United States. The first Air Force aircraft to reach Saudi Arabia were F-15C fighters from Langley Air Force Base, Virginia. During the afternoon of 8 August, a squadron of twenty-three air superiority fighters touched down at Dhahran Air Base two hundred miles south of Kuwait. Refueled seven times en route by SAC KC-10 tankers, the F-15s arrived fully armed.[11] Upon landing, they were told by their Saudi hosts to get out of the heat (120 degrees Fahrenheit) and rest while Saudi F-15s flew combat air patrols. When the Americans were ready, Saudi

---

[9]See the GWAPS Statistics report.

[10](S) Hist, MAC, 1990, especially pp 198-200. The European bases that provided the half way staging bases were Zaragoza and Torrejon in Spain and Rhein Main and Ramstein in Germany.

[11]The F-15s were armed for two reasons: in case they ran into Iraqi aircraft contesting their landing, and as a means of ferrying ammunition to the theater.

pilots (including veterans of "Red Flag" exercises at Nellis Air Force Base) took them on orientation flights. Meanwhile, a second F-15 squadron arrived from Langley.[12]

By mid-September nearly eight hundred U.S. aircraft (mostly Air Force, but including approximately 100 Marine aircraft) had deployed to airfields on the Arabian Peninsula.[13]

Their arrival doubled the number of military aircraft normally available to Saudi Arabia and other states on the Arabian Peninsula–neighboring Oman, the United Arab Emirates, Qatar, and Bahrain. Nearly two hundred aircraft from the United Kingdom, France, Canada, and Italy had joined U.S. and Arab aircraft on these bases. In addition, throughout the fall of 1990 the U.S. Navy maintained three carriers (with more than two hundred aircraft) in the Eastern Mediterranean, the Red Sea, and the Gulf of Oman–all within striking distance of enemy forces.[14]

The deployment of so many aircraft and troops to the Arabian Peninsula proceeded more quickly than smoothly. CENTAF had to change the destination of some aircraft en route, while the deployment involved shuffling some squadrons from one base to another before the onset of the campaign. American aircraft soon crowded Arab airfields, an inviting target for air or terrorist attack. Once deployment sorted itself out, U.S. and other foreign aircraft fit reasonably well in an exceptionally complex operational environment of more than twenty airfields. The second deployment phase in December and January stretched base infrastructure to its limits. Fortunately, since World War II, the U.S. Army Corps of Engineers had helped to build the airfields on the peninsula; in the last forty years they constructed more than was strictly necessary to house the

---

[12]Five unarmed E-3 Airborne Warning and Control System (AWACS) aircraft arrived at Riyadh just before the F-15Cs reached Dhahran. (S) Contingency Hist Rpt, 1st Tactical Fighter Wing, Aug-Sep 1990, AFHRA 881102; intvw, GWAPS with Col (Prince) Bandar A Bin Mohammed (RSAF), Cmdr, 13th Squadron (F-15s), Dhahran, 13 Jul 1992.

[13]For the deployment of US aircraft to the theater see Appendix 1.

[14]For US Navy and Marine deployments, see the Center for Naval Analyses (S) rpts, *Desert Storm Reconstruction Report* and *Marine Corps Desert Storm Reconstruction Report* (Alexandria, VA, 1991-92).

Saudi air forces. One suspects that the Saudis themselves were taking out an insurance policy to allow substantial reinforcement from abroad. The "overbuilding" proved to be a remarkably astute investment.[15]

Operations Plan 1002-90 did not specify which American aircraft would deploy to which airfield. Central Command possessed no peacetime forces of its own other than its small headquarters in Florida; Arab nations had not even permitted the Americans to locate their headquarters in the Middle East, let alone station substantial forces in the area. Consequently, U.S. planners could not be sure which airfields Arab nations would allow them to use in wartime. CENTCOM would receive its combat forces from other commands (like Tactical Air Command, Strategic Air Command, United States Air Forces in Europe, and Military Airlift Command) and it was still working out the details of an automated time-phased force and deployment list. Lacking a complete list in August 1990, CENTCOM had to improvise.[16]

With King Fahd's request for deployment of American forces on 6 August, Schwarzkopf returned to Florida where he could initiate deployment of ground forces and communicate more easily with Washington. He left Horner in Saudi Arabia as the acting commander of CENTCOM forward, since most early arrivals would be air force squadrons. Horner located his headquarters in the Saudi Ministry of Defense and Aviation at Riyadh, the capital about three hundred miles south of Iraq and two hundred miles west of the Persian Gulf. This command arrangement lasted three weeks until Schwarzkopf returned on 26 August. Meanwhile, Horner's deputy, Maj. Gen. Thomas R. Olsen, handled CENTAF's deployment from an office in Royal Saudi Air Force headquarters, also in Riyadh. Olsen reached Riyadh on 8 August with a portion of Ninth Air Force's staff from Shaw Air Force Base to form the nucleus of CENTAF headquarters.[17]

With most of Ninth Air Force's headquarters in Saudi Arabia, those remaining at Shaw could not handle a deployment for which so little

---

[15]See the GWAPS report on supporting the air base.

[16]See the GWAPS Planning report.

[17](S) Intvw, MSgt Theodore J. Turner, CENTAF historian, with Maj Gen Thomas R. Olsen, CENTAF Deputy Cmdr, Riyadh, 30 Sep 1990, GWAPS CHP 16A.

planning existed. Immersed in the problems involved in bedding down arriving units in the face of potential Iraqi invasion, those in Riyadh had difficulty communicating with bases in the United States and with the small group that remained at Shaw. Consequently, Tactical Air Command headquarters at Langley became CENTAF's rear headquarters.[18]

CENTAF had stored bombs at Seeb before the crisis broke, and Horner had planned to deploy some of his strike aircraft there: F-15Es and F-111s, together with EF-111 jammers. But, not surprisingly, it turned out that Oman did not want American strike aircraft prominently displayed at its international airport. The F-111s went to Taif, and the F-15Es to an isolated bare base at Thumrait, Oman, before eventually moving to another bare base at Al Kharj near Riyadh. Similarly, A-10 ground attack aircraft, originally scheduled for Riyadh's King Khalid International Airport, deployed instead to King Fahd Airfield under construction near Dhahran. Both Seeb and King Khalid airports received less controversial KC-135 tankers, as did Jeddah.[19]

Not surprisingly, there were considerable difficulties in the initial movement to Saudi Arabia. In the middle of the deployment, Maj. Gen. Lester Brown, acting Ninth Air Force commander after Horner's move to the Middle East, noted:

> The deployment was so rapid that transportation of logistic support items, bare base support equipment and communications gear lagged far behind. The result was that, even though they were on the ground in Saudi Arabia, [the] fighter units [in the initial deployment package] could not really function properly because they did not have the necessary support. For example, one squadron from the 363TFW flew sixteen hours to the beddown site at Al Dhafra–which was a bare base. When the aircrews and planes arrived, they found that there were only thirty SAC people on the base to meet them. . . . The aircrews had to disarm

---

[18](S) Olsen intvw.

[19]On the peregrinations of the F-15Es, see (S) hist, 4th TAC Fighter Wing in Southwest Asia, Aug 1990 - Jun 1991. B-52s did eventually end up at Jeddah, as Strategic Air Command had hoped.

> the missiles they had ferried over themselves. Even as late as today [13 August 1990] the 363rd at Al Dhafra has only enough food, water, and munitions to sustain it for twenty-four hours! . . . It will take at least until . . . 18-19 August before the necessary Harvest Eagle and other support equipment and supplies to maintain these units will arrive.[20]

A dozen airfields had to take air refueling tankers, mostly KC-135s. No other aspect of CENTAF's early planning fell so far short of what combat operations required. The planners at Shaw had failed to estimate how dependent air operations would be on air refueling, given the distances in the theater. They had called for sixty-eight tankers; in the end combat operations required over 230. The near doubling of aircraft deployed in December and January accounted for less than half the increase in tanker requirements. Even though the carriers would work in the Persian Gulf during the war, when original assessments had expected them to stay farther away in the Gulf of Oman, Navy strike sorties still depended on air force tankers. Nor had CENTAF planners anticipated how many strikes would have to hit targets deep in Iraq rather than in Kuwait or Saudi Arabia.[21]

In peacetime, tankers belonged to SAC; in spring 1990 that command had tried to persuade CENTAF that its estimate of the number of tankers it would require in war was inadequate. As late as 8 August, the Joint Chiefs of Staff and CENTCOM planned to have only twenty tankers in theater during the deployment's first forty days. Nevertheless, SAC managed to increase the number of tankers deployed in theater to eighty-five in the first forty days. This achievement depended on injecting SAC planners into the efforts in Riyadh and Washington. On 8 August, Brig. Gen. Patrick Caruana with a SAC team arrived in Riyadh aboard the flight of KC-10 tankers that had escorted the first F-15s to Dhahran.[22]

---

[20]Intvw, Maj Gen Lester P. Brown, "Desert Shield Deployment: USCENTAF HQ, An Interview Conducted with Maj Gen Lester P. Brown, Acting Ninth Air Force Commander and Col George L. Getchell, Ninth Air Force Chief of Staff," by David L. Rosmer, 9AF/USCENTAF Office of History, 13 Aug 1990.

[21](S) Brfg, Horner to Schwarzkopf, "OPLAN 1002 Air Operations," Apr 1990, GWAPS NA 256.

[22](S) Hist, SAC, 1990, pp 334-55.

That same day Headquarters USAF invited SAC to participate in the air campaign planning group in Washington. That command's cooperation paid dividends immediately. The SAC group recommended (their recommendation went directly to Schwarzkopf) that CENTAF needed a minimum of ninety-four tankers, with 114 optimal for forces contemplated in Operations Plan 1002-90. Schwarzkopf replied that so many tankers "almost blew my mind," but he supported the recommendation.[23]

Operational Framework

The process of creating an operational capability in Saudi Arabia was a complex one indeed. First, it demanded a set of realizable and politically realistic objectives. Then, one needed to place the forces in the theater with the base and logistical infrastructures to support sustained operations. And finally, one needed sophisticated operational plans that would place the strengths of one's forces against the weaknesses of the enemy; plans had to rest on a clear assessment of the enemy and his capabilities. In no fashion were these elements sequential; they occurred concurrently and depended on the personalities, intellectual preparation, training, and education of those who would be responsible for the conduct of the air campaign.

With Horner and his staff in Riyadh bedding down forces and cobbling together a defense against a possible Iraqi thrust into Saudi Arabia, there remained a conceptual gap in thinking through the problems involved in executing an air campaign. Fortunately, the air staff's deputy director of plans for warfighting concepts, Col. John A. Warden III, had begun building a planning cell in his "Checkmate" wargaming facility even before Schwarzkopf requested air staff assistance.[24]

---

[23](S) Notes, Lt Col Bernard E. Harvey, Checkmate, 17 Aug 1990, GWAPS CHP 9-4. See also (S) Rpt, Capt Johnson (USN), J-3/JOD, sub: CINCENT Trip, 17 Aug 1990, GWAPS, NA 203; (S) Brfg, Warden to Schwarzkopf, "Instant Thunder," 17 Aug 1990, GWAPS, CHSH 5.

[24] While a student at National War College, Warden had considered using Alexander the Great as a means of studying operational art in war. In the end he settled on writing an extended study of the air campaign, but stayed away from the term "strategic" bombing for obvious reasons. His study was eventually published: John A. Warden, *The Air Campaign, Planning for Combat* (Washington, DC, 1988). Warden made clear to GWAPS interviewers that the *Strategic Bombing Survey* as well as the thinking of Gen Hayward Hansell had heavily influenced his writing of *The Air Campaign* and in his thinking of

On 6 August Warden assembled key personnel to think about how air power could force Iraq to abandon Kuwait. On 8 August Schwarzkopf requested help from the air staff, and since the Chief of Staff, Gen. Michael Dugan, was out of town, Gen. Loh, Vice Chief of Staff, passed the request to Warden.[25] Because Checkmate had already performed basic ground work for a proposed air campaign against Iraq, Warden was able to brief Loh the next day. Warden's briefing quickly went to the Chairman of the JCS, then to Schwarzkopf, and eventually over to Horner in Saudi Arabia.[26]

The development of Warden's plan need not concern us overly; what is important is the operational concept that Checkmate articulated. The code name, "Instant Thunder," underlined the planning group's rejection of the U.S. approach to air war in Vietnam. That effort had involved a slow, gradual escalation of air attacks on the North Vietnamese; that escalation had allowed the enemy maximum time to adapt. With respect to Iraq, Warden's group advocated a massive and intense application of air power right from the start. Planners sought levels of destruction to the Iraqi military, the political system, and portions of the economy that would either force Saddam to quit, or other Iraqis to remove him; a proposed Presidential briefing, dated 13 August, suggested an intense first night attack to incapacitate Iraq's leadership. Significantly, Warden's briefing only minimally dealt with the problems of the Kuwaiti Theater of Operations (KTO) and Iraqi ground forces.[27]

The air staff plan attempted to identify vulnerabilities in Iraq and its military structure. At Instant Thunder's heart, its operational approach was

---

how the air campaign against Iraq should be designed. Intvw, Col John Warden with GWAPS personnel (Williamson Murray, Barry Watts, and Thomas Keaney), 21 Feb 1992.

[25] In his memoirs Schwarzkopf indicates that he initiated the request to the air staff for an air campaign plan. Schwarzkopf, *Hero*, p 313.

[26] (S) Intvw, TSgt Theodore J. Turner, CENTAF Office of History, "Oral Interview with Lt Col David Deptula," 1 Nov 1990; intvw, Lt Col David Deptula with GWAPS personnel (Williamson Murray, Barry Watts, and Thomas Keaney), 20 and 21 Dec 1991; intvw, Col John Warden with GWAPS personnel (Williamson Murray, Barry Watts, and Thomas Keaney) 21 Feb 1992.

[27] "'Instant Thunder,' Proposed Strategic Air Campaign," 13 Aug 1990, 2300 hrs, GWAPS CHP 35-6. Gen Powell may have used Checkmate slides to brief the President on 15 August 1990.

to "conduct powerful and focused air attacks on strategic centers of gravity." The air offensive would involve "round-the-clock operations against leadership, strategic air defense, and electrical targets " with the aim of achieving "strategic paralysis and air superiority." The air staff planners estimated that with sufficient air forces, CENTAF could complete such a campaign in five or six days. Early briefings for an air war against Iraq identified eighty-four targets which Checkmate estimated were essential to Saddam's regime.[28] Above all, the air staff plan moved a possible air campaign beyond merely servicing targets to a search for targets sets, the destruction of which would have interrelated or synergistic effects on the Iraqis. The argument was that the destruction of certain carefully selected groups of targets which were interdependent would cause larger problems in both political and military spheres than the elimination of large numbers of targets that possessed no coherent interrelationships.[29]

At the center of Iraqi power, Warden argued, lay Iraqi leadership. One could attack this target set best by cutting off the regime's capacity to communicate with its military and people. At this early point in the process, intelligence had identified only a few targets in this crucial target set; by January, Coalition plans would expand this category to more than thirty targets.[30] For attacking Iraq's command and control systems, planners targeted mostly radio and television sites but did not yet possess the intelligence base required for a systematic attack on the telephone network.

On the economic side, Warden and his planners selected electricity and oil as the most likely targets to achieve larger effects. Here historical literature, particularly from World War II, buttressed their thinking.[31] There was a certain irony in this because the *Strategic Bombing Survey*

---

[28] *Ibid.* The number of targets in the initial briefing reflected the state of intelligence available concerning Iraq. As more intelligence became available with a refocusing of intelligence assets, the number of strategic targets would grow to over 300 by the beginning of the air war.

[29] In particular, the personal log for Lt Col David Deptula for 11 August 1990, when the Instant Thunder concept was being worked up by the air staff, has a sketch of a flow plan for attacks on Iraq in support of the air campaign with a final category: "Desired Effect." The diagram became the prototype for the Master Attack Plans utilized during the war. Lt Col David A. Deptula, Personal Log, 9 Aug to 20 Aug 1990, entry for 11 Aug, copy in possession of the author.

[30] (S) Instant Thunder Campaign Plan, 17 Aug 1990, Annex C, GWAPS, CHSH 9, p 15.

[31] Intvw, Col John Warden with GWAPS personnel (Williamson Murray, Barry Watts, and Thomas Keaney), 21 Feb 1992.

had singled out electricity as a target particularly worth hitting for its impact on long-term industrial production; in Iraq's case the planners were looking for immediate effects. By hitting the electrical network, they hoped to gain political leverage on the Iraqi population as well as to affect communications and other systems depending on electricity. The collapse of the electrical network would also have a considerable impact on the military, since back-up power is rarely reliable. Radar installations and communication centers, dependent on computers, were particularly vulnerable. However, air staff planners hoped to limit long-term damage by attacking transformer stations and by avoiding generators.[32]

There were, inevitably, weaknesses in the initial plan that Warden and his staff prepared. Their conception was overly optimistic; it underestimated the number of targets that an air campaign would have to attack; and its estimate on the time necessary for such an air campaign to achieve success failed to take into account the frictions of the war, from bombing inaccuracies to bad weather. Moreover, Warden's conceptions paid little attention to the ground threat, which had considerable effect on the plan's reception by U.S. air leadership in Saudi Arabia. Finally, the plan's assumption that a relatively short air campaign, attacking little of Iraq's political infrastructure, could separate Saddam and his regime from the Iraqi population underestimated the strength of the Ba^cthist control.

Nevertheless, whatever the weaknesses in the air staff plans, they exercised an important, and in the end mostly beneficial, influence on the development of the air campaign. Other conceptions for an air campaign against Iraq suggest how valuable Warden's effort was. In early August, Tactical Air Command developed an approach that aimed to begin "with demonstrative attacks against high value targets . . . (and then) escalate as required until all significant targets are destroyed . . . . This strategy allows time and opportunity for Hussein to reevaluate his situation and

---

[32] *Ibid*, p 18; (S) Brfg, Col. Warden to Gen Schwarzkopf, "Iraqi Air Campaign Instant Thunder," 17 Aug 1990, GWAPS, CHSH 7-11.

back out while there is something to save."[33] Air effort would concentrate on targets "that reduce his ability to project power, [i.e.] field armies and infrastructure to support offensive operations."[34]

In effect, this approach represented a replay of the flawed air campaign against North Vietnam, especially its gradual and cumulative escalation of pressure. But some in the Navy were no more imaginative. The initial suggestion by naval commanders on the scene was for an air campaign that would separate the theater into route packages (as had been the case in Vietnam).[35] Other senior admirals suggested a roll back which would chew up the enemy's air defense and targets in a fashion quite similar to the Vietnam experience.[36] None of these alternatives suggested the use of air power to achieve rapid operational level effects on Iraq's military and strategic position.

Warden's concept for a "strategic" air campaign received considerable interest from Schwarzkopf. CINCCENT may well have doubted that an air campaign could be decisive, but it did provide an immediate–and probably the only military option if Iraq initiated a conflict before substantial American ground forces arrived. Consequently, he proved to be an enthusiastic listener when briefed on the conception. And at his urging the team that had briefed CENTCOM journeyed to Saudi Arabia to brief Horner and his staff.

For those who deployed in early August, including Horner, the problems associated with Iraq looked quite different. The most pressing problem was how to beddown and organize the steadily increasing flow of forces. The difficulties involved in the airlift and adjusting to a hostile

---

[33] Fax from General Griffith TAC/XP to General Alexander, AF/XOX, 11 Aug 1990, "CENTCOM Air Campaign Plan," GWAPS, CHSH-14. This could not be found in the archives of Tactical Air Command.

[34] *Ibid*, slide 12.

[35] Intvw, Maj Gen Buster Glosson with GWAPS personnel (Williamson Murray, Barry Watts, and Thomas Keaney), 9 Apr 1992. In fairness, the Navy's operational approach was undoubtedly influenced by the fact that it possessed no stealth aircraft.

[36] Letter from Capt Stephen U. Ramsdell, to Director, Naval Historical Center, 14 May 1991.

and forbidding climate were daunting enough. But over the entire theater hung the Iraqi threat. After the war Horner reflected that:

> The idea was that we were to deter an Iraqi invasion of Saudi Arabia, and if an invasion did come, we were prepared to defend. . . .Those were some of the worst nights of my life, because I had good information as to what the Iraqi threat was, and, quite frankly, we could not have issued speeding tickets to the tanks as they would have come rolling down the interstate highway on the east coast. It was an opportunity the Iraqis did not take, but every night we'd get more forces, and we'd sit down and get a game plan of what we'd do if we came under attack.[37]

The threat led Schwarzkopf to push for the deployment of combat forces–both air and ground–at the expense of support forces. While that resulted in some difficulties initially, it made sense both in terms of deterrence and combat potential.[38]

Having briefed the major players in Washington and CENTCOM on his proposal for a strategic air campaign against Iraq, Warden arrived in Riyadh to brief Horner. The briefing was not a success.[39] Above all, many in Saudi Arabia thought that Warden's conceptions paid scant attention to the harsh realities of the military balance on the Arabian Peninsula (particularly the ground balance), the logistic difficulties that CENTAF confronted, or the imponderables that an air war might unleash. At the end of the briefing Horner asked Warden a series of pointed questions: Did he know when sufficient supplies would exist in theater to support such a campaign? What would happen if the Iraqi regime did not collapse after a five or six day campaign and CENTAF had used up its logistic base in theater? What could CENTAF do against the Iraqi Army with so few ground forces presently in theater?[40]

---

[37]Speech By Lt Gen Chuck Horner to Business Executives for National Security, 8 May 1991, GWAPS, Horner Files.

[38](S) CENTCOM J-5 After Action Report, p 16.

[39](S) Harvey notes, 20 Aug 1990.

[40]Intvw, Maj Gen Larry Henry with GWAPS personnel (Williamson Murray and Barry Watts), Aug 1992; (S) Harvey Notes, 20 Aug 1990.

Despite his obvious disdain for Warden and his obvious concern with a possible Iraqi offensive, Horner kept Checkmate's draft plan and immediately established his own planning cell to develop it with planners from Checkmate.[41] At the time, Horner did not appear interested in employing air power much beyond battlefield support for the army.[42] But he would steadily move towards a larger conception of air power beyond merely attacking Iraqi ground forces. Several factors combined to push CENTAF toward wider options. First of all, at that point there was not much army to support, if an Iraqi ground offensive did occur; one needed greater leverage on Saddam Hussein than merely destroying tanks. In addition, even army generals like Schwarzkopf and Powell were looking for broader applications of air power than just supporting "the ground commander's scheme of maneuver."

Horner now asked Brig. Gen. Buster Glosson to take charge of his planning cell. The cell's official title was the Special Planning Group, but its secrecy soon won it the nickname of the "Black Hole." Glosson was not uncomfortable with the Washington origin of either Warden's plan or his staff, because he had only recently joined Central Command after a Pentagon tour. Indeed he found the Checkmate connection useful and in coming months made increasing use of Warden's staff to exploit the Washington intelligence community.[43] After the war Glosson commented that he carried "as much baggage from the Vietnam War as any other officer in the United States Air Force." Like many fellow officers who had been junior officers during the war, he had devoted much of his

---

[41] Horner sent Warden home, but significantly kept three of the planners to join the special planning cell which eventually became known as the "Black Hole." One of those he kept was Lt Col David Deptula who played a crucial role in transmitting the conceptions that Checkmate had begun into the planning and developing of a strategic air campaign against Iraq.

[42] Intvw, Gen Michael Dugan with GWAPS personnel (Williamson Murray, Barry Watts, and Thomas Keaney).

[43] (S) Intvw, MSgt Theodore J. Turner, CENTAF historian, with Brig Gen Buster C. Glosson, Riyadh, 17-27 Oct 1990, GWAPS CHP 5A.

postwar career to correcting those deficiencies. Moreover, his time as a student at National War College had influenced him considerably, particularly in thinking about air power and the operational level of war.[44]

Glosson found much of interest in Checkmate's conceptions. But he also believed the plan had crucial weaknesses: too little emphasis on counterair operations, excessive expectations, and not enough recognition of the staying power of Third World nations. A cryptic comment in his notebook on 23 August suggested: "need air campaign for fifteen rounds not three; six days is dumb."[45]

Over the long-term development of CENTAF's air campaign plan, Glosson kept one of Warden's planners, Lt. Col. David Deptula, and collected a number of officers from combat units now arriving in Saudi Arabia. While such a staff provided him with personal connections to fighting units, it did not provide a group with any special preparation to think about how one might utilize air power to achieve operational-level effects. The situation was considerably different in the case of the Army. In mid-September when confronted with the necessity to plan for a ground campaign into Kuwait and Iraq, the Army was able to pull into Riyadh a group of officers specially trained in operational art, all graduates of the School for Advanced Military Studies at Leavenworth.[46] As a result, the Army was able to build a sophisticated operational planning staff at short notice–one that could immediately think in terms of the operational employment of ground forces.

---

[44] Intvw, Maj Gen Buster Glosson with GWAPS personnel (Williamson Murray, Barry Watts, and Thomas Keaney), 9 Apr 1992. Glosson argued in this interview that instead of a Clauswitzian approach to war, much of the Air Force's senior leadership had consistently taken a Jominian view throughout the Cold War. Moreover, he argued that Air Force leaders had never understood operational art and had made little consistent effort to think about the higher levels of war. All too often Air Force leaders had become managers instead of warriors.

[45] Glosson Journal, 23 Aug 1990; intvw, Maj Gen Buster Glosson with GWAPS personnel (Williamson Murray, Barry Watts, and Thomas Keaney), 9 Apr 1992.

[46] CENTCOM J-5 After Action Report and Supporting Documents, GWAPS, NA 259.

Horner made clear to Glosson that he wanted "an executable air campaign plan by mid-September."[47] An essential point in the discussions between Horner and his chief planner was the clarification of what the CENTAF Commander had gleaned of the President's objectives during his early August meeting with Bush. As roughly sketched out, these political objectives were to 1) remove the Iraqis from Kuwait; 2) eliminate production and storage of weapons of mass destruction; 3) end Iraq's capacity to threaten its neighbors over the next five to ten years, regardless of whether Saddam remained in power; and 4) insure that the full conventional military capabilities of the United States would be used. There was a limiting factor: the desire to hold American military and Iraqi civilian casualties to a minimum.[48] In early October, Glosson journeyed to Washington to brief the national leadership, including the President, on plans for an air campaign; he utilized that opportunity to ensure that there was direct agreement between the President's political conceptions and CENTAF's view of its political objectives.[49]

From the initial formulation of political and military objectives in August to the onset of operations in January, there remained great consistency in the planning for the air campaign. What did change was the role of the air campaign in American strategy. In August–and much of September–air operations were the sole means of effectively striking the Iraqi military and political infrastructure. As increasing numbers of ground troops arrived, the emphasis shifted towards a combined air-ground strategy–one in which the air campaign would not only attack the heart of Iraqi power, but would prepare the way for an eventual ground offensive. Those ground forces would liberate Kuwait and complete the job of destroying the Iraqi military. Not surprisingly, there was some considerable tension between these two approaches, and those tensions carried over into the execution of Desert Storm.

---

[47] What is of considerable interest is the fact that Glosson's Special Planning Group used the "s" word from the first in its draft operations order for CENTAF's air campaign: "This operation will be a strategic air campaign against vital Iraqi centers of gravity . . . " [(S) COMUSCENTAF, Draft Operations Order, 27 Aug 1990, Offensive Campaign–Phase I, p 3].

[48] Intvw, Maj Gen Buster Glosson with GWAPS personnel (Williamson Murray, Barry Watts, and Thomas Keaney), 9 Apr 1992.

[49] *Ibid.*

Warden's initial briefings for Instant Thunder had noted that "psychological operations [would be a] critical element in the campaign; destroy Iraqi TV and broadcast systems–substitute U.S. broadcasts; separate regime from support of military and people."[50] But almost immediately, psychological operations disappeared from discussions of an air campaign against Iraq.[51]

The President's objectives now formed the framework within which Glosson's special planning group worked out its operational concepts for the coming air campaign. CENTCOM's objectives in the plan's last formulation before the onset of Desert Storm were to: 1) destroy Iraq's military capability to wage war; 2) gain and maintain air supremacy; 3) cut Iraqi supply lines to the KTO; 4) destroy Iraq's chemical, biological, and nuclear capabilities; 5) destroy the capabilities of the Republican Guard, Saddam's elite ground force; and 6) liberate Kuwait City with Arab forces.[52]

To achieve these military goals the CENTCOM and CENTAF planners developed a four-phased approach.[53] Phase I would be a "strategic" air campaign to cripple Iraq's political and military leadership. Destruction of Saddam's command and control system was essential to achieving this objective. But the air campaign aimed also to destroy Iraq's ambitious weapons development programs–how ambitious would emerge only after the war–in the nuclear, chemical, and biological areas. Phase II aimed at gaining air supremacy over Kuwait; consequently it remained closely

---

[50](S) Warden Brfg, 11 Aug 1990, "Instant Thunder," GWAPS Folder #35.

[51]As we will discuss at the end of this study, psychological operations played a minimal role in the operational air campaign against Iraq, while it was given a centerpiece role in the air campaign against Iraqi ground forces in the Kuwaiti Theater of Operations.

[52](S) HQ USCENTCOM, Combined OPLAN for Offensive Operations to Eject Iraqi Forces from Kuwait, 17 Jan 1991, pp 2-4. For further discussion of this point see Chapter 2 of the GWAPS Effectiveness report.

[53] By 2 September 1990,the conception for Phase I had been largely formulated with the initial planning work; the planning for the two succeeding phases was much less complete. By early October,Glosson would brief the first three phases to President Bush. See COMUSCENTAF Draft Operations Order, "Offensive Campaign–Phase I," 2 Sep 1990; and Lt Col David A. Deptula, "Instant Thunder (Offensive Campaign Phase I) Planning Assessment, Talking Notes of Lt Col David Deptula as presented to SECAF and XOXW upon return from first trip to AOR," 24 Sep 1990.

connected in the execution and timing to Phase I; the two phases would have to run concurrently. Phase III would prepare the battlefield by interdicting the Iraqi Army in the KTO along with direct attacks on its forces. Finally, Phase IV would be a ground offensive with air power to "support the ground commander's scheme of maneuver."[54]

CENTCOM's January operations plan for the conduct of the war against Iraq noted that "execution of the phases is not necessarily discrete or sequential; phases may overlap as resources become available or priorities shift."[55] The heaviest emphasis in the early days would lie on destroying Iraq's air defenses and in bombing high value strategic targets. Nevertheless, such attacks would continue to the last days of the war. Similarly, attacks on the Republican Guard and other ground forces would begin on D-Day, but become increasingly intense as the ground war approached.

The senior leadership both in Washington and Riyadh regarded the Republican Guard as a "strategic" target of essential importance to the regime's continued political stability. Moreover, as Powell noted after an early briefing on Instant Thunder, even if the air campaign forced Iraq to disgorge Kuwait, he did not want Saddam to retain his massive army. To allow Iraq to do so would allow the Iraqis to intimidate their neighbors after U.S. forces had gone home.[56] The Chairman commented on 11 August:

> I won't be happy until I see those tanks destroyed. . . . The campaign I laid out for the President: sweep the air and leave the tanks to pick off piecemeal–if we go this far . . . I want to finish it: destroy Iraq's army on the ground.[57]

Some within the Air Force, Warden being a prime example, believed that air power alone could defeat Saddam Hussein. What, however, their arguments missed was the crucial role that the ground war would play in

---

[54] USCINCCENT OPORD 91-001 for Operation Desert Storm, paras. 1D, 3A, and 3B. OPORD contained in a message USCINCCENT to CJCS, 161735Z Jan 1991.

[55] (S) HQ USCENTCOM, Combined OPLAN for Offensive Operations to Eject Iraqi forces from Kuwait, 17 Jan, paragraph 3a.

[56] Intvw, Col John Warden with GWAPS personnel (Williamson Murray, Barry Watts, and Thomas Keaney), 21 Feb 1992.

[57] Quoted by Memo (S) Subj: "Instant Thunder" Brfg to CJCS, 11 Aug 1990, Lt Col Ben Harvey, GWAPS CHSH #14.

convincing the world–especially the Arab world–of the complete defeat of Iraq's army. Without pictures on world TV showing Iraqi soldiers surrendering in droves, Saddam could soon have claimed that his army had remained in the field, bloodied but unbeaten, too formidable for the cowardly Americans to attack. Such propaganda would have gone down all too well in parts of the Arab world–in effect a replay of the infamous "stab in the back" legend that the German Army had stood unbeaten on the Western Front in November 1918.

Senior air commanders, especially Horner and Glosson, refused to claim too much for air power; better for the campaign to speak for itself. The problem, of course lay in translating concepts into plans and then into reality. An important part of this process was the assessment that coalition air commanders had to make of their opponents.[58] In the period before the war, the intelligence community and many so-called experts estimated that Iraq possessed exceptionally capable military forces.[59] Senior air leaders, on the other hand, felt that cultural and political impediments existed within the Iraqi military that would degrade its capacity to use the complex technological systems under its control.[60]

The air campaign against Iraq largely confirmed their net assessment of Iraqi military weaknesses and corresponding Coalition strengths. At the time, however, it represented a substantial leap of faith. Had such assumptions proved faulty, they might have resulted in heavy losses for the Coalition. The calculation of substantial superiority of Coalition air

---

[58] For the net assessment of the actual capabilities of the opposing sides see chapter 2 of this report.

[59] For an unclassified overestimation of Iraqi military capabilities see the study by the US Army War College's Strategic Studies Institute: Stephen C. Pelletiere, Douglas V. Johnson, II, and Lief R. Rosenberger, *Iraqi Military Power and U.S. Security in the Middle East* (Carlisle, PA, 1990).

[60] Senior air commanders from the Coalition's Arab air forces confirmed this assessment. In fact most estimated that the Iraqis were considerably inferior to the Saudi and other Gulf air forces; one source estimated that there were only twenty Iraqi pilots good enough to match the best pilots in the Gulf air forces in air-to-air combat and a further twenty capable of matching their counterparts in the air-to-ground arena. Consequently, out of an air force of nearly 500 pilots, Arab sources calculated that the Iraqis possessed barely fifty first-rate pilots. Intvw, Maj Gen Buster Glosson with GWAPS personnel (Williamson Murray, Barry Watts, and Thomas Keaney), 9 Apr 1992.

capabilities over those of the Iraqis allowed air planners to take substantial risks in developing the air campaign. They could think in terms of degrading rather than destroying Iraqi systems; moreover, their assessment allowed planners to spread scarce resources–especially in terms of precision bombing aircraft–across a broad spectrum of targets.

Tactical Framework

The urgency of the planning task caused Glosson to ask more from CENTAF's intelligence staff than they could provide. Checkmate planners had used target photography in Washington, not yet available in Riyadh; intelligence officers had worked with Checkmate to select aiming points on target photographs. But coordinates were of little use to planners or pilots unless accompanied by target photographs. The failure of the intelligence community to make existing imagery promptly available to the planners who desperately needed it seemed inexplicable to Glosson. So began his rocky relationship with a community vital to his work.[61]

Glosson established his own channels to intelligence analysts in Washington through Checkmate and later through Rear Adm. J. M. McConnell on the Joint Staff. They helped Glosson's Special Planning Group–the Black Hole–come to grips with growing target lists. Checkmate had begun with photography on eighty-four targets that looked promising, but over the next five months the Black Hole became acquainted with ten times that many targets, and still important targets would remain that intelligence failed to identify until after the war–if then. In many cases spaceborne and airborne reconnaissance assets simply could not substitute for ground-based assets.[62]

Precise intelligence was all the more important to Black Hole planners because they relied heavily on precision bombing. They needed to know exactly where the Iraqi leadership conducted business and how communications ran between Baghdad and army divisions, air bases, and missile sites. If intelligence could identify key nodes in the Iraqi com-

---

[61] (S/NF) Memo, Col James R. Blackburn Jr, Dir of Targets, HQ USAF, subj: USAF/INT Targets/MC&G Support to Desert Shield, 17 Oct 1990, GWAPS NA 269.

[62] See GWAPS Planning report.

mand and control network, precision-guided bombs, some of which could penetrate bunkers constructed of reinforced concrete, could disable the entire network.

Unfortunately, one of CENTAF's real weaknesses lay in its intelligence staff. It was not that intelligence was not available, or that there were not suitable, highly-trained officers in the field. But substantial problems emerged in getting intelligence in a timely fashion to the operators through organizational structures. For that reason, a number of the senior commanders in the Gulf War would criticize intelligence when the war was over.[63] But there is, of course, another side to the story: the disinterest that the operational community in the Air Force has displayed towards its intelligence branch throughout the past several decades. As a result, a considerable gap existed between real-time needs of operators and planners, and the desire of the intelligence community to maintain peacetime procedures and security classifications. In the end such difficulties did not prove crucial to the outcome of the war, but only because planners and air commanders established work-arounds with the help of those in intelligence services willing to work outside of normal channels. But in an environment where American forces were less dominant, this gap might have proven costly.

The Black Hole relied on the F-117 "stealth" fighter as its principal platform to attack targets in the Baghdad area. Analysis predicted that attacks by F-111s and Navy A-6s on targets in Baghdad would be extremely dangerous so the F-117 became the weapon of choice. Designed to give enemy radars a minimal picture, the F-117 promised to deliver laser-guided bombs in Baghdad without significant losses. Although F-117s had been operational since 1983, their only combat test had come in December 1989 in Panama. The F-117 had never had to

---

[63]Horner commented in a speech in spring 1992: "We ran into a problem that our intelligence systems were primarily designed for peacetime. You think about it, it makes sense. You have peacetime for ten or fifteen years, and you have war for, in this case, six weeks, and then you hope to enjoy a long period of peacetime. So as a result you tend to develop intelligence capabilities that look into a country, count its garrison. . . . And you tend to atrophy your capability to identify where his forces are deployed in the field." Horner, "Address to Business Executives for National Security."

deal with formidable air defenses like those protecting Baghdad.[64] But Glosson had flown against the F-117 when he had taken his F-15 wing to Red Flag, and his experience on the Nevada range had at least convinced him that F-117s could get inside enemy air defenses.[65]

The Air Force had kept its fifty-six F-117s at Tonapah, Nevada, an airfield whose existence remained secret–along with the F-117–until 1988. Before August 1990, Horner could not count on getting F-117s in the Middle East. Nevertheless, he hoped for some stealth aircraft. Eighteen F-117s arrived on 21 August. The Pentagon targeteers put as many as eight F-117 sorties on a single target for Instant Thunder, but Glosson and Deptula eventually hit on attacking as many targets as possible by sending each F-117 sortie against two targets with a 2000-pound laser-guided bomb (LGB) for each.[66] The ability to strike large numbers of targets with F-117s in a short time expanded again when President Bush doubled U.S. forces in November. The number of F-117s climbed.[67]

For precision bombing in less formidable areas, the Black Hole planned on using F-111Fs and eventually F-15Es. The latter, however, would only be useful for precision bombing after receiving their laser targeting pods, part of the Low Altitude Navigation and Targeting Infrared for Night (LANTIRN) system. When the first F-15E squadron arrived in August, it had only LANTIRN navigation pods–no targeting pods. The latter would eventually reach the theater in time to be used during the air campaign. The F-111Fs also posed a problem, but one more quickly solved. CENTAF had not expected to get F-111Fs; instead Operations Plan 1002-90 called for F-111Ds, which lacked precision-bombing capability. In early August the Secretary of the Air Force and Checkmate urged a

---

[64] *Ibid*; (S) study, Ronald H. Cole, *Operation Just Cause* (Washington, DC, 1990).

[65] Intvw, Maj Gen Buster Glosson with GWAPS personnel (Williamson Murray, Barry Watts, and Thomas Keaney), 9 Apr 1992. Intvw, Maj Gen Larry Henry with GWAPS personnel (Williamson Murray and Barry Watts), Aug 1992.

[66] See Richard P. Hallion, *Storm Over Iraq: Air Power and the Gulf War* (Washington, DC, 1992), p 153.

[67] (S) Horner called for F-117s in his April 1990 briefing to Schwarzkopf [(S) Brfg, GWAPS NA 256]. See (S) intvw, Maj Gen Thomas R. Olsen (Ret) with GWAPS personnel, 9 Mar 1992.

switch to F-111Fs to increase CENTAF's precision-bombing capability.[68] Consequently, when eighteen F-111s arrived at Taif on 25 August, they were F models from European Command rather than D models from Tactical Air Command.[69]

Since the planners in the Black Hole eventually decided not to risk conventional (non-stealthy) aircraft on missions against Baghdad where many crucial targets lay, only missiles could hit targets in the capital area during daylight hours. The Air Force had also developed a conventional version of its Air Launched Cruise Missile (ALCM). Strategic Air Command was eager to see conventional Air Launched Cruise Missiles tested in combat in limited numbers if it could launch them from B-52s that flew out of the United States and which did not touch down in the Middle East. This would be the longest air combat mission on record.[70] However the Navy possessed the sea-launched Tomahawk cruise missiles in considerable numbers. And they would form the heart of daytime attacks on Baghdad.

The Navy and Marine corps also contributed planners to the original Checkmate effort and then to the Black Hole. At first Navy and Marine planners hoped to use their A-6 precision bombers against targets in the Baghdad area, but computer modeling of the threat persuaded them to leave that job to F-117s and Tomahawks. By bringing half the six carriers, deployed by mid-January, in the Persian Gulf (with the other half farther away from Kuwait in the Red Sea) and attacking targets mostly in Kuwait and southern Iraq, the Navy sought to reduce dependence on Air Force tankers. The Marines preferred to keep their aircraft employed in Kuwait in behalf of their ground forces. They got their aircraft as close to the battlefield as they could, with AV-8s north of Dhahran at Al Jubayl and FA-18s (with their A-6s) south of Dhahran at Bahrain.

---

[68]Crucial to this deployment option was the disappearance of the Soviet threat in Europe which allowed the F-111Fs to deploy to the Middle East.

[69] Issue paper, Maj "Sky King," Checkmate, subj: F-111F Deployment, 12 Aug 1990, GWAPS CHSH 59-3.

[70]On the Tomahawks, see Frank Schwamb, et al. *Desert Storm Reconstruction Report, Vol II,: Strike Warfare* (Washington, DC, 1991).

Beyond phases and strategic objectives, the air campaign needed target sets that aimed at getting maximum synergies and interrelated damage from air strikes. Then, planners had to keep two limiting factors in mind: air attacks must inflict *minimum* casualties on the Iraqi population (as well as limited damage on the civil infrastructure of the country). As Glosson noted after the war, "the American people would not have stood for another Dresden."[71] Secondly, attacking air forces could not suffer heavy losses, again due to the pressures exerted by public opinion.

Early on, Warden and his staff had created ten target sets or categories. This was a crucial conceptualization, especially when one considers that the eighty-four targets on Warden's list on 21 August had grown to 218 by 11 October, 237 by 20 December, and 481 by 15 January.[72] These target sets were: Leadership; Command, Control, and Communications; Strategic Air Defenses; Airfields; Nuclear, Biological, and Chemical Research and Production; Naval Forces and Port Facilities; Military Storage and Production; Railroads and Bridges;[73] Electrical Power; and Oil Refining and Distribution Facilities. Schwarzkopf added the Republican Guard as a category and Scuds soon emerged as a separate target set. After the beginning of Desert Storm, two more categories appeared: fixed surface-to-air missile sites in the KTO and breaching sites for the ground offensive.

Organization

A crucial difference in the conduct of the air campaign against Iraq and Rolling Thunder against North Vietnam lay in the fact that now there was *one* individual responsible for the conduct of the campaign. In Vietnam, no less than six competing command authorities had muddled the execution of operations. Schwarzkopf now assigned the conduct of air operations against Iraq to one commander: Gen. Horner, as the Joint

[71] Intvw, Maj Gen Buster Glosson with GWAPS personnel (Williamson Murray, Barry Watts, and Thomas Keaney), 9 Apr 1992.

[72] See Watts and Keaney, GWAPS Effectiveness report, Target Sets.

[73] The original category was only railroads. Highway bridges were added when it became apparent that they represented a crucial portion of the transportation network.

Forces Air Component Commander (or JFACC). The concept of a JFACC had originated in the mid-1980s after serious debates among the Services. That debate reflected the pressures from Congress for "jointness," as well as the self-imposed difficulties that U.S. forces had encountered in the Grenada operation. Several members of the air staff, supported by the Air Force Chief of Staff, Gen. Charles Gabriel, pushed heavily for the creation of a JFACC position to provide a clearer focus for any future air campaign. Integral to the concept was a belief that the JFACC would not have to be an Air Force general but would reflect the composition of the units conducting the campaign–a campaign that relied heavily on carrier aviation would most naturally have an admiral as JFACC.[74]

Early on, Schwarzkopf made clear that Horner would be the JFACC; as Schwarzkopf indicated to Glosson: "If you aren't part of the air campaign under Horner, you don't fly."[75] In Horner's terms, the various Service air components and Coalition air forces were under his "control" rather than "command;" but the choice of wording reflected a desire not to exacerbate interservice or Coalition tensions. Nevertheless, whatever Horner's sensibilities or the complexities of interservice politics, his draft operations order of 27 August 1990 made clear that the "JFACC will conduct, in the near term, a theater air campaign to seize the initiative by attacking, isolating, and incapacitating the Iraqi military leadership and destroying Iraq's ability to conduct military operations."[76]

The creation of a Special Planning Group answered two crucial problems. First, most CENTAF planners were embroiled in the beddown of arriving units; they also had to put together the daily Air Tasking Order (ATO) that prepared Coalition air forces to meet any Iraqi offensive. Thus, Horner needed a Special Planning Group to plan a complex "strategic" air campaign. Equally important was the need for security, not only against Iraqi espionage, but also against premature disclosure to allies; the

---

[74] I am indebted to Col Robert Gaskin, USAF (ret) for recounting the interservice squabbles that eventually resulted in the creation of the JFACC position. Col Gaskin was the action officer for XOXID in debates which lasted a number of months and in which this author sat on several occasions.

[75] Intvw, Maj Gen Buster Glosson with GWAPS personnel (Williamson Murray, Barry Watts, and Thomas Keaney), 9 Apr 1992.

[76] COMUSCENTAF draft operations order, 27 Aug 1990, Annex C, p 1.

Coalition had not yet discussed any offensive action against Iraq, and there were many in the U.N. and in the U.S. for that matter, who had proven dubious even of the idea of an embargo of Iraq.

Consequently, development of an air campaign demanded stringent security precautions.[77] It was not that the U.S. needed to hide its planning from the Saudis or other Coalition members; rather the secrecy surrounding the Special Planning Group reflected the requirement to prepare a coherent plan before one briefed the Saudis. Due to diplomatic and political sensibilities, any plan would have to be briefed first to King Fahd; there could be serious diplomatic repercussions, if the Saudis discovered plans for offensive operations before they reached concrete form.[78] Finally, one needs to note the political sensibilities in the United States, where substantial portions of the public and Congress remained dubious about American participation in the crisis.

In December, Horner formalized the de facto arrangements between his two planning cells. Both the original CENTAF planners and the Special Planning Group now officially came under Glosson. The latter's title was Director of Campaign Plans–the organizations underneath him were: 1) Guidance, Apportionment, & Targeting No, 2) the Air Tasking Order shop. In addition, Horner also appointed Glosson as the commander of 14th Air Division, containing fighter units that would conduct much of the air campaign. There appear to have been two reasons for Horner's decision. First, it brought planning and execution functions of his staff together. Secondly, it formalized the close relationship between himself and Glosson, who otherwise would have had to report to Horner through the Deputy Chief of Staff for Operations.

Horner's principal device for unifying the air efforts not only of the U.S. Services but also of the Coalition as a whole was the daily Air Tasking Order (ATO). Through the months of Desert Shield, the diverse air forces of the Coalition accustomed themselves to the necessity of getting all sorties into CENTAF's air tasking order. Meanwhile CENTAF

---

[77] Notes from Ninth Air Force "Warrior" Brfg by Lt Cols Sam Baptiste and Jeff Feinstein to GWAPS, 4 Dec 1991, notes taken by Barry Watts.

[78] "Extract of Major Comments and Questions, Notes from Horner Brief," Col John Warden, 20 Aug 1990, GWAPS, CHP 35-10.

prepared air tasking orders for the first two days of the Desert Storm air campaign. Horner did not want orders prepared in advance of the campaign for more than the first two days, because after that initial period unexpected changes would require flexibility.[79] In fact, the planners did prepare skeleton outlines for further days in the campaign.

Since the war, there has been considerable controversy over the JFACC and the air tasking order. Admittedly, and not surprisingly, there were problem areas. Nevertheless, without a JFACC or an ATO there was little possibility of running a coherent air campaign: the possibilities of blue-on-blue fratricide would have multiplied; and the Iraqis would have found it relatively easy to slip aircraft into Coalition airspace because of competing authorities.[80] The only alternative to the JFACC-ATO approach would have been a modified version of the route package approach of the Vietnam War; each Service would have controlled its own geographic area independent of any larger control. The result would have been a less coherent, more factionalized and fractionalized air campaign.

What made the articulation of the air campaign against Iraq substantially different from earlier efforts lay in both its process and its conceptualization. In the earliest days of Instant Thunder, Colonel Deptula had hit on the idea of using a "Master Attack Plan" as an intermediate step between the target list and the ATO. The Master Attack Plan was an effort to coalesce numerous inputs into a coherent conception before one began the process of building an ATO of thousands of sorties. By giving only the basic information about combat sorties, the Master Attack Plan required relatively few pages instead of the hundreds consumed by the ATO. With a Master Attack Plan one could work on the overall conception of the campaign–an impossibility with ATOs, given the size of those documents. Consequently, Deptula's Master Attack Plan became the principal vehicle for designing the structure of the air campaign.[81] By

---

[79] Partial sets of ATOs for Desert storm are in GWAPS CATO and GWAPS HQ USAF Ops Ctr CSS 6. See also AFHRA 882196-214.

[80] In one case the Iraqis almost managed to slip two F-1s out into the Gulf due to competing airspace control between AWACS, Marine ground control, and Navy control. In the end, the system reacted and a Coalition F-15 shot down the Mirages.

[81] Succeeding versions of master attack plans for the first three days are in GWAPS BH 4-1 and CHC 16.

beginning the ATO process with a Master Attack Plan, the Black Hole's planners were now able to build a coherent picture of what they were attempting to accomplish with the air campaign and to track that campaign on a day-to-day basis.

Final Preparations

As more intelligence on Iraq became available, the size of the task on which Coalition air forces would embark slowly emerged. Especially troubling was the growing fear that the most dangerous weapon in Iraq's arsenal might prove to be anthrax, a fatal disease sometimes transmitted by cattle or sheep to farmers.[82] Although biological weapons might be more dangerous, CENTCOM predicted that Iraq was more likely to use chemical weapons. If Iraq had succeeded in producing chemical warheads for its missiles, a chemical attack on Riyadh or Israel was possible. Even conventional missile attacks on Israel might provoke an Israeli retaliation that in turn would threaten Arab participation in the Coalition. CENTAF planned to bomb fixed launch sites at the air campaign's outset, but Iraq possessed mobile launchers. U.S. Space Command assured CENTCOM that its satellites could see Scud launches in time to provide sufficient warning for those in the target area to take shelter and don gas masks. Whether Army Patriot surface-to-air missiles could shoot the Scuds down remained to be seen.[83]

Army and Marine ground forces had reason for special concerns about Iraqi artillery because of its superior range and the heavy emphasis that the Iraqis had placed on it in their defensive doctrine.[84] Schwarzkopf, however, placed more stress on air strikes against Iraqi armor, because he and Powell wanted to destroy Iraq's potential for future offensive operations. In any case, Schwarzkopf insisted that air power destroy half the Iraqi ground forces before beginning Phase IV, the ground offensive. Coalition air power was to pound Iraqi ground forces

---

[82] See GWAPS Planning report.

[83] See GWAPS Space report.

[84] The Iraqis had been working very closely with the South Africans and the Canadian artillery expert, Gerald Bull, during the last stages of the war with Iran. As a result, they possessed weapons with range superior to many in the ground forces of the Coalition.

so heavily that they could not exact many Coalition casualties during a ground campaign. This was an unprecedented demand.[85]

CENTAF categorized the job of destroying the Iraqi Army in its holes as Phase III of the air campaign. This did not fully square with Schwarzkopf, who divided the job between Phases I and III. For Phase I, the strategic air phase, Schwarzkopf ordered CENTAF to begin bombing the Republican Guard in southern Iraq. After the Guards had led the invasion of Kuwait, Saddam had pulled them back into a second echelon and placed less capable forces on the front lines in Kuwait. Thus, the Republican Guard was in position to launch a major counterattack once the direction of a Coalition offensive became clear. They could also stop front line forces from deserting. Since the Republican Guard was also an essential political prop for the regime, Schwarzkopf argued that they were a strategic target; consequently, he wanted them to be attacked as soon as possible.[86]

Although accepting Schwarzkopf's desire to see the Republican Guard bombed early, Horner and Glosson held the line on the first night of the campaign–there would be no diversion of air power to bombing ground forces on that night. In CENTAF's view the first three phases of the campaign plan had merged. Schwarzkopf's notion that the Coalition needed a Phase II for suppression of enemy air defenses in Kuwait and southern Iraq had never made sense to Horner and his planners, who intended to attack the Iraqi air defense system at its heart right at the start. The decision to attack the Republican Guard from the first day on, however, still left a pattern by which targets in Baghdad and northern Iraq would absorb most of the sorties for the first week; the bulk of the effort would then shift to Iraqi ground forces.[87]

---

[85](S) Rpt, Combat Analysis Gp, 21 May 1991, in Vol VI of CENTCOM J-5 After Action Rpt, GWAPS NA 259.

[86]Schwarzkopf, *Hero*, especially pp 319-20.

[87](S) Intvw, GWAPS with Maj Gen Glosson, 9 Apr 1992; (S) intvw, Center for Air Force History with Glosson, 12 Dec 1991.

Since the air assault on Iraqi ground forces would mostly come after the meticulously planned first two days, Phase III received relatively little attention in the Black Hole in the early planning stages. Checkmate ran computer spreadsheets which did suggest air's ability to destroy half Iraq's deployed force (including tanks and artillery) in less than a month. Nevertheless, throughout the prewar period the problem of taking apart the Iraqi Army in the KTO never received the attention or concentrated analysis that the air campaign against Iraq received during the same period.

The Coalition buildup in aircraft and munitions did keep up with intelligence estimates of the Iraqi buildup in the KTO to more than thirty divisions by the end of December. Indeed more than 300,000 tons of bombs reached the theater before the end of the war; Coalition air forces, however, would expend less than a third of that enormous quantity. The rest filled bomb dumps throughout the theater and especially the new depot at Al Kharj southeast of Riyadh. In August and September, C-ENTAF had been short of precision weapons because most of the bombs stored in the theater were "dumb bombs"–many dating from the Vietnam War. By November, however, CENTAF's precision munitions inventory had expanded considerably and was improving.[88]

A Coalition offensive had become likely by early November; President Bush announced his decision to double the size of the American deployment and bring VII Corps from Europe. This decision followed a CENTCOM Desert Storm briefing at the White House on 11 October. While the air portion of the briefing was persuasive, the Phase IV plan to send Coalition ground forces straight into prepared Iraqi fortifications in Kuwait raised the specter of heavy casualties. Schwarzkopf later explained that he could not divide his ground forces for a flanking movement unless he got VII Corps. Bush then gave CENTCOM VII Corps and virtually doubled the air deployment as well. Although CENTAF believed it possessed sufficient strength to wage an effective air campaign, the additional aircraft, and especially the increased numbers of precision bombers (F-117s, F-111Fs, and F-15Es), provided an abundance which made planning easier.[89]

---

[88] The series of Checkmate briefings reporting its findings on Phase III are in GWAPS CHSH 6 and 8.

[89] Schwarzkopf, *Hero*, pp 356-67.

Like VII Corps, many of the new Air Force units deploying to the Middle East came from Europe. Of the nearly 300 Air Force fighters that arrived in the Arabian Peninsula in the last two months before Desert Storm, more than a third were from USAFE. Thirty-two more F-111Fs from Lakenheath AFB, England, joined the thirty-six already at Taif. A dozen more F-4G Wild Weasels came from Spangdahlem Air Base, Germany, to Shaikh Isa on Bahrain. Twenty-four air-to-air F-15Cs arrived at Al Kharj from Bitburg AFB, Germany, and twenty-four F-16s flew from Hahn AFB, Germany to Al Dhafra in the United Arab Emirates. Another sixty-six F-16s arrived from the United States to make a grand total of 210 F-16s in the theater–by far the most numerous strike aircraft, with 132 A-10s a distant second.[90]

In addition to direct contributions to CENTCOM's force structure, European Command prepared for air and special operations missions into Iraq from Incirlik, Turkey. Not until the actual opening of the air campaign in January did Turkey grant permission for air operations, and special operations would remain taboo. Since European Command had sent all its F-111F precision bombers to CENTCOM, Task Force "Proven Force" had to make do with dumb bombs dropped by eighteen F-111Es and thirty-six F-16s. As early as September, the Black Hole had included provisional targets for Proven Force in the Master Attack Plans for the first two days. Beyond that, no firm arrangements were made even when the Proven Force commander, Maj. Gen. James L. Jamerson, visited Horner in early January. Horner could not count on Turkey's approval, and he had plenty of air power even without Proven Force.[91]

While CENTAF's forces grew, they were not idle. Not until the end of October could American aircraft use live ordnance on Saudi ranges, but short of that, the squadrons had engaged in as realistic training as possible. This was not without cost, and a series of accidents culminated in early October when an RF-4C and an F-15E flew into the ground. All four crewmen died. Horner then raised the minimum training altitude for fighter aircraft to 1,000 feet. Only the B-52s could continue to practice

[90] For a complete list of aircraft deploying to the theater November 1990 - February 1991, see GWAPS Statistics report.

[91] (S) Hist, Joint Task Force Proven Force, 13 Dec 1991; (S) intvw, CMSgt Jerome Schroeder, Proven Force historian, with Maj Gen James Jamerson, Ramstein Air Base, Germany, 27 Mar 1991.

missions at 500 feet. Although safety considerations inspired the new rules, they pointed toward an air campaign that would largely abandon low altitude in favor of altitudes above 10,000 feet. Since the air plan aimed to destroy Iraq's air defense system and the ability of Iraqi aircraft and surface-to-air missiles to control medium altitudes in the first two days, Coalition aircraft would be able to fly above the Iraqi antiaircraft artillery with relative impunity. But that factor would carry with it important consequences on the accuracy of aircraft not carrying precision-guided munitions in the Coalition inventories.[92]

Even if CENTAF could deconstruct the Iraqi air defense system, thousands of Coalition aircraft would still be in danger of flying into each other. Requiring all sorties to be included in a single air tasking order helped, but Horner attempted to further reduce the risk by conducting increasingly larger exercises. Beginning with hour-long exercises of a dozen aircraft in September, the training program culminated in November with a week-long exercise involving more than 2,000 sorties–a third of them on a single day. Like much of the rest of the exercise program, Imminent Thunder also attempted to deceive Iraqi intelligence. Its well-publicized name echoed Instant Thunder. Unlike Instant Thunder, most of Imminent Thunder's sorties were close air support. On board Navy ships in the Persian Gulf, the press watched a Marine amphibious operation near Mishab, twenty miles south of Khafji and forty miles south of Kuwait. Although rough water caused the Marines to cancel the hovercraft landing, even casual readers of the western press knew that the Marines were practicing amphibious landings. Iraqi focus on the Kuwaiti coast gave Schwarzkopf's flanking movement in the opposite direction a better chance of surprise.[93]

CENTAF Imminent Thunder exercised the so-called "D-Day Plan" which Horner's planners had been developing since August. At the beginning, they had intended to use the D-Day Plan to respond to an Iraqi invasion of Saudi Arabia. The bulk of Coalition sorties would attack Iraqi forces on the move into Saudi Arabia and Kuwait together with their supply lines. By September, however, Iraqi forces seemed unlikely to move south in view of the U.S. buildup; moreover, it was clear that the

---

[92] (S) Intvw Maj Gen Thomas R. Olsen (Ret) with GWAPS personnel, 9 Mar 1992.

[93] (S) Msg, CINCCENT to JCS, subj: Exer Imminent Thunder, 041800Z Dec 1990, AFHRA 882245.

Iraqis were putting a major effort into developing defensive positions in the face of growing Coalition forces. The Bush administration's second deployment made plain the likelihood of a Coalition offensive. At the end of November the United Nations Security Council called upon member nations to use force against Iraq if it did not withdraw from Kuwait before midnight 15 January. Iraq's only response was to release the foreign hostages it had taken in Kuwait during August. This relieved Horner of concern about the American and British hostages that Iraq had placed at sites that it wished to discourage the Coalition from bombing.[94]

Horner knew that the most likely air plan to be executed was the one developed by the Black Hole. Despite that plan's secrecy, there had been considerable speculation in the press about an offensive air campaign. In September, Secretary of Defense Cheney had fired the Chief of Staff of the Air Force, Gen. Michael J. Dugan, for talking to reporters about the possibility of defeating Iraq with an air campaign. Nevertheless, few even among Horner's staff knew the details of the campaign plan. Except for a handful of British and Saudi planners in the Black Hole, Coalition air forces remained in the dark about their targets until forty-eight hours or less before D-Day.[95]

By mid-January 1990, Horner could call upon the approximately 2,400 aircraft, three-fourths of them American and nearly 50 percent of them from the USAF. More than half of the Coalition fleet of aircraft could attack, while the rest could help them get to their targets safely or move troops and supplies. Six Navy carriers (three in the Persian Gulf and three in the Red Sea) carried more than 400 aircraft, while the Marines had more than 200 on shore. Two Navy battleships and sixteen cruisers, destroyers, and submarines carried over 400 Tomahawk cruise missiles. Allied fighter aircraft included British, Saudi, and Italian Tornados; Saudi F-15Cs; Mirages from France, Kuwait, Qatar, and the United Arab Emirates; British and French Jaguars; Bahraini F-16s; and Canadian CR-18s. Horner had spent considerable time with the air leaders of the allies and the other U.S. Services, and had included their forces in exercises. By mid-January all were familiar with the kind of air war that would come.

---

[94] UN Security Council Resolution 678, 29 Nov 1990.

[95] (S) Horner intvw, 4 Mar 1992.

Only 27 percent of the Air Force combat aircraft deployed in support of Desert Shield and Desert Storm. Yet, that overall percentage was deceiving. Fully 75 percent of the Wild Weasels, most of the stealth aircraft, and virtually all aircraft capable of flying precision-guided munitions were in the Middle East by January. In addition, 46 percent of USAF tanker assets supported the air campaign directly, while 80 percent of the strategic airlift went to support of the forces in the Middle East. Moreover, 63 percent of the laser-guided bombs, 43 percent of the CBUs (cluster bomb units), and 52 percent of the HARMs in the inventory went out to the combat theater.[96] All of this suggests that without the ending of the Cold War, it is doubtful whether the U.S. could have mounted such an air campaign in the Middle East.

The Final Plan

By the end of December, most of the forces for the air campaign were in place;[97] by then staffs were working out the final iteration of plans to destroy the Iraqi military. The final plan looked to achieve synergistic effects by attacking a wide variety of targets. Given the overcentralized nature of Iraq's society and political life, and the weaknesses inherent in its military system, Horner's planners hoped to break apart the controlling system in a political as well as a military sense. By degrading the electrical power network, one would exacerbate the difficulties caused by attacks on the command and control sector. And by attacking the integrated air defense system both directly and by raids on the regime's overall command and control system, one could separate the controlling mechanisms from the "shooters" on the airfields and in the missile batteries.

In turn, attacks on those facilities would keep attrition of Coalition air assets within tolerable limits for sustained operations. A sustained period without losses would then allow Coalition air forces to destroy targets, such as nuclear, chemical, and biological research facilities–of no immediate threat–at leisure. Attacks on oil refineries and distribution facilities would pressure Iraq's military and civilian society, while the attacks on transportation (railroads and bridges) would isolate its army

---

[96] Maj Dan Draper, LGXX (FA)/31017/25/25 Apr 1991, "Comparison of Logistic Tail Vice Aircraft Deployed to South West Asia."

[97] Among the exceptions were three of the Navy's carriers which were still on their way to the theater. One, in fact, would not arrive until after the war had begun.

and allow its destruction. Finally, the Republican Guard represented more than just an element of Iraqi ground forces; it represented an essential element in the stability of the regime, because they served to protect Saddam against his own armed forces. The air assault on Iraqi ground forces would begin against the Republican Guard on the first day and build until nearly all available sorties were attacking Iraqi divisions throughout the Kuwait Theater of Operations. When bombing had reduced the effectiveness of those units by at least 50 percent, Coalition ground forces would eject the remnant from Kuwait.

Gaining air superiority was essential to further military operations.[98] There were two fashions with which one could address Iraqi air defenses. The traditional approach would have involved a roll back campaign–one in which Coalition air power would steadily move its operations northwards and destroy Iraqi defenses on a gradual basis. The initial CENTAF draft operations order of 27 August reflected such an approach. As it noted: "Target priorities will be designed to roll back the IADS (integrated air defense system) and atrite [sic] enemy forces. Campaign will be expanded to include interdiction of C3 nodes, military support facilities and key choke points in northern Kuwait as forces are made available."[99] But the Master Attack Plan evolved independently of the initial operations order (and in fact the operation would soon be updated from the iterations of the Master Attack Plan). From the first, the authors of the Master Attack Plan envisioned attacking the heart of the enemy's integrated air defense system with F-117s at the beginning of the war.[100]

CENTAF's August operations order had noted: "Iraq's integrated air defense system [code-named KARI] . . . maintains track on every civilian and military aircraft over Iraqi airspace and consolidates the information into an overall air picture at the Air Defense Operations Center (ADOC) in Baghdad."[101] The implications of such a centralized system led planners to consider an attack to paralyze KARI at its center and degrade the capacity of the intercept operations centers and section operations

---

[98] This is a point often ignored by US Army thinkers and largely reflects the fact that since the first months of the North African campaign in 1943, one of the crucial contributions that air power has made to US military operations is that air superiority has allowed US ground forces to operate in an environment free of an enemy air threat.

[99] COMUSCENTAF, draft operations order, 27 Aug 1990, Annex C, p 2.

[100] See "Instant Thunder" brief, 17 Aug 90/ 2100, "Campaign Flow."

[101] COMUSCENTAF Operations Order, 27 Aug 1990, Offensive Campaign–Phase I, Annex B, p 6.

centers to coordinate defensive responses. The conceptualization of the first night's attack led to the belief that direct attacks could paralyze the Iraqi air defense system, while conventional air packages, protected by SEAD aircraft, could suppress the separate pieces of the enemy's air defenses.[102]

But how to attack KARI's controlling center without heavy losses in fighting through the defenses deployed around Baghdad–defenses that after the war Horner described as among the strongest in the world?[103] The answer was to rely heavily on stealth to attack the command structure of the enemy's air defenses. Yet the planners also were to provide the Iraqis with a large SEAD package that appeared to give them what they expected: a massive attack on Baghdad itself.[104]

By early January, the Black Hole had evolved a complex, carefully orchestrated plan for the first days of Desert Storm–a plan that aimed at operational level effects on the Iraqi air and ground defenses and at the destruction of Iraq's long-range capabilities that represented such a threat to the stability of the region: namely its nuclear, biological, and chemical programs. Of course there were weaknesses in the planning effort. But those weaknesses reflected deeper organizational and cultural patterns that had been established in the Air Force even before its birth.[105] Yet in many ways the final plan represented an intellectual triumph over much of the cultural baggage that had distorted the air war against North Vietnam. In the end, the Black Hole made a considerable effort to move beyond self-imposed limitations and to maximize the potential of aircraft and weapons technology.

---

[102]Conversation with Lt Col David Deptula, 24 Jun 1992; and "Instant Thunder" brfg, 16 Aug 1990/2100, "Campaign Flow."

[103]Lt Gen Horner, Address to Businessmen for National Security, May 1991.

[104]See Chapter 3 of this report for a fuller examination of how this was done.

[105]See in particular Barry Watts, *The Foundations of USAF Doctrine* (Maxwell AFB, 1985).

2

Net Assessment of the Opposing Sides

No single, numerical comparison can convey the balance between the opposing sides in the Gulf War. The crucial factors determining the outcome mainly concerned issues such as military preparation, peace-time training, doctrinal conceptions, and the complex interrelationships among training, technological capabilities, and the educational sophistication of those who did the fighting.

Moreover, the military ethos and political framework within which opposing military forces had developed played a major role in the outcome. This chapter will assess these factors as they applied to the opposing sides, first by looking at the Iraqis and then in turn at the Coalition. What it will attempt to convey is a sense of how these strengths and weakness matched up; finally, it will estimate how the two sides assessed the strengths and weaknesses of their opponents and sought to manipulate the situation to their strategic and operational advantage.

The Nature of the Theater

Iraq is the valley created by confluence of two great rivers, the Tigris and Euphrates, between whose banks the great civilizations of early man developed. In comparative terms laid out on a map of the eastern United States, Iraq would reach from Raleigh to southern Canada and from Washington, D.C. to eastern Indiana [see Map 1]. The great majority of its population of 17.6 million exists within the geographic confines of the Mesopotamian Valley.[1] Its people consist almost entirely of city and town dwellers, or farmers; only a few Bedouins inhabit the great deserts lying west and south of the rivers. While Iraqi culture has, of course, drawn heavily from the desert traditions of the original Arab tribes and conquerors, current Iraqis have little contact with their desert roots [see Maps 2 and 3].

---

[1]Congressional Quarterly, *The Middle East*, Seventh Edition (Washington, 1990).

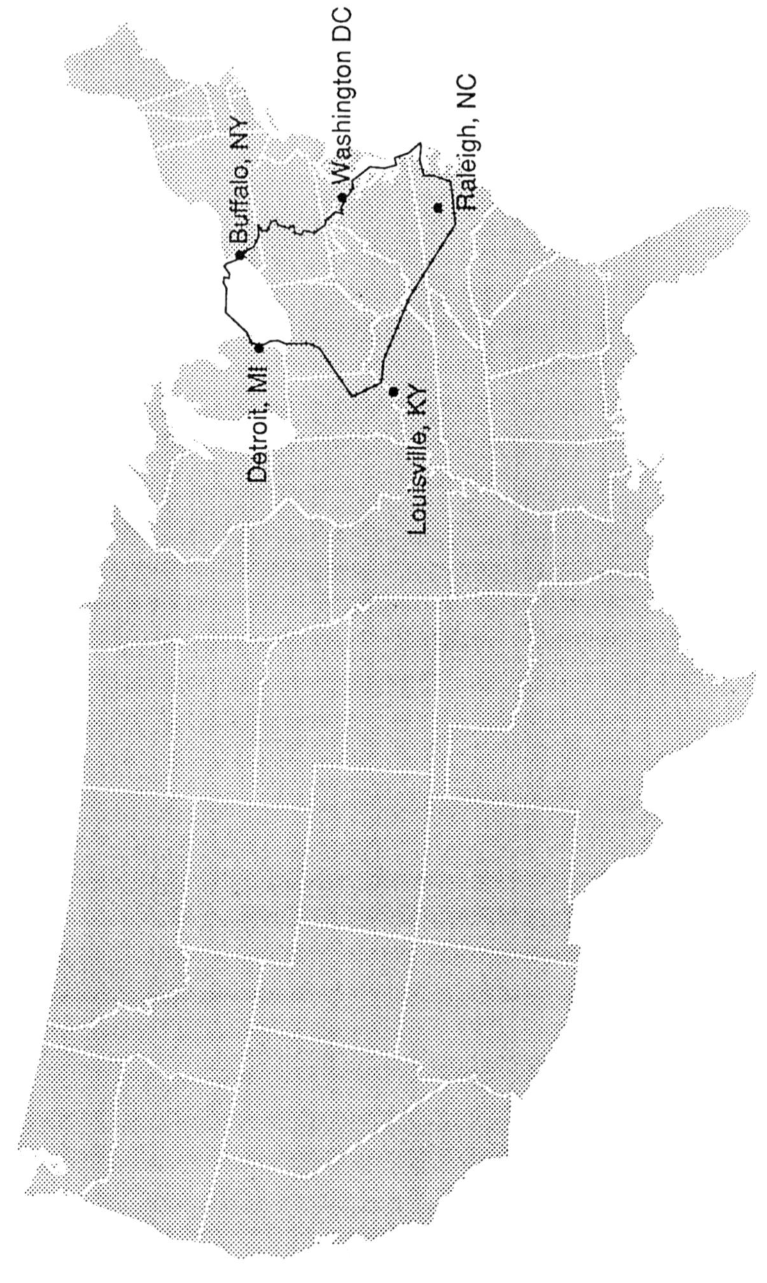
Buffalo, NY
Washington DC
Raleigh, NC
Detroit, MI
Louisville, KY

Map 2
Iraq Population Contours

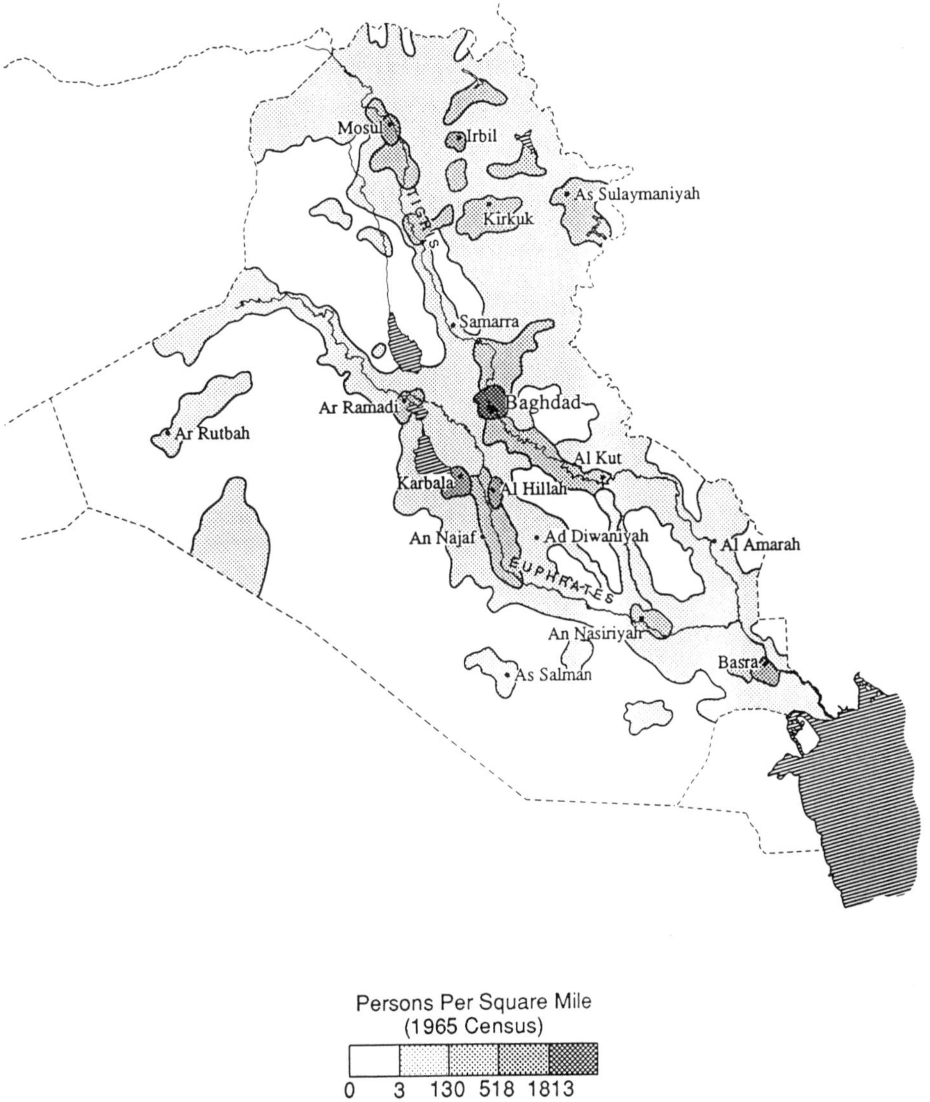

Persons Per Square Mile
(1965 Census)

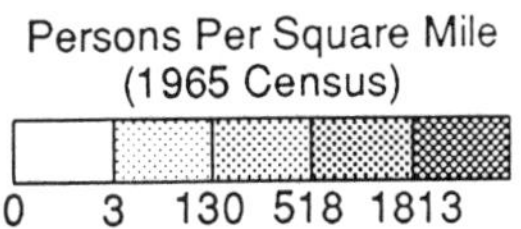

Map 3
Iraq Land Utilization

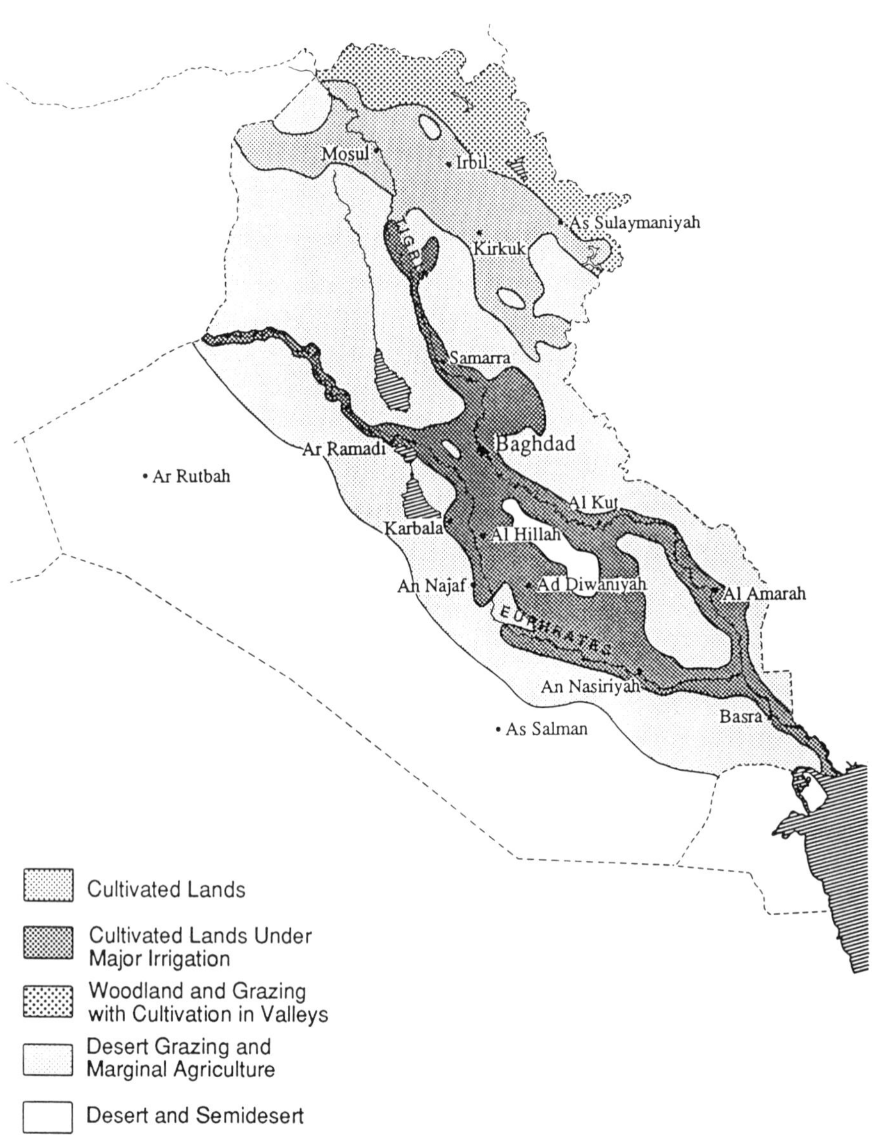

Nor for that matter has the Iraqi military, particularly the army, fought in those deserts. Instead the nation's great experience in war, its conflict with Iran, came in the terrain to the east of the rivers. From the border with Turkey in the north, a series of high mountains descends into rugged hills over a distance of three hundred miles. In this area, with sharply pointed terrain features, the Iraqis fought numerous battles with Iranians and Kurdish guerrillas. Map reading was relatively easy in a landscape of peaks and valleys. To the south, the Iran-Iraq frontier encroaches on the Mesopotamian valley with its relatively dense population; it then curves southward into a region of swamps and complex irrigation canals. In this area, the heaviest fighting of the Iran-Iraq conflict played itself out. Here, too, navigation represented few significant difficulties; moreover, terrain proved most suitable to the defensive tactics the Iraqis used to blunt Iranian attacks.

Significantly, the Iraqis had little experience in the deserts to the west and south. What little knowledge of the western deserts existed remained confined among truck drivers and construction crews working the pipelines and roads to Jordan and Syria. But even those Iraqis who drove through the desert felt that the great trackless spaces represented an area that was mysterious and hostile.[2]

And they were right. The desert spaces lying west and south of the Mesopotamian valley are thoroughly inhospitable to human beings. Scorching heat in summer, sudden deluges and terrible sand storms in winter, and virtually no water at most times of year would make this area a difficult challenge to military organizations even in peacetime. Beside the lack of water, navigating in a trackless wilderness with few points of reference–or in some areas constantly changing ones–represents as great a challenge as navigation at sea.

The first military force to grapple with operations in the desert, particularly the deep desert, was the British army in the Second World

---

[2]The Egyptian commentator Mohammed Heikal confirms this judgement: "The reason for Iraq's failure to protect its flank was later explained by a captured officer. The Iraqis assumed, he said, that the Coalition would not attempt to operate in the featureless desert, because of the risks of losing their way." Mohammed Heikal, *Illusions of Triumph, An Arab View of the Gulf War* (London, 1992), p 311. See also his analysis on p 269.

War. In a series of experiments stretching back to the 1920s and then pushed with great enthusiasm in the 1940-1941 period, the British learned to operate significant combat forces in a desert environment.[3] That process, however, took more than a decade of hard work and specialized training. But the Iraqi military in 1991 had little experience in desert conditions. Once the confrontation with the Coalition began, the Iraqis had little time to solve the problems involved in operating in such a region. As a result, both in their deployment and estimation of Coalition capabilities, the Iraqis assumed that Coalition forces would not and could not utilize the trackless spaces west of Kuwait. But the Global Positioning System combined with high levels of logistics and personnel training allowed Coalition forces to adapt to the desert in a fashion the Iraqis never expected.[4] Consequently, the deserts of western and southern Iraq represented a plus to Coalition forces, an advantage, however, that was not entirely clear before the ground campaign.

For allied airmen, the desert theater also presented significant advantages. The terrain laid the Iraqi Army open to the prying eyes of all forms of overhead reconnaissance. While the desert allowed the Iraqis to spread their forces out, the army divisions that poured into the KTO became an open book to the prying eyes of Coalition intelligence. Admittedly, the sameness of terrain and lack of clear points of reference were significant problems to allied aircraft in identifying which enemy positions were which, and after the ground war began in identifying the positions of Coalition forces.

Middle Eastern weather provides distinct climatic periods: summer with extraordinarily dry and hot conditions, and winter, lasting from November to April. Rainfall during the latter season averages only four inches a year around Kuwait; heavier rains fall the further north one moves. Nevertheless, throughout the winter, strong and violent storms

---

[3]For the best description of this effort see John W. Gordon, *The Other Desert War: British Special Forces in North Africa, 1940-1943* (New York, 1987).

[4]In a fashion that few of the so-called "experts" in the civilian world expected.

move through the area, bringing heavy rains and blowing sand storms in their wake. Unfortunately, Desert Storm's onset coincided with a period of particularly bad weather in the Gulf.[5] However, in any year the pattern of winter weather is not conducive to smooth, unimpeded military operations. If the bad weather that occurred in January and February was exceptional, it should not have been unexpected.

In the end, neither weather nor terrain represented significant advantages to the Iraqis, despite the fact that the war took place on their land. Ironically, their lack of knowledge of the desert turned to the advantage of the Coalition. From the point of view of employing air power and ground-based, technologically sophisticated systems, the desert with its flat and featureless terrain represented a significant advantage for Coalition military forces.

The Iraqis

Saddam Hussein invaded Kuwait and persisted in the face of worldwide opposition, a U.N. embargo, and the projection of immense military power into the Gulf as a result of ideological and political factors. Foremost among these were the nature of Iraqi tyranny, its ideologic world view, and its strategic goals. Iraq's military forces reflected its society, and the political and ideological framework of those forces played a crucial role in determining the outcome of the Gulf War.

The current regime in Baghdad draws heavily from an ideology developed in Syria in the 1930s.[6] This Baᶜthist ideology combined diverse threads of Fascism and Marxism with an intense Arab hostility to European colonialism. Above all, it aimed at rejuvenating the Arab world by rejecting Western political conceptions and replacing them with "Arabic" values. By utilizing the West's science and technology, the Arabs, Baᶜthist theory argued, could return to their rightful position as *the* dominant world civilization.

---

[5]Heikal, *Illusions of Triumph, An Arab View of the Gulf War*, p 307.

[6]The discussion in this chapter on the nature of the Iraqi political regime draws heavily from the penetrating book by the Iraqi exile Samir al-Khalil, *The Republic of Fear, The Politics of Modern Iraq* (Berkeley, CA, 1989).

In Iraq, the Baʿthist seized power briefly in 1963, but then fell from power. However, in 1968 they regained power; this time they set about making a stable and obedient polity out of a nation whose history had revolved around the success or failure of military coups. The new regime embarked on a ferocious purge of all centers of power in Iraq. Saddam Hussein, already assistant secretary general of the party, assumed control of internal security for the regime. Under his driving leadership, a pervasive sense of fear spread throughout the country. By 1979, firmly in control of state security, he moved against his fellow Baʿthists. In June, he replaced the president, while holding the families of his colleagues in the Revolutionary Command Council hostage. At the same time, he thoroughly purged the party's lower ranks. Then he moved against the leadership.[7]

When the dust settled, Saddam had created an extraordinary police state, one firmly grounded in Baʿth ideology and its paranoiac world view. His combination of ideology with an effective secret police reaching into all levels of society gave his regime enormous staying powers. On the other hand, it knew little of the external world and its ideological preconceptions insured that it would understand less.

The Iran-Iraq War

Having eliminated internal opposition, Saddam moved against Iran. Khomeini's revolution had thrown that nation into turmoil, while purges of the Iranian military placed the Islamic Republic's ability to defend itself in doubt. Since Iranian oil reserves lay close to Iraq in an area inhabited largely by Arabs (although of Shiʿte faith), Saddam concluded that he could easily expand Iraq's economic base, while seriously damaging his hated rival, Khomeini, by invading Iran.

---

[7]According to Khalil, Saddam carried out the purge of the party's top leadership in public: "The production that Saddam managed had all the hallmarks of his personal style. The first to 'confess' was Revolutionary Command Council member ʿAbd al-Husain Rashid whose family was held hostage. The confession was filmed and then, as one version of the story has it, shown to an all-party audience of several hundred leaders from the entire country. A grief-stricken Saddam addressed the meeting with tears running down his cheeks. He filled in the gaps in Rashid's testimony and dramatically fingered his former colleagues. Guards dragged people out of the proceedings and then Saddam called upon the country's top ministers and party leaders to themselves form the actual firing squads." *Ibid*, p 72.

Ba^cthist ideology provided Saddam with an extraordinary set of goals. As he suggested in January 1980, "We want our country to achieve its proper weight based on our estimation that Iraq is as great as China, as great as the Soviet Union, and as great as the United States."[8] In this context, Saddam meant not just Iraq, but an Arab world dominated by Iraq's Ba^cthist Party–one that with its oil reserves and attendant economic power could compete with the super powers.

The fact that Saddam possessed no experience beyond the world of Iraqi politics complicated the task. Moreover, he possessed no military experience, nor any background in military or strategic issues. His political instincts warned him to insure the political reliability of Iraq's military; much like Stalin, he equated professional competence with political independence. Consequently, his regime liquidated many of its best military commanders as threats to the nation's political stability. Moreover, there was little place in Saddam's Iraq for bearers of bad news or those who disagreed with the regime's policies.[9] Few who spoke their minds or who disagreed with the leader survived in positions of power.

Nevertheless, one should not take the regime and its military as fools. Within a limited arena, the Iraqis could mobilize popular support and economic resources–thanks to oil revenues–to confront opponents who operated within similar frameworks. The Iraqis possessed the political tools of control to force Iraq's population to obey; moreover, against military organizations with similar backgrounds, Iraqi commanders eventually proved sufficiently competent to force Iran to make peace on the basis of *status quo ante bellum*.

However, Saddam's decision to attack Iran initially resulted in a catastrophic war. After some initial successes, the Iraqis soon tumbled back onto their own territory in humiliation. Defeat came first in the air. Saddam had begun the war with major strikes to knock out the Iranian

---

[8]Speech of Saddam Hussein, 2 Jan 1980.

[9]Some reports stated that Saddam had shot a number of senior officers on the night of the invasion of Kuwait for disagreeing with his decision.

Air Force. The attack achieved little. Iraqi "bombs either missed the targets or misfired, partly because the crews did not possess the degree of expertise needed and partly because their Soviet warplanes, fitted with mediocre avionics, lacked accurate targeting equipment."[10]

Some Iraqi squadrons refused even to fight, while those that did, accomplished little in the air-to-air or air-to-ground arenas.[11] The Iranians, still possessing sophisticated U.S. aircraft and U.S.-trained pilots, and at least a modicum of the expertise that the Shah had purchased, gained the upper hand in the air war. Threatened with the loss of his air force, Saddam dispersed Iraqi aircraft to neutral territory in Jordan, Kuwait, Saudi Arabia, and Oman.[12] On the ground, the Iranians proved equally intractable and fierce. Moreover, Khomeini articulated his country's aim as being nothing less than the complete overthrow of Saddam's regime. The result was a series of defeats that came close to breaking Iraq.

But Saddam rallied his military to hold against fanatic Iranian assaults. Luckily for the Iraqis, the Iranians had their own troubles. In a fit of religious zeal, they completed the destruction of the Shah's military as the war continued. Without effective military leadership from senior levels down to non-commissioned officers,the revolutionary youth of Iran died in huge numbers before superior Iraqi firepower. The Iran-Iraq war settled into a war of attrition, in which the two sides faced each other across complex trench systems. The Iraqis relied on superior firepower to defeat the many Iranian offensives; the Iranians counted on superior numbers and religious fanaticism to break the Iraqis. As the war continued, the Iranians battered their way into southern Iraq, although they never achieved a decisive breakthrough. The result was a frightful blood bath for both sides.[13]

---

[10]Dilip Hiro, *The Longest War, The Iran-Iraq Military Conflict* (New York, 1991), p 40. The complete failure of this Iraqi attack on the Iranian Air Force probably contributed to an Iraqi belief in January 1991 that their air force could also survive a first strike by Allied air forces, should the Gulf confrontation turn into war.

[11]*Ibid*, p 41-2.

[12]*Ibid*, pp 41-2. See also Kenneth R. Timmerman, *The Death Lobby: How the West Armed Iraq* (Boston, 1991), pp 19-20.

[13]For discussions of the Iran-Iraq War, see Hiro, *The Longest War, the Iran-Iraq Military Conflict* ; Khalil, *The Republic of Fear, The Politics of Modern Iraq* ;
Anthony Cordesman, *The Iran-Iraq War and Western Security,1984-1987* (London, 1987).

Only desperate measures kept Iraq in the war. Saddam mobilized the population for war; to maintain morale, he allowed a peacetime economy to function. This approach of guns *and* butter provided domestic stability, but at the expense of Iraq's currency reserves and only with extensive borrowing from Arab neighbors. Confronting defeat, Saddam turned to an economic strategy and one of terror.[14] Iraqi aircraft attacked Iran's petroleum export facilities as well as tankers carrying Iranian oil. But these attacks failed to dissuade Iran from its political goal of toppling Saddam's regime. Both nations then resorted to firing Scud missiles at each other's cities. Heavy casualties resulted on both sides, but the repressive apparati of revolutionary police states stomped out waverings in popular support.

Finally, in 1988 a series of Iraqi victories led to the collapse of Iranian morale. In the spring, the Iraqis, going over to the offensive, regained much of the territory lost earlier in the conflict.[15] The Iraqis planned these attacks carefully, and set-piece battles against a debilitated opponent broke the Iranians. In each attack the Iraqis gained surprise; helped by U.S. intelligence, they possessed a thorough picture of Iranian dispositions, while the enemy operated in the dark.[16] Saddam's high command preplanned everything to the last detail, while Iranian weaknesses allowed the Iraqis to win without displaying much flexibility. They operated only within a highly structured framework.[17]

---

[14]Jaffee Center for Strategic Studies, *The Middle East Balance, 1987-1988* (Boulder, CO, 1988), Chapter 5.

[15]For an excellent discussion of the ending of the conflict see: Hiro, *The Longest War, The Iran-Iraq Military Conflict*, pp 199-212.

[16]Anthony Cordesman, *The Iran-Iraq War and Western Security, 1984-1987; Strategic Implications and Western Security*, pp 36-39. This intelligence information gave the Iraqis a healthy respect for the intelligence capabilities of the Americans.

[17]There were a number of "experts" both within and outside of the US government who discussed the Iraqi military in the most glowing terms before the Gulf War. Those assessments in turn drove the estimates that Coalition ground forces would suffer horrible casualties if it came to a direct military confrontation. What such analysis missed was the fact that Iraqi battlefield performance was strictly conditional. Within the context of a Middle Eastern war against an opponent with roughly equivalent levels of training and technology, the Iraqis were capable of performing effectively. But against an opponent whose capabilities, both in terms of technology and personnel, were on a more advanced

The war's cost was appalling. Estimates on the number of dead vary; conservative sources suggest a combined total of 367,000, of whom 262,000 were Iranian and 105,000 Iraqis. Military and civilian wounded approached three-quarters of a million.[18] Despite the war's costs, Saddam emerged in a stronger position than at the conflict's onset. The Ba^{c}thist regime in Baghdad had proved extraordinarily stable; undoubtedly, its ruthlessness enabled it to survive. It had mobilized its people and forced them to make extraordinary sacrifices; its security apparati reached into every level of Iraqi society; no matter how unpopular the conflict, no political disturbances occurred. Nevertheless, the performance of Iraqi military forces left much to be desired.

On the other side of the ledger, supporting the regime's demand that Iraqis persevere in the costly conflict to the end, lay extensive efforts to bribe the populace. Iraq pursued costly building projects; imports from outside kept shelves stocked with food stuffs and consumer goods; the peacetime economy continued in full swing. To do this, the regime imported millions of workers from Egypt and elsewhere in the Arab world. However, oil revenues could not meet the expenses of the war, much less the demands of servicing a peacetime economy. Only massive borrowing in the Arab world could keep the peacetime economy afloat and support the massive military effort required by the war. When the conflict was over Iraq was virtually bankrupt; its oil revenue could barely cover the interest on the national debt.

The regime's guns and butter approach had an interesting side effect that would impact on the military confrontation with the Coalition. When it became clear that the war with Iran was going to last a long period of time, the Iraqi military instituted a series of reforms to make military service as attractive as possible. Besides higher pay, considerable survivor benefits, and disability payments to the wounded, the regime provided for extensive periods of leave for soldiers in the combat theaters. Such policies would be in place when the Gulf crisis occurred,

---

level, the Iraqi military proved incapable of functioning effectively. For one of the most optimistic estimates of Iraqi military competence see Stephen C. Pelletiere, Douglas V. Johnson II, Leif R. Rosenberger, *Iraqi Power and U.S. Security in the Middle East* (Carlisle, PA, 1990).

[18]Hiro, *The Longest War, The Iran-Iraq Military Conflict*, p 250.

and consequently, throughout the lead up to the war, as much as 20 percent of the Iraqi Army may have been on leave at any given time.[19]

The people of Iraq greeted peace with enormous enthusiasm. But behind that enthusiasm lay much war weariness. The army's attitudes reflected national feelings. The long struggle with Iran certainly did not create a battle-hardened military force, eager to embark on other struggles.

In retrospect, the Iran-Iraq war did nothing to lessen Saddam's ambitions. Despite the fact that his country was almost bankrupt with a staggering debt, Iraq continued extensive armaments programs as well as the construction of monuments to glorify the war.[20] The Iraqi military obtained the most sophisticated weapons systems possible from Soviet and western suppliers; at the same time, it pushed efforts to produce special weapons, including nuclear devices. When these ambitious programs combined with a steady drop in oil prices, Iraq verged on bankruptcy. In 1989 it failed to pay the interest on its foreign debt; so serious did the financial situation become that some major arms suppliers suspended arms sales.[21]

Not surprisingly, Saddam leapt at the opportunity to settle with Kuwait in 1990; at one fell swoop he could eliminate a significant portion of his debt, while adding the oil resources of the Emirate to those of Iraq. America's reaction came as a surprise; but here Saddam's substantial misestimations of U.S. power and resolve worked against the Iraqis.

---

[19]See Chapter 6 of this book for examination of Iraqi leave policies and the impact they had on the army's readiness to meet Coalition forces in "the mother of all battles."

[20]See in particular Samir al-Khalil, *The Monument* (Berkeley, CA, 1992).

[21]Elaine Sciolino, *The Outlaw State: Saddam Hussein's Quest for Power and the Gulf Crisis* (Boston, 1991), pp 140, 188.

Above all, Saddam calculated that air power was an insignificant factor. As he suggested to CBS newsman Dan Rather in August 1990: "The United States depends on the Air Force. The Air Force has never decided a war."[22] Since air power could not play a crucial role, Saddam calculated that ground war would prove the final determinant of any military confrontation with the United States. Here the Iraqis believed they could inflict such heavy casualties that the Coalition would disintegrate and American willpower would collapse. As Saddam suggested to the U.S. Ambassador in July 1990: "Yours is a society which cannot accept 10,000 dead in one battle."[23]

One senses from Saddam's speeches as well as his actions a pervasive belief that the United States dared not resort to war.[24] Consequently, many Iraqis, including the military, did not take the threat of Coalition military action as seriously as they should have.[25] Military preparations aimed to deter the Coalition from attacking rather than to place Iraqi forces in the best military position.[26] Yet on paper those Iraqi military forces and their newly acquired capabilities represented a formidable challenge if the Coalition were to resort to war.

The Iraqi Military[27]

Saddam's gamble rested on how well his military would perform. There were some experts in the West who felt that the Iraqi military

---

[22]CBS Interview (Dan Rather) with Saddam Hussein, 29 Aug 1990, transcript in FBS-N25-90-170.

[23]Quoted by Jim Hoagland, *Washington Post*, 13 Sep 1990, p A33.

[24] Department of the Army, 513th Military Intelligence Brigade, Joint Debriefing Center, "The Gulf War: An Iraqi General Officer's Perspective," 11 Mar 1991, JDC Rpt #0052; and (S/REL UK) "Analyses of Source Debriefings," JDC Rpt #065.

[25](S/REL UK) Department of the Army, 513th Military Intelligence Brigade, Joint Debriefing Center, 11 Mar 1991, "Analysis of Source Debriefings," JDC Rpt #065, p 7.

[26]The stationing of much of their military forces in Kuwait and in southeastern Iraq made more sense from a political and diplomatic perspective, than from a military perspective.

[27]I am indebted to Dr. Caroline Ziemke for her help in the preparation of this section on the Iraqi military, both army and air force.

represented a highly competent military force.[28] One of the U.S.Army's major intelligence organs noted in September 1990 that the Iraqi Army

> . . . can conduct multi corps operations over 100 km or more and is capable of coordinating air and artillery, timing of movements and operations, coordinating complicated logistics requirements, and getting supplies, equipment, and troops to the right place at the designated time. The Iraqi army is distinguished by its flexibility, unity of command, and level of mobility. The army is highly qualified in planning, C-2, logistics and maintenance, but limitations placed upon commanders' initiative, especially in exploiting success, reduce these advantages.[29]

Nevertheless, Desert Storm indicated that the Iraqi military forces did not function at such high levels of effectiveness against Coalition forces. Within the Iraqi Army and Air Force, there existed considerable weaknesses and deficiencies; in the Iran-Iraq war, the Iraqis either worked around those weaknesses or placed their own strengths against the weaknesses of their opponent. The issue is not that the Iraqi military were grossly incompetent. In fact, throughout the Gulf War, they exhibited considerable powers to work around the damage imposed by Coalition air attacks.[30] But the point is that along with their strengths the Iraqis possessed serious weaknesses.

The greatest weakness of Iraq's military posture lay in the regime itself. Saddam possessed little understanding of the external world beyond Iraq.[31] Ba^cthist ideology distorted the few glimmerings of other nations that penetrated inside Saddam's tight-knit circle. Moreover, the dictator himself was largely ignorant of military factors–an ignorance that

---

[28] The study by Pelletiere, Johnson, and Rosenberger, *Iraqi Power and U.S. Security in the Middle East* is a case in point. For a brief sampling of such attitudes one might consult the testimony given before the House and Senate Armed Services Committees in the period immediately before the outbreak of the war; in particular see the testimony by Gen David Jones and Adm William Crowe, both former Chairmen of the Joint Chiefs of Staff.

[29] US Army Intelligence and Threat Analysis Center, "How They Fight–Desert Shield Order of Battle Handbook," Sep 1990, p 43.

[30] The Iraqi ability to hide their Scuds is a case in point, as was their capacity to maintain some form of communications to front line units throughout the war. For further discussion of the Scud campaign see Chapter 4.

[31] Nor for that matter did much of the Iraqi Army.

the experiences of the Iran-Iraq War had not corrected. Finally, his tyranny had so cowed military and civilian advisers alike that few, if any, dared mention unpleasant truths.

The Iraqi Army

The history of Iraq's army is intertwined with the nation's political history. It has represented the only coherent symbol of the Iraqi nation. As such, it was not loath to interfere in politics; between 1936 and 1956, it launched no less than five major coups, including an attempt in 1941 to join the Axis. Nevertheless, the army displayed little competence on the battlefield in that period. In the 1941 coup, a couple of under-strength British brigades from an army in desperate shape in the Middle East sufficed to rout the entire Iraqi Army.[32]

The Iraqi Army's participation in politics came at a high cost. Bloody purges followed each coup. The success of the 1956 coup only embroiled the army deeper in politics. Military men dominated cabinet and policy-making positions.[33] None of this contributed to the professionalization of the officer corps or to bettering military effectiveness. The disastrous performance of Iraqi forces in 1967 and 1973 against Israel further underlined the ineffectiveness of a politicized military.

The Ba^cth Party's control of Iraq after 1968 further exacerbated the military's weaknesses. The army's central role in maintaining internal order continued under the Ba^cthists, but its political independence did not. Iraq's new leaders did not miss the lessons of previous decades. A series of bloody purges removed all influential officers who lacked close ties to the party; political loyalty became the sole criteri for promotion. By 1971, Saddam, as the director of state security, was confident that "with our party methods, there is no chance for someone who disagrees with us

[32]The British had just lost Greece, were in the process of losing Crete, and had suffered a major defeat at the hands of Rommel (the first of many). In these desperate circumstances the British put together a rag-tag force and regained their position controlling Iraq and its strategic oil fields.

[33]Khalil, *The Republic of Fear*, pp 21-22.

to jump on a couple of tanks and overthrow the government."[34] The party and its security organs maintained a vigilant watch over everything in the military.

With Saddam's seizure of power in 1979, the emphasis became loyalty to the tyrant as well as party. In terms of the dictator's priorities, political control of the army became a basic principle on which the survival of the regime rested. With the army's previous history of launching coups, Saddam could not afford a cocoon of "professionalism." The first years of the war against Iran underlined the costs of a system that equated political loyalty with military competence. The war's desperate situation eventually forced Saddam to make changes, and the Iraqi Army showed some improvement during the conflict. But improvements came within a framework that satisfied political criteria. Initiative, flexibility, and rapid decision-making never became a hallmark for Iraqi operations. Iraq won the war against Iran because their opponent was less professional and even more determined to impose ideological [religious] purity.[35]

In the two years between the war with Iran and the Gulf conflict, the Iraqi Army went through an extensive expansion. The regime made major efforts to upgrade equipment as well as to expand the quantitative basis; it purchased large numbers of T-72s from the Soviet Union along with less sophisticated weapons and tanks from China. The Republican Guard, already a major force by the end of the war with Iran, continued its expansion as well. In the end, however, this continued expansion of Iraq's military forces may only have succeeded in diluting the quality of the army; certainly the events of 1991 suggest a hollow military indeed.

The overall picture of the Iraqi Army, then, was spotty. It had shown considerable powers of sacrifice in the Iran-Iraq war. Saddam's tyranny reinforced that spirit. The army possessed extraordinary engineering skills; as it had shown on numerous occasions during the Iran-Iraq War,

---

[34] Ronald E. Bergquist, *The Role of Air Power in the Iran-Iraq War* (Maxwell AFB, AL, 1988), p 22.

[35] (/REL UK) Department of the Army, 513th Military Intelligence Brigade, Joint Debriefing Center, "Analysis of Source Debriefings," JDC Rpt #065, p 3.

its ability to construct extensive field fortifications was unsurpassed. It also possessed extensive skills in camouflaging its positions and in building extensive dummy positions to mislead its opponents. On the other hand, the army remained politicized; it had little tolerance for initiative, nor much capacity to adapt; its soldiers possessed few of the educational or cultural aptitudes required by modern armed forces.[36] And its general officers had few of the leadership or intellectual capabilities of leaders on the other side of the hill.

The Iraqi Air Force

In most respects the Iraqi air force mirrored the weaknesses of the ground forces. [For the location of major Iraqi airfields see Map 4.] Throughout its history, the air force has remained subservient to the army. Iraq has consistently identified itself as a continental power, while the army's role as an internal guardian of order has given it the dominant position among Iraq's military institutions.

Two events in the 1980s, however, caused the Iraqis to reconsider the external threat. The 1981 Israeli attack on the Osirik nuclear reactor had set back Iraqi nuclear ambitions considerably; that raid also underlined Iraq's vulnerability to air attack.[37] Moreover, the relative impunity with which Iranian aircraft attacked Baghdad in the early days of the Iran-Iraq war represented a further warning. The result was that Iraq devoted considerable resources to build up its air defenses and to purchase up-to-date fighter aircraft. Nevertheless, even with this effort to build up the air force and air defenses, the primary focus in the Iraqi Air Force remained on the air-to-ground mission rather than on the air-to-air task of gaining air superiority.[38]

---

[36] *Ibid.*

[37] For more detailed examination of Iraq's efforts to acquire nuclear weapons see Michael Eisenstadt, "'The Sword of the Arabs: Iraq's Strategic Weapons," Policy Paper No. 21 (Washington Institute for Near East Policy, 1990); and Jed C. Snyder, "The Road to Osirak: Baghdad's Quest for the Bomb," *Middle East Journal*, Autumn 1983.

[38] This reflected the fact that by the end of the Iran-Iraq War the Iranian air force had almost entirely collapsed due to the loss of its US-trained pilots and aircraft. Consequently, the Iraqi air force no longer confronted the problem of gaining air superiority over the battlefield, while the crucial mission remained the support of Iraqi ground troops locked in their desperate struggle with the Iranians. (S/WN/NC/NF) SPEAR, Naval Intelligence Command, "Iraqi Threat to U.S. Forces," Dec 1990, p 3-63.

Map 4
Iraqi Air Bases

That Iraq would see the army as the decisive combat arm is not surprising. What seems less explicable is that the Air Force, charged with providing air defense and air support for ground forces, has proven so ineffective in both roles, not only in the war against Iran but in the Gulf War as well. While technically impressive, the Iraqi air defense system demonstrated weaknesses even during the Iran-Iraq War. Early in the Iran-Iraq War, the Iranian Air Force flew at will over Iraqi cities; the Iraqis made little effort to intercept intruders, because their defenses were incapable of distinguishing between friend and foe. In short, the primary role of Iraqi air power in the early 1980s was as a deterrent. Consequently, there was little willingness to risk aircraft losses or to fly dangerous missions. Far from criticizing his air force for its lack of offensive initiative in 1981, Saddam saw its inactivity as a reasonable strategic proposition: "We will not use our air force. We will keep it. Two years hence our air force will still be in a position to pound Bani-Sadr [then prime minister of Iran] and his collaborators."[39]

Like the army, the air force did improve during the war. Its strikes against Iranian tankers and Kharj Island–the crucial terminal for Iranian oil exports–showed considerable sophistication. However, at least in attacks on Iranian tankers, Iraqi aircraft operated in a risk-free environment.[40] Nevertheless, one Iraqi pilot made the enormous mistake of attacking the USS *Stark*, which created a serious international incident.

However, the attacks on the Kharj terminal were complex air operations in a hostile arena. In addition, in November 1986, Iraqi F-1s used "buddy" refueling techniques to strike the Larak Island oil facilities–a distance of nearly 1,200 miles from their bases.[41] Still, the Iraqis launched such raids only after long preparation and planning; also, these

[39] Maj Gen Edward B. Atkeson (USA, ret), "Iraq's Arsenal: Tool of Ambition," *Army*, Mar 1991, p 24.

[40] The Iraqis were not in a position to intercept Iranian aircraft, while the attackers undoubtedly received considerable mission support from the Gulf States on the southern side of the Persian Gulf. See (S/WN/NC/NF) SPEAR, "Iraqi Threat to U.S. Forces," Appendix C.

[41] Yet as one commentator on the Iran-Iraq War noted during the war: "in practice the two air forces proved to be equally incompetent." Efriam Karsh, *The Iran-Iraq War, A Military Analysis*, Adelphi Papers 220, Spring 1987.

raids exploited Kuwaiti bases for recovery, and only utilized a small portion of Iraq's air assets–the best pilots and aircraft. More significantly, the Iraqis failed to maintain such efforts for prolonged periods of time. As a result, these operations appeared to be spectacular, but proved neither decisive nor long-lasting. At best they shut Kharj down for short periods of time and lowered Iranian oil exports. But never did they stop Iran's ability to export oil.[42]

In the air-to-air arena, the Iraqis displayed little initiative and skill. As the U.S. naval intelligence reported shortly before Desert Storm:

> Air-to-air engagements [on both sides of the Iran-Iraq War] were correspondingly unimpressive. Both sides appeared to overestimate the capability of their adversary and had an exaggerated fear of radar guided missiles. Iraqi avoidance of air-to-air engagements was continuous throughout the war. Lock-on by Iranian fighters would generally cause Iraqi aircraft conducting offensive counter-air/strike missions to abort the mission and return to base. Even when the odds were overwhelmingly in favor of the Iraqi air force, survival still dominated their tactics. Any engagements that did occur were noteworthy for a lack of aggressive maneuvering. High speed, maximum range missile launches were followed by egress and return to base by both sides.[43]

The failure of the Iraqi Air Force to play a decisive role in the Iran-Iraq conflict did not prevent Saddam from investing heavily in air power during peacetime. The Iraqis spent considerable sums to upgrade their aircraft inventory by buying more Mirage F-1s and a number of MiG-29s. Moreover, they continued efforts to expand their air bases and to provide airfields with multiple runways and taxiways as well as hardened shelters capable of withstanding even nuclear blasts.

---

42 Defense Intelligence Agency commented on the Iraqi Air Force's performance in the Iran-Iraq War in the following terms in early 1990: "Despite an overwhelming advantage over Iran in numbers of operational aircraft, Iraq has failed to take full advantage of its air superiority. Iraqi effectiveness has been limited by conservative employment doctrine, unsophisticated tactics, and the political leadership's reluctance to employ the air force more aggressively." Defense Intelligence Agency, "Iraqi Ground and Air Forces [sic] Doctrine, Tactics and Operations," Feb 1990.

43 (S/WN/NC/NF) SPEAR, "Iraqi Threat to U.S. Forces," p 3-63.

Yet the seventy-five years of air warfare have consistently underlined that the crucial element in aerial combat lies in the capabilities of aircrews. The Iraqis had, of course, just completed a major war against Iran–a conflict during which they had suffered significant pilot losses. Moreover, they were now taking on newer and more complex model aircraft even as the war with Iran ended. Consequently, rebuilding the Iraqi Air Force took place within the framework of upgrading to significantly more complex equipment.

The picture of fighter pilots available to western intelligence suggests that there were few first-class operators in the Iraqi Air Force.[44] During the war against Iran, Iraqi pilots had earned "their qualifications and status with a minimum expenditure of personal effort and risk."[45] Basic training provided little on which to upgrade fighter pilots to more sophisticated aircraft; moreover, the Iraqis conducted basic instruction on a rigid and inflexible pattern. Pilots and instructors executed their maneuvers "solely by reference to instruments with little attention paid to outside, visual references." Consequently, most Iraqi pilots had difficulty transitioning to the more advanced stages of air-to-air training.[46]

Not surprisingly the products of such a system were unexceptional.Iraqi pilots lacked the preparation to "respond proficiently to dynamic tactical situations," while they had "relatively poor air-to-air maneuvering and lookout skills." For the most part, "their overall situation awareness [was] extremely poor." Those who flew the Mirage went from basic pilot training in Iraq to France, where over 80 percent washed out of the coursethat had little impact on the Iraqi Air Force, which qualified virtu-

---

[44]One of the most accurate prewar analyses of Iraq's military capabilities was that performed by the SPEAR Department of the Navy's Operational Intelligence Center: (S/WN/NC/NF) "Iraqi Threat to U.S. Forces." SPEAR's accuracy in the assessment business largely reflected the fact that it was one of the few intelligence organizations in the American military that combined individuals with operational backgrounds in about equal numbers with intelligence officers. The relationship clearly brought out the best in both and SPEAR's studies were close to the mark when Desert Shield moved into its execution phase. For a less sophisticated examination of the Iraqi air force that was more positive as to its capabilities see: (S) Defense Intelligence Agency, "Iraqi Ground and Air Force Doctrine, Tactics and Operations, Feb 1990.

[45](S) *Ibid*, p 3-63.

[46](S) *Ibid*, pp 3-62 and 3-63.

ally all who flunked the French syllabus upon return.[47] The Soviets were not so demanding and generally passed everyone; the Iraqis, however, regarded Soviet training as decidedly inferior to what the French provided.[48] On the other hand, the Soviets assessed less than half the students whom they passed as possessing the ability to fly in frontline Soviet fighter outfits, which in turn were considerably below American standards.[49]

Follow-on training in the Iraqi Air Force was no more remarkable. After the war with Iran, Iraqi Air Force leaders considered an ambitious program to upgrade pilot skills. However, one suspects that Iraq's financial difficulties prevented implementation of any serious upgrade program. The training that occurred was not particularly challenging; "Intercept tactics and training [were] still predominantly conservative, elementary, and generally not up to western standards." [50]

The emphasis in Iraqi air operations against Iran had rested on support for ground forces. Consequently, the best pilots in the Iraqi Air Force have traditionally gone into ground attack units. Air-to-air units had the leavings.[51] The basic issue here is that the Iraqis, whatever the technological sophistication of their equipment, did not possess the basic flying skills to exploit fully the capabilities of their aircraft.

---

[47](S) *Ibid*, p 3-63.

[48]How much the former Soviets had to learn from the Gulf War as well as their own mis-estimates of the balance of skill and technology between the east and the west is suggested by a short article written by a former Soviet advisor to the Iraqis as the Gulf War was actually unfolding: "I feel that the Iraqi fighter pilots were trained just as well as the pilots of, for instance, France and Finland with whom we in recent years have been in contact repeatedly. In truth, I will not take it upon myself to compare their professionalism with the combat skills of American pilots but, in constantly seeing the prevalence of Negroes and mulattoes among the U.S. pilots on the TV screens, I could draw some conclusions." "Former Soviet 'Advisor' Describes Experiences in Iraq," *Komsomolskaya Pravda*, 23 Feb 1991, Foreign Military Affairs, JPRS-UMA-91-014. For a thorough examination of the Russian military's examination of the air war in Desert Storm (which also tells much about how to think through the significance of the air war) see: Benjamin S. Lambeth, *Desert Storm and its Meaning: The View from Moscow*, Rand Rpt R-4164-AF (Santa Monica, CA, 1992).

[49](S/WN/NC/NF) SPEAR, "Iraqi Threat to U.S. Forces," p 3-61.

[50](S/WN/NC/NF) *Ibid*, p 3-64.

[51](S/WN/NC/NF) *Ibid*, p 3-63.

The Iraqi Air Defense System

Beyond its aircraft, Iraq depended on a complex air defense network. The Iraqi system was highly centralized; four sectors, each with a Sector Operations Center (SOC), controlled air and air defense assets. The focus of that network was on meeting two threats: long distance Israeli air attacks or that posed by the Iranian Air Force, what little remained after the war. Under each SOC, Intercept Operation Centers (IOCs) ran ground control intercepts and SAM defenses and coordinated the flow of information from individual radar stations and visual reporting sites to the SOCs.

Information collated at the center then flowed back down to antiaircraft units, air bases, and SAM sites.

At the center, the Air Defense Operations Center (ADOC) in Baghdad made the crucial decisions, while a French-designed computer system (KARI-Iraq spelled backwards in French) tied the network's diverse pieces together.[52] KARI also possessed "land line and/or command microwave radio links (either troposcatter or line-of-sight)" to lower echelons. Redundant land lines tied the section centers to the national command level, while the Iraqis placed their intercept centers near existing telecommunication trunks capable of carrying both voice and data communications. The French designed system modems so that each node could easily switch from one form of communication to another.[53] The Iraqis also provided extensive protection to both types of centers by placing them in hardened shelters.

As the war with the Coalition loomed, the Iraqi leadership viewed the strategic purpose of its air defenses as providing the means for the nation to ride out an air campaign. The defenses were to inflict heavy enough losses on the attackers to bring on a ground campaign. The primary tools for defending Iraqi air space were SAM and antiaircraft

---

[52] (S/WN/NC/NF) *Ibid*, pp 3-7 to 3-29.

[53] (S/WN/NC/NF) *Ibid*, pp 3-17, 3-25.

forces. On paper, active air defenses were indeed impressive: five hundred radars located in no less than one hundred sites, SA-2 batteries, SA-3 batteries, SA-6 batteries, SA-8, and ROLAND I/II systems covered different areas of the nation. The air defense system controlled about 8,000 antiaircraft pieces, but the percentage devoted to the defense of strategic targets as opposed to the defense of the army in the Kuwaiti Theater of Operations is not known. Nevertheless, the Iraqis deployed approximately 4,000 fixed and mobile antiaircraft artillery pieces and SAMs around Baghdad [see Map 5].[54]

Not surprisingly, the Iraqis tied the SAMs closely to computer KARI. However, antiaircraft artillery relied on barrage firing on preset azimuths to hit attacking aircraft. The Iraqis believed that a combination of SAMs and antiaircraft artillery would impose sufficient attrition on attacking forces; at medium to high altitudes SAMs would shoot down many Coalition aircraft; should the attackers go low, then antiaircraft guns would inflict heavy casualties. Finally, Iraqi aircraft, protected by hardened aircraft shelters, could intervene at selected moments to add to Coalition losses.

Unfortunately for the Iraqis, KARI possessed a number of weaknesses. French experts oriented the system to protect Iraq from attack from the east (Iran) and west (Israel). Coverage towards Saudi Arabia was weak. SAM and antiaircraft defenses were strong in some sectors; admittedly, Baghdad was an extraordinarily heavily defended target [see Map 5]. Strong air defenses also protected Basra, Scud-launching sites in western Iraq, and Iraq's northern oil fields. But much of the rest of the country lay open–a factor that allowed allied aircraft to approach targets from different directions. Moreover, the layout of the western and central sectors created a dead zone pointed directly at Baghdad from Saudi Arabia.[55] Not surprisingly, Iraqi defensive systems could only handle

---

[54] (S/WN/NC/NF) *Ibid*, p 3-13.

[55] Intvw with Gen Henry, GWAPS, 28 Aug 1992; "Electronic Combat in Desert Shield/Desert Storm," Brig Gen Larry Henry, GWAPS NA 358.

threat levels consistent with Middle Eastern force structures.[56] Indeed, to the Iraqis, the system's capacity to track targets seemed more than sufficient.[57]

But what Coalition air forces could throw at the Iraqis was something well beyond the capacity of Iraqi information, command and control, and weapons system capabilities.[58] The largest weakness, however, lay in the fact that Iraqi operators and pilots could not handle either the technological or tactical competence of Coalition forces. Exacerbating their deficiencies was the low level of training and preparation among Iraqis in comparison to the levels of their opponents.

The Coalition

The greatest potential weakness of Iraq's opponents lay in the fact that they were a Coalition. At the highest level, intense negotiations, cajoling, and careful handling all combined to achieve general agreement among the partners to use force against Iraq. The Coalition of Saudi Arabia, Britain, France, the Gulf States, Syria, Egypt, the U.N. and myriad other nations was neither inherently stable, nor naturally united.[59] Yet,

---

[56]The misapprehension that they were confronting a threat consistent with their Middle Eastern experiences marked Iraqi behavior throughout the prewar and wartime periods. Their mis-estimate of American capabilities was similar to the mis-estimate that the North Vietnamese made in 1962 in calculating the power of the United States. They may well have won the Second Vietnam War, but they inherited a nation that American firepower wrecked from one end to the other and they lost an entire generation of young men. See Bernard Fall, *Last Reflections on a War* (New York, 1967).

[57](S/WN/NC/NF) SPEAR, "Iraqi Threat to U.S. Forces," p 3-20.

[58]This is suggested by the fact that the northern SOC at Kirkuk only went down for a few days during the war; yet it proved incapable of handling the air strikes put into northern and central Iraq from Turkey by the American forces, operating out of Incirlik. Undoubtedly, there were a number of factors at work, such as "Proven Force's" SEAD efforts, but the zero loss rate is indeed suggestive. For the continuing operation of the Kirkuk SOC see (S/WN) Defense Intelligence Agency, "Desert Storm BDA Imagery Review, DDX-2900-489-91, May 1991, Vol. II, p 95.

Map 5

Iraqi IR SAM and AAA Threat

Saddam's efforts to break up the Coalition prior to 17 January 1991 showed little success, a result more of his inept diplomacy than of the Coalition's inherent strengths.

On the operational side, Coalition members deployed great military power as the crisis built towards its military climax.[60] In most of history, coalitions have found it particularly difficult to cooperate in the military sphere in the early part of a conflict.[61] In this war, the differences in the operational style of national military forces did not prove to be as great a hurdle.

The major non-Arab contributors, the United States, Great Britain, and France, all held the common experience of cooperating within the NATO framework. While the French have remained outside of NATO's command structure since 1962, they have had extensive direct and indirect contacts and working experience with their NATO allies in the field. Consequently, neither British nor French forces had significant difficulties in working with Americans. On the air side, both the British and the Saudis had participated in "Red Flag" exercises, so their pilots had regularly integrated themselves into American practices and employment concepts.

The three major NATO powers deployed exceptionally professional forces to the Gulf. Since the 1950s, the British have relied on all-volunteer forces rather than on conscription; in the early 1970s, the

---

[59] The French minister of defense resigned shortly before the shooting war began to protest the anti-Iraq policy of his government and because he felt participation in the war would permanently damage French standing in the Arab world.

[60] See Chapter 1 for a discussion of the actual forces deployed.

[61] See in particular Edward Spears, *Liaison, 1914: A Narrative of the Great Retreat* (London, 1936) and *Assignment to Catastrophe* (London, 1954) for the problems that confronted the British and French in the opening years of World War I and World War II.

United States embarked on a similar road. While the French still held to conscription, the forces they deployed to the Gulf came largely from professional units. While Coalition forces lacked combat experience, they did have extraordinarily high levels of professional skill. Coalition soldiers, airmen and sailors were experts in the profession of arms, at both tactical and operational levels.

Moreover, many of the Coalition's Arab air forces had worked with the Americans. Most flew American aircraft and many had received training in the U.S. Only the Syrians, with a long history of dependence on the Soviets for equipment and training, had little common experience with their allies. Consequently, whether one talks about air or ground operations, there was considerable commonality in thought pattern, concepts of operations, and tactical frameworks within which Coalition forces would operate.

The Americans

The bulk of the Coalition's military strength rested on the capabilities of the American forces deployed in the Persian Gulf. And it was on the capabilities of those U.S. forces that success or failure in the Gulf would depend. The American political system had regained much equilibrium since the Vietnam war. Under Presidents Reagan and Bush the nation again projected an image of strength and determination on the international scene. Nevertheless, beneath that exterior, substantial doubts assailed U.S. leaders and those recording American attitudes. Above all, Vietnam had created a sensitivity in all levels of leadership to the loss of American life, and this sensitivity carried over into the conduct of operations and strategy. Moreover, that sensitivity carried over into a specific and general unwillingness to put Iraq's population at hazard.[62]

Throughout the lead-up to, and the conduct of this war, concerns over possible American battlefield casualties expressed this factor most directly; this was a direct reflection of the impact of Vietnam on the American psyche.[63] From the onset of the crisis, this fear of heavy losses was a

---

[62] See Gen Glosson's comment in Chapter 1 of this report.

[63] Gen Glosson in his prewar briefing to American fighter pilots underlined that no target was worth the loss of an American aircraft. Glosson implied that our aircraft would be able to return to attack a target that had not been destroyed, but once an aircraft

major factor in decision-making in Washington. Saddam was a careful observer of these debates and as war approached, he made clear his belief that this American fear represented a weakness, especially when compared to the level of sacrifices that Iraq had borne in its war with Iran.[64]

The American Military

In 1973 the United States had withdrawn the last of its military forces from South Vietnam; the collapse of that polity followed shortly thereafter. The impact of the war on the American military was serious in the short run. For some in the military, defeat resulted from unwillingness of politicians, media, and even the people to stand behind the fighting man.[65] For others defeat resulted from the failure of national leaders, military as well as civilian, to create an effective strategy for the conflict.[66] Some veterans felt the military had performed badly on all the

---

or aircrew had been lost, one was in an irrevocable situation. Glosson's attitude stands in stark contrast to the attitude of army air force commanders in World War II, whose attitude was that any losses were justified so long as bombers attacked the target. Intvw, Maj Gen Buster Glosson by GWAPS personnel (Williamson Murray, Barry Watts, and Thomas Keaney), 14 Apr 1992. Glosson's comments to F-16 pilots were confirmed by Maj John Nichols, member of 401st Tactical Fighter Wing, GWAPS, 20 Jul 1992.

[64]But, as with almost everything that he did in this war, Saddam's attitude may have backfired against him. Saddam's boasts "that America would not tolerate thousands of dead GIs, but that Iraq was ready for such sacrifices" directly impacted on the morale of his troops. Department of the Army, 513th Military Intelligence Brigade, Joint Debriefing Center, "The Gulf War: An Iraqi General Officer's Perspective," 11 Mar 1991, JDC Rpt #0052.

[65]Frederick Downs, in his dispassionate account of his service in Vietnam, recounts an incident that happened to all too many servicemen after their tours in Vietnam: "In the fall 1968, as I stopped at a traffic light on my walk to class across the campus of the University of Denver, a man stepped up to me and said, 'Hi!' Without waiting for my reply to his greeting, he pointed to the hook sticking out of my left sleeve. 'Get that in Vietnam?' I said 'Yeah, up near Tam Ky in I Corps.' 'Serves you right.' As the man walked away, I stood rooted, too confused with hurt, shame and anger to react." Frederick Downs, *The Killing Zone: My Life in the Vietnam War* (New York, 1978), preface, no page.

[66]Harry Summers notes at the beginning of his work: "'You know you never defeated us on the battlefield,' said the American Colonel. The North Vietnamese pondered this remark for a moment. 'That may be so,' he replied, 'but it is also irrelevant.'" Summers, *On Strategy: A Critical Examination of the Vietnam War* (Carlisle, PA, 1987), p 1.

levels of war.[67] But virtually all military professionals agreed that there was room for improvement.[68]

In the 1970s,improvement dealt with reestablishing the discipline and respect essential for military effectiveness. In the 1980s, with Reagan's swelling defense budgets, the U.S. military carried out a massive re-equipment of its forces, as well as a rethinking of how best to employ its growing combat power. This two-part process played a major role in the Gulf. Throughout the Reagan buildup, there was a major debate in the U.S. over the weapons that the military needed after the drawdown of the 1970s. Arguments revolved around issues of quantity and quality. The so-called military reformers argued that the U.S. should not buy complex, sophisticated weapons because they were not only expensive, but unreliable. Instead, they argued the American military needed cheaper and less sophisticated weapons, ones that were more reliable and available in larger quantities, and which required less support.[69] On the other side, the American military argued that with technological advances, rapidly evolving computers, and sophisticated volunteer soldiers (or airmen, or seamen), the U.S. military needed to ride the technological wave.

In almost every case Secretary of Defense Casper Weinburger supported "high tech" solutions in purchasing the next generation of U.S. weapons. While not all of those weapons proved out, the superiority as well as reliability of the new technologies played an important role in the

---

[67] Maj Gen Buster Glosson, when he talked to a group from GWAPS, emphasized his belief that Summers was wrong and that we had performed no better on the tactical level during the Vietnam War than we had performed on the other levels of war and that we had gotten large numbers of men killed because our performance on the basic tactical level had been so inadequate. Intvw, Maj Gen Buster Glosson with GWAPS personnel (Williamson Murray, Barry Watts, Thomas Keaney, and Alexander Cochran), 9 Apr 1992.

[68] Virtually every senior officer that GWAPS interviewed for this study indicated their profound dissatisfaction with the leadership under which they had served in the Vietnam War and their desire to insure that this time the same mistakes would not occur at any level.

[69] For two of the more publicized critics of the American military see Gary Hart and Bill Lind, *America Can Win: The Case for Military Reform* (Bethesda, MD, 1986); and James Fallows, *National Defense* (New York, 1982).

Gulf.[70] On balance, technological sophistication significantly enhanced, rather than undermined, the performance of well-trained American forces.

But the superiority of American (and Coalition) equipment explains only a portion of the success. On the second day of the ground offensive, a platoon of Marine M1A1s–manned by reservists–ran into a battalion of Iraqi tanks deploying to counterattack. Despite the fact that the Iraqis outnumbered the M1A1s, and the encounter engagement took place at close range in daylight conditions, the Marines destroyed thirty-four enemy tanks in less than ten minutes; they suffered no losses to themselves.[71] This single example underlines that the crucial factor in the Gulf War lay in the superiority of training that Coalition forces had received during the previous decade. That training advantage overshadowed whatever combat experience Iraqi forces had gained against Iran.

Vietnam had shown serious shortcomings in the tactical preparation of American forces. Above all, the Army had felt those failings; and if it did not always own up in public to its failures in Vietnam, it grappled seriously in both tactical and operational domains. In the 1970s, it rewrote its basic doctrinal manual, FM 100-5 and then packaged the new manual in such a fashion that an explosive debate occurred throughout the Army over the directions that doctrine should take.[72] That, in turn, led to a new FM 100-5–one substantially reworking the 1970s version to re-emphasize maneuver and battlefield flexibility. The crucial point is

[70]The distances at which US M1A1 could acquire, hit, and then destroy targets in comparison to the T-72 tanks that the Iraqis deployed suggests the advantages that the high-tech equipment gave US forces in all arenas in which our forces engaged the Iraqis in the Gulf War. M1A1s were capable of acquiring and killing Iraqi tanks at ranges of more than 3,000 yards; the Iraqis using T-72s could acquire and fire at US tanks at ranges barely more than 1,000 yards unless direct visual conditions were operative.

[71]Lt Col J.G. Zumwalt, "Tanks! Tanks! Direct Forward!" *Proceedings of the U.S. Naval Institute*, Jul 1992, pp 78-80. What is significant about this engagement, as opposed to most others in the Gulf War, was the fact that it occurred at relatively close range and with both sides caught by surprise. Thus, the combat conditions should have negated some of the technological advantages of US weapons systems. The results, however, were the same: the utter destruction of the enemy forces and minimal damage to US forces.

[72]For a careful study of Gen Depuy's formulation of the new version of FM 100-5 see Paul M. Herbert, *Deciding What Has to be Done: General William E. Depuy and the 1976 Edition of FM 100-5, Operations* (Leavenworth, 1988).

that not only has the Army rewritten basic doctrine twice since Vietnam, but that doctrine has become an essential preparatory element for combat.

Similarly, in its professional education, the Army emphasized warfighting skills at every level. In the mid-1980s it created the School for Advanced Military Studies (SAMS); that specialized school provided the top graduates of the Command and Staff College with a second year of intensive study concentrating on the operational level of war–the employment of military forces within a theater to destroy the enemy. In their succeeding assignments, the graduates of SAMS provided the Army with an intellectual leavening that broadened its understanding of war. Above all, it prepared its graduates to think through employment of ground forces to achieve goals larger than simply battering enemy divisions on the front lines.

The Air Force and the Navy followed similar paths during this period.[73] The air war against North Vietnam was one of the most controversial aspects of our mishandled efforts in Southeast Asia. Ill thought-out political considerations had dominated the conduct of air operations. Yet, postwar claims that political naivete was solely responsible for the failure of the air campaign missed a basic issue. The organization of American air power had also been less than satisfactory; to all intents and purposes Air Force and the Navy had waged entirely separate air campaigns. But even within its own domain the Air Force hardly provided coherent direction:

> The absence of a single air commander produced chaos. The 2nd Air division in Saigon, the air force headquarters with direct control over fighter wings participating in the campaign, received guidance not only from PACOM and PACAF, but also from [Thirteenth] Air Force in the Philippines. . . .To simplify the multi-layer air force command arrangement, PACAF changed the 2nd Air Division to the [Seventh] Air Force in early 1966. The confusion then increased, however. Instead of providing [Seventh] Air Force with complete control over the 2nd Air Division assets, PACAF gave the [Seventh] Air Force 'operational' direction over the fighter wings, while the [Thirteenth] Air Force retained 'administrative' control. The ultimate result of this bizarre

---

[73]Since this study is largely concerned with air power it will discuss the US Navy and the Marine Corps only in so far as their air power capabilities affected the battlefield in the Gulf.

arrangement was the creation of the [Seventh]/[Thirteenth] Air Force in Thailand, which then assumed *administrative* control of the fighters!

A discouraging aspect of the air war lay in the exchange ratios between American aircraft, naval as well as air force, and their North Vietnamese enemies. In the last two years of World War II and in Korea, American pilots averaged exchange ratios of well over ten-to-one in air-to-air combat against their opponents. Yet, from 1965 to 1968 the ratio of American kills versus losses against North Vietnamese aircraft in air-to-air combat was barely two-to-one. When the raids against North Vietnam stopped in 1968, the Navy rethought its approach to air-to-air combat. "Top Gun" resulted, and its impact on the skills of Navy fighter pilots showed in 1972, when they established a twelve-to-one exchange ratio against their North Vietnamese opponents. The Air Force, however, suffered an even worse air-to-air exchange ratio during the initial months of Linebacker I than the barely 2-to-1 it had posted during the 1965-1968 period, even though, by the year's end, an influx of more seasoned pilots enabled it to achieve a 2-to-1 exchange ratio for 1972.[75]

The success of "Top Gun" resulted in substantial changes in how the Air Force approached its tactical business after 1973. The Air Force established "Red Flag" to address the tactical problems of air warfare across the board. "Red Flag" taught a whole generation of air force pilots and commanders how to deal with enemy defensive *systems* from fighters to SAMs and AAA, as well as how to get bombs on target. It was in the hard-to-measure areas of training and preparation for countering threats that Coalition air powers, especially Americans, enjoyed enormous advantages over their Iraqi opponents. One pilot in a "Weasel" squadron underlined the advantage in a comment made during the war:

> Going into the first combat mission, I don't think I was ever scared. . . .I've trained for eight years for this; Major Moore has trained for ten or eleven years. . . .The fact that I see stuff shooting at me is a little different, but I was well prepared for it. In fact, when the SA-2 launched, I didn't feel scared at all. . . .I knew exactly what to do. In fact I didn't think at all. It was instinct. I knew I had to get out of

---

[74]Mark Clodfelter, *The Limits of Air Power; The American Bombing of North Vietnam* (New York, 1989), p 128.

[75](S) USAF Tactical Weapons Center, Project Red Baron, *Air-to-Air Encounters in Southeast Asia* (Nellis AFB, 1973-74).

there. I'm sure that's what Major Moore was thinking. He knew exactly what he had to do in the back seat; I knew exactly what I had to do in the front seat. He's getting out the chaff; he's putting on the pod. I'm moving the jet. It's just like we have trained for years and years . . . they train us a lot better than you can imagine. So we can handle any threat we see up there–air-to-air or ground-to-air. Anything that comes up. We've seen it before; we know exactly what to do when we get it. It's all instinct. The reason we are all doing well in this war is the fact that we are all well trained.[76]

An F-111 pilot commented at a NATO conference 1992 in the following terms:

> Training saved our lives! We trained for the low and the medium altitude war. Eighty percent of our training was for the low level altitude environment, but we found that training for a low war made fighting high a little bit easier. We also had local airfield attacks; we also had our HHQ composite force exercises; we had tanker exercises, and we had all kinds of training down in Saudi Arabia. Our training allowed us to verify the operability of our systems, prior to the war. We made sure that bombs would indeed come off the jet, when you push the pickle button, which did not always happen, unfortunately. And of course, we fought like we trained.[77]

The appearance of precision-guided munitions in the late 1960s began a revolution in weapons technology; the arrival of stealth aircraft in the 1980s significantly extended that revolution. The training and preparation of American aircrews for combat allowed U.S. forces to maximize the potential of these revolutionary changes in weapons technology. The training programs prepared pilots for the actual environment in which they would fight and extended their capacity to adapt to the conditions of combat.

There was one last, intangible advantage to the Coalition. Western military forces had spent the previous forty years in preparing to fight

---

[76] TSgt Charles L. Starr, "Special Study, History of the 35th Tactical Fighter Wing (Provisional): Operations Desert Shield and Desert Storm," GWAPS NA 277.

[77] (S) Capt Kelly, "F-111 Operations–Desert Storm," Appendix 21 to Annex C to 1730.13.7/AFOOAT/S-078/92, 20 Feb 1992, NATO.

Soviet ground and air forces. Western military organizations had thoroughly prepared in their training, doctrine, and exercises for a great clash with the Warsaw Pact. That clash never occurred, but Western forces that entered the Gulf confronted an opponent, much of whose doctrine, training, and equipment largely derived from the Soviets. Consequently, many aspects of the Iraqis' style of war and doctrine were familiar to Coalition military leaders as well as pilots and tank crews; the enemy's tactical doctrines and styles of fighting were ones that U.S. forces were thoroughly prepared to disassemble. Even more advantageously, Iraqi forces lacked the staying power and depth of Soviet forces. Finally, desert conditions in western and southern Iraq–and Kuwait–magnified the superiority of Western technology over Soviet technology.

Preparing to fight in the Central European environment over the past several decades against a vastly more numerous foe conveyed a number of other advantages to U.S. forces in the Gulf. On the ground and in the air, that preparation forced them to develop maximum skills to utilize the advantages conveyed by western technology. In the aerial arena which not only demanded the rapid achievement of air superiority but the conduct of operations deep behind the enemy's front lines to stem the forward movement of Soviet echelons, U.S. air forces developed highly sophisticated means of attacking, deceiving, or jamming Soviet air- and ground-based air defenses. Electronic warfare became more than an arcane art, and the suppression of enemy air defenses (SEAD) became a realizable goal. These skills and technologies, which would have presented considerable difficulties to Soviet air defense systems, were beyond the experience or comprehension of Iraq's air defenders.

Conclusion

In the comparatively static kind of ground warfare–reminiscent of the Western Front in World War II–that dominated the Iran-Iraq War, the Iraqi regime had demonstrated enormous staying power; in that conflict it proved that it could mobilize as well as drive its military to suffer extraordinarily heavy casualties. But because of its striking misestimates of the U.S. and its allies, as well as the willingness and ability of Coalition leaders to attack Iraq's military weaknesses, Saddam Hussein's regime would ultimately fare far less well against the Coalition than it had against revolutionary Iran.

In retrospect, Iraq's strengths and weaknesses appear to have been different from what many Western observers and military analysts outside the theater assessed them to be prior to the war. Its greatest strength may have lain in the ruthlessly effective political control that Saddam had established over his nation. Even the catastrophic defeat of his air force and air defenses, the bombing of targets throughout Iraq for forty-three days, and the destruction of the bulk of his army in the Kuwait theater did not suffice to overturn the regime. Like Stalin's Soviet Union in 1941, military disaster on the frontiers did not quite manage, given the limited objectives under which the Coalition prosecuted Desert Storm, to decapitate Saddam Hussein's "Republic of Fear."

On the other hand, the Iraqi military, outside of its utilization of mobile Scuds, displayed little capacity to adapt to the very different kind of warfare, with its emphasis on advanced technology and operational art, that the Coalition imposed on it. The Iraqis had just finished a long and exhausting war against Iran, a conflict that certainly had not turned their army into the "battle-hardened force" that some in the West perceived. While Iraq's opponents possessed little direct experience with combat–at least in the lower ranks–Coalition air and ground forces had undergone complex training and preparations for the actual conditions that they eventually encountered. Those preparations were far more realistic than anything that occurred in the Iraqi military.

It was at the strategic level that the Iraqis made their greatest miscalculations. To put it simply, they proved incapable of changing their assumptions in the light of what was actually happening. As Dr. Norman Cigar has noted:

> Such [strategic and political] assumptions, by their very nature, are usually deeply held. Their rejection or modification requires painful soul-searching and the willingness to admit a mistake in one's original basic calculations, if not the rejection of one's entire analytic framework. This is never easy–even in the face of overwhelming evidence . . . [yet Saddam] remained intractable to the end, being willing to risk war, and believing until relatively late into Operation "Desert Storm" that Iraq would acquit itself well on the battlefield.

---

[78]Dr Norman Cigar, "Iraq's Strategic Mindset and the Gulf War: Blueprint for Defeat," *Journal of Strategic Studies*, p 23.

Only the complete collapse of his military forces eventually led Saddam to recognize what was happening and to request a ceasefire.

A quote from an Iraqi newspaper in summer 1990 underlines the greatest imbalance between Iraqi and Coalition forces. An Iraqi reporter commented as follows on reports that American troops were requesting Chapstick and insect repellant:

> There is no army in the world that requests such supplies. This runs counter to the existing concept of the military, which [demands] toughness, rigor, manliness, and adaptability to conditions. . . .What kind of soldier is this that puts cream on his lips? What is the difference between U.S. soldiers and singers and dancers?[79]

The difference was that the Americans took care of the needs of their troops in the most fundamental ways; the Iraqis did not. Against the Iranians, who were equally disdainful of basic human needs, this did not matter; against the Americans it did. Saddam assured his people and the world that Iraq was happy to suffer hundreds of thousands of casualties, while America could not even suffer casualty lists in the thousands. To the poor bloody Iraqi infantryman, this casual statement underlined the tyrant's disinterest in whether the infantryman lived or died. And that disinterest factored into his willingness to fight. This had not mattered in the war against Iran, because Saddam's regime retained control of the battlefield and its rear areas. In this war, the Iraqis did not control the battlefront or even the air over their own nation. On the other side of the hill American soldiers, sailors, marines, and airmen knew that their leaders cared.[80]

---

[79] Hamza Mustafa, "American Troops and their Hurried Requests," *Al-Jumhuriyya*, 17 Aug 1990, p 4.

[80] To a great extent this was true of the Vietnam war, as much of the literature of war underlines. Particularly worthwhile in this respect is the brilliant novel by the former Secretary of the Navy: James Webb, *Fields of Fire* (New York, 1978).

3

The Opening Days: Final Plan and the Scripted War

This chapter will examine the conduct of the first two days of the air campaign against Iraq; to set the stage, it will discuss the immediate and long-term objectives of the air operations. In this short span of time, Coalition air attacks achieved a solid basis from which Allied air commanders could mount systematic attacks against strategic targets in Iraq, the enemy's military forces, and the infrastructure that supported those forces. The success of these first strikes ensured the possibility of a sustained offensive against the present dangers of Iraqi military power as well as Iraq's long range potential.

When the Gulf War ended with U.S. troops on the Euphrates and the outskirts of Basra, commentators hailed the ground campaign as a masterpiece of "operational art." Indeed, it was; the conception of a wide sweep, deep into Iraq behind the entrenched Iraqi forces, a clever deception effort, thorough logistic planning and deployment, and effective execution by U.S. and Coalition armies represented an enormous achievement. Yet, the most impressive operational achievement of the Gulf War was the successful battle for air control, fought, and largely won, on the opening day of Desert Storm. That air battle, against the Iraqi air defenses, broke the enemy's capacity to defend himself from the blows that would fall throughout the remainder of the war. It placed Iraq and its military forces, in the words of a senior commander, in the position of a "tethered goat, being pounded to death from beyond its reach."

This air battle sought to achieve operational effects beyond the mere destruction of targets; on opening night, Coalition aircraft found enemy air defenses that were on full alert and that had received plenty of strategic warning. By way of comparison, the February ground war occurred against an opponent whom air attacks had pounded for weeks and whose morale had clearly suffered. This chapter aims to provide the reader with a sense of what that operational employment of air power hoped to achieve, how Coalition air forces went about that task, and what the opening blows achieved.

Deployment of American forces into the Gulf had accelerated in late November in response to President Bush's decision to prepare for the worst case: war. Arriving forces were soon to wage offensive air *and* ground campaigns. The addition of VII Corps and more air units represented an insurance policy; the two Army corps and a Marine corps could now defeat the Iraqi Army, if the air offense failed to force Iraq to disgorge its gains. Nevertheless, the buildup of powerful ground forces had resulted in a gradual shift in the emphasis of Coalition military plans. In August and September, the balance of forces between the opposing sides had precluded anything outside of defensive ground operations; offensive operations would have to rest entirely on air power. By November, Allied ground forces were in a position to launch a limited ground offensive; by early January the logistical and operational strength of ground forces had reached the point where Coalition armies could strike deep and hard.

On the operational level, this resulted in a shift from an almost exclusive concentration on an air campaign aimed at centers of gravity in Iraq to an air campaign with divergent goals: the first, a strike at the Iraqi homeland–a "strategic" air offensive; and the second, "preparation of the battlefield" in the Kuwaiti Theater of Operations, to use U.S. Army terminology. The first three phases of the air campaign–strategic offensive, destruction of enemy air defenses in the KTO, and preparation of the battlefield–would begin concurrently, although initially emphasizing the first.[1] The fourth phase, ground invasion, would not begin until the ground war was initiated by either the Iraqis or the Coalition.

For the air war, a tight-knit group of officers under Glosson had carefully planned operations for the first two days. The offensive sought to attack a wide variety of targets in order to achieve synergistic effects. The plan emphasized an "inside-out" campaign in which air operations would begin at the center of Iraqi power and aim at functional effects

---

[1]In terms of the changing perspectives of the commanders, Schwarzkopf, who had been one of the strongest supporters of the "strategic" bombing options in the early days of Desert Shield, blew up at Horner just before the beginning of the air campaign in front of the latter's staff because of the supposed lack of emphasis in CENTAF plans on the Republican Guard.

rather than levels of destruction.[2] Crucial would be attacks against certain target categories whose destruction or degradation would affect others. These effects in turn would cascade through other sectors of Iraqi defenses or military efforts.

This approach by the Special Planning Group (hereafter referred to as the "Black Hole") represented an effort to utilize air power as an operational rather than a tactical instrument. The first air attacks did not seek the absolute destruction of single targets or target sets, but rather damage to a wide variety of targets. The combination of damage to these targets would, hopefully, degrade Iraq's defensive responses for the remainder of the campaign. Degradation to the electrical system, communication nodes, discrete elements in the air defense system, and certain leadership targets would, planners in the Black Hole believed, mutually reinforce difficulties in other areas as well as the defects in the Iraqi system.

Glosson and his deputy in charge of the strategic air campaign, Lt. Col. David Deptula, believed that such an approach would exacerbate inherent weaknesses in the Iraqi military due to the political biases of their system.[3] The air campaign thus represented an effort to maximize operational effects by causing complex frictions within the enemy's military organizations and structure. This may well have been intuitive rather than doctrinal, but it reflected an imaginative understanding of the operational conduct of war.[4] The interplay between plans and operations in this first and decisive period of the war suggests much about the operational potential of air power, as well as the inevitable frictions

---

[2]See GWAPS Effectiveness report, Chapter 1 for a closer examination of the synergistic effects that the planners aimed to achieve in the first series of air attacks. The discussion in this chapter, particularly in regards to the SEAD plan, also aims to bring out how the air campaign aimed to achieve an impact well beyond the direct destruction of mere targets.

[3]Intvw, Maj Gen Buster Glosson, with GWAPS personnel, 9 and 14 Apr 1992. Also see the intvw, Lt Col David Deptula with GWAPS personnel, 20 and 21 Dec 1991.

[4]Maj Gen Larry Henry commented to GWAPS interviewers that the SEAD plan had aimed at throwing sand into the Iraqi gear box to cause the structure to break down at critical moments, particularly during early phases of the war. Intvw with Maj Gen Larry Henry with GWAPS personnel, 28 Aug 1992.

involved in any combat–or as Clausewitz suggests, "the factors that distinguish real war from war on paper."[5]

A number of factors contributed to the success of initial air plans. The plans themselves represented a realistic mix of understanding the enemy and his *actual* capabilities and a keen appreciation of Coalition strengths. Above all, Coalition air leaders proved flexible and adaptable to the actual conditions they confronted. Finally, the Iraqi system and its commanders did not or could not adapt either to the weight of attacks or to the form that the air offensive took.

The Operational Problems in Projecting Air Power

The discussions in much of the rest this chapter center on the operational employment of air power against targets through out Iraq and Kuwait. However, that application depended on the complex movement of aircraft from bases not only scattered widely throughout Saudi Arabia and the Gulf States but which were situated hundred of miles from the Iraqi frontier. The Saudis had constructed those bases to confront diverse threats from Israel in the west to Iraqi, Iranian, and possible Soviet threats from the north.

Saudi Arabia is an enormous country; Map 9 suggests its extent. Superimposed on a map of the United States, it would run from South Dakota to eastern North Carolina. From north to south it would run from Minnesota to southern Alabama. Over the past three decades the Saudis have constructed a considerable number of bases to protect those frontiers. Consequently, when Coalition air forces deployed into the Arabian peninsula they found themselves at bases separated by great distances from Iraq. Just to reach Iraq, F-117s, faced a journey of more than 665 nm (nautical miles). F-111Fs and EF-111s at Taif had a 525-nm trip to reach the Iraqi boarder. Many other USAF fighters had almost as long a haul. F-16s at Al Dhafra and Al Minhad had flights of nearly 528 nm, while F-15s at Dhahran, Al Kharj, and Tabuk, as well as the F-4Gs at Shaikh Isa all had flights of approximately 250 miles before they reached Iraqi air space. [See Map 7] In fact, they often had longer distances, because the missions formed up on tanker tracks and then crossed the frontier as integrated packages.

---

[5]Carl von Clausewitz, *On War*, translated and edited by Michael Howard and Peter Paret (Princeton, 1976), p 119.

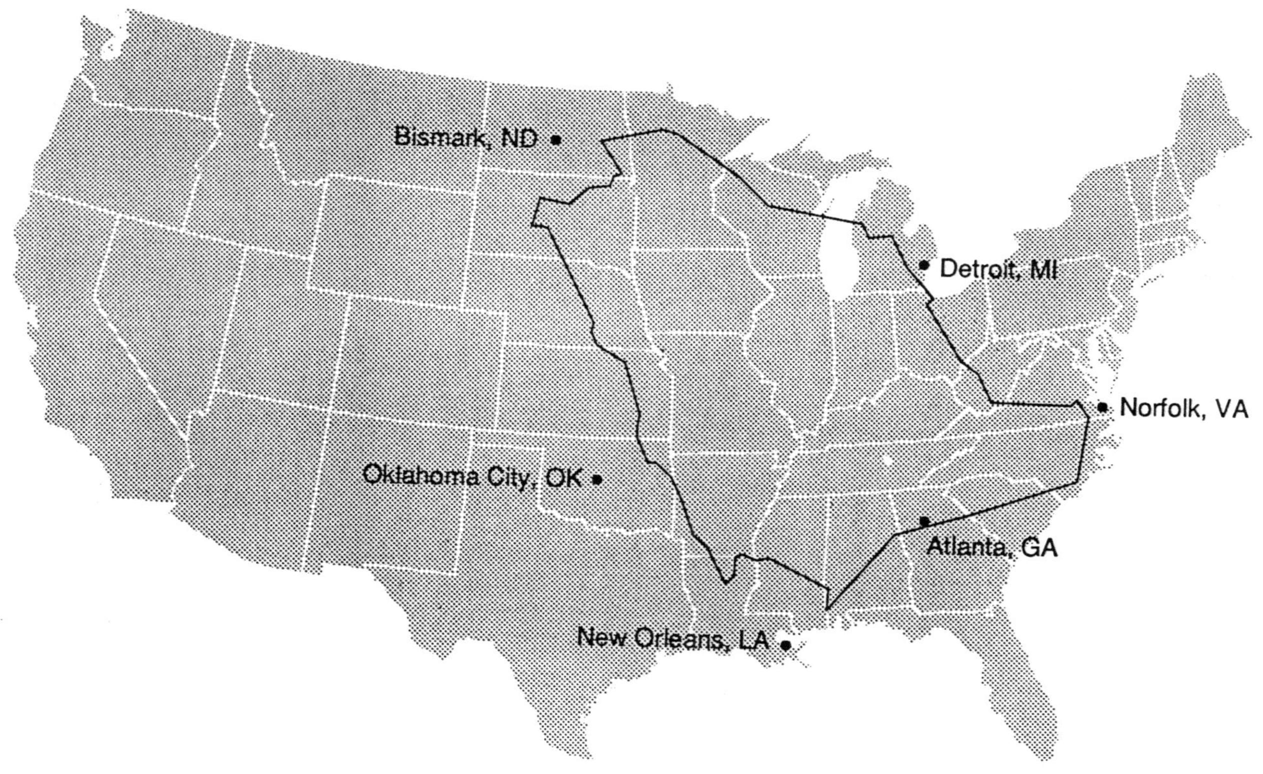

Bismark, ND
Detroit, MI
Norfolk, VA
Oklahoma City, OK
Atlanta, GA
New Orleans, LA

Map 7
CENTAF Deployment by Aircraft Type and Selected Distances to Iraq

The problems confronting naval aircraft were just as daunting. Carrier aircraft from the Red Sea had to fly approximately 600 miles to reach Iraq. For aircraft flying from the entrance to the Persian Gulf, distances would have been over 800 miles, depending on the location of the carrier. However, by 17 January, the carriers had moved into the Persian Gulf. But even then their aircraft had distances of 300 miles to fly before they reached Iraqi territory. [See Map 8]

Given the distances of Iraqi targets from Coalition bases, Allied aircraft required extensive mid-air refueling to execute their missions. By January CENTAF had established a series of tanker tracks running across northern and central Saudi Arabia for tankers to pick up Coalition aircraft as they came off airfields and accompany them to final drop off points just short of enemy territory.[6] From that point allied aircraft had to fly considerable distances to reach their targets. [See Map 9 for a depiction of the general pattern of tanker tracks]. But the fact that the movement of aircraft involved not only north-south flights to the Iraqi frontier but east-west movements as well, given the placement of aircraft on the Arabian Peninsula, only served to exacerbate the difficulties of providing tanker support when needed.[7]

Not surprisingly, since tankers and aircraft often came out of different airfields, the process of refueling required careful coordination. Admittedly, the process depended on the experience and expertise that the Air Force and Navy had built up over the past forty-five years in extending aircraft range by mid-air refueling. Moreover, with the large number of aircraft flying, along with numerous changes in the air tasking order (ATO), the tanking operation depended on the flexibility of aircrews and tankers in adapting to difficulties in the aircraft flow.[8]

---

[6]The RAF confronted the need to establish an east-west track to serve their Tornados. They solved the problem with typical British imagination. "These two problems always meant that we had something to negotiate with the other middle airspace users, even artillery. Despite this, we were always welcome, and I even suspect that the challenge used to brighten their day. We also had our little triumphs like the occasion the Prince of Wales visited the RAF Headquarters, and the American airspace team, being typical schizophrenic Republicans, were desperate to meet him. We had them around the corner of the building, and at the right moment, pushed them forward to be introduced, handshakes, photos, and all. They were very impressed, not to mention grateful. The result of this gratitude was 'Olive Trail'–an east/west refueling route for the Tornados when all the other trails were north south. If the visitor had been the Princess of Wales we could have named our price." (S) Squadron Leader Minns, HQ STC, "Airspace Control," Appendix 2 to Annex C to 1730.13.7/AF00AT/S-078/92, 20 Feb 1992, Nato.

[7](S) *Ibid.*

[8]One of the Weasel crew members commented during the war: "We went up on another mission and couldn't find our tanker. I [don't] know if you would call it skill or

Map 8
Naval and Mari
Corps Air
Deployment an
Selected Distanc
Iraq

ISRAEL
Cairo West
JOR-DAN
IRAQ
IRAN
EGYPT
Tabuk
KUWAIT
300 nm
550 nm
KC-130
Jubail
AV-8
King Abdul Aziz NB
King Fahd
Dhahran
Bahrain
F/A-18
A-6
EA-6
KC-130
QATAR
Doha
Aircraft Carriers
Ranger,
Midway,
America,
Roosevelt
F-14
A-6
F-18
A-7
EA-6
E-2
KA-6
Abu Dhabi
Sharjah
Dubai
Al Minhad
Al Ain
Bateen
Al Dhafra
Seeb
KKIA
Riyadh
Al Kharj
UAE
Aircraft Carriers
Saratoga,
Kennedy,
F-14 EA-6
A-6 E-2
F-18 KA-6
A-7
Jiddah
Ta'if
SAUDI ARABIA
Masirah
OMAN
RED SEA
SUDAN
Khamis Mushayt
Thamarit
Nautical (Miles)
0 100 200 300
(All Times Assume
420 Knots Enroute)
ARABIAN SEA
YEMEN
ETHIOPIA

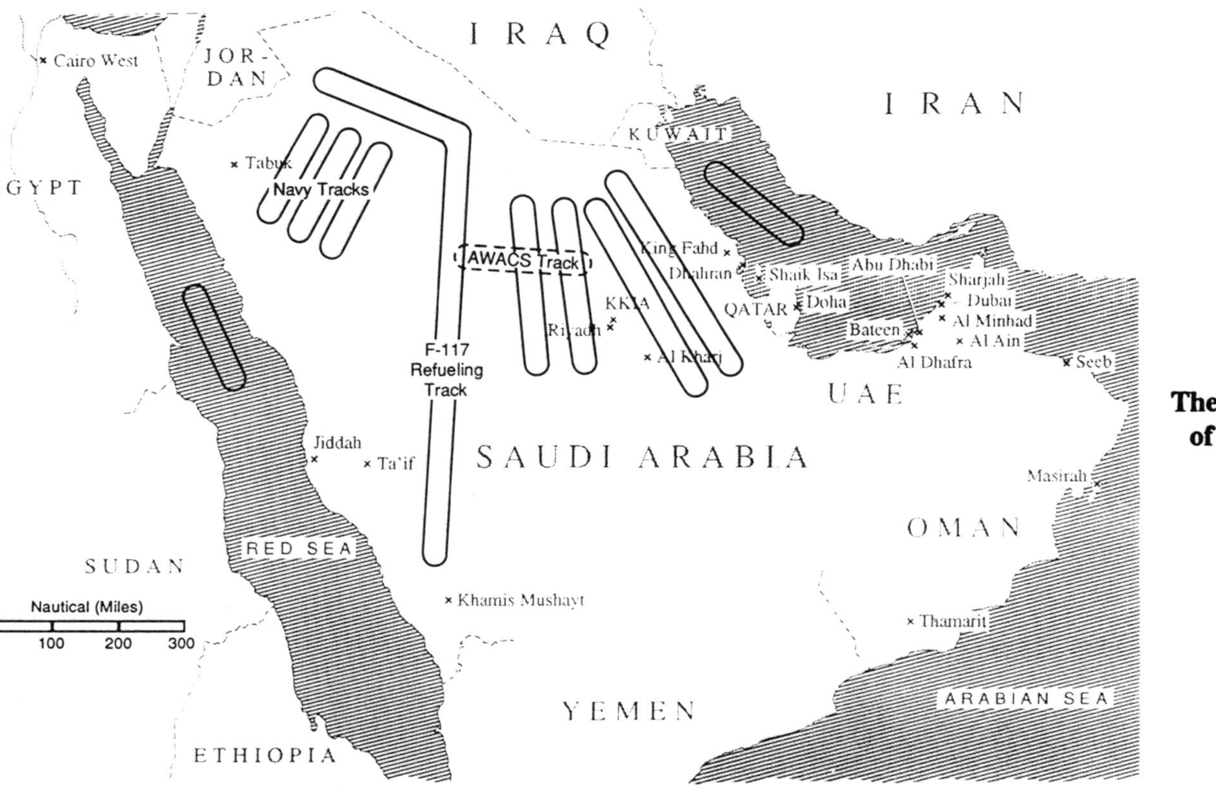

Map 9
The General Pattern of Tanker Tracks

But refueling Coalition aircraft was only one part of a larger problem in coordinating movement of strike packages to the frontier. A package targeted against the Baghdad area might contain F-16 fighter bombers from Al Dhafra and Al Minhad, F-15 air superiority fighters from Al Kharj, F-4G Wild Weasels from Shaikh Isa, and EF-111s from Taif; in addition, Navy and/or Marine SEAD aircraft such as EA-6Bs and F/A-18s with fighter support aircraft might also support the effort in its flight into Iraq. The aircraft would join up at the southern end of a tanker track (or tracks), refuel, and then move across the frontier as a coherent, articulated force that could jam enemy radars, fire HARMs at SAM sites threatening the package, attack enemy fighters that rose to challenge, and then bomb the target.

Here again peace-time training paid large dividends. A substantial portion of the aircrew, particularly mission and package commanders, had flown in "Red Flag" or the Navy's equivalent exercises at Fallon and "Top Gun;" they were thoroughly familiar with coordinating, planning, and flying such missions. The Navy undoubtedly had an advantage here: carrier air groups on board the carriers possessed a broad spectrum of aircraft, because the carrier might have to operate by itself; therefore each possessed air superiority, SEAD aircraft, and bomb droppers, and those aircraft operated together on a day-to-day basis.[9] But Red Flag had provided the Air Force with a solid basis on which to plan and execute strikes involving multiple types of aircraft.

To illustrate how such strike packages assembled, we can look at the war's biggest package, Package Q, flown on day three of Desert Storm.[10] This mission was to strike at Baghdad with seventy-two F-16s, fifty-six from Al Minhad (388th Tactical Fighter Wing) and sixteen from Doha (401st Tactical Fighter Wing); it received the support of eight F-15Cs from Tabuk as air cover against enemy fighters; eight F-4G Wild Weasels from Shaikh Isa to attack enemy air defenses; and two EF-111s

---

luck, but I locked onto the biggest contact I had on the radar and it happened to be a tanker. He had no other aircraft on board. He wasn't our tanker, but he had his boom down and was ready to pass some gas, so we went up and topped off with gas and made it home. Otherwise we would have had to divert to another airfield. . . .The unexpected can happen at a moment's notice. . . .We were flexible [enough] to cope with it." TSgt Charles L. Starr, "Special Study, History of the 35th Fighter Wing (Provisional): Operations Desert Shield and Desert Storm," GWAPS, NA 277, pp 159-60.

[9]The Air Force with its new composite wing structure is moving toward a similar system in which each wing will control most of the aircraft necessary to accomplish its mission without requiring the support of other wings.

 [10]For a discussion of the actual course of this mission see Chapter 4.

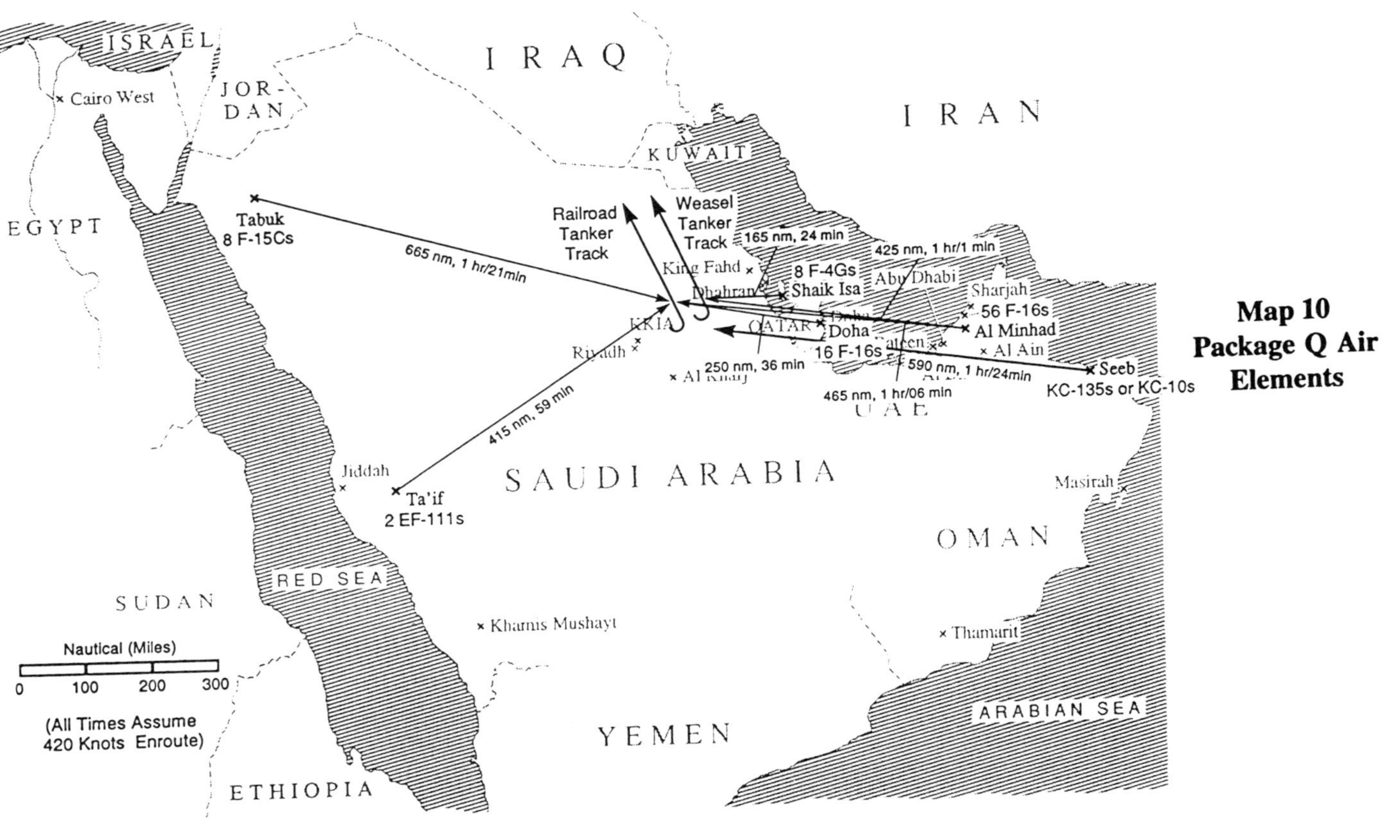

Map 10
Package Q Air Elements

Figure 1
Time Flow: Package Q
19 January 1991

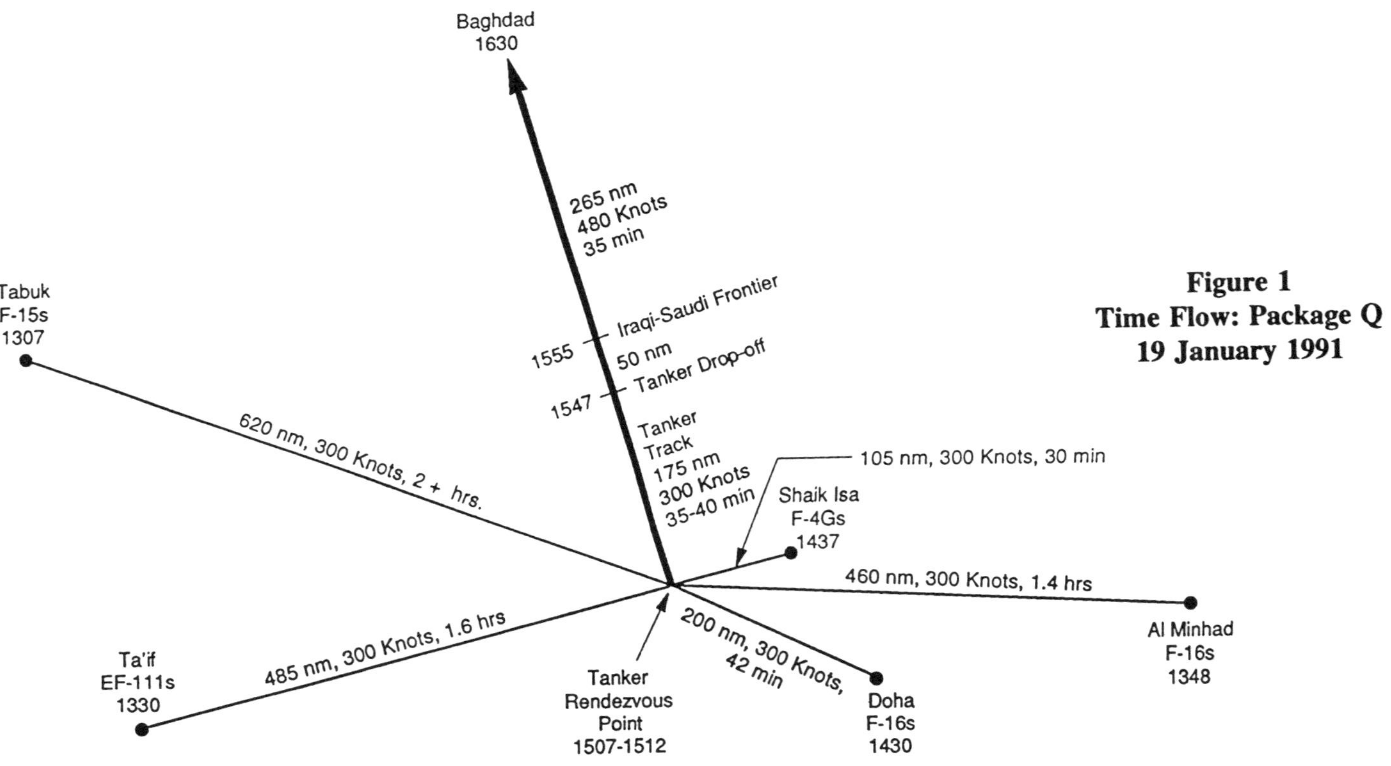

from Taif to jam enemy radars.[11] With a time on target of 1630L the strike package would have to cross the frontier at 1555; aircraft would begin dropping off tankers at approximately 1547.[12] The tankers, of course, would have to be ready in their tanker orbits at the right position to refuel Package Q's aircraft in the flight to Iraqi airspace.

Beyond the articulation of tanker support, Package Q also depended on a number of airborne platforms to coordinate and control its progress as well as to warn its mission commanders as to the tactical situation in Iraq. AWACS (Airborne Warning and Control System) and ABCCC (Airborne Battlefield Command and Control Centers), specially configured aircraft with complex communications equipment and controllers on board, would coordinate and update as the package marshaled its component parts and then launched them into Iraq. Meanwhile, Compass Call EC-130s would begin jamming the signals from enemy communication centers in Iraq; at the same time AWACS would also provide warnings of enemy aircraft threats, navigational assistance, airspace control, and changes to the tactical mission. In particular, Package Q would depend on AWACS for a coherent evaluation of the emerging enemy air-to-air threats in the theater. Finally, RC-135 Rivet Joint aircraft would monitor the enemy's electronic signals to evaluate how he was reacting to the raid's progress. All these platforms would be airborne and on station to provide support for the strikers as they moved up to and eventually into Iraqi airspace. Their station times in orbits over Saudi territory and their knowledge of the intent and mission responsibility for Package Q would, of course, have been arranged ahead of time in the ATO process.

To get to tanker tracks Railroad and Weasel, Package Q's aircraft would have to leave four different bases at four different times. [See

---

[11]The Master Attack Plan called for three such large daylight strikes against targets in the Baghdad area on day three; however the first two were cancelled due to weather, while the third, Package Q, did fly. When we get to day three we will discuss the difficulties that this package ran into during the course of its operation in Iraqi territory. Unfortunately the ATO for the third day is not in the GWAPS files. Consequently, while we are describing Package Q, this chapter is forced to discuss the movement up to the Iraqi frontier in general terms. The reconstruction has been accomplished with the help of Lt Col Robert Eskridge and Maj Theron Severance, both of the GWAPS Staff.

[12]Again, the ATO for Day Three does not exist in GWAPS files; as a result, we have reconstructed probable takeoff times and tanker rendezvous times on the basis of known distances and flying times.

Map 10 for a depiction of distances travelled to tanker tracks by the mission packages.] Each tanker track had somewhere between five and eight tankers. The lead tanker would be the low man in the cell; succeeding tankers would stack up (offset to the right) with one mile separation distances and each 500 feet higher in altitude. Mission commanders would plot out the times required to join up with tankers and determine their launch times on that basis. At approximately 1346 the first F-15 began rolling at Tabuk. The fifty-six F-16s from Al Minhad began launching next around 1401; their sister aircraft from Doha lit their afterburners later, at 1431. The EF-111s from Taif needed to begin rolling by 1408. Finally, Weasels from Shaikh Isa would not have to take off until 1443. Like a finely tuned watch, mission commanders adjusted their speeds so that aircraft arrived at the tanker tracks on the mark; the ATO had already coordinated call signs, targets for the various missions, and times on target for the segments within Package Q.

As depicted in Figure 1, aircraft movement to the jump off point seems a relatively easy task. It was, but only because Air Force, Navy, and Marine flight crews had prepared carefully and thoroughly to fly such missions for more than forty years. Practice had created a state of mind in which the operators can and do change and adapt flexibly to actual conditions. All of this carefully planned and organized articulation only involved getting Package Q to the *frontier* with Iraq. We will discuss the actual fate and operational experience of the package in the next chapter.

The Iraqi Strategic Framework

There is little evidence with which to examine Iraqi preparations and conceptions. Even if Iraqi records were available, substantial elements of uncertainty would remain, because so much rested on Saddam's enigmatic mind. Nevertheless, the actions and experiences of the Iraqis in previous wars allow substantial judgments. In the largest sense, it appears probable that Saddam, and therefore his military leaders, never expected war.[13]

---

[13] Department of the Army, 513th Military Intelligence Brigade, Joint Debriefing Center, "Analysis of Source Debriefings," JDC Rpt #065, 15 Mar 1991.

TIME FLOW: PACKAGE Q
19 January 1991

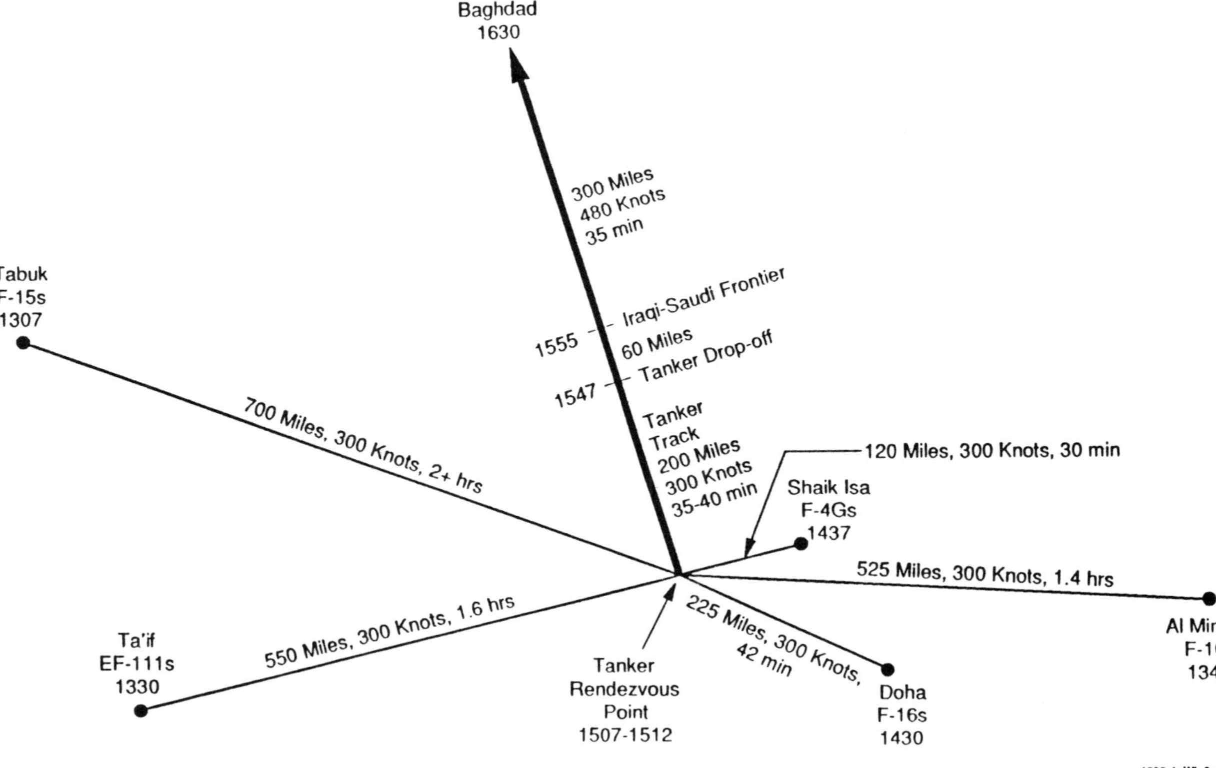

The Iraqis appear to have calculated that the Coalition possessed serious fault lines, not only between Western and Arab members, but among the Western partners as well.[14] Saddam's estimation of the United States and its performance in the Vietnam War led to a belief that President Bush would not launch American forces into a conflict.[15] As the Iraqi press noted early in the crisis: "We know that Washington's threats are those of a paper tiger. America is still nursing the disasters from the Vietnam War, and no American official, be it even George Bush would dare to do anything serious against the Arab nation."[16] Even as the buildup of Coalition forces reached ominous proportions in late December, the Iraqis failed to change their fundamental misperceptions of American resolve.[17]

On the strategic level, Saddam aimed at three distinct objectives: 1) to retain Kuwait, 2) to avoid humiliation, if forced from Kuwait, and 3) if forced from Kuwait, to maintain control over the Iraqi Army.[18] If it came to war, he believed that he could achieve substantial gains. This reflected two assumptions: first, that air power could not play a war-winning role, if the Coalition unleashed its forces;[19] and second, that none of the powers in the Coalition–especially the United States–could sustain

---

[14]See footnote 66, Chapter 2.

[15]The Soviet diplomat Evgeniy Primakov commented after the war on the basis of his conversations in Iraq both before and during the conflict that "it seems that Saddam Hussein up to the last moment still was operating on [the basis] that the 'multinational forces' would not initiate military operations." Quoted in Norman Cigar, "Iraq's Strategic Mindset and the Gulf War: Blueprint for Defeat," *The Journal of Strategic Studies*, March 1992, p 8.

[16]*Ibid*, p 3.

[17]In the last month before the war, the statements of many American congressmen which received great attention from the media and which both C-Span and CNN broadcast in excruciating detail did nothing to disabuse Saddam of his notion that the Americans would not use force.

[18](S) CIA Brfg, "Iraqi Strategy and Conduct of Operations in the Gulf War," 25 Jun 1992. The SPEAR intelligence analysis done immediately before the war underlined that the survival of the air force and the Republican Guard were essential to the future political stability of the regime. See (S) SPEAR, *Iraqi Threat to U.S. Forces*, p 3-4.

[19]As Saddam noted before the war: "Air power alone will not decide the battle." Cigar, "Iraq's Strategic Mindset and the Gulf War: Blueprint for Defeat," p 18.

heavy casualties.[20] Underlying both assumptions, influenced by Iraqi experiences against Iran, was a belief that only ground operations could be decisive and that casualties would be high on both sides.

The Iraqis did recognize that in case of war, Coalition air forces would soon dominate the skies over Iraq. However, they believed that their military, industrial, and political infrastructure could absorb any level of punishment that Coalition air power could impose. At the same time, their air defenses would inflict losses on attacking aircraft sufficient to force the Coalition to begin ground operations. The resulting "Mother of All Battles" would lead to such heavy casualties that Iraq would achieve at least a moral victory, if not an actual one.[21]

Such assumptions obviously affected Iraqi preparations. The Iraqi military did recognize that there would be a separate air campaign if war were to come; but they estimated its duration, depending on success of defensive efforts, at no longer than approximately a week. During that time, they estimated that Coalition air attacks could inflict only limited damage on their ground forces and infrastructures. Saddam confidently assessed that the Coalition would then have to attack on the ground and that "the [Iraqi] lads will show themselves and [the attackers] will see them [i.e. the Iraqis] as they raise their heads [still] safe and sound and ready for battle."[22]

The Iraqis never intended to contest for control of the air. They hoped to preserve most of their air assets for use when the ground war started, or even for the postwar period after the war's outcome.[23] The Iraqis placed a high value on active and passive defenses to deflect the air campaign. SAM and antiaircraft defenses provided the basis for defense against air attacks; from the Iraqi perspective, these weapons would inflict sufficient attrition on attacking aircraft; equally important,

---

[20](S) CIA Brfg to GWAPS, 25 Jun 1992.

[21](S) *Ibid.*

[22]Quoted by Cigar, "Iraq's Military Mindset and the Gulf War: Blueprint for Defeat," p 18.

[23]CIA Brfg to GWAPS, 25 Jun 1992.

such defenses would degrade the accuracy of Coalition air strikes.[24] Again, the Iraqi leader seriously underestimated the U.S. capabilities in his comments before the war:

> When powder and smoke rise [from the battlefield], aircraft are forced to approach to within five kilometers in order to see their targets. . . . When they approach to a distance of five, ten, twenty, or thirty kilometers, our weapons are able to shoot them down. They [i.e., the Americans] will [only] be engaging in Rambo stunts [in that case].[25]

As for the threat that stealth aircraft represented, the dictator was equally dismissive: stealth aircraft, he noted, "will be seen by a shepherd in the desert as well as by Iraqi technology, and they [i.e., the Americans] will see how their Stealth falls just like . . . any [other] aggressor aircraft."[26]

On the passive side, the Iraqis carried out massive efforts to protect everything from tanks and ground equipment to nuclear and chemical facilities. They constructed bunkers and berms throughout Iraq and Kuwait. From August to January, Iraqi engineers moved millions of tons of dirt; those efforts paid considerable dividends. Moreover, the Iraqis removed much of the equipment from research facilities in the period before the war; how much still remains uncertain, but UN inspections suggest that the dispersal effort was quite considerable.[27]

Finally, there was an offensive element to Iraqi strategy: the Scuds. Here, Saddam hoped to intimidate the Saudis by hitting targets throughout the Arabian Peninsula. More importantly, he calculated that he could involve the Israelis in the war by firing Scuds at the Holy Land. Any Israeli countermoves, involving attacks on Iraqi soil, would, he believed,

---

[24] SPEAR reported before the war that "the limited number of fighters compared with Iraq's large number of SAMs . . . makes the SAM the logical choice as the primary air defense weapon." (S/WN/NC/NF) SPEAR, *Iraqi Threat to U.S. Forces* , p 3-51.

[25] Quoted in Cigar, "Iraq's Strategic Mindset and the Gulf War: Blueprint for Defeat," p 19.

[26] *Ibid*, p 19.

[27] See particularly David Kay, "Arms Inspections in Iraq: Lessons for Arms Control," unpublished paper, 12 Aug 1992, GWAPS, NA 375.

break up the Coalition.[28] Many senior leaders in Washington certainly felt so, and the pressure to find the Scuds would continue to absorb Coalition air assets throughout the war. In the end, Saddam's strategy depended on his military organizations imposing heavy enough losses on the Coalition both in the air and on the ground for Iraq to emerge with its prestige intact. If he achieved even the semblance of a stalemate with the Coalition, Iraq would achieve enormous political dividends in the Arab world.

The First Night

U.S. Central Command stated the following as its theater objectives for Operation Desert Storm:

1. Attack Iraqi political/military leadership and command and control.
2. Gain and maintain air superiority.
3. Cut Iraqi supply lines.
4. Destroy Iraqi supply lines.
5. Destroy Republican Guard Forces.
6. Liberate Kuwait City with Arab forces.[29]

The achievement of these objectives was to involve a three-phased air campaign. It would lead to a ground offensive to complete destruction of Iraqi military forces in the KTO.[30] In fact, these three air phases began concurrently and continued right to the end of the war. Only the relative weight of effort involved in each changed.

---

[28]One staff officer in Riyadh recounted that when word first came in the control room where he was present that a Scud had impacted on Israel, the Saudi officers cheered.

[29](S) Headquarters US Central Command, "Combined OPLAN for Offensive Operations to Eject Iraqi Forces from Kuwait," was issued to all Coalition forces. It used slightly different language than that quoted above for reasons discussed in the Effectiveness report of this study. The Operational Order, quoted above, was issued to US forces only: HQUSCENTCOM, OPORD 91-001, paras. 1D, 3A, 3B, GWAPS, CHC 18-1. See Also Title V pg 74.

[30](S) *Ibid.*

But underlying the planning for the air campaign was a belief that Coalition air power needed to achieve air supremacy early in the war. To do so it had to suppress Iraqi air defenses to the point where Coalition aircraft could accomplish their missions in a relatively benign environment. Consequently, the destruction of Iraqi air defenses would be essential to the success of the air campaign over succeeding weeks. Four individuals, Lieutenant General Horner and Brigadier Generals Larry Henry and Buster Glosson, and Colonel Deptula, supported by planners and electronic warfare experts, designed a SEAD campaign that eviscerated Iraqi air defenses.

At the same time that Checkmate had begun its design for Instant Thunder, Gen. Robert Russ, Commander of Tactical Air Command ordered his Inspector General, General Henry, to fly to Saudi Arabia and support CENTAF. Henry, a backseater in the F-4, had a career in which he commanded both an F-4E squadron and then a wing of F-4G Wild Weasels. While a student at National War College in 1982, he had carefully studied the tactics that the Israelis had used in the Beka'a Valley to deceive and then destroy the complex air defense system that the Syrians had established with the help of Soviet advisers.[31] With this background, many in the Air Force regarded Henry as one of the premier SEAD experts in the tactical air forces. The problem with regard to the Iraqi air defenses as opposed to those of the Syrians on the Beka'a Valley was that Saddam's defenses represented an order of magnitude increase in their complexity, extent, and numbers, as well as the distances over which the Coalition would conduct the air campaign.

Henry had worked with Horner on previous exercises; in particular, they had looked at the problem of how one might disrupt a Soviet invasion of northern Iran by attacking Soviet command and control systems. The actual problem in the Middle East in mid-August was, of course, quite different. CENTCOM confronted the possibility of an Iraqi invasion of Saudi Arabia from Kuwait, and Iraqi forces not only held the airfields, but a large number of mobile SAM systems (SA-6s). In the event of an invasion, they would naturally move these systems forward to cover advancing spearheads.[32]

---

[31]Intvw, Maj Gen Larry Henry with GWAPS personnel, 28 Aug 1992.

[32]*Ibid.*

Henry and Homer decided to go after the enemy's command and central systems that would control the SAMS. HARMs were weapons that homed in on the various signals and signatures that enemy radars emitted. By striking the emitters they would at a minimum destroy the capacity to track targets and control SAMs; in many cases where the emitter and the SAM site were coterminous the HARM would eliminate both. None of the planners believed that the Iraqis could put up much of a defense once their command and control system collapsed. With destruction of the air defense system, Coalition air power could concentrate on Iraqi armored units in the open. In addition, they also estimated that Iraqi fighters would not interfere significantly with Coalition air attacks due to the superiority of allied crews and tactics.[33]

Here Warden's efforts in the Pentagon paid considerable dividends. The Instant Thunder briefing makes clear that the Checkmate conception provided for a mass SEAD attack on Baghdad at the opening of the campaign–one that would mislead the Iraqis into believing that the Coalition was beginning the war with a major raid on the capital. But the principal weapon for the attack would be HARMs that would attack the radar sites. The Checkmate briefings by Warden may not have received a warm reception from Horner, but they did receive considerable attention from Glosson and Henry.[34]

These influences eventually formed the basis for the SEAD effort that Coalition air forces used against the Iraqis with such devastating effect in January.[35] The final result was a plan that attacked the heart of Iraqi defenses; it aimed to break the connections between nodes in the KARI system and to swamp the defenses. From the first, Coalition air attacks

---

[33]"Electronic Combat in Desert Shield/Desert Storm," Brfg by Brig Gen Larry Henry, CENTAF/EC, post war, GWAPS NA 358. Also intvw, Maj Gen Larry Henry with GWAPS personnel, 28 Aug 1992.

[34]Instant Thunder Brief, "Campaign Flow," 16 Aug 90/2000.

[35]Intvw, Maj Gen Larry Henry with GWAPS personnel, 28 Aug 1992.

would place constant, relentless offensive pressure on the Iraqis; they would overload enemy defenses to the maximum extent. And they would attack Iraqi air defenses from the inside out–in other words incapacitate the center where the Iraqis made their decisions. Above all, the initial waves would overload the Iraqi system with a massive attack at its heart. There would be no roll back or incremental approach; confronted with a massive attack at the war's onset, the Iraqis would have no time to adapt to Coalition tactics and attacks.[36]

With the command and control system breaking down, Iraqi defenders would have to operate in an autonomous mode–one in which they had had little preparation to handle. The underlying principle of the SEAD plan was to attack KARI as a whole. It would not be necessary to kill all the SAM sites; it would be enough if the Coalition SEAD assets intimidated the Iraqis to the point that those running SAM sites would refrain from turning radar on.[37] Finally, the plan to suppress enemy air defenses aimed to defeat the SAM threat, so that allied aircraft could operate at medium altitudes which would minimize the threat posed by Iraqi AAA.[38]

In effect, the planners looked to maximize the inherent inefficiencies and frictions within KARI. They believed that the Iraqis could not operate effectively without centralized direction; once the system began to break down at the center, it would no longer function at all. As Henry noted after the war, the SEAD campaign aimed to throw sand into the Iraqi gear box.[39]

Coalition air operations before initiation of hostilities set the Iraqis up for what was coming; these operations also indicated to Coalition air commanders the weaknesses within the Iraqi defenses. Early on, Glosson

---

[36] *Ibid.*

[37] As Gen Henry put it to the GWAPS interviewers, "we wanted every Iraqi SAM site to know that if they kept their radar on long enough to acquire, track, launch, and guide a missile into an allied aircraft, they were definitely going to pay with a HARM down their throat." Intvw, Maj Gen Larry Henry with GWAPS personnel, 28 Aug 1992.

[38] In World War II the most serious threat at low altitudes proved to be AAA and Allied fighters that beat up well protected German airfields suffered appalling losses.

[39] Intvw, Maj Gen Larry Henry with GWAPS personnel, 28 Aug 1992. See also intvw, Maj Gen Buster Glosson with GWAPS personnel, 9 Apr 1992.

and Henry recognized a significant electronic and command and control gap between western and central sectors in Iraqi air defenses; Coalition air power would utilize this gap throughout the war.[40]

Over the five and a half months of peace, electronic monitoring also determined the pattern and nature of Iraqi defensive operations. Allied planners deliberately chose H-hour as 0300L (3:00 a.m. local or Riyadh time) on the morning of 17 January because it was at that time that Iraqi defenses were weakest.[41] Finally, over this period, the Coalition gradually built up the number of sorties flying close to the border with Iraq. Consequently, the Iraqis became accustomed to armadas of aircraft–F-15s on CAP (combat air patrol), AWACS, tanker tracks, and assorted other aircraft moving in and out of training areas located immediately south of their border with Saudi Arabia.[42]

American preparations resulted in a carefully prepared script for the first two days. They also involved a carefully laid out deception effort. With similar air operations occurring across the length of the Saudi-Iraqi frontier day in and day out, enemy controllers became familiar with similar patterns. The Iraqis would see little difference over the night of 16-17 January, until the full weight of Coalition air power fell on their defenses.

On the day before Desert Storm, Coalition forces displayed no change in the intensity of operations; F-16s did substitute for F-15s on combat air patrol missions, so that the latter could gain down time in the hours immediately before war. The pattern of activity in the last minutes of peace was sufficiently familiar to mislead Iraqi controllers. The enemy failed to react until the initial strikes had commenced.

In the last hours before war, the mood among senior leaders was one of cautious optimism. Senior American airmen were veterans of the mishappened air campaigns against North Vietnam; to them, the preparations in the

---

[40]*Ibid*

[41]This account will use local Saudi time on all occasions, unless otherwise specified.

[42]*Ibid.* Gen Henry in his postwar briefing on the SEAD planning referred to this area directly south of the border as the "junkyard." Brig Gen Larry Henry, CENTAF/EC, "Electronic Combat in Desert Shield/Desert Storm," GWAPS, NA 358.

Gulf at the tactical and operational levels were significantly different from that conflict. At the strategic level, the Coalition possessed clear goals that appeared attainable. Nevertheless, these men remembered the terror, confusion, and uncertainties reminiscent of Southeast Asia, and they knew the terrible environment into which they were committing their forces.

In the early morning of 17 January, F-4G Weasels of the 35th Tactical Fighter Wing (P) taxied out onto the active runway. At the end of the taxiway, maintenance crews had set up a spotlight and an American flag. One crew member recalled: "I didn't see it [the flag] when I stepped out of the van. When I got to the jet I saw the light shining on it. That brought chills down my spine. It really meant something that we were Americans and were fighting for America."[43]

At 0239, twenty-one minutes before H-hour, Army Apache helicopters, led by three Air Force MH-53s, attacked two Iraqi early warning sites up on the frontier.[44] This first mission opened a corridor for several packages of aircraft with early missions. [See Maps 11 and 12 for depictions of the flow of allied air operations during the first night.] A package of F-15Es, a four ship in the lead, moved through the gap to attack Scud sites in western Iraq; two EF-111s supported that strike by jamming Iraqi radars. Another eighteen F-15Es followed to attack other fixed and mobile Scud launchers. Along with the first package, the EF-111s moved forward to provide jamming for the attackers on the Scud sites; they were later supposed to jam into the Baghdad area; in fact they never did support the first stealth strikes on the enemy's capital.[45]

---

[43]Starr, "Special Study: History of the 35th Fighter Wing (Provisional): Operations Desert Shield and Desert Storm, 2 Aug 1990–2 Aug 1991," GWAPS NA 277, p 151.

[44]This appears to have been the only time that army air assets actually were included in the Master Attack Plans or the ATO.

[45](S) Master Attack Plan, "First 24 Hours;" GWAPS Database; and (S) Reconstruction of aircraft mission profiles by AFSAA (Air Force Studies and Analysis), GWAPS.

Map 11
Day One [H-21(0239) to H+20(0320)]

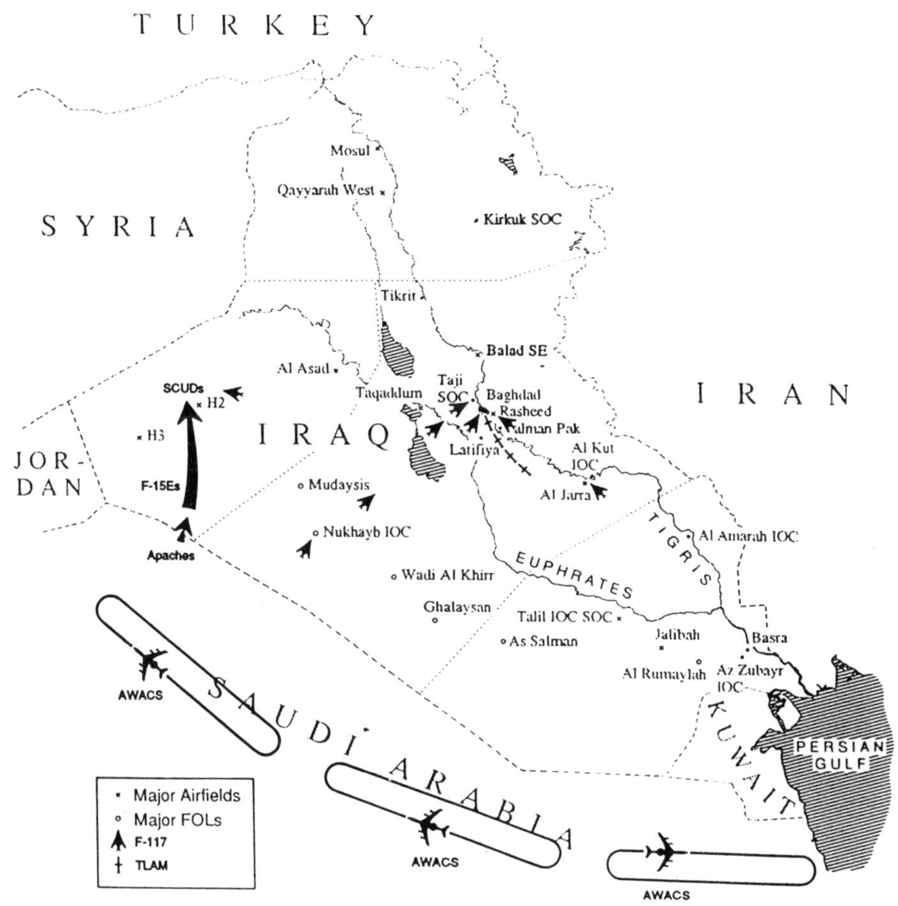

Map 12
Day One (0320 to 0430)

U.S. air power was already deep in Iraq as these opening moves by conventional aircraft occurred. Two F-117s had already crossed the frontier and were on their way to Baghdad when the early warning sites came under attack from the Apaches at 0239. Six more F-117s crossed the border shortly thereafter. By the time that the EF-111s were to have turned on their jammers (0258) at Baghdad, the first F-117s would already be within range of acquisition and targeting radars from the capital's redundant SAM defenses, as well as within the lethal range of the missiles themselves.[46]

The first F-117 attack came at 0251 with a bomb on the Nukhayb Intercept Operations Center; Nukhayb was the central reporting node with the best chance of detecting the F-15Es. Moreover, it was best positioned to coordinate Iraqi defensive efforts against succeeding allied SEAD attacks.[47] Ironically, in view of the controversy that erupted after the war,[48] the EF-111s never provided jamming into the Baghdad area during the first strikes, so that the F-117s that attacked the first targets in the capital, including the AT&T Building and the Telecommunications Center, flew into, over, and through the heart of the fully operating air defenses of Baghdad with no support from electronic countermeasures.[49] As American television made clear with stunning clarity, the first F-117s hit their targets, and telephone and television communications between Baghdad and the outside world thereupon ceased.

---

[46] (S) *Ibid.*

[47] (S) Master Attack Plan, "First 24 Hours;" GWAPS Database.

[48] For reports that indicate the F-117 did not operate without jamming support see: Bruce D. Nordwall, "Electronic Warfare Played Greater Role in Desert Storm than any Conflict," *Aviation Week & Space Technology*, 22 Apr 1991; and Michael A. Dornheim, "F-117A Pilots Conducted Precision Bombing in High Threat Environment," *Aviation Week & Space Technology*, 22 Apr 1991.

[49] (S) Master Attack Plan, "First 24 Hours," GWAPS Database; (S) reconstruction of aircraft mission profiles by AFSAA (Air Force Studies and Analysis), GWAPS; intvw, Lt Col David Deptula with GWAPS personnel, 20 Dec 1992; and GWAPS Database.

Within five minutes, six more F-117s struck at the Baghdad air force headquarters (targeted twice), the Air Defense Operating Center (ADOC), the presidential palace, the AT&T Building (a second time), the Tallil Sector Operations Center (SOC), and the Salman Pak Intercept Operations Center (IOC). These aircraft had also been in Iraqi airspace before the first strike on the early warning sites.[50]

Meanwhile, the U.S. Navy had launched fifty-two TLAMs (Tactical Land Attack Missile–Tomahawks) against leadership, chemical, and electrical power targets in and around Baghdad; their time on targets (TOTs) ranged between 0306 and 0311.[51] The Master Attack Plan placed twelve Tomahawks against electrical generating sites, six against the Baᶜth Party headquarters, eight against the presidential palace, and twenty against a variety of chemical facilities at Taji. The timing of the missile attacks, shortly after H-hour, reflected the fact that the Navy could not estimate the arrival of these weapons at their targets exactly due to factors such as wind. Nevertheless, almost concurrently with the first wave of F-117 attacks, the Tomahawks began hitting their targets around Baghdad.[52] The results were widespread system shut downs in the electric grid. Where Iraqi power went down, the results forced the affected units–including crucial command and control centers–to rely on less satisfactory back-up power.

As the first F-117s withdrew, their missions completed, F-15Es and EF-111s approached their targets, while F-15Cs and F-14s moved up ready to pick off any Iraqi fighters that enemy controllers had scrambled. The enemy aircraft that scrambled were not only scarce but badly prepared for the arena of air-to-air combat. According to post-flight review of F-15E infrared imagery, one MiG-23 crossed over in front of a

---

[50](S) Master Attack Plan, "First 24 Hours;" GWAPS Database.

[51](S) Master Attack Plan, "First 24 Hours;" GWAPS Database.

[52](S) Master Attack Plan, "First 24 Hours;" (S) reconstruction of aircraft profiles by AFSAA; Harold P. Myers, "Nighthawks over Iraq: A Chronology of the F-117A Stealth Fighter in Operations Desert Shield and Desert Storm," Special Study 37FW/HO-91-1.

MiG-29 and was shot down by his comrade. A MiG-29 also flew into the ground–hardly an auspicious beginning, while the F-15Es were approaching H-2 and H-3.[53]

At approximately the same time that the F-15Es were beginning their strikes on the Scud sites at H-2 and H-3, other Iraqi fighters launched. AWACS picked up bandits moving south in the general direction of the F-15Es as two flights (Penzoil and Citgo) were refueling. The lead pair in Penzoil swept forward at .95 mach at 30,000 feet. As the flight neared the forward operating location at Mudaysis, the first group of bandits turned back north almost immediately to land again. However, another aircraft, soon identified as a MiG-29, made its appearance thirty miles to the north at 11,000 feet and climbing. AWACS called possible multiple aircraft, but there was no individual breakout at final lock-on which occurred at twenty to twenty-two nautical miles. Finally, certain that the target was a "bandit," the F-15 fired his AIM-7M at sixteen miles. After firing, the lead F-15 executed a hard turn to the east as the missile impacted the MiG-29. The Iraqi pilot apparently undertook no evasive action but continued to climb straight into the missile.[54]

Citgo flight by now had dropped off the tankers and was rapidly moving up into Iraqi airspace. As it approached Mudaysis, it picked up two trailing groups of Iraqi fighters tracking F-15Es coming off their targets. Because it was approaching midnight (Zulu or Greenwich mean time) and the IFF (Identification Friend or Foe) were due for change, the F-15s were unsure whether or not the tracking group consisted of Iraqi aircraft. However, the fighters then turned north (still out of range); but another group of Iraqi aircraft now climbed out of Mudaysis airfield.

---

[53]"4th Tactical Fighter Wing in Southwest Asia," Aug 1990-Jun 1991, Unit History, 12 Nov 1991, GWAPS NA 168, p 44; "Tim Bennett's War," *Air Force Magazine*, Jan 1993, p 36.

[54]Abstracted from (S) "Desert Storm Air-to-Air Engagements, 33d Fighter Wing Air-to-Air Engagements, Desert Storm," 3 Mar 1992, pp 1-11.

One of the aircraft (later identified as a Mirage F-1) failed to turn on his radar until the last minute. At 8.5 nautical miles, seconds after the Iraqi pilot had turned on his radar, Citgo's flight lead fired an AIM-7M. Seconds later, the missile hit and resulted in a large fireball, followed shortly thereafter by a second fireball as the wreckage impacted on the ground. The remaining Iraqi fighters flew to the west and the comparative safety of H2/H3 airfields underneath their SAM coverage. Citgo flight then turned back rather than hazard a flight into the SAM belt.[55]

By now, fifteen minutes after H-hour, the Iraqis knew that they were under attack. In fact, they had known that something was going on from the strike against early warning sites near the border at 0239; shortly before Hellfire missiles from the Apaches had struck the radar sites, one station managed to get out word that it was under attack. Antiaircraft defenses around Baghdad then opened up with a furious barrage against what their radar screens showed as an empty sky. The enemy fire subsided until the F-117 bombs brought the Iraqis back up to a frenzy of wild firing around 0300. By 0315 (Riyadh time), the air force headquarters, the Air Defense Operations Center, the Tallil and Taji Sector Centers, communications centers, and electrical plants had all come under attack from F-117s and Tomahawks. In some areas, power was already out.[56]

At this point, the full weight of U.S. SEAD forces attacked the Baghdad area to break the capabilities and the morale of the defenders. [For the attacks on Baghdad during the first hour see Maps 16, 17, and 18]. The intent behind the SEAD attack was that the opening F-117 and Tomahawk missile attacks would disrupt enemy defenses, but at the same time bring the air defenses up to full alert and readiness to engage attackers.[57] The planners also believed that General Michael Dugan's Septem-

---

[55](S) *Ibid.*

[56]*Ibid*

[57]The crucial point is that the staff of a SOC or IOC that had received a direct hit from a GBU-27–even if the weapon had not managed to penetrate the hardened concrete–would have received a severe shock that would hardly have made them capable of operating at full efficiency, especially if they had come under attack when none of their radars indicated that there were allied aircraft in the neighborhood. The Tallil SOC received three hits from F-117s in the first two days of the war; postwar inspection by DIA/DNA when the airfield fell into American hands at the end of the war revealed that the Iraqis could have continued to use the facility. The intelligence at the time suggested to both Checkmate and Black Hole planners that the Iraqis had abandoned using it,

ber remarks–which had resulted in his removal from office–would lead the Iraqis to expect an all-out attack on downtown Baghdad.[58] Soon after the F-117 and Tomahawk attacks on Baghdad, Iraqi early warning radars showed Coalition aircraft massing south of the border for just such a raid.

In fact it was nothing of the sort. Two large SEAD packages were now moving forward into Iraqi airspace. From the west, three EA-6B jammers accompanied by three F-14 top cover, ten F/A-18, two A-6, and eight A-7 HARM shooters, and three KA-6 tankers flew in from carriers in the Red Sea; they would attack Baghdad's defenses from the west. In addition, slightly behind the western package, four A-6 bombers and four RAF GR-1 Tornados would strike Al Taqaddum airfield; the effort would receive cover from four additional A-6s with TALD (Tactical Air Launched Decoy) decoys to further confuse Iraqi defenders.[59] In the south, twelve F-4G Weasels were flying north against Baghdad's southern defenses. Along with the Weasels, EF-111s would jam the Iraqi radars to further the confusion.[60] Finally, backing up later packages were EC-130 Compass Call aircraft that also jammed Iraqi com munications from orbits just inside Saudi Arabia.[61]

At approximately the same time that the first BQM- 74s reached the capital, the A-6s were each close enough to drop the Navy's air-launched decoy, the TALDs.[62] In all, the Navy SEAD strikes against Baghdad and Al Taqaddum dropped twenty-five decoys within the space of twenty minutes.[63]

---

largely because of the threat of further Coalition air attacks. Discussion with Lt Col Allan W. Howey, 12 Jul 1992.

[58] See particularly, intvw, Maj Gen Larry Henry with GWAPS personnel, 28 Aug 1992; see also intvw, Maj Gen Buster Glosson with GWAPS personnel, 14 Apr 1992.

[59] (S) Master Attack Plan, "The First 24 Hours," 16 Jan 1991, GWAPS Database; and Center for Naval Analysis, "Desert Storm Reconstruction Report," Vol. VIII, "C^3/Space and Electronic Warfare," p 3-3; and GWAPS Database.

[60] (S) Master Attack Plan, "The First 24 Hours," 16 Jan 1991, GWAPS BH 1-3-1; and GWAPS Database.

[61] AFEWC, "Operation Desert Storm Electronic Combat Effectiveness Analysis," Jan 1992, p 9-15.

[62] (S) Center for Naval Analysis, "Desert Storm Reconstruction Report," Vol. VIII, p 3-8.

[63] Center for Naval Analysis, "Desert Storm Reconstruction Report," Vol. VIII, "C^3/Space and Electronic Warfare," p 3-9.

Map 13
Day One (0300 to 0310)

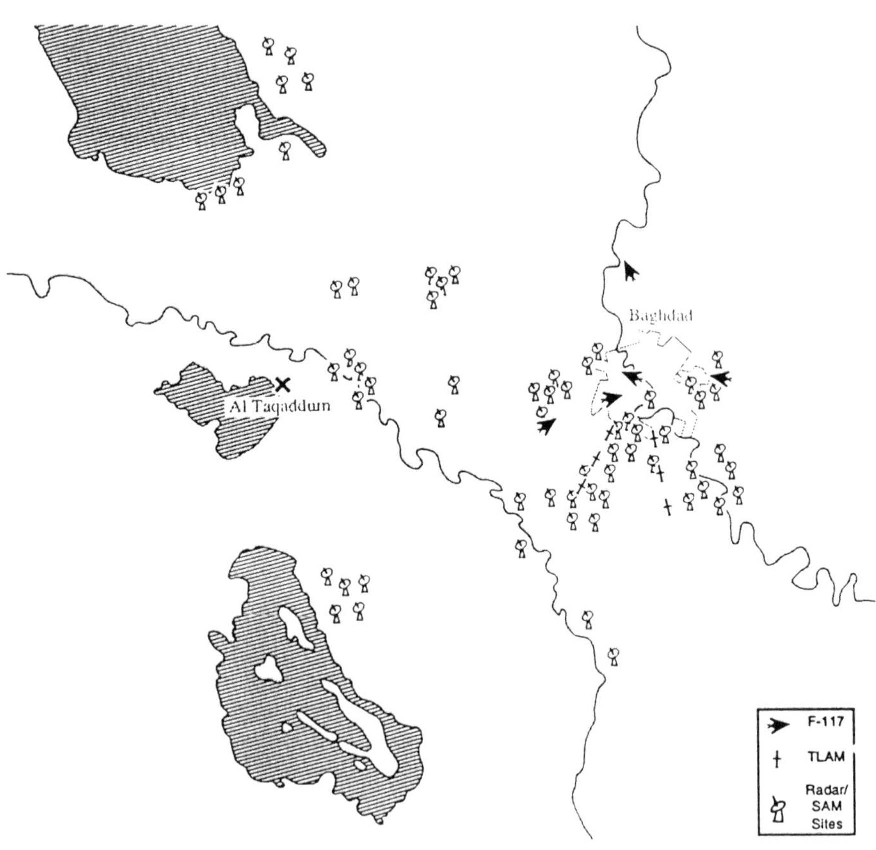

Map 14
Day One (0346)

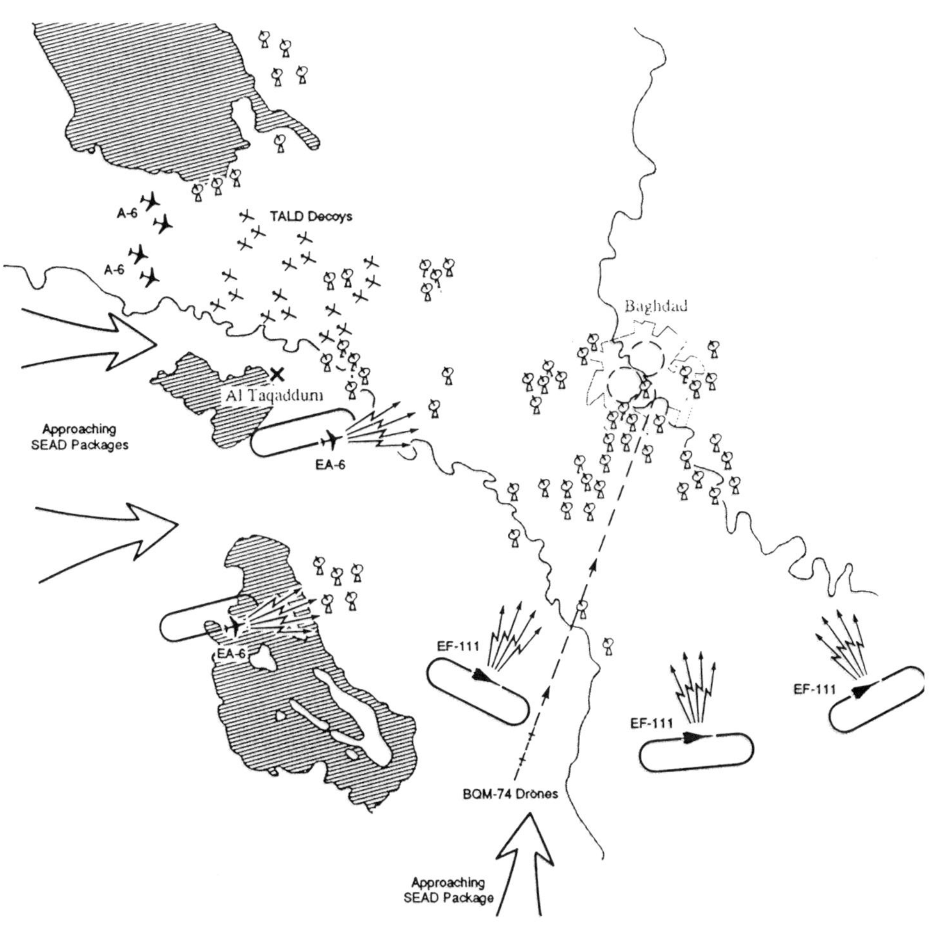

Map 15
Day One (0348 to 0355)

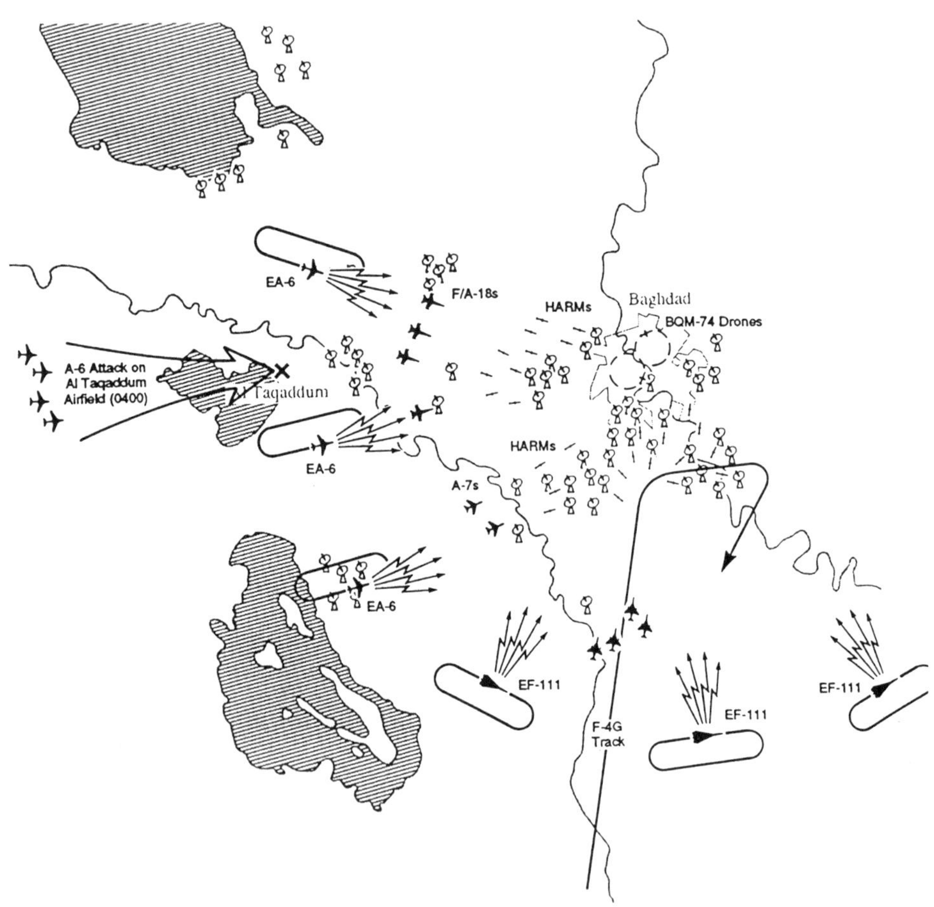

The combination of BQM-74s and TALDs further increased the numbers on their radar screens that Iraqis were seeing.[64] At the same time, the jammers forced radar sites to up their power to handle the electronic jamming. Up to the arrival of the drones over Baghdad and the appearance of TALDs, Iraqi radar activity had been sporadic. Most

[64]The large number of aircraft that the Iraqis claimed on the next several days to have shot down, undoubtedly reflected their success against air force drones and navy decoys.

emitters had been blinking–turning their radars on and off and thus providing no consistent source. "Once the drones started to orbit over Baghdad, the Iraqi target acquisition/tracker/fire control radar activity not only became steady, but increased. . . .[P]ost-attack analysis confirmed that Iraqi 'lethal' activity increased dramatically in the immediate area of the drones."[65]

All of this activity had precisely the result that the planners had hoped.[66] At this point, the HARM shooters began to fire. F/A-18s and A-7s from the Navy SEAD package fired forty-five HARMs in their prebriefed mode–at targets already designated as known SAM sites–and six more at targets of opportunity. The F-4Gs, however, possessed the capability of identifying active SAM sites from the air; consequently, their backseater Electronic Warfare Officers (EWOs) could mark active sites from the aircraft's equipment and then fire at the site by programming the HARM on board the aircraft.

The SEAD package of F-4Gs headed straight for Baghdad, and then just short of the capital swung northeast. As the aircraft did so, the EWOs picked sites that intelligence had identified.[67] If those sites were not operating, they then went after targets of opportunity. The Weasel wing reported:

> The WILD WEASELs picked up SAM activity 100 NM from Baghdad. At 0037Z SA-8s, radar AAA, and I-HAWK came up. From 0048Z on, the

---

[65]Message from AFEWC, Kelly AFB, 182100Z Sep 1991, Subj: "Constant Light Report No. 11–Air Force Unmanned Aerial Vehicle (UAV) Effectiveness," GWAPS CH3, 3-4A. Interestingly, Col Warden had apparently alerted Glosson and Henry about the possibility of using drones: Message 080103Z Sep 1990, HQ USAF Washington, DC, same GWAPS folder.

[66]After the war a major NATO Conference in Belgium assessed the contribution of SEAD to the Gulf War in the following terms: "The Joint SEAD campaign and SEAD support of the Gulf War will long be remembered as an outstanding success. The role played by EC assets, and in particular the EC-130 Compass Call, was critical to that success." (S) AAFCETLP Gulf War Conference Report, 1730.13.7/AFOOAT/S-078/92, 20 Feb 1992 NATO.

[67]Starr, "Special Study, History of the 35th Tactical Fighter Wing (Provisional): Operations Desert Shield and Desert Storm," p 148.

activity was very heavy. The WILD WEASELs had radar contacts on the drones. We did not observe any hits on the drones by Iraqi air defense. The 35th TFW felt the drones were highly effective in stimulating the threats. This provided a "target rich" environment for the WEASELs.[68]

In all, the southern strike of Air Force Weasels fired twenty-two HARMs with ten shots assessed as successful (a 46 percent success rate).[69] Overall, there is no exact evidence as to the damage done to the Iraqi air defenses by the first strike; there were, however, significant numbers of radars that ceased operating when incoming HARMs would have impacted. While the Baghdad SEAD strike went in, two other similar SEAD packages, also supported by drones and decoys to stimulate the defenses, struck the enemy defenses in the west–near Scud bases–and in the east around Kuwait City and Basra. These attacks achieved similar levels of success against the Iraqi defense system.

Evidence indicates that the tactic of using drones to stimulate the defenses achieved its aim. Over their operating period on the first night, there was a 22 percent rise in active lethal radars seeking to acquire targets. Moreover, the correlation between F-4G HARM firings and the cessation of activity by radar sites suggests that 45 percent of the HARMs fired by Weasels caused the targeted emitters to go off the air.[70] Data for the Navy SEAD packages is less clear.[71] Nevertheless, there is no reason to believe that the Navy's strikes were any less successful in achieving the desired functional effect. The crucial point is that Weasel and Navy

---

[68]Air Force Intelligence Command, Air Force Electronic Warfare Center, "Operation Desert Storm, Electronic Combat (EC) Effectiveness Analysis," January 1992, p 11-9. The Hawks were US surface-to-air missiles possessed by the Kuwaitis; they and their supporting systems had been taken over by the Iraqis.

[69]*Ibid*, p 11-9.

[70](S/NF) Institute for Defense Analysis, "Desert Shield/Desert Storm, Suppression of Enemy Air Defenses," Phase I Report, IDA Document D-1076, p I-3.

[71]By and large in the first several days the Navy fired its HARMs at pre-briefed targets in a preemptive mode. It is much harder to correlate preemptive firings with specific emitters going off the air.

SEAD attacks intimidated Iraqi air defenses and operators beyond the mere destruction of individual SAM sites. As the wing commander of the F-4Gs noted:

> The key is that very early on while the F-15s maintained air superiority, the weasels maintained suppression of enemy air defense[s] as far as I am concerned, because they beat them down quickly, efficiently and the enemy knew if he turned his radar on, he'd be dead. As a result of that, they are not turning their radars on. If they do anything, they are blinking them off and on just to be able to say they are doing it and to maybe get some cuts on where the strikers are coming in. They're firing their missiles off ballistically. For the most part they are completely ineffective, and I hold that almost exclusively at the value of the suppression of the enemy air defenses during that first week.[72]

Almost concurrently with SEAD attacks on Baghdad, the next wave of F-117s hit Sector and Intercept Operations Centers (in some cases), command and control centers, and leadership targets.[73] Like the first wave, this one also had a high rate of mission success with pilots reporting ten hits out of sixteen bombs dropped.[74] The targets also involved a significant number of command and control nodes in the air defense system.

While we do not have a detailed picture of what was happening within the Iraqi system, there was clearly considerable confusion and misinformation; undoubtedly, the Iraqis found it difficult to grasp what

---

[72]Starr, "Special Study: History of the 35th Tactical Fighter Wing (Provisional): Operations Desert Shield and Desert Storm," p 179.

[73](S) Master Attack Plan, "The First 24 Hours," 16 Jan 1991; GWAPS Missions Database.

[74]SMSgt Harold P. Myers, "Nighthawks over Iraq: A Chronology of the F-117A Stealth Fighter in Operations Desert Shield and Desert Storm," p 8.

exactly had happened over the past several hours.[75] To add to their confusion, the second F-117 strike came immediately after what had seemed to be a massive strike against Baghdad–one that had only fired missiles at SAM sites; the drones had dropped no bombs, and now with no apparent aircraft overhead, bombs were once again falling on the KARI's control centers.

Unfortunately, because of bad weather over their targets, the third wave of F-117s on the first night had less success; its pilots reported only five hits out of sixteen bombs dropped. For the short run, its misses were less important because the targets were mostly chemical and biological bunkers.[76] But the cause of the misses, bad weather obscuring the targets, presaged the weather problems that plagued the unfolding of the strategic campaign. At the same time that the F-117s attacked the chemical/biological bunkers, four F-111Fs struck the bunkers at Salman Pak. Again, not as many bunkers were damaged as had been planned.

While SEAD packages beat up the air defenses around Baghdad, B-52s and British GR-1 Tornados struck at the forward operating bases located near the Saudi frontier. The fear here was that the Iraqis might move their fighter aircraft forward and then launch a strike against an AWACS or tanker, thereby disrupting the flow of operations. On the next morning, bomb damage assessment (BDA) provided mixed evidence regarding how much physical damage these strikes had inflicted.[78] Nevertheless, they achieved their larger purpose because the Iraqis never again attempted to use the forward operating locations.

---

[75]An indication of this is the extraordinarily high number of aircraft that the Iraqis claimed their defenses had shot down in the first night's action, some of which were probably drones (TALDs and BQM-74s).

[76]Myers, "Nighthawks over Iraq: A Chronology of the F-117A Stealth Fighter in Operations Desert Shield and Desert Storm," p 9. The hour chosen was one in which the breaking of these bunkers, if they contained anthrax spores, would do the least damage to the surrounding population.

[77](S) Master Attack Plan, "First 24 Hours," 16 Jan 1991.

[78]Capt William Bruner, who was in the Black Hole at the time, felt these strikes had largely failed in a physical sense (conversation, 8 Apr 1992). Lt Col Richard King, who was involved in BDA (bomb-damage assessment) in Washington DC, recalls that runways at several bases were cratered (written annotations to draft of this chapter, Feb 1993).

During the course of the night, a number of other missions went after Iraqi airfields, while Coalition fighter aircraft covered the movement of allied aircraft into and out of the country. RAF GR-1 Tornados employed JP233 scatterable mines and cratering bomblets to restrict Iraqi use of several critical airfields. JP233 required the Tornados to overfly the targeted runways and taxiways at extremely low altitudes and maintain straight-and-level flight while the submunitions were being dispensed. One RAF pilot remembered his mission during the first night in the following terms:

> We flew our familiar parallel track formation at 200 ft auto TF with pairs at two-four miles width and forty seconds between following aircraft, to allow freedom of movement for any aircraft that might be threatened en-route. At about forty miles from the target I commented to my backseater on the heavy AAA in the two o'clock when we turned at point J where we changed from parallel track to twenty second trail and since Jane's, All The World Fireworks Displays, was now in the twelve o'clock, it became apparent to both of us that the AAA was, in fact, emanating from our target . . . deep joy! We got speed up above 500 kts and I took the auto pilot out and manually TFR'd whilst I watched the bomblets of the front four-ship explode from right to left in front of me in amongst the firework display. Thirty seconds later we then attacked at about 520 kts and 180 ft radar altitude, through what seemed to be a solid red and white wall of tracer. My backseater confessed to me later that, rather than look out at the tracers, he chose to concentrate very hard on his radar display upon which the double wire airfield perimeter fence, common to all Iraqi airfields, stood out like the proverbial dog's balls and made a superb aiming offset. It was obvious that the US formations that had attacked before us had stimulated the defenses into action. The barrage was fully developed by the time we arrived eight minutes after the first bomb drop. None of it seemed aimed at us since it was all pointed more or less vertically upwards but it was nevertheless a fearsome sight. We heaved a great sigh of relief when all the aircraft checked in off target.[84]

For the first night, the RAF lost no aircraft despite their extreme exposure to enemy flak with their low-level mission profiles.

As soon as the conventional force packages began moving into Iraq, F-15Cs and F-14s had established CAPs near the airfields that represented

---

[84](S) Flt Lt Bruce MacDonald, "Tornado GR-1 Low Level Operations," Appendix 16 to Annex C to 1730.13.7/AF00AT/S-078/92, 20 Feb 1992, NATO.

particularly serious threats to the attackers. The planners' belief was that if Coalition air superiority fighters struck hard and fast at Iraqi aircraft attempting to launch, they would deter the enemy from even flying.[80] The conception proved correct; shoot downs of Iraqi aircraft in the immediate vicinity of their own airfields did not encourage others to fly.[81]

In almost every respect, the first night's work represented an enormous success. A crucial indicator was the fact that when it was over, Coalition air forces had lost only a single F/A-18 in the SEAD package against Baghdad. At the time, it was believed that its loss resulted from a SAM, but it now appears that a MiG-25 may have scored a victory (if so, it would represent the only air-to-air kill the Iraqis got during the entire war).[82] Considering that Horner, Glosson, and others had expected far heavier losses on the first night (estimates had ranged as high as twenty to twenty-five aircraft), the loss of a single aircraft appeared miraculously low.[83] There had even been fears about a possible mid-air collision between allied aircraft–even one involving a tanker.[84] The apparent results of the night's bombing and missile attacks also met expectations, especially in comparison with the experiences of previous wars. The first two waves of F-117s had achieved stunning successes in the teeth of enemy defenses: twenty-three hits out of thirty-three bombs dropped. One of those reported as having missed, the attack on the H-3 sector center, in fact appears to have done its job, since the Iraqis failed to use the center during the rest of the war.[85]

---

[80]Intvw, Maj Gen Buster Glosson with GWAPS personnel, 14 Apr 1992.

[81]Glosson's conception was solidly supported by SPEAR's analysis of Iraqi capabilities. See (S) SPEAR, "Iraqi Threat to US Forces," p 3-63.

[82]Discussion with Cmdr Mark Fitzgerald, SPEAR, Naval Intelligence Command, 15 May 1992. During the Gulf War, Fitzgerald was on the *Kennedy* and led the first A-7 package into Iraq on the opening night of the war. He saw a MiG-25 pass overhead in afterburner and headed toward the F/A-18s. Lacking any solid evidence of SAM activity in the vicinity of the F/A-18 lost on the first night, Fitzgerald believes that the Hornet most probably fell to the MiG.

[83]Intvw, Maj Gen Buster Glosson with GWAPS personnel, 14 Apr 1992. Horner in particular had cautioned Deptula against believing that the plan would function as smoothly as it had been laid out; but even Deptula found the success of the first night beyond his expectations. Intvw, Lt Col David Deptula with GWAPS personnel, 20-21 Dec 1992.

[84]Intvw, Lt Col David Deptula with GWAPS personnel, 20-21 Dec 1992.

[85]Testimony of Lt Col Robert Eskridge, former member of the Black Hole, 16 Sep 1992.

The damage to the enemy's systems had been significant; how significant is difficult to separate from that inflicted by subsequent attacks over the succeeding forty-eight hours.[86] But the first night attacks had substantially degraded enemy air defenses. KARI no longer operated as an integrated system.[87] Many Iraqi radars and SAM sites no longer functioned. On 18 January, intelligence sources reported that much of Baghdad no longer had electricity.[88] Of the Sector Operations Centers, F-117s claimed hits on all except H-3, and that one no longer functioned. Laser-guided bombs had also hit many Intercept Operations Centers, and even if those sites still operated, their effectiveness no longer matched their original capabilities. Nevertheless, in the first day's euphoria, Horner interjected a note of hard-headed realism that proved to be astonishingly close to the mark. At the 1700 staff meeting on 17 January, he warned: "We are at Day One of a thirty-to forty-day war."[89]

The First Day

Dawn brought no relief to the Iraqis: the pounding that had begun in the night continued right through to the war's end. [For maps depicting the air operations on the rest of the first day see Maps 16, 17, and 18]. Between 0830 and 1200, after exhausting flights from Barksdale AFB, Louisiana, seven B-52s arrived at launch positions in Saudi Arabia and fired thirty-five CALCMs (Conventional Air Launched Cruise Missile) at targets throughout Iraq.[90] One missile crashed into Saudi Arabia shortly

---

[86]Without Iraqi documents, it is impossible to calculate the actual damage as "documented" historical truth. What matters most in terms of this study was the continued success of Coalition air operations in attacking targets throughout Iraq for the remainder of the war without significant losses. In fact, even with full and complete access to Iraqi documents, this historian doubts whether one could arrive at a hard judgement, for example, on the individual contributions of F-117 attacks on communication nodes and command and control centers, the damage to the electrical network due to TLAMs, or the level of success achieved by the SEAD attacks of the first night; because the pieces of the first night's raids were so closely interrelated their accomplishments were too interwoven for individual contributions to be readily quantifiable in isolation.

[87]This is not to claim that the enemy air defenses no longer retained substantial lethality. As the Third Day's attack on Baghdad discovered, the enemy on occasion could react with some considerable effectiveness.

[88]Desert Storm Master Chronology, electronic file, 28 May 1992.

[89](S) TSgt Barton's notes of the TACC, 1700 Brfg, 17 Jan 1991, GWAPS, NA 200.

[90]The first B-52 had taken off from Barksdale AFB at 0636 on 16 Jan for the flight

after launch; at least twenty-eight hit their targets, while a further three may have impacted in the target area. The attack by CALCMs on the Al Musayyib Thermal Power Plant suggests both the accuracy of the weapons system and the problems with bomb-damage assessment that would soon plague the air campaign.

Map 16
Day One (0600 to 1300L)

to Iraq: Richard P. Hallion, *Storm Over Iraq, Air Power and the Gulf War* (Washington, 1992) p 163.

Map 17
Day One (1300 to 1830)

The B-52 strike underlines the effort required to support the first day's missions. The Barksdale bombers needed no fewer than thirty-eight KC-135 tanker sorties from Lajes in the Azores and nineteen KC-10 sorties out of Spain.[97] Of eight targets attacked, SAC intelligence

---

[97] *Ibid*, p 35.

Map 18
Day One (1830, 17 Jan to 0300L, 18 Jan)

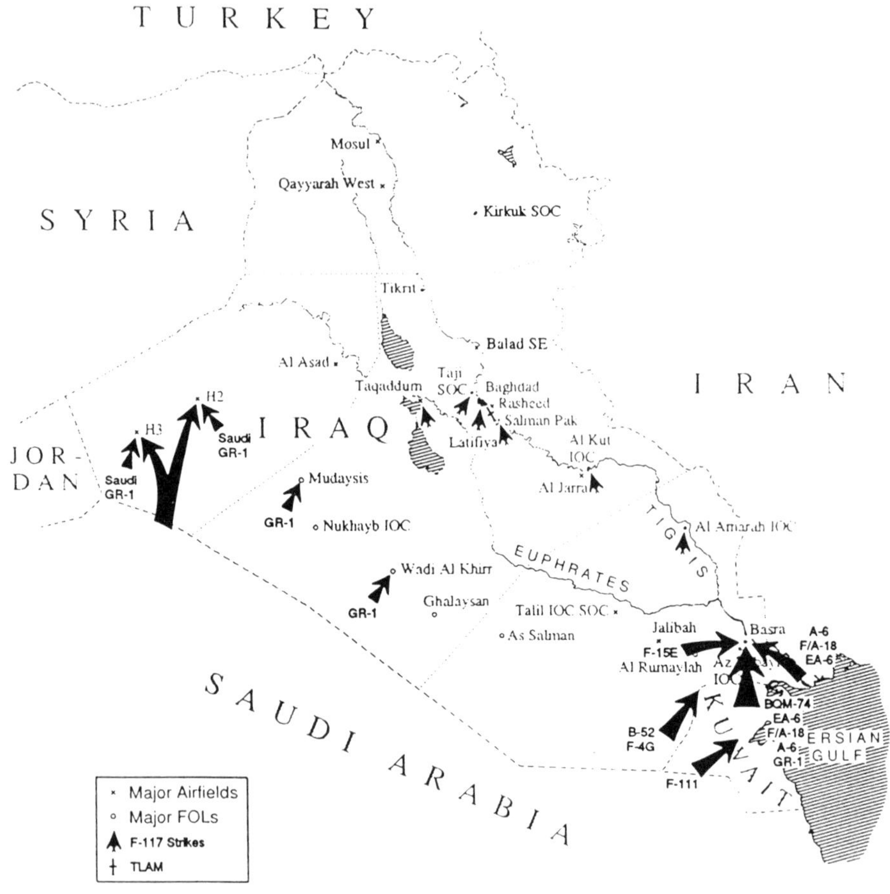

estimated that six ceased functioning, one was damaged, and one was missed by the missiles.[98]

Throughout the day, packages of Coalition aircraft moved through Iraqi airspace to strike assorted targets. A-10s attacked the enemy's early

[98]*Ibid*, pp 39-40.

warning sites along the frontier; here the aim was to eliminate the ends of the tentacles, so that the enemy would lose his sense as to what was coming. A-10s also struck enemy ground forces throughout the triborder area. F-16s struck the Republican Guard several times during the day, the first of many visits. Throughout the day, heavy Navy and Air Force SEAD packages went after Iraqi air defenses, both control centers and SAM sites. Overall, the weight of Coalition air attacks fell most heavily on the enemy air defenses. [See Table 2]

Table 2
Daylight Attacks on 17 January 1991

Target Category	Type and Number of a/c	Percentage
Airfields	4 GR-1, 4 A-7, 56 F-16	30.5%
Oil	20 F-16	9.5%
Telecomms/C^3	12 F-16, 5 B-52	8%
Strategic Air Defenses	24 A-10, 24 F/A-18	23%
Electricity	3 B-52	1.4%
Scuds	16 F-16	7.6%
SAMs	36 F-16, 6 F/A-18	20%[99]
	Total Aircraft: 210	

[99](S) Master Attack Plan, "First 24 Hours," 16 Jan 1991.

Meanwhile, Tomahawk missiles continued hitting targets in the Baghdad area; here the intent was to keep pressure on the capital twenty-four hours a day. Since the F-117s only operated at night, the missiles offered a means of striking the Iraqi capital during daylight.[100] Undoubtedly, the impact of six Tomahawks hitting the Iraqi Ministry of Defense between 1010 and 1017 did little to improve morale of those in the building or neighborhood.[101] The close groupings of the missile attacks on particular targets must have added to the Iraqi sense of helplessness; the fact that they could often see the missiles in flight, but could do little in response, could not have improved the defenders' psychological state.

Late in the day, a particularly heavy strike of thirty-two F-16s occurred against the airfield at Al Taqaddum and the Habbaniya Petroleum Storage Facility. The planners gave the remaining Iraqi defenses considerable respect. Four EF-111s provided jamming support; eight F-4G Weasels brought their HARMs to use against operating SAM sites,

Smoke pours from a burning petroleum refinery hit by Allied bombs.

---

[100]Intvw, Lt Col David Deptula with GWAPS personnel, 21 Dec 1992.

[101]GWAPS Database, TOTs acquired from the Center for Naval Analysis.

while sixteen F-15Cs provided top cover.[102] The fact that no fewer than twenty-eight support aircraft shielded the thirty-two strike aircraft from the enemy defenses and fighters suggests the extent to which stealth extended Coalition air capacity to attack targets deep inside the enemy's defensive system. In comparison, the F-117s that had executed the first strikes on *downtown Baghdad* had needed no SEAD or fighter support to attack their targets–against a fully functioning defense system. The fact that the F-16s did not possess precision-guided munition capabilities and therefore lacked the ability to hit their targets with the lethality of the F-117s further underscores the difference.

The first day's effort ended with heavy attacks in early evening. Seven B-52s struck the Tawakalna Division of the Republican Guard; F-111Fs, supported by EF-111s, attacked Saddam Hussein's residence in his home town of Tikrit, north of Baghdad.[103] But the main show in the early night hours of 18/19 January centered on F-117s and Navy and Marine attacks against the air defense systems in eastern and western Iraq. Unfortunately, due to weather problems, the last F-117 strike of Day 1 barely achieved 50 percent hits (ten hits and eight misses); a number of other targets were no drop because of weather.[104] At 2200, eighteen Marine F/A-18s, ten Marine A-6s, and four RAF GR-1s attacked airfields, bridges, and petroleum facilities around Basra; a major Navy package followed the Marines into the area at the same time that sixteen F-15Es struck targets near Basra. Two separate SEAD packages supported the three strikes; in the first, four Marine EA-6Bs provided jamming, while six Marine F/A-18s fired HARMs at the remaining SAM sites. A second SEAD package consisted of four Navy EA-6s and six F/A-18s. To the west, Navy SEAD protected nine A-6s and eight RAF GR-1s in pounding the H-2 and H-3 airfields and runways.[105]

At the end of the first day's operations, the Iraqi air defense system had received a severe blow. It is impossible to estimate at what point it

---

[102](S) The Master Attack Plan, "The First 24 Hours," 16 Jan 1991; and GWAPS Database.

[103](S) *Ibid.*

[104]GWAPS Database; (S) Master Attack Plan, "The First 24 Hours," 16 Jan 1991; and Myers, "Nighthawks Over Iraq: A Chronology of the F-117A Stealth Fighter in Operations Desert Shield and Desert Storm," p 9.

[105](S) Master Attack Plan, "First 24 Hours," 16 Jan 1991; and GWAPS Database.

no longer operated as an integrated system; the Iraqis themselves still probably do not know. But while in some areas the system, particularly in the Baghdad area, could operate autonomously, its sectors were under severe pressure and no longer represented an effective defensive system. As the successful operations of Coalition aircraft throughout the first day underlined, enemy air defenses could not prevent allied air power from using medium altitudes with impunity. In the end, the Coalition plans and the attacks that had resulted from them had created maximum confusion and friction within the enemy's system.

Perhaps the second greatest surprise of the first day–after the light losses suffered by Coalition air forces–was the failure of the Iraqi fighters to put up *any* significant opposition. The enemy flew 120 sorties on the first day, but many of those were not "shooter" sorties.[106] In fact, during the first *three* days of the air war, the Iraqis flew slightly more than 100 air-to-air sorties, a dismal performance in view of their numbers. As Glosson supposed, the presence of F-15s and F-14s on combat air patrol over Iraqi airfields discouraged the enemy from flying.[107] The loss of three MiG-29s, three F-1 Mirages, and two MiG-21s over the course of the first day further discouraged Iraqi pilots from engaging the allied air offensive.[108] One suspects that the Iraqis never intended to commit their aircraft to meet the first waves of air attacks; rather they intended to save their air force to support the army in the ground battle.[109] But the lack of response was indeed a surprise.

On the other side, Coalition air losses remained extraordinarily light. During daylight air attacks, the RAF lost one GR-1, while the Kuwaitis lost an A-4, both to SAMs; during evening operations, the allies lost three more aircraft, all within forty-five minutes, but in different operational

---

[106]"Conduct of the Persian Gulf War: Final Report to Congress," Apr 1992, p 204.

[107]In one case the Iraqis had approximately eight aircraft cranked up and ready to go. USAF F-15s shot the first two down shortly after they became airborne; the other six aircraft then shut down. Intvw, Maj Gen Buster Glosson with GWAPS personnel, 14 Apr 1992.

[108]The MiG-29s and Mirages were shot down by F-15s; F/A-18s shot down the MiG-21s.

[109]Perhaps Saddam viewed his air force as the Germans viewed their navy in World War I–as being a major player in the postwar balance of power and therefore as being too valuable to risk losing in action.

areas. The USAF lost its first aircraft, an F-15E, the British another GR-1, and the USN its second aircraft, an A-6E, the first two to antiaircraft fire, the latter to a SAM. In all, the Iraqis managed to damage thirteen Coalition aircraft.[110]

The overall loss rate for the first day of the war was indeed astonishing, especially when one considers that Iraqi air defenses were among the best-equipped in the world. The first day's success established a number of essential preconditions for the destruction of Iraq's military power at minimum cost to Coalition forces. It was now clear that allied air power would soon enjoy air supremacy over Iraq and Kuwait; that would allow allied ground forces to redeploy at their own convenience, while the Iraqis remained entirely blind as to what was occurring. Secondly, Coalition air forces could now attack Iraqi ground forces at their leisure; there would be no need for a ground campaign until air attacks had severely attrited enemy forces. Finally, there would be sufficient time to attack those strategic targets, the destruction of which would lessen Iraq's threat to regional stability.

The Second Day

As with the first day, the Black Hole had carefully scripted what would occur on day two. The pattern of Coalition air operations again suggests an effort to spread confusion and friction throughout the enemy's command system; in other words Horner and the planners aimed to further degrade Iraqi capacity to defend themselves against the air campaign. To a great extent, the conduct of operations on day two extended the successes that air attacks had gained at the start; nevertheless, by the end of the day, weather was having a severe impact on the conduct of the campaign.

Nor was poor weather the only friction that began to crop up by the second day. In planning Desert Storm, the Black Hole air planners had recognized that once the campaign got past the scripted first two days bomb damage assessment (BDA) from intelligence would quickly become important for evaluating previous strikes, deciding which targets to strike in succeeding days, retargeting when necessary, and uncovering new targets as the war unfolded. Unfortunately, for much of the air campaign, BDA did not arrive from the formal intelligence channels in a timely manner, and the

---

[110]GWAPS Database, 25 Jun 1992.

air planners in Riyadh found themselves increasingly forced to obtain BDA from alternative sources.[111] Those sources included Glosson's special relation with Admiral McConnell in Washington, the use of video recordings from aircraft like the F-117 and F-111F that could provide imagery of their own strikes, the Black Hole's ad hoc relationship with Checkmate, and informal relationships with operationally oriented organizations such as the Navy's SPEAR (Strike Projection Evaluation and Anti-Air Warfare Research) in Suitland, Maryland.

This report cannot give a detailed examination of the BDA problems that emerged during Desert Storm between the commanders, their operational planners, and the formal intelligence organizations. Suffice it to say that there were problems,[112] and that the blame for these problems did not lie exclusively on the intelligence side of the house.[113] (The reader interested in more insight into BDA problems should consult Chapter Four of the Summary report.)

As with the previous day's operations, the second day began with F-117 attacks. [For a depiction of air attacks on Day Two, see Maps 19, 20, and 21.] The planners paid special attention to air defense controlling centers (SOCs and IOCs); again their emphasis was on disruption rather than on sheer physical destruction. Some considerable retargeting took

---

[111]The postwar criticism by such figures as Generals Schwarzkopf and Horner underlines that there were some considerable problems. In turn, their criticism is backed up by the logs in the TACC, the notes taken by air force historians in the TACC throughout the war, and by personal journals kept by crucial players such as Glosson and Deptula.

[112]Horner's frustrations at intelligence at times spilled over into the TACC Log. On 30 January he noted: "Target–SA-2 missiles–will be hit by Scud hunters in the east if not required for a higher priority target–Target is ___ This sentence is incomplete because the ops intel interface is also incomplete!" TACC, CC/DO, Current Ops Log, 30 Jan, GWAPS, NA 215.

[113]On the extraordinary difficulties involved in having operations and intelligence work together successfully one might best consult F.H. Hinsley, *British Intelligence in the Second World War*, three volumes (London, 1979, 1981, and 1984-88). It took the British nearly half the war to get their intelligence operations working successfully and they were confronting a situation that threatened directly the very survival of the nation.

Map 19
Day Two (0300 to 0800L)

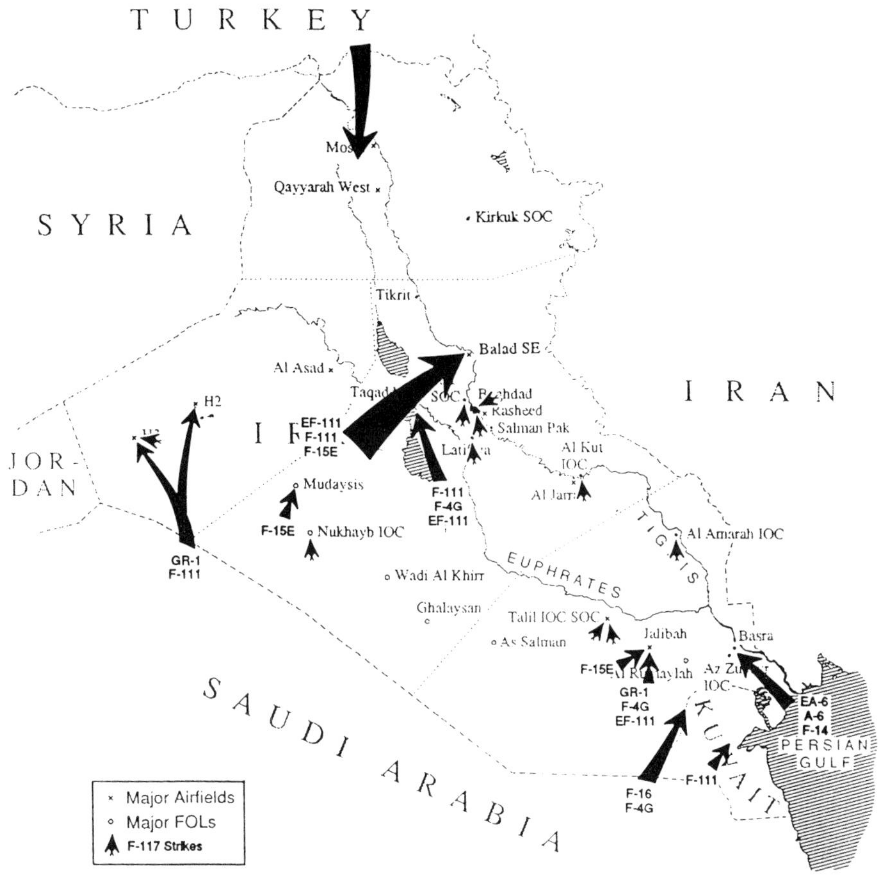

place in the case of the chemical and biological warfare bunkers because so many had escaped damage due to the bad weather that had plagued F-117 strikers early on 17 January.[114] The F-117s achieved hits with thirteen out of nineteen bombs dropped, a considerable improvement over the

[114](S) Master Attack Plan, "Second 24 Hours," 18 Jan 1991.

Map 20
Day Two (0800L to 1800L)

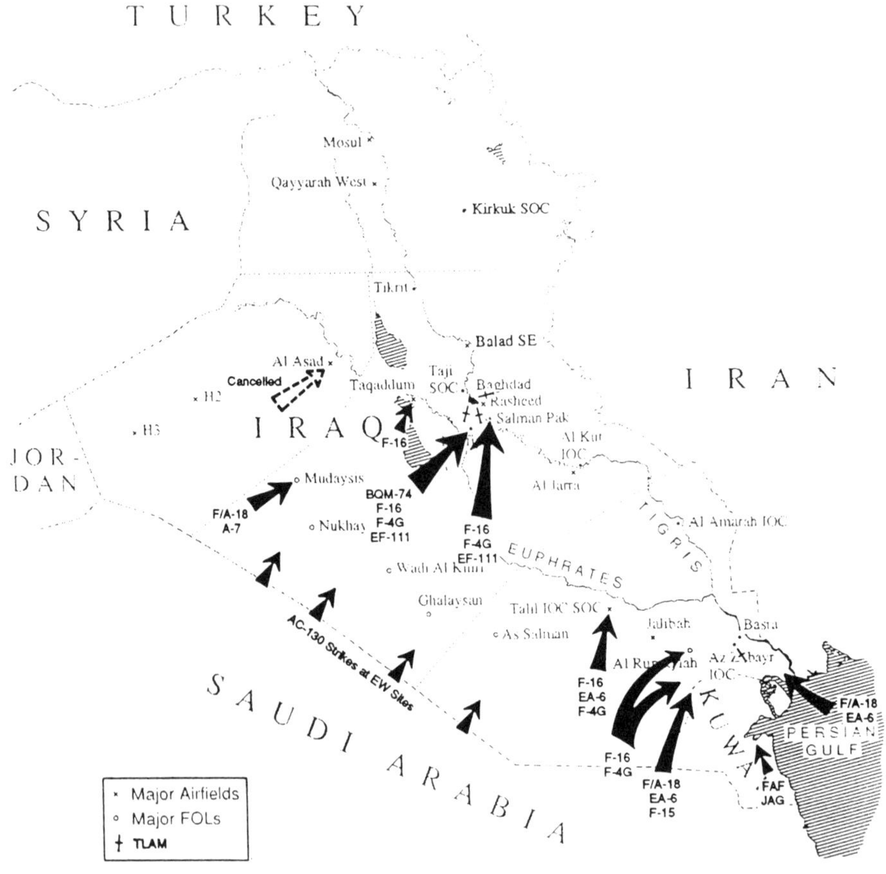

success rate of their past two waves.[115] Along with F-117 strikes in the early morning hours, other packages struck airfields and Scud sites throughout Iraq. The major Iraqi air bases at Balad, Al Taqaddum, and

---

[115]Myers, "Nighthawks Over Iraq: A Chronology of the F-117A Stealth Fighter in Operations Desert Shield and Desert Storm," p 9.

Map 21
Day Two (1800L, 18 Jan to 0300, 19 Jan)

Jaliba all received extensive attention from F-111Fs and GR-1s.[116] If the Iraqis aimed to display more willingness to engage Coalition aircraft on 18 January, these strikes were meant to discourage them.

The pattern of attacks displayed some change. Believing that the first day's effort had degraded Iraqi defenses, the planners put larger packages in against the various target sets under attack. The morning's initial strike, a large package of Navy aircraft–ten A-7s, sixteen F/A-18s, and

---

[116](S) Master Attack Plan, "Second 24 Hours;" and GWAPS Database.

eighteen F-14s along with four GR-1s–targeted the Al Asad area at 0930, but bad weather interfered with much of the mission.[117]

At 1000 hours two large packages hit the center of Iraq on each side of Baghdad. EF-111s provided SEAD, while forty F-16s attacked munitions, Scud, and military production targets on Baghdad's west side. Shortly after, package J with forty-four F-16s struck Scud-related manufacturing and fuel targets east of Baghdad. Substantial SEAD support covered both packages to suppress Baghdad's defenses: BQM-74 drones were included in the effort, four EF-111s jammed enemy radars, and eight F-4Gs provided HARM support against those radars still brave enough to operate.[118] Finally, twenty-four USAF and four Saudi F-15Cs provided top cover for strikers and ECM aircraft.

Beginning at 0930 air attacks went against Republican Guard units located along the Kuwaiti-Iraqi frontier. The Marines led off with twenty-four F/A-18 sorties against the Republican Guard divisions– divided equally among the Tawakalna, Madinah, Hammurabi; eight F/A-18s and four F-15Cs provided air coverage for the attackers and their ECM package of four EA-6Bs. Two hours and fifteen minutes after the last F/A-18 mission, thirty F-16s struck Tawakalna. At 1610 sixteen F-16s hit targets associated with the airfield at Al Rumayla, just north of the Kuwaiti-Iraqi frontier. As the fighter bombers worked the airfield over, thirty more F-16s again struck Tawakalna. Fifteen minutes later twenty-four F-16s hit Madinah. Significantly, as was the case with many early packages, Air Force, Navy, and Marine SEAD assets covered the strikers; in this case four F-4Gs and two Marine EA-6Bs.[119]

Two other features on the second day were the constant hammering of Iraqi positions near the border by A-10s and sustained attacks by naval air on the enemy navy and other positions in the Basra area. The former discouraged the Iraqis from unleashing a ground campaign; the latter removed the latent threat represented by Iraqi naval forces at the top of the Persian Gulf.[120] The attacks on naval targets were a major focus of

---

[117]The notation in the Master Attack Plan for 18 January 1991, indicates that the package was cancelled because of weather. GWAPS Database and Navy data suggests that a portion of the mission may have struck an alternative target.

[118](S) Master Attack Plan, "Second 24 Hours," 18 Jan 1991, and GWAPS Database.

[119](S) *Ibid.*

[120](S) *Ibid.*

naval air operations in the first weeks of the war; more than 1,000 strikes of naval fixed-wing aircraft hit the Iraqi navy, its bases, and often sites that could threaten Coalition maintenance operations.[121] The destruction of Iraq's naval assets eventually allowed the carriers to move up into the central portions of the Persian Gulf and thus relieve some of the need for tanker support.

The evening and night of 17/18 January proved most disappointing to the F-117s. The Master Attack Plan called for a large number of strikes on targets in the Baghdad area. Unfortunately, the weather was so bad around the capital that no F-117 dropped on its primary target, while few alternates were open. Strikes by other aircraft did go in despite weather conditions. Package T from carriers in the Red Sea struck the power plant and TV station at Hadithek in western Iraq. At 2100, three B-52s again hit the Tawakalna Division, while two four-ship formations of B-52s struck targets near Tallil between 2200 and 2230. The final action of the day saw eight F-111Fs hit bridges along the Euphrates behind the Republican Guard, while three-ship formations of B-52s dropped on the Tawakalna, Madinah, and Hammurabi.[122]

Iraqi air defenses were still capable of putting up opposition to Coalition air strikes. On an evening strike by B-52s in the KTO, one of the Weasel crews reported:

> I worked an SA-2 about twenty-five miles away. We [received] good data on our computer so we had a pretty good shot. As we fired the missile, it came off the left toward the north[; then] we got the indications on the computer that we had been launched on. I looked out of the left side of the jet and watched the first two missiles coming at us. There was a glow in the clouds and then they popped up through the clouds with a wavering orange plume. I called out to Mark (Buccigrossi [the backseater]) that they were coming up. He got them in [sight]. . . .I tried to keep my air speed up because we were at 29,000 feet. I broke into the missiles. The only way I knew the missiles were gone, I called out 'missiles are boom and boom.' [sic] I said I've got two more coming up on the right side and Mark said 'what are you going to do now?' I said, 'Get the pod and chaff going.' I kept the airspeed up. Again Mark kept his eyes on the missiles and called out

---

[121](S) Frank Schwamb, et al, *Desert Storm Reconstruction Report*, Vol. II, *Strike Warfare* (Alexandria, VA, 1991), p D-2.

[122](S) Master Attack Plan, "Second 24 Hours," 18 Jan 1991, and GWAPS Database.

> the explosions on those two missiles. Then the last two I picked up on the left hand side. We had now gotten down to about 15,000 feet because of all our maneuvering. That put us right in the middle of the triple 'A'. Missiles were coming up from the left and Mark said, 'What are you going to do now?' I'm thinking to myself I can't go right because of the triple 'A' off to the west and higher than us now, but the good news was that it wasn't at us. There was still a lot of small arms firing at us. It looked like guys with a fire hose waving it around. I was able to get the airspeed up and climb out. . . .We got out of there and spent three to five minutes in after burner.[123]

An additional strategic factor to the Coalition's advantage had opened up 18 January: the Turks granted permission for USAF aircraft from Europe to begin attacking targets in northern Iraq from Incirlik. Air operations from that direction confronted the Iraqi leadership with a threat from an entirely new point on the compass. It further overloaded their air defenses and placed enemy airfields in this area within easy range of U.S. aircraft. Moreover, it robbed the Iraqis of the possibility of shifting air assets to the north to escape Coalition air attacks.

USAF aircraft operating out of Incirlik–the name for the task force was "Proven Force"–were also within easy range of the Mosul and Kirkuk airfields and other targets in northern Iraq. Unfortunately, the potential of bases in Turkey failed to pay a full set of dividends: lacking aircraft and systems capable of laser designation, Proven Force could not attack targets with the same accuracy as the F-111Fs, F-15Es, and F-117s operating out of Saudi Arabia.[124] The first strike from the north occurred on the second night when ten F-111Es dropped cluster bombs on early warning radar sites just over the border. The next day, the first F-16 daylight mission against Kirkuk was canceled because some Turkish authorities did not yet understand that their government had authorized air strikes from Turkey.[125] But the Iraqis were on notice that there were now no sanctuaries, even in northern Iraq.

---

[123]Starr, "Special Study, History of the 35th Fighter Wing (Provisional): Operations Desert Shield and Desert Storm," GWAPS, NA 277, pp 156-57.

[124]Not until the end of the war did F-4s from Clark with a precision-bombing capability arrive at Incirlik. Unfortunately, their laser designation pods did not arrive until after the war.

[125](S) 7440 Composite Wing (Prov), "Bomb Damage Assessments," 18 Jan–27 Feb 1991; see also Maj Scott Norwood, "Daylight Tactical Air Operations in Northern Iraq, 17 Jan to 27 Feb 1991," GWAPS NA.

The second day's air action underlined the continuing success of efforts to degrade KARI and suppress individual elements of the Iraqi air defense system with SEAD packages. Iraqi air activity declined by about one third compared with the first day.[126] While Coalition fighters failed to shoot any Iraqis down, allied losses fell to only three aircraft: a Navy EA-6B, a Marine OV-10, and an Italian GR-1. Furthermore, the Iraqis damaged only one Coalition aircraft, an F-111E.[127] Due to weather and other factors, Coalition air forces flew two hundred fewer sorties, but all in all it was a most successful day.

It was during this period that the conduct of operations solidified the inclination of Coalition air forces to fly strike missions at medium altitudes. Even before the air campaign against Iraq had begun, there had been an unspoken predisposition to fly and execute strikes above 10,000 feet. Such an approach made obvious sense because it placed Coalition aircraft above the envelope within which most Iraqi antiaircraft guns and infrared SAMs were effective. Nevertheless, this tactical approach was intuitive rather than directed. And it reflected the obvious belief that attacks on KARI and SEAD against enemy missile sites and radar would allow Coalition aircraft to operate with low losses at or above 10,000 feet.[128] Consequently, during Desert Shield most units began to train for medium altitude delivery; the Vietnam experience undoubtedly reinforced such a tactical approach. As one F-16 wing commander noted, he had emphasized to his crews during the period before 17 January that his experience in Vietnam underlined that enemy air defenses were most successful against low-flying aircraft.[129]

The aircraft most wedded to low-level strikes were RAF and Saudi Tornados and B-52s. In the latter case, the mission to attack runways dictated low-level delivery. The Tornado JP-233 weapon systems had to be delivered at low altitude, and the Tornados continued dropping it until 24 January. During this period the Tornados experienced the bulk of the losses

---

[126]DOD, *Conduct of the Persian Gulf War: Final Report to Congress* (Washington, 1992), Table VI-6, p 204.

[127]GWAPS Database.

[128]Precrisis training for most NATO aircraft had stressed low-altitude delivery to minimize the MiG and SAM threats in Europe.

[129]Intvw, Col Ray Hout with GWAPS (Wayne Thompson), Shaw AFB, 9 Mar 1992. Horner's and Glosson's emphasis that no fixed target during the air campaign was worth an aircraft undoubtedly reinforced such proclivities.

they would suffer during the air campaign. By then it was obvious that most Iraqi aircraft were remaining in their shelters and that the few Iraqi fighters that rose to challenge Coalition raids were easily being shot down.[130]

The B-52s changed tactics more quickly than the Tornados and stopped low-level attacks after the first three nights. Strategic Force Planners were told that CENTAF could not afford to lose a B-52. On the second night, a B-52 had turned back in the face of heavy ground fire, and during a low-level attack on an oil refinery that night an SA-3 had damaged another B-52.[131] In general, the decision to leave low altitude seems to have been reached on a unit-by-unit basis that recognized the obvious realities of the situation.[132] Horner never ordered the departure from low altitudes, but he did suggest to the RAF on 19 January that he thought that their low-altitude losses were unnecessary.[133]

The decision not to bomb at lower altitudes carried with it a number of important consequences. On the positive side, it minimized the casualties that Coalition aircraft would take throughout the course of the air campaign; the low casualty rates played a crucial role in allowing the continuation of air operations for a period entirely determined by the needs of Coalition air and ground forces in "preparing the battlefield." On the other hand, the decision to bomb from medium altitudes did have a severe impact on the accuracy of munitions other than precision-guided in attacking fixed positions or equipment. In effect, that decision robbed platforms such as the F-16 and the F/A-18 of much of their ability to attrite enemy ground forces,while allowing those aircraft to remain invulnerable to enemy defenses.[134] This is not to say that their attacks did not play a role in the collapse of Iraqi ground forces; clearly their bombing attacks had a considerable impact on Iraqi morale. In the final analysis,

---

[130]A.D. Kitcher, RAF Strike Command, Operations Research Branch, "Operation Gramby: JP-233 Analysis," Nov 1991, GWAPS, NA 515B.

[131](S) SAC History, "Desert Shield/Desert Storm," SAC, 1990, pp 251-53.

[132]CENTAF's obvious concern with losses undoubtedly served to reinforce the tactical and operational chances that individual units made.

[133]CENTAF TACC Historian's notes, TSgt Barton, 20 Jan 1991, GWAPS, NA 200.

[134]In the case of the A-10, the medium altitude decision robbed its 30 mm gun of much of its accuracy. However, the Maverick missile did provide A-10s with the means to attack targets accurately from medium altitudes. The F-16s had the capability to fire Mavericks but since few of the pilots in the F-16s were qualified to use the missile system, virtually no F-16s flying from the south used Mavericks.

the decision to attack from medium altitude made both operational and tactical sense, and it certainly carried with it important implications for the post-Gulf War arena of air power employment.

Conclusion

What had the air offensive thus far achieved? Allied air attacks on the enemy's air defenses had degraded enemy capabilities to the point where the campaign could continue at acceptable levels of attrition *for as long as Coalition military and political leaders deemed necessary.* The plan to combine attacks on the enemy's air defenses, his centralized command and control system, SEAD efforts such as electronic countermeasures and HARMs, and destruction of much of Iraq's electric network had succeeded beyond the most optimistic forecasts. Moreover, Allied air attacks against Iraq gained a measure of air supremacy in two days at minimum cost to attackers. An almost flawless flow of operations and the relatively low cost of these successes certainly surprised the planners.[135] To a great extent, these two days contradicted General Helmuth von Moltke's assertion that war plans do not survive first contact with the enemy.

This success did not mean that the air offensive had destroyed all the individual components of KARI or that some sectors could not operate autonomously; throughout the remainder of the war, the Iraqis would cobble together bits and pieces of their air defense systems in response to continuing attacks. The crucial point was that the Iraqis now possessed *no effective* defenses against the attacks on their civil and military infrastructures. Perhaps the most telling statistic was the fall in the activity levels for Iraqi SAM/AAA radars by more than 90 percent.[136] While the decline in early warning radar emissions was not as drastic, the crucial fact was that from the first attacks on the Iraqi integrated air defenses, Coalition air forces gained a measure of air superiority sufficient to operate in Iraqi airspace largely with impunity.

Yet one must also note that the attacks on targets in downtown Baghdad had focused on functional effectiveness rather than physical destruction. The concept had been to inhibit and confuse the Iraqi defensive systems, and barely any attacks had occurred against Iraq's political infrastructure. For all the spectacular footage of Iraqi antiaircraft fire over the first few days of the war, F-117s had only dropped *fourteen*

---

[135]Intvw, Lt Col David Deptula with GWAPS personnel, 20-21 Dec 1991.

[136]DOD, *Conduct of the Persian Gulf War: Final Report to Congress*, p 202.

bombs on targets within the heart of the capital in the first twenty-four hours of the war and only *one* during the second twenty-four hour period.[137] Tomahawk missiles had carried considerable weight with thirty-nine impacting on targets in downtown Baghdad during the first day and eighteen missiles on the second day.[138] But the small size of the missile warhead as well as its inability to penetrate hardened targets had limited its effectiveness.

The planners had foreseen this situation. Their aim was to return to a number of critical targets that the first days,attacks had only partially damaged with large conventional force packages of F-16s beginning on the third day. Such attacks would underline the regime's inability to protect itself as well as complete the destruction of a number of large, complex headquarters sites upon which the regime depended for its military and its political control of Iraq.[139]

The imponderable was whether the air attacks of the first two days had wrecked the Baghdad defensive system sufficiently to allow such packages of F-16s to fly within the capital's vicinity without suffering significant losses themselves or without placing the civilian population of the capital at needless hazard.[140] Those two basic questions would not have answers until the first large package of F-16s actually flew against the capital. If the operational approach of using F-16s against large high-value targets in the capital did not work, then the planners faced the challenge of attempting to deconstruct these significant military and political targets that harbored the control apparatus of the regime with individual F-117 sorties. And this would represent a lengthy process that

---

[137]GWAPS Database. The second twenty-four hour period was considerably influenced by the weather.

[138]*Ibid.*

[139]The guidance letters put out by Glosson for D+3, D+4, and D+5 (before it was changed) explicitly directed that at least one large package of F-16s (with twenty-four plus aircraft) attack Baghdad vicinity to make the air campaign visible to the Iraqi people. US Central Command Air Force, COMUSCENTAF Air Guidance Letter, ATO Planning guidance for D+3, Buster C. Glosson, Director of Campaign Plans (no date), p 6, GWAPS, Box 3, Folder 59, Daily Planning Material.

[140]Any kind of SAM threat over the capital where the attacking aircraft were threatened by guiding SAMs would force the pilots to drop their bombs and drop tanks so that they could take effective countermeasures. Such an action would, however, place civilians on the ground in considerable hazard since the pilots would obviously have no means of controlling the fall of these objects.

would carry with it less psychological impact on the regime and demand a consistent and clear focus to the strategic air campaign.

What did these successes over the first two days mean in terms of the strategic and operational balance of power? On the Iraqi side, the intensity of the offensive as well as the level of damage that the attackers inflicted undoubtedly came as a surprise. Coalition attacks on communications, electricity, and air defenses had sowed confusion within a tightly controlled system. The loss of electrical power forced the military to utilize backup power in many places. The effect of these raids magnified the confusion, uncertainty, and frictions attendant on waging of war. Moreover, the nature of Saddam's tyranny probably exacerbated the frictions resulting from Coalition air attacks.

From the Allied perspective, events would soon bear out Homer's pessimism that things never go flawlessly in war. Extraordinarily bad weather, the on-going diversion of some assets to the Scud problem-forced by political considerations–as well as the other uncertainties of "real war" would exercise great strain on the conduct of the "strategic" air campaign. On the other side, the storm systems that dominated the weather in the Persian Gulf throughout this period seemingly gave credence to Saddam's belief that he could wait out the air campaign for the ground war without suffering catastrophic damage. Where he miscalculated was in the duration, accuracy, and intensity with which Coalition air forces could wage the air campaign even in the face of considerable difficulties and frictions.

4

Friction and the Conduct of Operations 18 January to Al Firdos

Allied aircrews had executed the first two days of attacks against Iraq in almost flawless fashion. Air power had shut down much of Iraq's electric system; its air defenses, where still operational, were largely ineffective and intimidated; and Coalition air losses had been extraordinarily low. Stealth aircraft had attacked the heart of enemy air defenses from the first moments of the war; a carefully planned SEAD campaign had severely damaged many radar sites and jammed the remainder successfully. Not surprisingly, planners and commanders greeted the successes of the first days with euphoria. The American public, led to expect heavy losses by the "experts", were equally enthusiastic. Unfortunately, the air campaign now ran into some substantial difficulties and frictions. In retrospect, many of these frictions lay beyond the control of planners and leaders; some might have been foreseen, at least in outline; but most reflected the uncertainties that distinguish "real war from war on paper."[1]

This chapter will discuss the ongoing operational air campaign within the framework of these frictions: the extraordinarily bad weather, the political impact of Scud attacks on Israel and Saudi Arabia, and the difficulties in putting together coherent operational plans and orders within short periods and under great pressure on a sustained basis instead of a single plan for the initial two days of operation refined over a long period of time.[2] These frictions came together on day three of the air war. For that reason we will begin with a detailed examination of operations on 19

---

[1]Clausewitz, *On War*, p 119.

[2]The history of the 614th Tactical Fighter Squadron suggests some of the difficulties that just one friction could cause; on the second day the squadron struck the airfield at Al Rumayla. The squadron historian then notes: "The damage to the airfield could not be assessed for approximately two weeks due to the overcast skies, but in the meantime, the airfield was hit quite a few more times by additional packages." 401st Tactical Fighter Wing, "614th Tactical Fighter Squadron, Desert Shield/Desert Storm."

January 1991. Thereafter this chapter will concentrate on more general topics that reflect the general pattern of operations through 13 February.

The Third Day

On day three, friction began to affect the air campaign. The difficulties underlined that the first days' success did not indicate that the rest of the war would proceed flawlessly. In an oral interview after the war, Horner suggested that he had not allowed his planners in the Black Hole to proceed beyond Day Two in their laydown of air operations.[3] This certainly followed Moltke's advice that war plans do not survive first contact with the enemy; in fact, the Black Hole had prudently worked up an outline for the third day's master attack plan before the war began.

But a number of imponderables confronted planners in their thinking before the war about the third day's operations. By that point, Coalition air forces would have flown several thousand sorties against Iraq and its military forces: what level of success would SEAD and attacks against strategic targets have enjoyed? What would Bomb Damage Assessment (BDA) show? How effective would enemy air defenses prove? There were consequently a number of issues that the conduct of operations and the flow of intelligence would have to resolve before planners could make final decisions on the targets for the third day.

The planning system would rest on a three-day cycle; the first day would involve casting the Master Attack Plan, during which planners, utilizing up-to-date BDA, would integrate strategic and other targets with re-attacks and available platforms.[4] Then on the second day, the Air Tasking Orders (ATO) cell would take the plan and coordinate the details, such as call signs, IFF (identification) codes, comjam procedures, and tanker tracks, into an Air Tasking Order. On the third day, the air units would execute the plan under the direction of the current operations portion of the TACC (Tactical Air Control Center).

---

[3](S) Intvw, R. Davis, P. Jamison, and B. Barlow, AF History Program with Lt Gen Horner, Shaw AFB, SC, 4 Mar 1992.

[4]Intvw, Maj Gen Buster Glosson with GWAPS personnel, 14 Apr 1992; Intvw, Lt Col David Deptula with GWAPS personnel, 20-21 Dec 1991.

Unfortunately, the complexities involved in such a cycle were not clear before the war. Not surprisingly, planners in the Black Hole underestimated the time required to complete the Master Attack Plan under wartime conditions. In the event,they did not complete the Master Attack Plan for day three until 2000 on *18 January*. The euphoria of the first day may have also added to the problem of getting down to work on the third day's plan. To add to planning troubles, timely bomb-damage assessment simply failed to emerge from the intelligence system.[5] As work proceeded on the Master Attack Plan, the building of the third day's Air Tasking Order had to begin; here, the Tactical Air Control Center (TACC) was not yet ready to handle the coordinations involved in working up the Air Tasking Order under the demands of wartime conditions and the severe constraints of time. None of this is surprising; under the actual conditions and pressures of war, human systems and organizations rarely work at optimal levels, especially at the beginning. It takes them time to adapt; and indeed the system did adapt.

In the end, CENTAF's Director of Operations (DO), Maj. Gen. John Corder, finally threw up his hands and ordered both Black Hole and the Air Tasking Order cell to give the TACC what they had.[6] The result was less than satisfactory.[7] As Corder suggested after the war, it took nearly six days for the Black Hole and the Air Tasking Order cell to work into a cycle in which the Master Attack Plan flowed smoothly into an Air Tasking Order.[8]

The cancellations over the next week support Corder's assessment. Over the first two days of operations, the number of cancellations were under fifty for each day; on the third day the number of cancellations rose to 456 and on the fourth reached 431. The sixth day would see 331

---

[5]Weather, as well as a lack of the right kinds of airborne reconnaissance platforms, were major contributing factors.

[6]Intvw, Maj Gen John Corder with GWAPS personnel, 18 May 1992, GWAPS, NA 361.

[7]Intvw, Maj Gen Buster Glosson with GWAPS personnel, 14 Apr 1992; Intvw, Lt Col David Deptula with GWAPS personnel, 20-21 Dec 1991.

[8]Intvw, Maj Gen John Corder with GWAPS personnel, 18 May 1992 GWAPS, NA 361. The after-action report of the 50th Tactical Fighter Wing supports Corder's contention: 50th Tactical Fighter Wing, "Desert Shield/Desert Storm," GWAPS, NA 379

sorties cancelled.[9] Not until 23 January (the seventh day of the war) did the process of translating the Master Attack Plan into an executable Air Tasking Order function with some coherence. On that day, the cancellations fell to manageable levels–105 cancellations and on the next day to thirty-one.[10] Some of these were admittedly due to weather, but others were the result of the failure of tankers or other aircraft to show up at the right time, or other causes.

These Air Tasking Order difficulties translated directly into the operational world. As an F-16 pilot recorded about a mission flown on day four:

> I came off the target with lead and number four in sight, jinked to get my egress steerpoint, checked for number four again–he was gone. Checked for lead again–he was gone, so I came out a singleton between a four ship of F-4G Weasels–not fun! And now the real fun begins. There were no fragged tankers for us! There are planes all over the sky bootlegging tankers. We get enough fuel to divert but decide to dial-up-a-tanker and beg for fuel to get home. And now it's pitch black with some weather.[11]

Similarly, a large package scheduled to attack the Al Taji Rocket Production Facility near Baghdad on the morning of the third day cancelled because there was no Weasel support available.[12]

---

[9](S) GWAPS Database, "USAF Sorties by Day: Scheduled, Added on, Flown, and Cancelled." Despite problems with the weather, the exceedingly high number of cancellations suggests difficulties in the Master Attack Plan–ATO process and that those problems were causing considerable problems in the coordination of tankers, SEAD assets, CAP sorties, and maintenance. There would be equally bad periods of weather later in the war, and those periods would drive up the number of cancellations, but never did the number approach the numbers on the third and fourth days of the war. Only on 30 January would the number of sorties reach over three hundred (310) during the rest of the war.

[10]*Ibid.* The daily cancellations for this period were:

19 January: 456	22 January: 331
20 January: 431	23 January: 105
21 January: 256	24 January: 31

[11]Capt Mike Boera, 10th Tactical Fighter Squadron, 50th Tactical Fighter Wing, "Desert Shield/Desert Storm," p H-15.

[12]401st Fighter Wing (Provisional), "614th Tactical Fighter Squadron, Lucky Devils, Desert Shield/Desert Storm, 29 Aug 1990–29 Mar 1991," GWAPS, no page numbers.

Along with the problems of working into a coherent planning cycle, the weather turned nasty. A series of lows began moving through the theater and directly affected the ability of Allied aircraft to strike targets in Iraq. There were some periods of good weather; often good weather and bad weather alternated over the period of a day, but weather now became a major factor in the conduct of operations.[13] The sortie cancellations on 20 January underline the impact that weather could have on operations. On that day, there were 300 sortie cancellations due to weather alone.[14]

Bad weather had already affected F-117 operations on the night of 18/19 January when roughly two of every three planned strikes either missed or could not be dropped due to weather.[15] While the F-117 "no drops" and misses attributed to weather improved to one out of two on the night of 19/20 January, half the planned effort from the F-117s against strategic targets was still frustrated by weather in the target areas. These initial difficulties were a harbinger of weather problems that would persist throughout the campaign. Black Hold planners would soon begin scheduling precision strikes in areas such as Baghdad according to the weather fronts as they moved through the theater of operations. Nonetheless, significant losses of F-117 strikes to weather would recur in early February on ATO Days 17 and 18, and ATO Days 40 and 41, during the ground campaign, would see the F-117s nearly grounded by weather.[16]

While weather impacted other air operations on 19 January, a significant number of strikes did go in against targets–either through breaks in the clouds or dropping by use of radar, generally an inaccurate means

---

[13]Kenneth R. Walters, Maj Kathleen M. Traxler, Michael T. Gifford, Capt Richard D. Arnold, TSgt Richard C. Bonam, and TSgt Kenneth R. Gibson, "Gulf War Weather," Mar 1992, USAF Environmental Technical Applications Center.

[14]Notes from the TACC, taken by TSgt Barton, 21 Jan 1991, 1700 Brfg, GWAPS, NA 215.

[15]GWAPS Missions Database, Manual Strike Counts done by Task Force Six (see Effectiveness report, Appendix 1).

[16] *Ibid.* On ATO Day 40, the F-117s did not fly at all; the following day the weather was still so bad that F-117 pilots only managed a half dozen strikes.

of weapons delivery. But throughout the day, weather cancelled force packages and affected the tactics and accuracy of those who did bomb.

The third day kicked off with F-15Es striking Scud and air defense targets. [For targets on Day 3 see Maps 22, 23, 24, 25]. The next large package, F-16s, targeted the Madinah and Hammurabi Republican Guard divisions, but cancelled because of weather. At 0500 Package C was to strike Tikrit South and the Scud depot at Qubaysah, but air and ground aborts for maintenance again washed out much of the mission.[17] At the same time, the Navy was having no better luck in southeastern Iraq; the carriers cancelled Package D, which had been scheduled to strike the naval base at Umm Qasr.[18]

The major morning efforts came between 0600 and 0730. At 0600 four B-52s pounded the Madinah Division with a second wake-up call; half an hour later, thirty F-16s were to hit Hammurabi and Tawakalna. Fourteen F-16s cancelled, setting a pattern that continued over the next several hours.[19] Suggesting the difficulties in the Air Tasking Order process, the planners had scheduled two large strike packages to hit Baghdad from 0700 to 0730. By putting so many aircraft together in one strike, planners hoped to minimize coordination of SEAD and tankers and at the same time keep sortie utilization rates up.

Besides scheduling difficulties, there was some overconfidence among commanders and aircrews after the successes of the first two days. One senior officer in the Black Hole exclaimed over the possibility of "darkening the skies over downtown Baghdad." But overconfidence was not only in the Black Hole; the F-16 wings proved receptive to the idea of using their aircraft to go downtown as well, as their F-105 and F-4 predecessors had gone against North Vietnamese defenses in the Red River Valley. In fairness, two large SEAD packages had struck Baghdad's defenses in the first two days, while a number of conventional strike

---

[17]GWAPS Database.

[18](S) Master Attack Plan, Third 24 Hours, 18 Jan 1991 and GWAPS Database.

[19](S) *Ibid.*

packages had probed right up to the capital's suburbs. Thus far, the enemy had inflicted only minimal damage on the attackers. Consequently, there was reason to believe that attacks had already attrited enemy defenses to the breaking point.

Map 22
19 January (0300 to 0800)

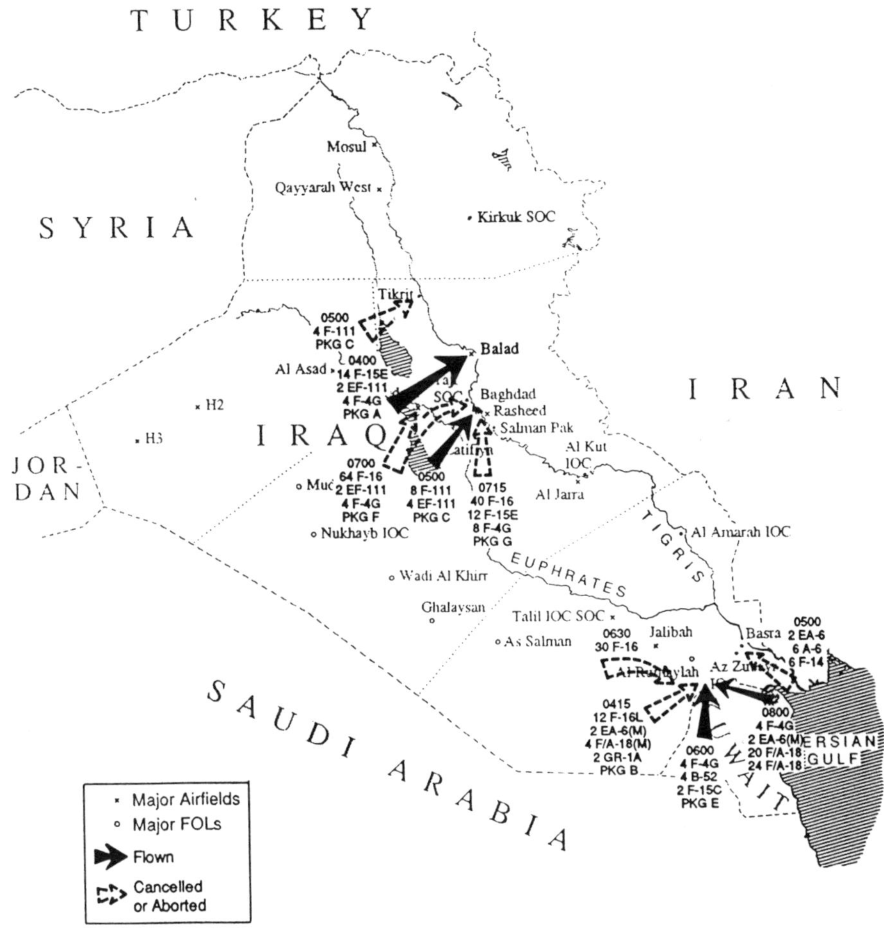

There was also a tactical reason for planning large F-16 strikes against a number of targets in the Baghdad area. Large structures such as the Ministry of Defense or the Air Defense Operations Center would require a considerable number of F-117 and Tomahawk missile attacks to destroy them completely. Whatever the inaccuracies of the F-16 plat-

Map 23
19 January (0830 to 1700)

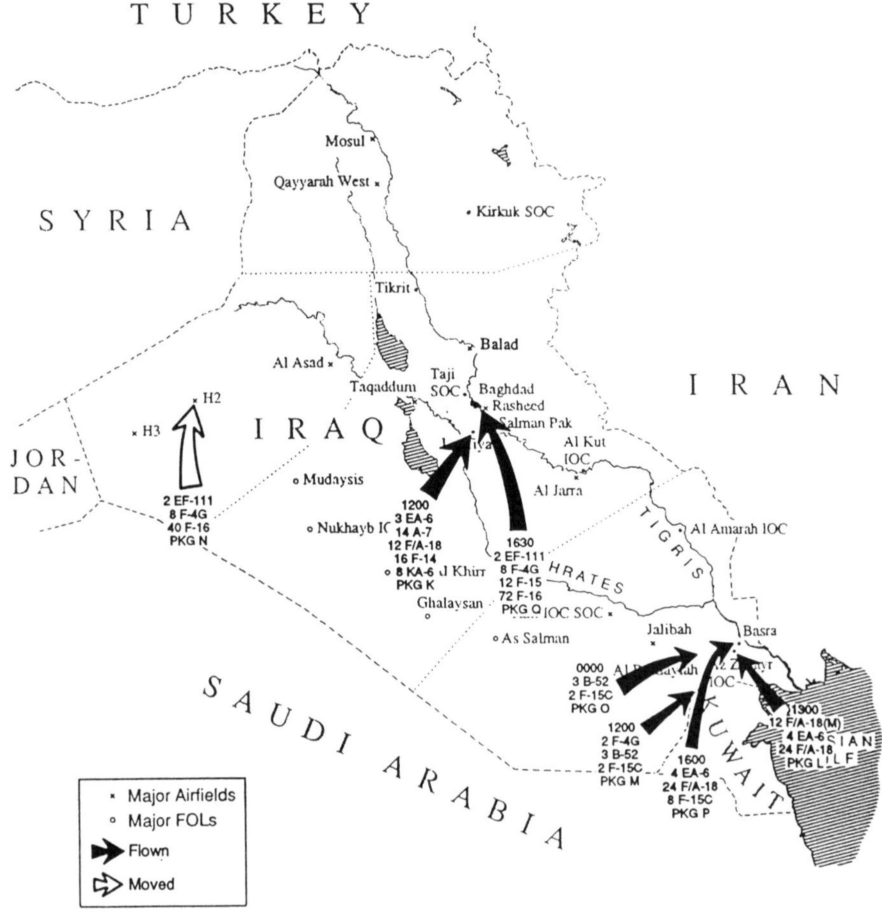

form, the size of such structures provided area targets where pinpoint accuracy was less of an issue than in most cases. The destruction of several of the Iraqi government's larger buildings in Baghdad would obviously have had psychological effects on both government and people.

Map 24
19 January (1700 to 2000)

Moreover, the attacks would underline that American air power could reach anywhere in Iraq without serious loss.[20]

Map 25
2000, 19 January to 0300, 20 January

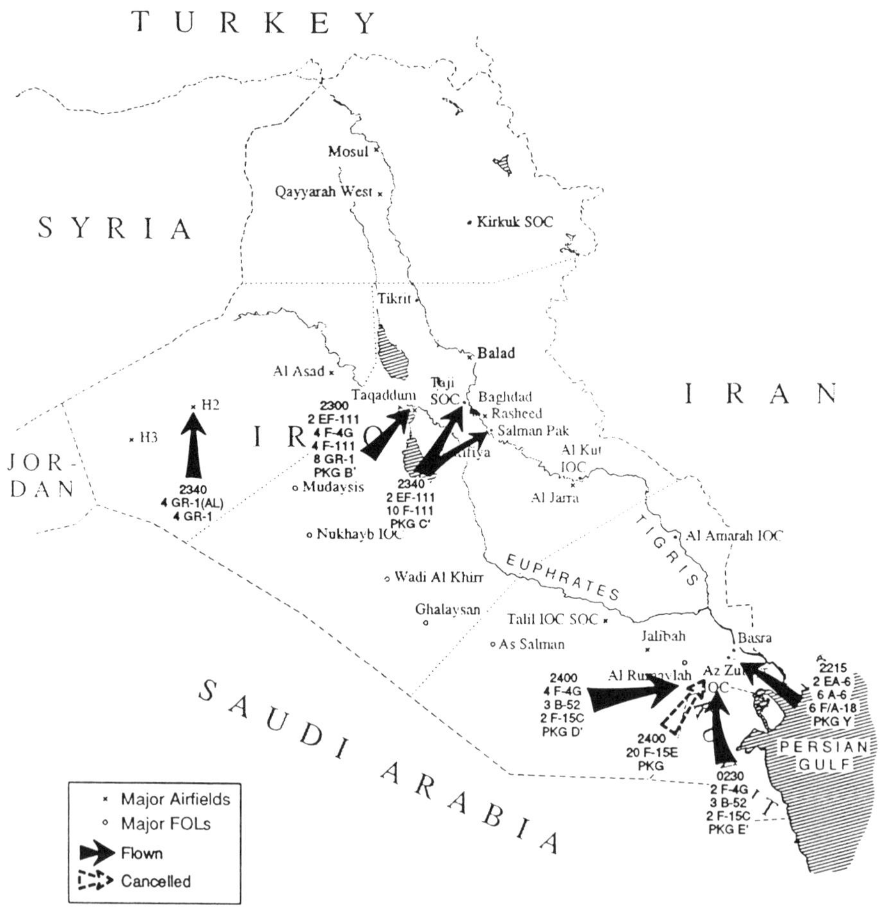

---

[20]Conversation with Lt Col David Deptula by phone, 22 Sep 1992.

The morning efforts against the Iraqi capital were only the first of several such efforts planned for 19 January. The first package was to strike Al Taqaddum air base and the Habbaniya chemical warfare production centers west of Baghdad at 0700. Supported by two EF-111s, four F-4Gs, and sixteen F-15Cs, forty-eight F-16s were to attack these targets.[21] Fifteen minutes later, a second large package of forty F-16s was to strike targets in Baghdad: among others, the headquarters of the Internal Security Agency, Military Intelligence, Air Force, and Baᶜth Party.[22] The second strike would receive support from eight F-4Gs, while twelve F-15Cs ran interference against Iraqi fighters. To underscore Coalition air superiority, the last aircraft in each group of eight F-16s was supposed to carry leaflet bombs to cover downtown Baghdad with Coalition propaganda.[23] A third strike of sixteen F-16s would then pound Taji at 0745 to complete early morning attacks on the capital. In fact, virtually none of these sorties flew because of weather, tanker, or scheduling difficulties–or a combination of these factors.[24] Only one package of eight F-16s struck a target.[25] In its case, the Weasels failed to show, and therefore it went after the alternate, Salman North, just over the frontier, instead of Taji.[26]

Meanwhile, heavy attacks began on the Republican Guard, attacks that lasted all day. At 0600 four B-52s struck the Madinah Division; two hours later twelve Marine F/A-18s struck both Madinah and Hammurabi Divisions. Four F-4Gs, two Marine EA-6Bs, and four Marine F/A-18 antiradiation missile shooters suppressed enemy air defenses, while four F/A-18s provided air cover.[27] The near one-to-one relationship between support aircraft and bomb droppers for a target in the Kuwaiti Theater of Operations (KTO) stands in sharp contrast to the relatively weaker SEAD

---

[21](S) Master Attack Plan, Third 24 Hours, 18 Jan 1991; and GWAPS Database.

[22]GWAPS Database of sorties flown and targets attacked.

[23](S) Master Attack Plan, Third 24 Hours, 18 Jan 1992, p 3.

[24]GWAPS Database.

[25]*Ibid.*

[26]401st Tactical Fighter Wing, "614th Tactical Fighter Squadron, Desert Shield/Desert Storm," GWAPS, no page numbers.

[27]*Ibid*; GWAPS Database.

support packages that were to accompany missions into central Iraq during the day.

At 0900 three more B-52s struck the Hammurabi Division. Further flights of B-52s hit the Republican Guard four more times during the day. Finally, starting at 0730 and continuing every half hour until 0830, large packages (upwards of ten) of F-16s pounded Madinah and Tawakalna. Throughout the remaining daylight hours into evening, F-16s continued working over the Republican Guard. The attention that the Iraqi elite force received reflected Schwarzkopf's priorities rather than those of his corps and division commanders. However, it is well to remember that air planners and commanders (as well as policy makers in Washington) had seen these units as political and strategic targets as much as military targets.[28]

But Baghdad and surrounding areas were *the* day's primary targets. At 1200 a major Navy strike package of aircraft from *Kennedy* and *America* hit Scud production and fuel sites west of the capital. Again Navy aircraft received heavy coverage from SEAD assets: five EA-6s, six F/A-18s, and three A-7s suppressed enemy air defenses, all in support of eight A-7 and ten A-6 strikers.[29] The heavy support reflected a stronger emphasis on SEAD sorties in the Navy's strike community–a considerably heavier emphasis than in the Air Force's tactical air forces (with the possible exception of units from Europe).

Three hours later, a package of forty F-16s, covered by eight F-4Gs and two EF-111s, was to hit targets in Baghdad. The Master Attack Plan called for sixteen F-16s to strike the Military Intelligence Headquarters, while eight would hit the Ministry of Information.[30] It is not clear why, but between the Master Attack Plan and the actual conduct of the mission, the package shifted to attack Scud sites around H-3 airfield.[31] Since Horner and Schwarzkopf were already under great pressure due to the Scud men-

---

[28] *Ibid.*

[29] CNA Database; (S) Master Attack Plan, Third 24 Hours, 18 Jan 1991.

[30] (S) Master Attack Plan, Third 24 Hours, 18 Jan 1991, and GWAPS Database.

[31] GWAPS Database.

ace to Israel, it is possible that they diverted the mission–particularly since one more major package was still to come to strike Baghdad.

The first two attacks on Baghdad were to have formed the prelude to one of the more interesting episodes in the war: Package Q. This attack was the largest of the war and did in fact represent an attempt to strike a powerful blow to enemy defenses. Nevertheless, the raid illustrates how a number of small incidents–or frictions–none by themselves necessarily serious, can contribute to a less than satisfactory outcome: in this case the loss of two F-16s.

The Master Attack Plan called for seventy-two F-16s to attack targets lying on an axis from southeast to northwest across Baghdad in the heart of Iraqi defenses. The package commander and most of the aircraft came from the 388th Tactical Fighter Wing (Provisional), but some aircraft came from the 401st Fighter Wing. In the last chapter we described how Package Q moved out from its bases to link up with tankers on tracks running up to the border. Shortly after 1300, the first aircraft began to roll and the complex ballet to assemble the package began. Each section within the package had received a mission number and call sign. Each mission cell would consist of up to eight aircraft, but smaller numbers of aircraft could make up a mission cell, depending on the target. All of the various pieces needed careful coordination in order for the operation to function effectively.

Unfortunately, full coordination and planning did not take place for this mission. The Air Tasking Order reached mission commanders so late that some of those who led missions on 19 January received a brief outline of the day's mission upon landing after an exhausting day's flight on 18 January.[32] When mission commanders from the 401st began coordinating their portion of the mission on the morning of 19 January, they discovered certain crucial changes had taken place during the night. Their original target–as with much of the rest of the attack–had been the nuclear research

[32]Intvw, Maj John Nichols with GWAPS personnel, 20 Jul 1992. Maj Nichols was the mission commander of the last group of aircraft to attack Baghdad in Package Q.

facility southeast of Baghdad. But overnight, the Air Tasking Order had changed their target to three major sites in downtown Baghdad.[33]

A major employment problem in the revised tasking was the fact that F-16s would begin striking targets in southeast Baghdad and then work their way through increasingly alerted defenses to the heart of the enemy capital.[34] Such an approach would maximize the exposure of the F-16 train to enemy air defenses; however, it was too late to change the order in which the mission subsets would attack targets.[35] So little time existed between the arrival of the Air Tasking Order and launch time that neither the package commander nor his mission commanders could change the order of the attack.[36] In fact, it is not clear how it was determined that the package would attack targets from southeast to northwest–outside of the fact that that was the fashion in which the Master Attack Plan had listed the targets.[37] There was time to coordinate the raid with the units at other bases, but that time was hardly optimum.

For the crews, the mission appeared risky, but within safety margins; their feeling was that earlier SEAD packages had attrited enemy capabilities and that the SEAD allocated would be sufficient to suppress the remaining defenses. Because of distances and fuel consumption, the F-4Gs could carry only two HARMs; moreover they would not have much time in the target area because of their high fuel usage. The F-16s were also heavily loaded, carrying two Mark-84s, two external fuel tanks, two air-to-air missiles, ninety bundles of chaff, and fifteen flares.[38]

---

[33]401st Tactical Fighter Wing, "614th Tactical Fighter Squadron, Desert Shield/Desert Storm," GWAPS, no page numbers.

[34]This discussion of the events on the third day draws heavily on the oral testimony of two of its participants, Maj John Nichols and the Wing Commander, Col Jerry Nelson, who flew as a regular wingman on this mission, as well as the history of the 401st Tactical Fighter Wing (Provisional).

[35]Nevertheless, it is worth noting that those planning the mission "did believe that while the support package was a bit thin, it would suffice." Intvw, Maj John Nichols with GWAPS personnel, 20 Jul 1992.

[36]Much of the Air Tasking Order appears to have been passed to the units by phone. No complete ATO for the third day exists in the GWAPS files.

[37](S) Master Attack Plan, Third 24 Hours, 18 Jan 1991.

[38](S) *Ibid.*

Link-up and refueling with the tankers ran into problems. There was bad weather along the tanker tracks, and the tankers approached the release point too early. Consequently, they throttled back to minimum speed, which in turn seriously affected the accompanying fighters. The F-16s were soon close to stalling out, and some had to light afterburners just to stay airborne; four fighters coming off the last tanker fell so far behind that their mission commander ordered them to return to base.[39]

Fortunately, as the package reached Iraqi airspace, it broke out into the open. But Iraqi gunners greeted the Americans with a couple of high-altitude shots in the middle of several formations. Not surprisingly, there were difficulties in communicating among mission groups in the package; the mission commander of the flight attacking downtown Baghdad estimated that he received approximately 80 percent of the calls. Adding to the excitement of the flak exploding below, the Iraqis threw 100-mm shells into the formations. From the moment the package approached Baghdad's air defenses, the Weasels engaged enemy SAM sites. However, there was a problem with the Weasels allocated to the mission; either because of fuel, timing, or the decision of the package commander, not all appear to have made it to Baghdad;[40] moreover, some Weasels did not fire all their HARMs, which suggests that they had to leave because of fuel problems.[41]

Approaching their targets, the "downtown" aircraft (flying F-16s with newer model engines) passed F-16s on the way to, rolling in on, and leaving targets–all in a hostile environment. As Maj. John Nichols rolled in to strike his target, the Iraqi Air Force Headquarters, he heard the Weasels call that they were leaving. Unfortunately, cloud cover obscured the target; Nichols rolled off to turn to an alternate target, an oil refinery which was under attack by a portion of his formation.[42]

---

[39](S) *Ibid.*

[40]Intvw, Maj Gen Buster Glosson with GWAPS personnel, 14 Apr 1992.

[41]GWAPS Database. The database indicates that the Weasels only fired six HARMs; the leader of the Baghdad mission reports that it was not until after the Weasels had called in that they were leaving that the Iraqis began guiding their missiles from the ground. Intvw, Maj John Nichols with GWAPS personnel, 20 Jul 1992.

[42]GWAPS Database.

Up to this point, the Iraqis had fired most of their SAMs ballistically. Within a short time of the Weasel call that they were leaving, SAMs directly engaged Nichols' flight. Many SAMs were now guided and most of his flight had to take evasive action, which included "last ditch maneuvers" such as jettisoning fuel tanks and bombs. Approximately half of the flight struck the oil refinery; others were en route to alternate targets when SAMs engaged and forced them to jettison ordnance. SAMs hit one F-16 just as the last bombs were striking the oil refinery. As the flight egressed Baghdad, evading SAMs, another missile impacted near another F-16. Both aircraft were lost, but their pilots did survive the war. In all, the participants in the wild ride over the capital counted twenty SAMs in the air; one pilot dodged no fewer than six.[43]

The excitement for the survivors did not end when they left Baghdad. To bring an end to their day, a couple of MiG-29s started closing toward the rear of the F-16s as they exited the capital's environs; the F-15 top cover had apparently left with the Weasels. Nevertheless, all the F-16s had to do was turn on the MiGs, and the Iraqis ran. By the time that the F-16s approached the border some were almost out of fuel. One fighter would have crashed short of Coalition territory had not a KC-135 tanker from the Kansas National Guard crossed over into enemy territory. When the F-16 began refueling in Iraqi territory, it had only 800 pounds of fuel on board–in the words of the wing commander, flying as a wingman, "an eye-watering situation."[44]

Obviously, no one factor caused the loss of two F-16s and the possible loss of others. Rather a series of frictions–the lateness of the Air Tasking Order, not enough coordination time, a tactical approach that provided the Iraqis considerable warning, fuel problems for the Weasels and other aircraft, bad weather, insufficient attrition of the defenses–combined to create a dangerous situation, one ultimately catastrophic for two aircraft.[45]

---

[43] *Ibid.*

[44] Telephone conversation with Col Jerry Nelson, 2 Sep 1992.

[45] Luckily the pilots were able to eject successfully, although the Iraqis captured both.

There were a number of crucial lessons from Package Q. The most obvious was that enemy defenses in Baghdad remained lethal; consequently, it was not worth the risk to send conventional packages into the heart of those defenses, especially when F-117s could strike such targets with little risk. This was entirely the result of its stealthy qualities, which its precision-guided munition capabilities magnified. Consequently, enemy defenses never put F-117s in the position where they had to jettison bombs over populated areas, and the chances of civilian casualties that would allow Saddam to manipulate the American media were considerably lessened.

There was, however, a crucial operational turn that the mission's failure caused. Glosson and his planners had hoped that destruction or at least degradation of Baghdad's air defenses would allow them to run large packages of F-16s into the capitol's environs during the daytime. Their targets, as on the morning of day three, would have been the larger command headquarters and symbols of the regime, such as those of the Baᶜth Party, Republican Guard, and Military Intelligence. Most of these structures were so big that F-16s, even though less accurate, could hit such targets with a fair probability of success. As symbols of the regime, the destruction of such headquarters would have major political and military effects.[46]

The difficulties, however, into which Package Q ran, as well as the potential of inadvertent bomb release by aircraft under SAM attack, caused Horner and his planners to decide against sending any more F-16 packages against downtown Baghdad.[47] What speaks well for the American leadership in this air war was the fact that it did not repeat Package Q to prove some doctrinal beliefs of the high command at the expense of aircrew lives. American air commanders adapted to the situation as it was. There would be no more conventional packages into the heart of

---

[46]Conversation with Lt Col David Deptula, 31 Jul 1992.

[47]Intvw, Maj Gen Buster Glosson with GWAPS personnel, 9 Apr 1992; and intvw Lt Col David Deptula with GWAPS personnel, 20-21 Dec 1991.

[48]This had certainly *not* been the case in World War II or in Vietnam when senior air commanders had persisted in faulty operational approaches and tactics to the cost of large numbers of aircrew.

Iraqi defenses.[49] Moreover, F-16 packages would remain smaller–thus more manageable and easier to coordinate and fly–for the remainder of the war.[50]

Neither the difficulties encountered by the F-16s nor the problems that F-117s experienced on the third day stopped the continuing attacks on other portions of Iraq and occupied Kuwait. B-52s hit the Hammurabi Division three more times, as well as the Bayji oil refinery. They also launched a heavy attack on manufacturing sites in the Tikrit area. The Hammurabi Division also received a major strike by F-15Es, while the Navy attacked the bridges behind Saddam's elite force. Both chemical and ammunition storage areas received extensive attention from Navy and F-111 packages. Finally, RAF and Saudi Tornados continued the pressure on Iraqi airfields throughout the day, while French and British Jaguars and Kuwaiti A-4s struck Iraqi forces in and around Kuwait City.[51]

Over the course of the third day Coalition air forces continued their domination of the skies over Iraq. F-15Cs from the 33d Tactical Fighter Wing accounted for all the kills: two MiG-29s, two MiG-25s, and two Mirage F-1s fell to their missiles.[52] By now a clear pattern was emerging in terms of the relatively few air-to-air engagements taking place. Iraqi pilots generally failed to respond to radar lock-ons and displayed almost no capacity or willingness to maneuver between the time that Coalition aircraft locked on to them and the time that a missile impacted. In two cases they ran into the ground before the missile hit, hardly suggestive of combat effectiveness or good training.[53]

---

[49] One more mission of F-16s would go against the Iraqi defenses in Baghdad on the next day, but that would be the last F-16 strike against the capital during the war.

[50] On 20 January Gen Glosson told his chief planner, Lt Col David Deptula, that there would be no more packages greater than twenty-five aircraft: Deptula, personal notes, entry for 20 Jan 1991.

[51] (S) Master Attack Plan, Third 24 Hours, 18 Jan 1992 and GWAPS Database.

[52] Thomas P. Christie, Gary C. Comfort, and Richard E. Guild, "Desert Shield/Desert Storm Air-to-Air Performance Study," Institute for Defense Analysis, Apr 1992.

[53] "33d Tactical Fighter Wing Air-to-Air Engagements through 21 February 1991." See the SPEAR evaluation of Iraqi pilot performance in the war with Iran which almost exactly foreshadows how their pilots would or would not react in the air superiority arena. SPEAR, "Iraqi Threat to U.S. Forces," p 3-63 to 3-64.

Nevertheless, the continued existence of Iraqi combat aircraft in hardened shelters throughout Iraq did worry intelligence analysts that Saddam would launch his air force on a massive suicide mission, reminiscent of the 1968 Tet offensive.[54] We will soon address how the planners responded to this fear and helped the Iraqis pay the first installment on their reparation payments to Iran.

On the other side, Coalition air losses did rise. In particular GR-1 Tornados had a bad day on 19 January. The British and the Saudis each lost two; these aircraft were still using low attack profiles, which maximized exposure to Iraqi flak and IR SAMs. Besides two F-16s lost against Baghdad, the USAF lost an F-15E to SAMs and an F-4G to fuel problems (possibly due to battle damage).[55] Given the number of sorties flown, these losses were well below prewar expectations and were more than sustainable.

The Air Campaign, 20 January to Al Firdos

The remainder of this chapter aims to provide a more general sense of operations than our detailed examination of the first three days. Consequently, we will now turn to a topical approach of specific issues that impacted on or guided the conduct of air operations.

The first specific problem area was obviously the hunt for the Scuds, their launching sites, and support structure, undoubtedly the most frustrating and least satisfactory aspect of the air campaign. This section has singled out the Scud story for examination in isolation. The rest of the chapter will consider shifts in priorities as well as continued efforts to destroy the Iraqi Air Force, the impact of weather on operations, and arguments as to when the air effort should move to preparing the battlefield for the ground war.

---

[54] Intvw, Col John Warden with GWAPS personnel (Williamson Murray, Barry Watts, and Thomas Keaney), 21 Feb 1992.

[55] GWAPS Database.

Of all the aspects in the air campaign, the effectiveness of air operations in suppressing Iraq's Scud missiles remains the most unclear. As one recent report indicated well after the war: "To date, we have yet to confirm an Iraqi mobile SRBM [short-range ballistic missile] launcher kill resulting from U.S. aircraft attacks. . . ."[56] Without access to Iraqi (or for that matter Israeli documents) we cannot estimate crucial factors such as: How many missiles might the Iraqis have launched if the air campaign had not interfered, or interfered less successfully with their efforts? How many missiles and mobile launchers did air attacks destroy or damage? What constraints did air power impose on Scud launches? How likely was it that the Israelis might respond to the Scud bombardment and what effect might such an intervention have had on the Coalition, particularly its Arab members? Whatever the answers to such questions, the Scud campaign did play an important role in the conduct of the Coalition's air campaign.

At the strategic level, one deals with the greatest imponderable of all: what impact would an Israeli retaliatory strike have had on the Coalition, particularly its Arab members? This author suspects that within the framework of the focus against Iraq and provided that such strikes remained limited and did not involve heavy casualties, the Coalition would have held. Immediately after the war, Schwarzkopf, however, felt otherwise, telling David Frost: "there was no question about the fact that, had Israel entered the fray [in response to the first Scud attacks], I don't think we could have held [the Coalition] all together."[57] Further exacerbating fears about Scuds was a belief that their use might involve chemicals to broaden the impact of missile attacks.[58]

---

[56] Defense Intelligence Agency, "Defense Intelligence Assessment, Mobile Short-Range Ballistic Targeting in Operation Desert Storm," OGA 1040-23-91, Dec 1991, p 9. In fairness the report does indicate that did not evaluate the majority of aircrew reported kills."

[57] Schwarzkopf television Intvw with David Frost, 27 Mar 1991, p 3.

[58] On 2 September CENTAF's Draft OPORD underlined as a "planning constraint" the likelihood that "Iraq will attempt to employ chemical weapons against the U.S. and friendly regional states, including Israel, if the opportunity arises." (S) COMUSCENTAF Draft OPORD, Offensive Campaign–Phase I, 2 Sep 1990, p 2. The October SNIE on Iraqi military capabilities concluded that "Iraqi tactical use of chemical weapons is virtually

Horner was more optimistic in interviews after the war. His sources in the Arab world suggested that Israeli strikes in response to Iraqi strikes would not have bothered the leadership of most of the Coalition's Arab members.[59] But Horner did worry that the movement of Israeli aircraft through Saudi airspace might lead to an air-to-air confrontation with U.S. aircraft, while an Israeli move through Jordanian airspace might bring that country into the conflict on the side of Iraq.[60]

Whatever the fears about Israeli response, there was little doubt that attacks on Arab territory *whatever the provocation* would have serious political consequences. The larger point, however, is that, whatever tactical and operational difficulties resulted from the hunt for Scuds, the effort against the missiles, combined with the perceived success of the Patriot in defending against them, achieved the strategic objective of enabling the Israelis to stay out of the conflict. And it is on the strategic level that military organizations, nation states, and Coalitions win wars.[61]

The Iraqis had purchased large numbers of Scuds from the Soviets in the 1980s, and late in the Iran-Iraq War they fired some 190 missiles, which had been modified to provide ranges of 600 kilometers, at Iranian cities in an attempt to break their opponent's morale.[62] Even under the best of conditions, however, the Iraqi version of the Scud, the Al-Hussein, had a circular error of probability of more than 2,000 meters and carried less than 180 kilograms of high explosives. Consequently, they did not represent a significant improvement over German V-2s of World War II fame. They were not, then, a weapon possessing much military utility, but they did represent a distinct political and psychological threat.

---

certain if Iraq suffers serious battlefield defeats" and even suggested the possibility of "Iraqi chemical attacks if Baghdad believes a Coalition attack is imminent." (C/NF) "Iraq as a Military Adversary," pp iv and 16.

[59] Horner's greater optimism after the war was undoubtedly framed by the fact that the Iraqis had failed to shake the Coalition.

[60] Oral History Interview of Lt Gen Charles A. Horner by Perry Jamison, Rich Davis, and Barry Barlow, 4 Mar 1992, HQ Ninth Air Force, Shaw AFB, South Carolina, p 40.

[61] Alan R. Millett and Williamson Murray, "The Lessons of War," *The National Interest,* Winter 1988/1989.

[62] (S) Thomas P. Christie and William J. Barlow, "Desert Storm Scud Campaign," Institute for Defense Analysis, IDA Paper P-2661, p I-13.

The missile threat itself broke down into two distinct aspects. U.S. intelligence had discovered the locations of Iraqi fixed-launch sites constructed over the previous several years. Of sixty-four individual positions in western Iraq, U.S. intelligence identified those which had launchers and those still under construction without launchers.[63] All such sites received heavy attention in the war's opening days.

Unfortunately, the Iraqis also possessed a number of mobile missile launchers. By early January 1991, intelligence estimates of mobile launchers had climbed into the high twenties.[64] In addition, the Iraqis had purchased a number of Scud decoys from the East Germans and had then manufactured their own local copies.[65] As one of the senior officials in DIA admitted after the war, there was "no accurate accounting of numbers of mobile launchers or where they were based [or] hiding."[66] Postwar intelligence indicates that the Iraqis had approximately thirty-six mobile launchers.[67] By December 1990 overhead imagery had made clear that the Iraqis had dispersed these missile launchers to unknown locations.[68] U.S. intelligence could estimate the general positions of missile firing baskets, all approximately 600 kilometers (324 nautical miles) from targets in Israel and Saudi Arabia.[69] But finding and then destroying the missile launchers and transporters remained a problem that was not solved in the months before Desert Storm.

---

63 SRBM Fact/Information Sheet; Briefing, "Offensive Air Campaign," 20 Dec 1990.

64 Conversation with Capt William Bruner, who tracked Scuds in the Black Hole during Desert Storm.

65 (S) Thomas P. Christie and William Barlow, "Desert Storm Scud Campaign," Institute for Defense Analysis, IDA Paper P-2661, p I-13.

66 Intvw, Rear Adm J. "Mike" McConnell with Diane T. Putney, Center for Air Force History and Ronald H. Cole, JCS Historical Division, 14 Feb 1992, GWAPS NA 261.

67 DIA, "Mobile Short-Range Ballistic Missile Targeting in Operation DESERT STORM," p.9

68 DIA analysts who have gone back over the evidence believe that the Iraqis sent some of their mobile launchers into the field as early as August 1990. GWAPS discussion with DIA analysts 30 Sep 1992.

69 (S) DIA, "Iraqi Mobile SRBM Developments," DDX-1040-18-90, p 1-3.

Worries in Washington concerning the political and diplomatic fallout from Scud attacks had been considerable from the beginning.[70] In fact, the Scuds represented an area where some genuine divergence of views occurred between Washington and operational commanders in the Gulf. Most senior air commanders had believed that the Scuds did not represent a particularly credible *military* threat. As Horner noted, the Scud was "a lousy weapon."[71]

In the summary slides to a 20 December briefing for Cheney, Powell, and Wolfowitz, Horner predicted that the air campaign would "preclude" Iraqi missile attacks.[72] Apparently Horner did indicate that while he believed that Coalition air power would destroy fixed sites, mobile missile launchers represented a different order of difficulty, and that some would escape destruction.[73] Nevertheless, the records suggest that planners and commanders in the Gulf neglected to push preparations for an aggressive anti-Scud campaign to the full extent because they regarded Scuds as a weapon of little *military* consequence. In fairness, it was not yet clear, and would not be clear until the war, how successful the Iraqis would be in eluding Coalition aircraft with their mobile missile launchers.

---

[70] Paul Wolfowitz, Robert Kimmit, Dennis B. Ross, and John H. Kelley, in "The Gulf War Conference," pp 258, 262, and 267.

[71] Lt Gen Chuck Horner, "Speech at the Dadaelian Dinner," 11 Sep 1991, p 5. The circular error of probability for the Al Hussein (indicated above) certainly suggests the weaknesses of Iraqi Scuds as military weapons. Nevertheless it is worth noting that a Scud almost hit the *Tarawa* while it was tied up at an ammunition loading dock during the war.

[72] Brfg, "Offensive Air Campaign," 20 Dec 1990.

[73] In a March 1992 interview Horner recounted about the 20 December briefing: "I'm not as politically sensitive as I should be. [Cheney] is going in[to] detail, 'How are you going to get the Scuds?' I show him [that] we are going to put two laser-guided bombs in every one of the fixed Scud sites the first opening moments of the war. BOOM, BOOM, BOOM. I mean how high can you get?!! With regard to the mobile, I show him where all the things were [that we were] hitting, but I just said, 'You can't get them all!'" Intvw, Lt Gen Charles A. Horner, p 42.

In the end, air planners settled on a strategy against Scud sites that targeted fixed sites in the opening days of the war, devoted a large number of sorties in the opening days to attacks on the manufacturing centers for the missiles and their fuel, and launched a significant number of sorties to those areas where the Iraqis would likely deploy their mobile launchers. The effort did not represent an attempt at eyewash, but it did miss how sensitive Coalition political leaders would prove to a continuing succession of Iraqi missile launches.

Fortunately, there were limitations that affected Iraq's ability to fire its missiles at Saudi Arabia and Israel. Until August 1990, the great threat to Iraq was Iran. Consequently, while the Iraqis had made some preparations to fire Scuds at Israel–underlined by Saddam's ferocious speeches threatening to deluge Israel with fire–most of the Scud storage facilities were probably not located in western Iraq.[74] Most likely, what the Iraqis had managed to prepare were a number of protected holding pens for mobile launchers and their missiles. Such sites were carefully prepared along the highways running through the launch baskets in western Iraq so that they would be difficult to find and hit from the air.

In any event, there were limits on the numbers of Scuds that Iraq could fire at any one time. Moreover, moving Scuds into firing positions down the Euphrates and Tigris valleys, an area covered with villages and vegetation, was easier than across the open deserts to western Iraq. Very possibly, that explains why the Iraqis fired more Scuds at the Saudis than at the Israelis, although the latter were undoubtedly the target of preference. Finally, at the end of the war the Iraqis began to fire missiles at King Khalid Military City from Baghdad.

---

[74] This represents a supposition on the part of the author on the basis that the flat, unmarked terrain of western Iraq could only hide smaller storage sites for the missiles about to be launched against Israel. However, there was a limit to the number of mobile launchers that Iraq possessed and the evidence from the war indicates that in relatively short order, the Iraqis were moving Scuds out of their storage areas in central Iraq to the launch areas. The fact that they were able to move those missiles to their launch areas despite the considerable interest of Coalition air power in all movement demonstrates the elusiveness of mobile missiles, as well as the effectiveness of Iraqi efforts to avoid detection.

The Iraqis initiated their reply to Coalition air attacks with a barrage of Scuds aimed at Israel. Between 0259 and 0327 on the morning of 18 January (Baghdad time), they fired eight Scuds at the Israelis.[75] The missiles landed higgledy-piggledy without causing much damage, but fears that these weapons contained chemical or nerve agents magnified their psychological impact.

The effect of Scuds on the air campaign was immediate. Notes taken in the TACC the next morning suggest the pressure from Washington:

> 0825: Gen Glosson on the phone in Black Hole: We will spend the remainder of the day targeting Scud sites. Imagery shows we had not destroyed all that we had thought. I don't know what's going on. The alert birds (ground) will be sent up and they will just go back and forth to the tankers until we get them. . . .
>
> 0938: Gen Glosson: CINC is getting a lot of calls from Washington about the Scuds.
>
> 0948: Second bunch of A-10s found seven MELs [mobile launchers]; destroyed two. We are sending more A-10s. First site given was wrong. Actual site in SW corner of Iraq. These are supposed to be targeted at Riyadh.
>
> 0952: Gen Glosson: We have found nine of their twenty-seven TELs in the open. We need to go get them. . . .
>
> 1040: Crigger to Horner: A-10s are being sent to the seven TELs. Also the F-15s are on the way. . . .
>
> Horner: They (F-15s) should be there by now. Doesn't care if they get there <u>all</u> at the same time. Want those Scuds gone.[76]

From the first, political pressure from Washington was enormous. To a certain extent, the airmen were caught by overly optimistic estimates

---

[75] (S) Christie and Barlow, "Desert Storm Scud Campaign," Appendix A, Defense Support Program Scud Launch Log, p A-1.

[76] TACC NCO Log, Notes by TSgt Barton, 18 Jan 1991.

of the prewar period.[77] Nevertheless, despite pressures from above, Horner kept his eye on the larger strategic aims lying behind the air campaign. On 18 January, he commented to the morning stand up:

> Last night we had a very busy night because of the Scud launches. The Scuds will continue to be a problem, not militarily, but politically. Consequently, we need to turn our attention toward timely detection and destruction of Scuds, so that we don't allow him to pull our minds off our primary job: that's taking down his military machine and getting him out of Kuwait.[78]

Unfortunately, there were no easy methods for finding and destroying mobile missile launchers, especially at night. Air attacks in the first several days appears to have removed the fixed sites as possible launching pads.[79] The first week, however, was a particularly difficult time: four more missiles in the early morning hour of 19 January; then eight at Saudi Arabia on the 20th; seven at the Saudis on the night of 21/22 January; one at Israel early on the night of 22/23 January; four at Saudi Arabia (all at 2254 local) and one at Israel (2300) on the evening of the 23rd; eight at Israel on the evening of the 25th and three at Saudi Arabia over the night of the 25/26; and four at Israel and one at Saudi Arabia on the night of the 26th/27th.[80]

Iraqi firings during this period do suggest a pattern: heavy firing at Israel on the 18th, 19th, 25th, and 26/27th; heavy firing at Saudi Arabia on the 21/22nd, 22/23rd, and 25/26th. Thereafter, there was a fall off that lasted the remainder of the war; with the exception of a few days, the Iraqis were barely able to fire one shot a day; on many days they did not manage to get off any shots. Nevertheless, during the first ten days, when the Iraqis fired an average of five shots per day, there were periods

---

[77] In fairness to them it was impossible to estimate what the effectiveness of new technologies might be in locating mobile targets in a wide open area such as western Iraq.

[78] HQUSCENTAF, Office of History, "Daily Comments of Lt Gen Horner," 20 Mar 1991, Horner file in GWAPS.

[79] The Iraqis did not make any attempts to launch from the fixed Scud sites during Desert Storm. Whether they decided to forego their use prior to 17 January 1991, or were prevented from doing so by Coalition air strikes remains a matter of speculation.

[80] (S) Christie and Barlow, "Desert Storm Scud Campaign," Appendix A, Table A-1.

when activity dropped to zero; that fact alone suggests that from the beginning they were having considerable trouble in getting missiles out of their main storage areas.

Nevertheless, even this relatively low level of firings caused serious perturbations within the American leadership. The Army rushed out Patriot batteries to Israel. The military effectiveness of those batteries defending Israel (and Saudi Arabia) is a moot point. What was crucial is that they provided political and strategic reassurance to the civilian populations of Israel and Saudi Arabia; they underlined that U.S. forces were engaged in a significant effort to provide protection from Scuds. The far higher casualty rate that the Scuds caused in the Iran-Iraq War suggests that the Patriots did manage to provide a significant measure of protection during the Gulf War.[81] But the essential point was the political impact that the Patriots achieved in terms of civilian morale.

The main pressure came on the air commanders.[82] Horner and Glosson had to focus resources on trying to suppress and destroy Iraqi Scuds and their launchers. The platform that ended up being most affected by this requirement was the F-15E. The sensors on these aircraft included both LANTIRN and a synthetic aperture radar. An ideal choice for going after elusive mobile targets at night, the F-15Es soon became heavily engaged in the "Scud Hunt." The abundance of air assets forced a heavy reliance on scheduling in advance. Consequently, there were

---

[81] In the exchange of missiles between Iran and Iraq that took place in the winter and spring of early 1988, the Iraqis fired approximately 190 extended-range Scuds at Tehran and several other Iranian cities. They caused 2,000 deaths and a considerable number of injured. Approximately half that number of Scuds were fired during the Gulf war at targets in Israel and Saudi Arabia, but the number of casualties, civilian and military,were considerably under that number. That certainly suggests that the Patriots had a considerable impact on the effects that the Scuds were able to achieve; unopposed, the Scuds might have achieved far higher casualty figures with serious political implications. Hiro, *The Longest War*, p 200.

[82] For example,on 30 January Horner noted in the Current Ops Log: "CINC Meeting tonight–please keep info moving upchannel to CENTCOM–They get Mucho Heato from D.C. When they don't feed the info monster every three-four hours–Good news is wanted but beware once you start sating [sic] the monster becomes ever hungrier." TACC, CC/DO, Current Ops Log, 30 Jan 1701Z, GWAPS, NA 215.

times when Scud targets appeared vulnerable, but strikers were not always available.[83]

Planners had recognized before the war that mobile Scuds would represent a significant nuisance. However, they calculated that alert aircraft, A-10s and F-15Es, would suffice to suppress most of Iraq's launch capabilities. That, of course, was not the case. The first diversion of Coalition assets came with efforts to use AC-130 gun ships against mobile missiles, but the near loss of one of those aircraft in the high threat environment of western Iraq ended that approach.[84]

It was soon clear that only aircraft flying on station over the launch sites could attack the mobile launch platforms before they escaped.[85] Moreover, the suppression effort required significant air assets to shut down road traffic in western Iraq by day and night–a tall order indeed. As a result, anti-Scud efforts evolved into two approaches: the first to interdict missiles coming from storage sites to launch baskets; and the second to suppress launch activity by making the Scud crews believe that the accomplishment of their mission was a dangerous task indeed. On 20 January, Horner and Corder underlined the importance of the Scud search by creating a "Scud Chasing Log" in the TACC to track anything and everything that had to do with mobile missile launchers.[86]

---

[83] The NCO recorder in the TACC noted on 31 January: "With all of the aircraft in theater, I found it difficult to believe that we were actually 'short' [of available aircraft to strike Scud sites]. We do, however, have that problem. With the number of packages and individual missions scheduled in the ATO, there are, in fact, very few unscheduled aircraft available!" TSgt Barton's notes of conversations in the TACC,

[84] To evade an Iraqi missile fired at it, the AC-130 pulled so many Gs that it had to be returned to the United States for a major overhaul. "AC-130 Gunship Desert Storm Mission Summary," attch to 16SOS/CC to the Office of the Secretary of the Air Force, 14 May 1992.

[85] But even then they could have a difficult time. On 9 February the Current Ops Log reported: "Scud launch–Israel. Two F-15Es were on station and saw the launch but were unable to find the launcher. Two F-15Es on target immediately–two additional F-15Es closed within five minutes. No luck." TACC, CC/DO, Current Ops Log, 09 0036Z Feb, GWAPS, NA 215.

[86] (S) Christie and Barlow, "Desert Storm Scud Campaign," Appendix C reproduce the TACC Scud Log.

By the end of the first week, the Scud campaign showed focus and a measure of success, but it required a diversion of resources from the rest of the air campaign. The effort over the night of 23/24 January, for example, suggests the extent of resource diversion. From 1800 on the 23rd to 0800 on the 24th, four F-15Es remained on airborne alert fifteen to twenty minutes from western Scud launch baskets. If after four hours there were no launches or no reported activity, the F-15Es then struck Scud-related targets; at the same time four new F-15Es arrived on station. At all times during this period, eight F-15Es stood alert to replace airborne aircraft should they attack suspected Scud targets.[87]

At the same time in the east, four F-16s with LANTIRN navigation pods maintained the same airborne alert over eastern launch baskets. Eight F-16s backed up the airborne aircraft, while the airborne F-16 attacked preset targets after four hours. Meanwhile, twenty-four hours a day, two A-10s worked over each Scud Box area, while twelve A-10s stood ground alert with one hour reaction time.[88] In fact, the Iraqi launches against Saudi Arabia appear to have caused about as considerable a diversion of air resources as the attacks on Israel.

In addition, there were a number of preplanned missions against Scud targets and support facilities. At 2015 on the 23rd, twenty F-111Fs, supported by four F-4Gs, two EF-111s, and eight F-15Cs, struck suspected Scud sites and shelters at Qalat Salih airfield. At 0400 on the 24th, twenty F-111Fs, with a support package similar to that of the earlier F-111F strike, hit the H-2 airfield shelters. One hour later, eight GR-1s, supported by a Navy ECM package of one EA-6B and two F-14s, attacked the H-3 army barracks. Finally, late in the afternoon of the 24th, sixteen A-7s, supported by ten F-14s and two EA-6Bs, hit the lines of communications running into the H-1 airfield.[89]

---

[87] (S) Christie and Barlow, "Desert Storm Scud Campaign," Table III-3.

[88] (S) *Ibid.*

[89] (S) *Ibid.*

Three days later, the CENTAF Director of Operations, Maj. Gen. John Corder, detailed the effort against the Scuds in the TACC log. His report formed the basis for a later paper for Powell on the air resources devoted to suppressing the Scud menace. Horner commented at the end of Corder's notes: "victory & frustration–issue never in doubt, but a high price to pay to kill a pain in the ass."[90]

How effective were such efforts? It is hard to say in a tactical sense; the evidence of how many mobile Scuds and their launchers Coalition air attacks destroyed or damaged remains spotty. It does appear that a number of tanker trucks on the way to Jordan or Basra paid a severe price for having infrared signatures resembling mobile launchers; some Bedouins also may have paid a similar price for having elongated, heated tents in the desert blackness that looked like canvas-draped Scuds. In the end, the best one can say is that some mobile launchers may have been destroyed. Although Iraqi launch rates of modified Scuds–particularly of coordinated salvos–dropped over the course of the campaign, and while mobile Scud operations were subjected to increasing pressures and disruption, most (and possibly all) of the roughly 100 mobile launchers reported destroyed by Coalition aircraft and special operation forces now appear to have been either decoys, other vehicles such as tanker trucks, or other objects unfortunate enough to provide "Scud-like" signatures.[91]

By the end of January, the number of Scud launches had dropped dramatically. Over the last thirty days of the war, the Iraqis barely launched one missile per day. By 28 January, Horner at least was feeling confident enough about the Scud problem to joke in the TACC log: "28 [Jan] 1845Z–one Scud shot down another of our Patriots. . . .Have not had a successful Patriot launch to Iraq yet."[92]

By the end of the war, the Scud hunt had absorbed nearly 20 percent of F-15E sorties, 2 percent of A-10 sorties, 4 percent of F-16 sorties, and 3 percent of F-111F sorties. In addition, a significant number of sorties by B-52s, A-6Es, A-7s, F-117s, F/A-18s, and GR-1s also engaged in

---

[90] TACC Log, "Scud Suppression–Tactics and Procedures as of 27 2300Z, Jan 1991."

[91] See GWAPS Effectiveness report, Chapter 6.

[92] TACC, CC/DO, Current Ops Log, Horner note, 28 January, 1845Z, GWAPS, NA 215.

attacking Scud sites or production facilities.[93] Still, it is worth noting that the Iraqis were able to make a successful recovery in the last days of the war; while they never reached the number of launches of the first week, they were still able to cause considerable discomfort and casualties to their enemies.

The psychological impact of these missiles was considerable, not only on civilians in Israel and Saudi Arabia, but on Coalition soldiers and airmen as well. Yet one of the greatest successes that the Scuds achieved was the degree to which they caused "worst casers" in the intelligence community to overestimate the impact of future missile attacks. Luckily, pessimistic intelligence did not overly influence senior leadership in Washington.[94]

In terms of its indirect effects, the Scud was the most effective weapon in the Iraqi inventory; it drew off significant numbers of Coalition air sorties that could have found more productive utilization in other areas.[95] Nevertheless, the Coalition possessed an excess of air power

---

[93] Approximately 1,500 Coalition strikes altogether were focused against Iraqi ballistic missile capabilities. Half of those strikes hit targets such as culverts, overpasses, and fixed sites; 30% went after missile and fuel production facilities. Barely 15% (approximately 215 sorties) actually reported that they had attacked mobile launchers. Roughly another 1,000 "Scud patrol" sorties were planned against mobile Scud launchers but ended up attacking other targets.

[94] It is worth considering what the impact of such reports might have been on a weaker or less resolute leadership.

[95] There is a direct comparison between the effect of the Scuds in the Gulf War and the effect of the V-1 in the last years of World War II. The V-1 was a rather inexpensive weapon that possessed no great accuracy, but was nevertheless able to draw off considerable resources from both the Allied strategic bombing campaign and tactical air efforts to identify and attack the fixed sites. The British government feared–quite rightly–that the explosion of large numbers of V-1s in southern England might have a serious impact on the morale of the population and its willingness to see the war through to a successful conclusion. In the end, Allied air and ground forces mastered the threat but only after

over its requirements; it is difficult therefore to say how much more effective those sorties might have been against other targets. What is clear is that after 26 January–ten days into the war–the Iraqis had difficulty firing their missiles. In the first ten days, they fired forty-nine Scuds; in the remaining thirty days, they succeeded in launching only thirty-nine, 20 percent less over a period three times longer. However, what does suggest Iraq's capacity to adapt to Coalition air strikes was the considerable recovery of Scud firings in the last two weeks of the war. From the beginning to the end of the war, Scuds introduced a serious friction into the conduct of the air campaign–one that did not affect the final outcome, but only due to the absence of any other Iraqi successes.

There is, moreover, a larger issue: the question of might-have-beens. Except for the hit at the war's end that killed a large number of U.S. Army reservists, the Scuds achieved little damage and few deaths. Nevertheless, a Scud nearly hit the USS *Tarawa*, while that ship was tied up at the main dock at Dhahran–a dock piled high with ammunition. It does not take much imagination to visualize what an actual hit might have achieved in political and psychological terms.

Air Supremacy

For much of the first week, weather and continuing difficulties with the Air Tasking Order hampered the strategic air campaign. The Black Hole and Air Tasking Order schedulers did not get a full handle on the scheduling process until 23 January. Even then, substantial problems in scheduling and processing the Air Tasking Order remained until the end of the conflict. The constant flow of changes and new intelligence that occurred, at times even as Allied aircraft were launching, always perturbed the process. In particular, Checkmate and Admiral McConnell proved to be particularly useful conduits for getting time-critical intelligence out to Glosson and the Black Hole. [96]

Nevertheless, such interruptions in the plan's execution did not make the system run more smoothly or ease the lives of the crews and mainte-

---

the expenditure of resources far in excess of what the Germans had devoted to the V-1.

[96] Intvw, Maj Gen Buster Glosson with GWAPS personnel, 14 Apr 1992.

nance personnel. As late as the 25th, Horner was voicing displeasure with how the system was working: "I sure hope that it was well-coordinated [changes to the Air Tasking Order], because I hate to think of sending some guys up there [and] having fifty or sixty SAMs shot at him [sic] when he got jerked around with an alternate mission. . . .Yesterday we saw the air battle that almost got away from us."[97]

Overall, Horner believed that the air war was going in favor of his forces. On 23 January, he commented to the CENTAF staff at the 0730 briefing:

> Bean counters are concerned about holes in runways. They are missing the point. The point is [that] there's no power in Baghdad, no chemical attacks, and their nuclear capability is damaged. We've had [few] aircraft losses. Remember aircraft losses are wins for him. We are going to work on the Republican Guards now. We must keep the pressure on. We know the score is ninety-six to one, but we don't know what inning we're in.[98]

Horner's comments were particularly perceptive, because it remained unclear how much pressure the air campaign had imposed on the Iraqi regime. The direct results were obvious: control of the air, the shutoff of electrical power throughout much of Iraq, and the damage to much of the military and communications infrastructure throughout Iraq. Nevertheless, thus far the Iraqis had shown no sign of bending, much less cracking.

As discussed above, Scuds continued to cause great concern and diversion of effort, and there was no way to judge what effect air attacks were having on Iraqi morale. Moreover, bad weather was interfering on a continuing basis with Coalition operations against strategic targets. Finally, while the "strategic" air campaign had dominated events during the first three days, external events and factors now impinged on the conduct of the campaign.

---

[97] "Daily Comments of Lt Gen Horner, 25 Jan 1991, HQCENTAF, Office of History, 20 Mar 1991, Horner Files GWAPS.

[98] *Ibid*, 23 Jan 1991, 0730 Briefing.

The interference that continuing patterns of bad weather imposed is most noticeable when looking at F-117 strikes. Out of the first ten days of the war, weather affected half or more of the planned F-117 strikes on three days, one-third of them on two more days, and about one-quarter of the planned strikes on three other days. The weather on ATO Days 2 and 7 was the worst during this period; both these days saw two-thirds of the planned strikes end up as weather "no drops" or weather-induced misses.[99] After the war, Glosson admitted that by the end of January, the weather had the campaign "absolutely beat down."[100] He noted in his diary on 28 January:

> Bad weather again. Fourteen days on the calendar. . . .Due to the weather we have flown fewer than 100 sorties on Baghdad. Supposed to have flown 300. Whole pace of the campaign disastrously affected.[101]

The Euphrates Valley remained fogged in for one period of five straight days, and weather conditions forced diversion of precision sorties to targets outside of Baghdad. By 27 January Schwarzkopf was pushing Horner and Glosson to move the campaign's focus to Phase III, preparation of the battlefield for the coming ground campaign. But by that point, instead of having achieved ten days of target destruction in the strategic bombing campaign, weather had affected operations to such an extent, that the campaign had only reached levels of destruction planners had believed they would achieve the first four to five days of the war.[102]

Besides weather, other factors imposed friction on the air campaign. Coalition air commanders had expected more of Iraq's air-to-air fighters to come up and fight. While the Iraqis had flown approximately thirty-five shooter sorties per day in the conflict's first week, Coalition air-to-air kills virtually ceased after the third day.[103] The Iraqis were not only

---

[99] GWAPS Database; Manual counts, Effectiveness report from GWAPS.

[100] Intvw, Maj Gen Buster Glosson with GWAPS personnel, 14 Apr 1992.

[101] *Ibid*; Gen Glosson showed this particular entry to the interviewers from GWAPS.

[102] *Ibid*; also Intvw, Lt Col David Deptula with GWAPS personnel, 20-21 Dec 1992.

[103] DOD, *Conduct of the Persian War: Final Report to Congress*, Table VI-6, pp 204 and 216.

refusing to fight, but were in fact running at first sign of Coalition aircraft.

While this lack of serious opposition in the air eased the conduct of day-to-day operations, it presented the Coalition with a latent threat.[104] The Iraqis still possessed much of their air force and air capabilities sheltered in hardened shelters. Moreover, the media was not slow to comment on how few Iraqi aircraft the Coalition had shot down thus far in the war. Finally, fears surfaced that the Iraqis might launch an all out air assault to achieve the equivalent of the Tet offensive in January 1968.[105]

Since the Iraqi Air Force would not fight, Horner and Glosson determined to go after it in its lairs. The Iraqis had built nearly 600 shelters on various airfields. Some of these, such as the super-hardened shelters at Balad SE and Al Asad, were bunkers with sufficient strength to take over-pressures even from nuclear weapons.

On 21 January, F-111Fs began attacking these shelters; on the next night F-117s joined the effort. The attackers dropped 2,000-pound, laser-guided bombs. While the initial intent was to start with the main

---

[104] The lack of reaction by the Iraqi Air Force did cause some considerable uneasiness among Coalition aircrews, particularly the F-111F drivers. They reported on several occasions being intercepted by Iraqi aircraft that approached them and even illuminated them with searchlights without ever firing. The TACC log reports a ballad about "Baghdad Billy" that runs as follows: "I'm an F-111 Jock, and I'm here to tell/of Baghdad Billy, and his jet from hell./We were well protected, with Eagles in tight/ but that didn't stop, the man with the light./ RJ, AWACS,–they didn't see/ As Baghdad Billy, snuck up on me./ Then I found a spotlight shining at my six/ and my whoozoo said, hoolyy shit./ I popped off some chaff and I popped a flare/ but that Iraqi bandit, he didn't care./ I had tracers on my left, and tracers on my right/ with a load of bombs, I had to run from the fight./ I rolled my Vark over and took her down/ into the darkness and finally lost the clown./ When I landed back at Taif and gave this rap/ CENTAF said, I was full of crap./ I'm here to tell you, the Gods' honest truth/ that Iraqi bandit, he ain't no spoof./ You don't have to worry, there is no way/ you'll see Baghdad Billy if you fly in the day./ But listen to me son, for I am right/ watch out for Baghdad Billy if you fly at night!!!" There was never any evidence that the Iraqis ever intercepted an F-111 flying at night, much less managed to shine a spotlight on it. Nevertheless, the story has a tragic ending, because an F-111 appears to have flown into the ground attempting to escape from a nonexistent Iraqi aircraft. TACC, CC/DO, Current Ops Log, 9 Feb 1991, GWAPS, 215, and Intvw, Maj Gen Buster Glosson with GWAPS Personnel, 14 Apr 1992.

[105] Intvw, Col John Warden with GWAPS personnel, 21 Feb 1992.

operating bases in central Iraq, weather ended up focusing the bulk of the early effort on secondary fields in southern Iraq. As a result, estimating the number of Iraqi aircraft destroyed inside shelters became difficult. Nevertheless, video imagery of attacks on hardened aircraft shelters at Balad SE on 23 January showed hits against several shelters being followed by spectacular secondary explosions.[106] Regardless of the number of aircraft destroyed inside hardened shelters, the Iraqis were soon in danger of running out of shelters. In the end, the air attacks against the Iraqi Air Force's hardened shelters would destroy 375 of 594 (63 percent).[107]

Faced with the possibility that the entire air force might be lost, the Iraqis opted to fly what aircraft they could to Iran.[108] The move caught the Coalition by surprise. In fairness, the flight to Iran was a desperate move–in effect the Iraqis were making the first reparation payment to the Iranians for the Iran-Iraq war. Such flights provided Coalition fighter pilots with increasing opportunities to add to the box score of air-to-air engagements. In reaction to the flight of Iraqi aircraft to Iran, Glosson established CAP (combat air patrol) missions of F-15s and F-14s deep in Iraq as a barrier to the escape of enemy aircraft. In fact, some Iraqi pilots were so inadequately trained that they crashed their aircraft for lack of fuel in the journey to Iran. Thus, the shelter-busting campaign finished the Iraqi Air Force as a possible combat factor. Some of the remaining aircraft the Iraqis had to hide among villages and historical sites; absolute air supremacy now lay in the hands of Coalition air forces.

The Course of the Strategic Campaign

How the Coalition would utilize its air supremacy was now the crucial question. The opening of the campaign had seen a carefully plotted and integrated operational approach achieve great effects at rela-

---

[106] VCR film of F-117 and F-111 strikes, GWAPS files.

[107] DOD, *Conduct of the Persian Gulf War: Final Report to Congress*, p 154.

[108] At the beginning of the war with Iran when his air force had performed equally badly, Saddam had ordered it to fly its aircraft out to Kuwait, Jordan, and Saudi Arabia. But then at least he had a few friends.

An F-15 of the 1st TFW lands in Saudi Arabia after Desert Storm mission.

Bombs for the Iraqis.

Bombs for the Iraqis.

Iraqi aircraft shelters bombed by USAF.

Although the ex
ternal structure
may remain,
nothing inside
remains. Tallil
Air Base, Iraq.
7 March, 1991.
*Photo: D.A.
Deptula*

Hardened aircr
shelter Tallil
Airfield. A porti
of the reinforce
concrete roof th
has fallen in ca
be seen on the
left interior of
hangar.

Damage at Tallil Air Base, Iraq. 7 March, 1991. *Photo: D.A. Deptula*

Battle damage to hangar doors, Tallil, Iraq.

Soviet built Foxbat inside a NATO type Hardened aircraft shelter at Jalibah Airfield. Such damage to a shelter would normally have been characterized as "light" by air force intelligence.

Iraqi Republican Guard tanks sit destroyed after the Gulf War in the southern sands of Iraq. 27 March, 1991.
Photo: SSG Robert Reeve

Iraqi radar equipment after a bomb impacted in the immediate vicinity.

Victors and vanquished. Tallil Air Base Iraq. From left to right, Maj. Chip Setour, Lt. Col. John Turk, Lt. Col. David Deptula 82 ABN Div ALO Maj. Joe Abott, and Lt. Col. Phil Faye. *Photo: D.A. Deptula*

August, 1990 in "Checkmate". The Pentagon Washington, D.C. Navy, Marine, and Air Force planners refining "Instant Thunder". *Photo: D.A. Deptula*

6s being bombed up in preparation for night strikes against Iraq.

Royal Saudi fighter lands at base.

C-130 taking off from a forward operating strip. The "Hercules" transports provided the crucial logistical link between the main air bases in Iraq and the forces deploying for Schwarzkopf's outflanking move.

Hardened Aircraft Shelters, the most modern in the world, at Taif Air Base, Saudia Arabia, September 1990. These shelters hel the F-117s for the duration of the war.

Various aircraft. RF-4C's, F-5's and F-4G's of the 35th TFW.

‑-15 of 4th TFW in Saudi Arabia.

F-117 prepares for deployment to U.S.

F-16 Fighting Falcon 4th TFS on runway of a Desert Storm base.

B-52 redeployment to Middle East.

An A-10 close ground support Warthog from 23rd TFW uploaded with 30mm cannon ammunition, MK-87 cluster bombs, AIM-9 Sidewinders, and AGM-65 Maverick missiles.

F-117s deploying through Langley Air Force Bay on their way to the Gulf.

Br. Gen. Buster C. Glosson (L), Lt. Col. David A. Deptula (R), in the "Black Hole", 27 January, 1991.

Horner (front row seated) briefing army and navy senior officers on F-117 strikes against Baghdad in midwar.

tively little cost. However, after the first two days, those planning the course of the strategic air campaign were found to react to day-to-day pressures in their effort to achieve a variety of objectives. Many of these had been clear before the war, but the full complexity of the target sets only emerged as the war unfolded. However, some of the objectives that gained prominence during the campaign were not apparent before the war; the Scuds and the attacks against hardened shelters are cases in point. Moreover, the bad weather and pressures from Washington, particularly dealing with Scuds, added to complexities confronting Horner and his subordinates.

Early on the afternoon of 26 January, Horner sat down and wrote a detailed precis of the air campaign's achievements and future direction.[109] His notes provide a useful summary of his intentions, goals, and conceptions. It is well to remember that, when Horner wrote this memorandum, the shelter-busting campaign was just under way.

The CENTAF commander began by indicating that Coalition air forces had achieved air superiority. During the first days, allied air attacks had sought to limit Iraqi air activity by reducing the number of available operating surfaces at key airfields. By this point in the war, air attacks had been carried out against the bulk of the enemy's major bases and the enemy air force bottled up on the ground; a top priority would be eliminating the Iraqi air force at its airfields.[110] Unfortunately, the Iraqis

---

[109] At the 1700 staff briefing that afternoon, Horner noted to his officers, "Things appear to be going well. Had a good day today, weather has been good. We're getting some good results. If I had to summarize how we're doing, I'd say despite some pretty bad weather, probably four days of weather losses, we are doing well. But it does not mean that we will not be striking targets throughout Iraq. We will. But the goals of taking down the IADS; the goal of neutralizing his air force; the goal of severely crippling his ability to produce weapons such as biological, chemical, and nuclear [have been largely achieved]. Horner File: Daily Comments of Lt Gen Horner, HQUSCENTAF, 26 Jan 1991, 1700 Brief, Office of History, 20 March 1991. The chief planner in the Black Hole noted on 28 January: "Results to date–No electricity, water in Baghdad–No Allied air losses last forty-eight hours–No Iraqi air activity last twenty-four hours–leadership driven underground–NBC capability set back ten to fifteen years–oil refining capability reduced 70% to 80%–100% electricity out in Baghdad–no water–50% out nationwide" (Deptula, Personal Notes). The Black Hole kept a running status board that was mounted on the planning map of Iraq. The board kept track of the status of each target set.

[110] TACC, CC/DO, Current Ops Log, "Air Ops Summary of Air War, written by Lt Gen Horner after 8 1/2 days of Combat, 26 1100Z 91," GWAPS, NA 215.

had committed few aircraft, so that Coalition fighters had achieved a relatively small number of shoot downs. In all, Horner felt that he needed between 160 and 210 sorties to finish off the enemy base system and thus, the Iraqi Air Force. As for remaining Iraqi air defenses, he noted that Salman Pak was the only remaining intercept operations center that still functioned. Coalition aircraft would deal with the SAM threat by a combination of suppression–i.e., HARMs and ECM—and destruction: bombing the sites themselves.[111]

Turning to the strategic campaign, Horner underlined the importance of continuing efforts to isolate the Iraqi leadership. Parenthetically, he noted that the Rasheed Hotel was a key node, but that there would be political costs for attacking it.[112] Interestingly, he suggested that his goal remained the creation of an environment in Iraq "where the current leadership cannot control and provide the opportunity for new leadership to emerge."[113] Here he thought that he would need approximately 210 sorties. For both NBC (nuclear, biological, and chemical) and Scud targets, Horner emphasized the destruction of current stocks, as well as production, and research and development facilities.[114]

Two other categories remained in the strategic campaign in Horner's notes: 1) electricity and petroleum (POL), and 2) military storage. In the former case, the CENTAF commander emphasized destruction of refined POL products and several major electrical plants still apparently producing electricity.[115] Horner's impression that they were still functioning at this point probably reflects bomb damage assessment problems. From the number of sorties allocated to electricity and POL (thirty to each), Horner clearly did not believe much work remained against these target sets.[116] For the military support category–which included munitions storage facilities, missile research and development and production facilities, and

---

[111] *Ibid.*

[112] Coalition aircraft, of course, never attacked the Rasheed Hotel.

[113] *Ibid*, p 3.

[114] *Ibid*, p 3.

[115] In retrospect, it appears that these three plants were in fact inoperative by 26 January. Horner's impression that they were still functioning at that point probably reflects bomb-damage assessment problems.

[116] *Ibid*, p 4.

storage facilities–Horner allocated 200 sorties. Here the aim was at long-range effects beyond the tactical needs of the Gulf War.[117]

The final categories on Horner's list were the Iraqi ground forces. He hoped to isolate and destroy the Republican Guard; to achieve this goal he estimated the need for 10,000 sorties over a ten-day period. Finally, in terms of the other Iraqi ground forces in the KTO, the CENTAF commander could not come up with a total because he felt that the requirement would depend on psychological operations and how ground commanders shaped their requirements. He did estimate that CENTAF would need approximately 750 sorties per day for an indeterminate period against the ground forces in the KTO.[118]

At the end of his rough estimate of the situation, Horner calculated the number of sorties, type of platform, and time that would be needed to accomplish these tasks. For strategic targets, Horner calculated approximately 640 more F-111F and F-117 sorties over nine days to destroy the remaining strategic targets.[119] In conclusion, he summed up the overall situation. At the top of his list was the need to defend Saudi Arabia and solve the Scud problem. In terms of the strategic attacks on Iraq he suggested: 1) "protect our force from air attack, [2)] keep leadership isolated/C^2 degraded, [3)] destroy NBC capability, current and future, [and 4)] service as required SAMs, IADS [integrated air defense system]." To attack the Republican Guard he would rely on "penetration and heavy bombers;" to attack the enemy's artillery, supplies, and armor in the KTO, the Coalition would use its "attack aircraft."[120] Clearly, Horner was ready to refocus the air campaign on Phase III, preparation of the battlefield.[121]

---

[117] *Ibid*, p 4.

[118] *Ibid*, p 4. Despite the fact that Republican Guard units were also ground forces, they had been counted from the first as a separate category because of their political importance to the stability of the regime.

[119] Horner's numbers do not add up, but he was clearly thinking on paper rather than providing a detailed analysis for either his superiors or subordinates. For that very reason this document provides a particularly useful look into his mind at this stage in the campaign.

[120] Lt Gen Chuck Horner, "Air Ops Summary," TACC Log, CC/DO. GWAPS, NA 215.

[121] As early as 18 January Horner indicated to his staff his readiness to move quickly towards preparing the way for the ground forces: "I would suspect that in the next few days we will finish up valid targets in Iraq and begin to really shift our emphasis on[to]

There are a number of interesting aspects to Horner's estimation of the tasks remaining for Coalition air power.[122] He already felt relatively near to closure on most strategic target sets. The Scuds still remained as a problem; here political pressures undoubtedly played a role in his estimate. As for Iraqi ground forces, his emphasis lay on the Republican Guard; his focus was already moving away from the strategic air campaign against Iraq. Admittedly, from the first, air and ground commanders had regarded the Republican Guard as a strategic target–the destruction of which would carry political as well as military consequences. The attack on other Iraqi ground forces was of less consequence in Horner's mind, but that largely reflected Schwarzkopf's emphasis on the Republican Guard.[123]

Over the first four weeks of the campaign, Coalition aircraft struck a wide variety of strategic targets. The focus had shifted due to a variety of factors: long-range goals for the strategic air offensive, immediate military needs, political pressures, and the CINC's strategic and operational focus. In December, the planners had chosen to attack a broad spectrum of targets from the onset of the air campaign rather than concentrate on individual target sets, because they feared the Iraqis might bail out of the war under the pressures of air attacks.[124]

---

the military forces in Kuwait." GWAPS, Horner File: Daily Comments of Lt Gen Horner, HQUSCENTAF, 18 Jan 1991, 0730 Brief, Office of History, 20 Mar 1991.

[122] The persistence of these priorities is suggested by another notation in the TACC Log by Horner: "Priorit[ies]: 1. Defend from Air/Scud attack; 2. Kill Republican Guard; 3. Continue Strategic Campaign; 4. Kill Arty, Armor, Stocks, CPs in Rest of KTO; KEEP FOCUSED ON THE TARGET." TACC, CC/DO Current Ops Log, 28 Jan 1991, 0336Z, GWAPS, NA 215.

[123] We will deal with this issue in the chapter dealing with the ground campaign. Suffice it note that Schwarzkopf as the CINC would consistently demand from his air commander a very heavy emphasis on the attacks against the Republican Guard, while his ground commanders, Army as well as Marine, were requesting that air power emphasize the enemy's forces directly on their front rather than the Republican Guard. Horner and Glosson had no choice but to follow the dictates of their commander, but since there was no ground component commander (as there was for the air), the ground commanders did not participate in the final decision making processes. The unfortunate result was considerable bad feeling that the Air Force was not responding to the needs of the ground forces.

[124] Just because Saddam Hussein chose to stick the war out to the bitter end is no reason to criticize the prewar assumptions of the air commanders and planners. They had to go on the premise that the Iraqi leader would recognize the hopelessness of his nation's

Consequently, the first week of the strategic air campaign saw attacks on a broad spectrum of targets.[125] Nearly one quarter of the F-117 strikes during this period went against the Iraqi air defense system; 15 percent of the F-111 sorties also attacked portions of KARI.[126] The remaining F-117 sorties were spread fairly evenly among leadership (17 percent), command and control (14 percent), nuclear/chemical/biological (11 percent), military support (10 percent), and airfield target sets (10 percent). The F-111s, however, struck heavily against Iraqi airfields with 48 percent of their strikes; military support and Scud categories also received some attention.[127]

Over the course of the second week a distinctly different pattern emerged. CENTAF's efforts to eliminate the Iraqi Air Force now resulted in the shelter-busting campaign. More than 60 percent of the F-111F strikes attacked airfield targets, mostly shelters, while 26 percent of the F-117 sorties executed the same mission.[128] Because so many sorties hit airfields, the F-111s hit relatively few other targets–no other target category received more than 10 percent of their strikes.

The F-117s, however, expended a considerable portion of their attacks during the war's second week on nuclear/chemical/biological, military support, interdiction, and Scud targets, as well as against airfield targets.[129] Nevertheless, in combination significant numbers of F-111F and F-117 sorties went against bridges along the Euphrates. This effort

---

position and decide to bail out of the war. Consequently, there was a desire to hit as many high value targets as possible across the broad spectrum of target sets, so that even if the war ended early, the air campaign would achieve at least a minimum level of damage to all the targets sets.

[125] Our discussion in succeeding paragraphs will focus on the target sets attacked by the F-117s and the F-111Fs, because those aircraft were the premier precision munition strike aircraft and because the most accurate data exists on their attacks.

[126] GWAPS Mission Database; see Effectiveness report, Gulf War Air Power Survey Appendix 1, for the by-week strike summaries of F-117 and F-111 operations. Note that the strike data cited were based on manual counts done by Task Force Six.

[127] *Ibid.*

[128] *Ibid.*

[129] The RR category had originally included just railroad targets, but had broadened out during the planning phases of Desert Storm to include bridges as well. One might best think of this category in terms of interdiction.

was not just interdiction–although that concept was clearly involved–but was an effort to prevent the Republican Guard from retreating across the Euphrates. Coalition leaders wanted air power to destroy them in place.[130] In the end, of course, Saddam left them there right up to the start of the ground war.

By the war's second week, the impact of the attacks on KARI had become clear. The Iraqi air defense system no longer functioned except fitfully. Coalition aircraft consequently ranged back and forth across the full extent of the country at medium altitude with slight risk. In the end, as their shelters went up in clouds of cement dust–often with aircraft inside–the Iraqis could only fly their aircraft to seizure by a none-too-friendly Iranian regime. By the second week, Glosson was ordering tankers to fly into Iraq to fuel F-117 strikes against targets in the Mosul area, as sure a proof of air supremacy as one could wish.[131]

Nevertheless, during the second week of the war, Saddam undertook his second political initiative–the Scuds being the first–in reply to the pounding that Iraq and its military were undergoing from the Coalition: he ordered Iraqi commanders in Kuwait to open up the oil pipeline from the Kuwaiti oil fields–one that normally filled tankers lying off shore–and flood the Gulf. President Bush accurately characterized Saddam's actions as "environmental terrorism."[132]

Almost immediately, Horner and Glosson had their planners look into halting the flow by using precision-guided bombs against the shut off valves and pumping stations. They soon determined that a few GBU-15s would solve the problem. However, at that point Schwarzkopf intervened to prevent the mission. It appears that the Kuwaitis wanted to accomplish

---

[130] Intvw, Lt Col David Deptula with GWAPS personnel, 20-21 Dec 1991.

[131] Intvw, Maj Gen Buster Glosson with GWAPS personnel, 14 Apr 1992.

[132] *U.S. News and World Report, Triumph Without Victory, The Unreported History of the Persian Gulf War* (New York, 1992), p 262. Saddam's purpose appears to have been a desire to enlist the Western media in a campaign against the war because of the environmental damage that it was causing to the Gulf region. To a great extent, he succeeded as Western reporters flocked to the oil soaked beaches and decried–quite justifiably–the damage that it was causing with some clearly implying that the war must stop before more ecological damage resulted. However, what Saddam had not calculated was the capability of Allied air power to end this cynical effort to play on Western concerns.

the task using their own underground.[133] In the end, several days and millions of gallons later, F-111Fs ended Saddam's atrocity against nature by destroying the pumping station and severing the pipeline itself with well placed bombs.[134]

For the most part, the pattern of attacks by the F-117s and F-111Fs against strategic targets that was evident during the first two weeks persisted into the third. Attrition of aircraft shelters at Iraqi airbases continued, with the F-111Fs posting more than 200 strikes (41 percent of the F-111 total for the third week); the F-117s carried out some 50 strikes against airfield targets (18 percent of their strikes for that week).[135] The F-117s, though, did increase their effort against nuclear/chemical/biological warfare targets (more than 90 strikes totaling 32 percent of F-117 effort for the third week).[136] The other change, discussed in more detail below, that began toward the end of the third week was the shift of the F-111Fs to attacking Iraqi armor with 500-pound laser-guided bombs in the Kuwait theater of operations.

By the end of the second week, Horner and Glosson had come under increasing pressure to switch the air war away from strategic attacks against Iraq to Phase III, preparation of the battlefield in the KTO. As early as 26 January Horner suggested to the TACC his conviction that the air campaign could soon devote most of its attention to the enemy army:

---

[133] Intvw, Maj Gen Buster Glosson with GWAPS personnel, 14 Apr 1992; intvw, GWAPS with Edward W. Graham, U.S. Ambassador to Kuwait, 14 Jul 1992.

[134] See the report in the TACC log on 28 January for the first report of the success of this mission. TACC Log, 28 Jan, GWAPS, NA 215.

[135] GWAPS Mission Database; also see the Effectiveness report, Appendix 1.

[136] The question which remains, in terms of level of damage that these strikes achieved, is the extent to which the destruction of buildings and bunkers achieved effective damage. One suspects that by this point in the war the Iraqis were desperately engaged in moving everything that was not cemented down to the floor out of sites that were vulnerable to attack. Certainly the report of UN inspectors who had a chance to look at nuclear facilities suggests that the Iraqis made major efforts both before and during the air campaign to limit the damage that Coalition air attacks might achieve against such targets. See in particular International Atomic Energy Agency, "Consolidated Report of the First Two IAEA Inspections under Security Council Resolution 687 (1991) of Iraqi Nuclear Capabilities," 11 Jul 1991, Rpt #S/22788 p 5; and "Report on the Seventh IAEA On-Site Inspection in Iraq under Security Council Resolution 687 (1991), 14 Nov 1991, Rpt #S/23215.

"We are where we need to be to shift the emphasis to the Republican Guards."[137] Three days later he reemphasized his priorities:

> We're well into our attack on the Republican Guards. It is not going to be spectacular. It's going to be a lot of work. It should not be inordinately hazardous. We are not going to get a lot of feedback until suddenly they're defeated. We'll fight the weather the next couple of days, but keep the pressure on the Republican Guards. It's the target. When we have the Republican Guards in the bag, then we'll turn our attention to the ground forces in Kuwait.[138]

As early as the 27th, Schwarzkopf had directed Horner to shift his air assets except F-117s and F-111Fs to Kuwait.[139] At the end of the month, the Iraqi attack on Khafji moved the attention of senior commanders to the Kuwait theater; as the air campaign continued, ground commanders demanded that its focus move to preparing for the ground campaign. Unfortunately, there were few indicators as to what the air attacks in the KTO (Kuwaiti Theater of Operations) had achieved thus far against Iraqi ground forces, Republican Guard as well as regular army.[140] Not surprisingly, the CINC, clearly believing in the necessity for a ground campaign, pressured his air commanders to move on.

In late January, F-111F crews reported that their forward looking infrared receivers could pick up the distinct signatures of tanks and other Iraqi military equipment in the desert. This was because the metal cooled at a different rate than the sand of the surrounding desert. On 5 February, with the full support of Horner and Glosson, the F-111Fs dropped eight GBU-12s, destroyed five revetted positions and claimed four tanks and

---

[137] Daily Comments of Lt Gen Horner, 26 Jan 1991, 1700 Brief, HQCENTAF, Office of History, 20 Mar 1991, GWAPS, Horner File.

[138] Daily Comments of Lt Gen Horner, 29 Jan 1991, 1700 Brief, HQCENTAF, Office of History, 20 Mar 1991, GWAPS, Horner File. Here Horner was undoubtedly following the preferences of Gen Schwarzkopf.

[139] The chief planner in the Black Hole noted on the 28th: "Yesterday CINC shifted all but 111s & 117s to RG; OK but many production facilities not destroyed." Deptula personal notes.

[140] We will discuss in Chapter 6 the nature of these arguments as well as the probable impact that the air campaign was making on the Iraqi ground forces.

one artillery piece.[141] On viewing the tape, Horner noted in the TACC's Current Ops Log: "Just returned from watching video of F-111F/Pave Tack/500 laser-guided bombs blowing up tanks in Kuwait that ought to be required viewing at Army War College and A-10 Fighter Weapons School–classic of how to do the job right."[142] Horner, undoubtedly at Schwarzkopf's urging, promptly ordered the F-111Fs to shift entirely out of the strategic campaign.[143]

On 6 February, the F-111Fs embarked on what soon became termed their tank "plinking" effort.[144] There is some irony in both the focus during the war on tank "plinking" and in the debates thereafter, because the corps commanders were by and large more interested in efforts to destroy Iraqi artillery. In fairness to the F-111F attacks that now ensued, many of their attacks went in against artillery positions as well as tank units. On the night of 6/7 February, the F-111Fs dropped more than 140 GBU-12 laser-guided bombs on dug-in Republican Guard armor and artillery. After a return to other targets on 7 February while results were assessed, the F-111Fs resumed tank plinking on the night of 8/9 February.[145] From this point until the beginning of the ground campaign on 24 February, the F-111Fs would concentrate their efforts against Iraqi ground order of battle, particularly on Republican Guard units deployed along the Iraq-Kuwait border.

The division of effort between strategic platforms in the fourth week illustrates this change in focus. Some 73 percent of the F-111s' strikes went against enemy ground forces, 6 percent to oil, and 5 percent to

---

[141] TACC, Current Ops Log, 6 Feb 1991, 0730Z, GWAPS, NA 215.

[142] TACC, Current Ops Log, 7 Feb 1991, 1838Z, GWAPS, NA 215.

[143] On 9 February Glosson noted in his diary somewhat lugubriously: "Saddest day of the war: we are going to have to stop strategic air campaign before it is completed." Intvw, Maj Gen Buster Glosson with GWAPS personnel, 14 Apr 1992.

[144] Gen Schwarzkopf soon made clear that he did not like the term "tank plinking." As Horner commented after the war, however, CINCCENT's expression of disapproval at the term only insured that it would become enshrined in Air Force lingo. TACC, Current Ops Log, 8 Feb 1991, GWAPS, NA 215.

[145] GWAPS Mission Database; see Effectiveness report, Appendix 1.

military support.[146] The F-117s displayed no similar concentration of effort to oil, and 5 percent to military support; instead they attacked a wide variety of target sets: no less than six sets received more than 10 percent of the stealth effort for the week. What does, however, suggest the focus of the attack by both platforms was their combined effort against leadership (with 14 percent of the strikes) and command and control (with 20 percent of strikes). There was obviously a distinct effort to complete the paralysis of the Iraqi leadership that the war's opening strikes had failed to achieve.

In the early morning hours of 13 February–in fact during the last hours of Day 27 of the air campaign–two F-117s hit the Al Firdos bunker with one bomb apiece. Intelligence had identified twenty-five bunkers in Iraq that the enemy could use as critical command posts. Ten of these were inactive on 15 January and therefore not targeted. By early February, intelligence indicated that the Iraqis had activated the Al Firdos bunker for use as a command post. Within the week after identification it appeared on the Master Attack Plan.[147] *No one* in the planning cycle or in intelligence knew that the Iraqis were also using the bunker as a shelter for civilians.[148] The strategic consequences of this attack were considerable. To all intents and purposes the civilian losses ended the strategic air campaign against targets in Baghdad.

---

[146] *Ibid.* All the attacks against oil targets were flown by F-111Es flying out of Turkey.

[147] Intvw with assorted members of Checkmate, the Black Hole, and others involved in the air campaign.

[148] Those who worked in the targeting process made clear to those who interviewed them for GWAPS that they would never have targeted the Al Firdos bunker had they realized that it contained women and children. One of the ironies of the stealth/pgm war was that where the Al Firdos bunker would have provided substantial protection in terms of World War II attacks or even in terms of the B-52 strikes against Hanoi, precision platforms now rendered safe most unprotected sites, but made such hardened targets as Al Firdos exceptionally dangerous to those unlucky to be inside of them. The Iraqis as usual mounted a skillful campaign of disinformation. Not surprisingly some of the press swallowed Saddam's line; the Iraqis, of course, allowed no detailed inspection of the facility until after the war was over and they had had full opportunity to fix up the site to extract the maximum propaganda value.

The targets attacked by F-117s on day twenty-seven of the air campaign around Baghdad suggest the extent that the planners were going after the leadership and political centers of the Baᶜth regime:

Baghdad: Iraqi Air Force HDQS	Two hits
Baghdad Radrel Sta	One hit, one no guide
Baghdad: Ministry of Defense	Two hits
Baghdad Conference Center	Three hits, one no drop
Baghdad Auto Exch-Radrel	Two hits
Baghdad Auto TP Exch	One hit, one no guide
Baghdad Maydan TP Exch	Two hits
Iraqi Intelligence Service HQS	One hit, one no drop
Baghdad Radcom Xmtr-Rcvr	One hit, one no drop
Baghdad Intl Radcom Rcvr	One hit, one no drop
Baᶜth Party HDQS	Four hits
Al Firdos District Bunker	Two hits
Bag Dir of Gen Int Sec HDQS	One hit, one no guide
Bag Dir of Mil Intel HDQS	Two hits
Iraqi Intel Ser HQ	Three hits
Baghdad Presidential Bunker	Two hits
Baghdad Auto Mpur-Radrel	No Guide[149]

The number and nature of targets in Baghdad suggest that somewhere along the line civilian casualties were bound to occur. Unfortunately, they came in such a frightful fashion that political pressure ensured that targets in downtown Baghdad were put largely out of bounds for the remainder of the war.

The attack against Al Firdos raises an interesting point. Thus far, this book has argued that the Iraqi regime possessed great political stamina and corresponding great weaknesses in the military arena.[150] This leads to the conclusion that an air campaign against Iraq's military structure, unless followed by the complete occupation of the nation, would not have resulted in the regime's collapse.[151] To break Saddam's regime by

---

[149] GWAPS Missions Database.

[150] These strengths and weaknesses are entirely interrelated.

[151] Here we have verifiable evidence, in that well after the destruction of most of Iraq's military power and its humiliation in Kuwait, the regime is still maintaining its hold on power.

air power, an air campaign would have had to go after the political structure from the onset of war. But to do so would almost certainly have led to a series of incidents similar to Al Firdos. In the end, such an air campaign, even though targeted at breaking the Iraqi regime directly and therefore aimed more realistically at what might cause its collapse, could very well have achieved less.

13 February: Day 28 of the Air Campaign

To conclude this chapter, a summary of conventional air operations on 13 February will be given to suggest how much they had changed over the four weeks of war.[152] This day's operations came in the hours immediately following Al Firdos; the deaths at the bunker, however, had not yet affected the lay down of air operations.

As a prelude, it would be useful to describe an air-to-air mission flown on 6 February. The mission underlines the degree of air superiority that Coalition air power enjoyed by this point in the war. On that day, two F-15Cs, Xerex flight, were flying a barrier combat air patrol mission to prevent the Iraqis from slipping more aircraft away to Iran.[153] AWACS called an initial contact at sixty nautical miles (nm). The bandits consisted of two MiG-21s and two SU-25s flying to Iran at barely 300 knots at less than 1,000 feet altitude.[154] After considerable difficulties in identifying the targets, Xerex Two achieved a lock on one of the MiG-21s at twelve nm. Both he and the lead then fired AIM-7Ms, but the first flew by the MiG-21, while the motor of the second missile failed. A third AIM-7M also did not track its target. By this time the Iraqis had split into two separate flights. Xerex Two then closed to within 6,000 feet and shot both SU-25s down with AIM-9M Sidewinder, heat-seeking missiles. At the same time, Xerex One shot down the MiG-21s, also with AIM-9Ms. At no time in the engagement did the Iraqis take evasive action, and they appeared oblivious to missile attacks or the approach of F-15s to the rear of their aircraft.

---

[152] We have suggested the pattern of Stealth strikes above.

[153] The account of this mission is abstracted from "Desert Storm Air to Air Engagements, 53d Fighter Squadron Air to Air Engagements," Desert Storm, 3 Mar 1992, pp 12-17.

[154] There may have been more MiG-21s or other aircraft involved, but that remains unclear.

Obviously, the Coalition had established almost complete dominance in the skies over Iraq. No longer was it necessary for air superiority fighters to accompany strike missions in the KTO. Instead, F-15Cs and F-14s maintained a number of combat air patrol positions not just on the frontier, but deep in Iraq itself. In fact F-15s were flying CAP missions northeast of Baghdad, close to the Iranian border. [For the position of CAP missions in early February see Map 26.]

At the same time, SEAD missions no longer directly supported most KTO strike packages. Instead, both EF-111s and F-4G weasels flew orbits, either to jam the radars of enemy air defenses–in the case of the EF-111s–or to seek out and attack SAM sites that came up–in the case of the F-4Gs.[155] While SEAD packages still accompanied strike packages against targets in Iraq, there were few areas in Iraq outside of Baghdad where Coalition aircraft could not fly.

The first strike of 13 February came against a "killbox" in the KTO; four Navy A-6 all-weather day-night strike aircraft worked over two killboxes. [See Maps 27, 28, 29] With dawn, the pounding of the Iraqi ground forces swung into high gear. Three particular quadrants in the killboxes, AF6, AF7, and AG7, received the heaviest attention throughout the day–the first from forty A-10s, the second from sixty-eight F-16s, and the last from seventy-six F-16s. In addition, A-10s flew 222 sorties–210 of which their pilots judged successful in terms of identifying and attacking targets during the course of the day.[156]

---

[155] The Master Attack Plan called for round-the-clock coverage by EF-111s and EA-6Bs for electronic counter measures, by EC-130s, Compass Call for further ECM, and by F-4Gs to attack operating SAM sites in the KTO. SEAD support was of course available for those aircraft that had to strike targets deeper in Iraq. (S) Master Attack Plan, D+27, 13 Feb 1991, pp 1 and 5.

[156] (S) Master Attack Plan, D+27, 13 Feb 1991 and GWAPS Database.

Map 26
Allied Air Operations - Support Structure for Air Supremacy Early February 1991

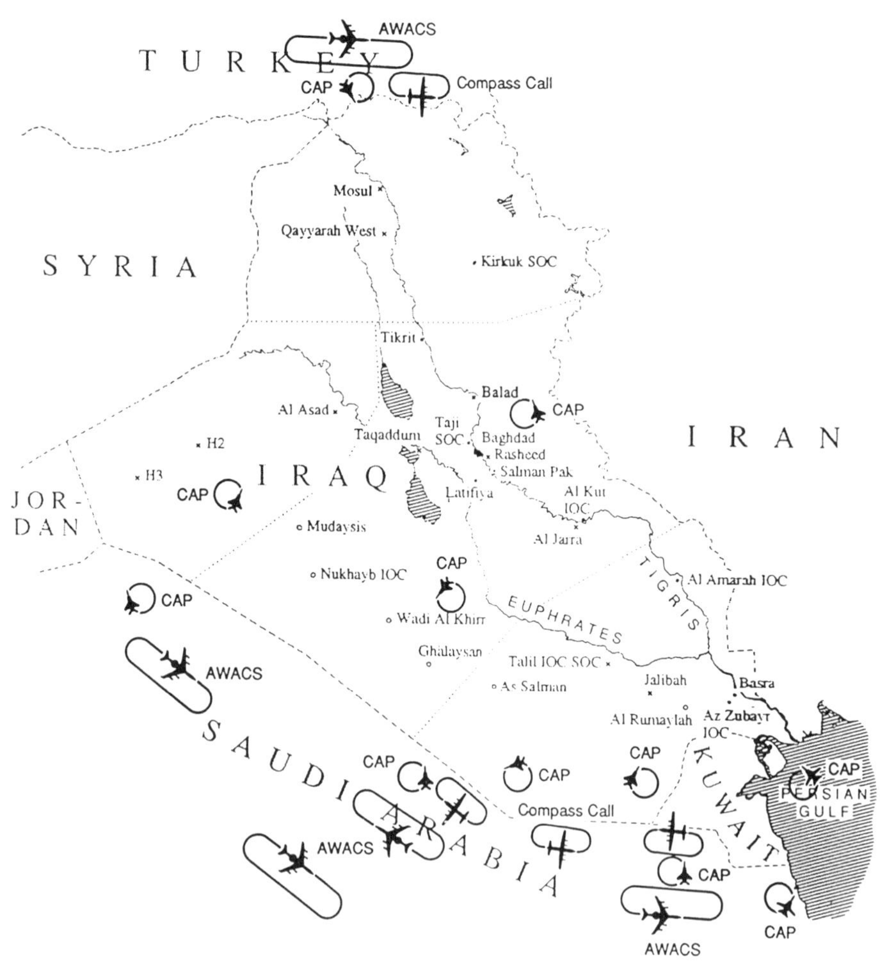

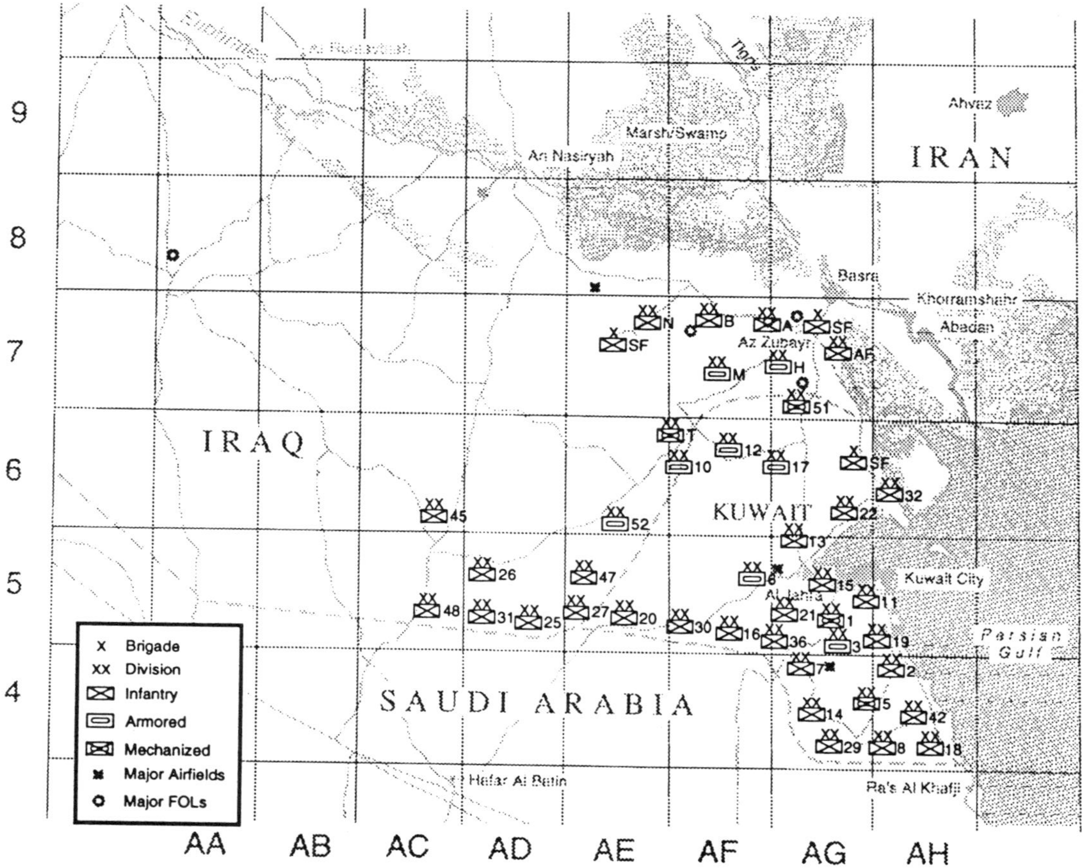

Map 27
Iraqi Army Deployment in the KTO

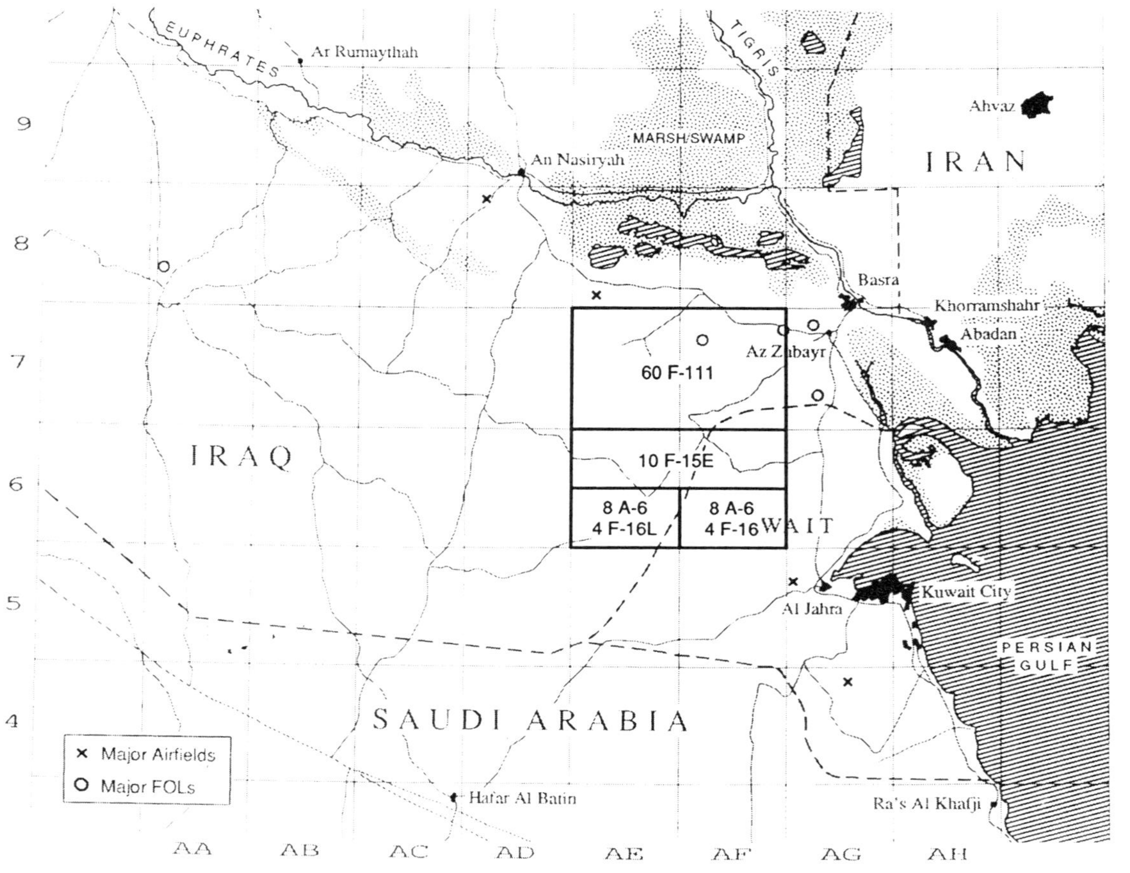

Map 28
Night LGB work
13 February

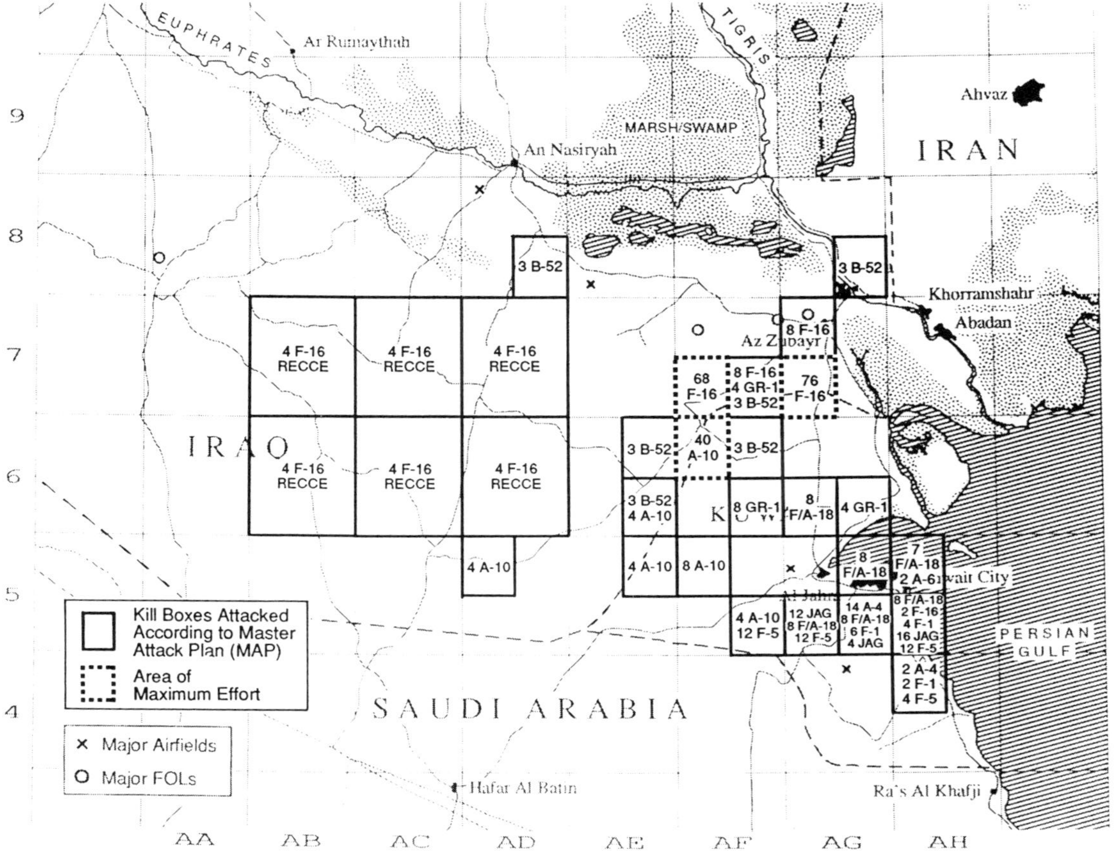

Map 29
Non-LGB
Attacks in KTO
13 February

At night, sixty F-111F sorties struck AF7 and AG7. Two killboxes to the south also received considerable attention from ten F-15Es, sixteen A-6s, and eight LANTIRN F-16s.[157] The emphasis on air efforts in the KTO throughout the day and night–as for much of the war–lay on the Republican Guard. Saddam's elite ground forces, chosen for their political reliability as much as for their military competence, remained in position along the Kuwait-Iraq frontier southwest of Basra. It was these boxes that received the attention of much of the air campaign for the rest of the war. In addition to these sorties, numerous other aircraft attacked targets in the KTO. Some were aircraft tasked to support Special Operations Forces, or assigned to JSTARS; some were aircraft on alert. The general picture then is of unceasing activity throughout the KTO.

The emphasis on the KTO did not mean that air operations against the rest of Iraq ceased; they continued, but at much reduced levels. A few F-16 sorties still flew against targets of opportunities in Iraq, while other attacks went against airfields and communication sites; British, Saudi, Proven Force, and Navy aircraft were particularly useful in sustaining pressure on the Iraqi airfields and Scud sites.[158] One suspects that the bombing of hardened shelters that occurred during the course of 13 February aimed as much at getting Scuds that were possibly hiding in the shelters as at finishing off the Iraqi Air Force.

Morning attacks against the Iraqi airfields like Al Asad and Taqaddum were multi-national as well as multi-service efforts. [See Maps 30 and 31 for depictions of air operations on 13 February.] At 0810, six RAF Tornados attacked Al Asad; two Tornados provided capability to attack active SAM sites (with Alarm anti-radiation missiles), while two Navy EA-6Bs covered by two F/A-18s provided ECM. Half an hour later, RAF Buccaneers lased for four Tornados in a second attack on the same field; three EF-111s, two F-4Gs, and two F-15Cs covered the strike. At the same time (0840), two more Buccaneers lased for another four RAF Tornados in a strike against Taqaddum hardened shelters.[159]

---

[157] (S) *Ibid.*

[158] (S) Master Attack Plan, D+27, 13 Feb 1991, and GWAPS Database.

[159] (S) *Ibid.*

Map 30
13 February (0300 to 1300)

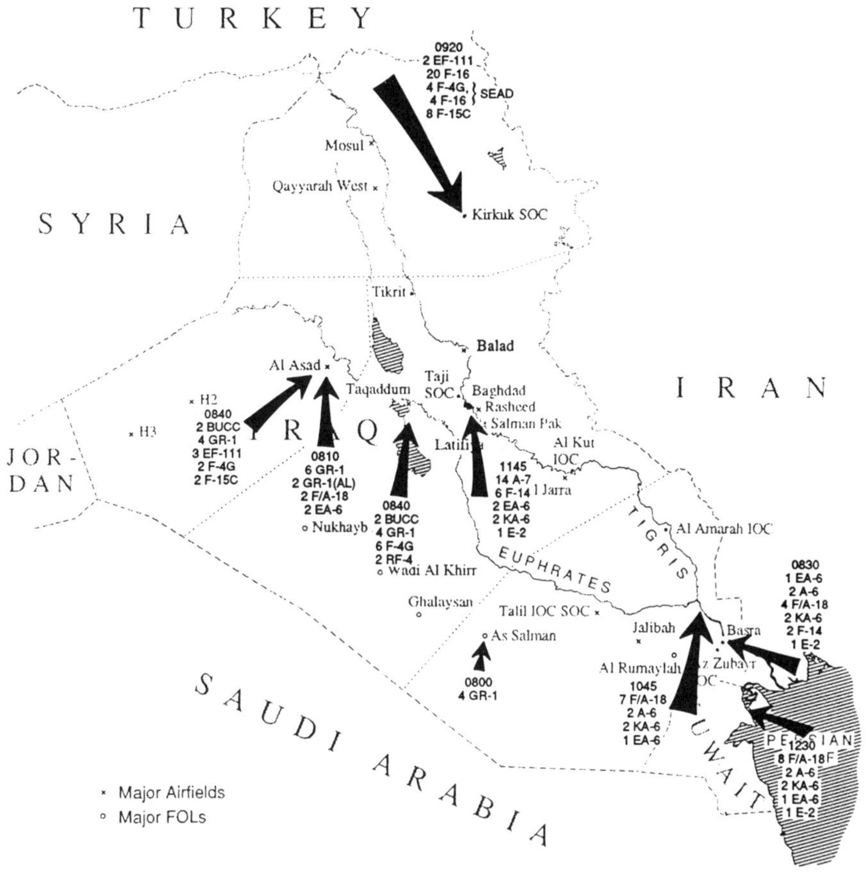

Major activity came at night: eight Tornados attacked Taqaddum in the early evening hours; F-111Fs struck the bridges just north of Basra. These attacks were the prelude to two major attacks that occurred just before midnight. A massive package of twelve B-52s, accompanied by no less than three EF-111s, four F-15Cs, and eight F-4Gs attacked the Taji Missile Repair Facility. At the same time, twelve F-111Es attacked Kirkuk from the north.[160]

---

[160](S) *Ibid.*

Map 31
13 February (1300 to End of Day)

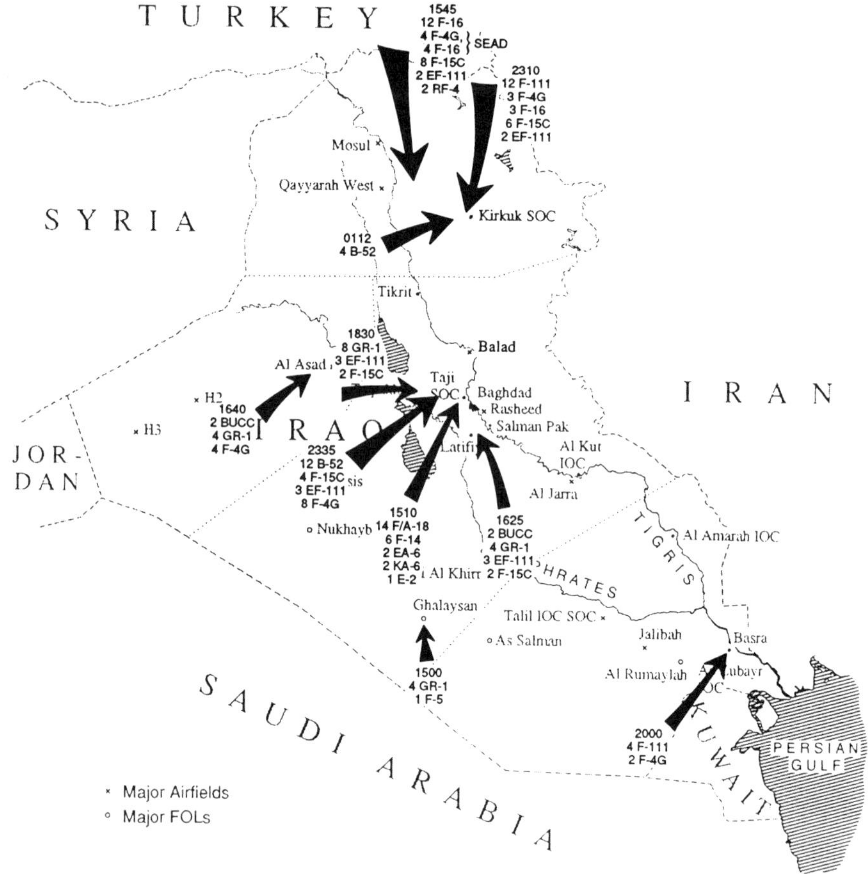

The pattern and weight of the attacks over the course of 13 February underline a number of ways in which the conduct of air operations had changed. Most notable was the general absence of interference from Iraqi defenses. Secondly, F-117s almost entirely carried the weight of the precision war against Iraqi strategic targets. The general focus of Coalition air efforts now lay within the KTO. Nevertheless, Coalition air planners had sufficient resources available so that they could keep substantial pressure on Iraq throughout the day and night.

Conclusion

The three-and-a-half week period of air operations that followed the opening two days of the campaign suggests a number of interesting aspects. Despite the Coalition's overwhelming success at the start of the war, a number of impediments to a coherent execution of the campaign now appeared. The enemy was able to affect the Coalition's plans to a considerable extent; mobile Scuds forced Horner and his planners to bleed off resources to search for and rarely find these elusive targets. The enemy's refusal to fly and fight forced Coalition air power to strike Iraqi airfields and deconstruct the Iraqi Air Force shelter by shelter. The shelter-busting campaign was successful in its aim but also pulled precision bombing assets away from the strategic campaign. Finally, the weather posed a considerable obstacle–and one that the planners had not entirely foreseen.

Such frictions in the conduct of the campaign are not surprising. The leaders of the air campaign for the most part adapted to these real conditions with considerable skill and imagination. By 13 February, they had reached the point when the air campaign was already substantially damaging the infrastructure of the Iraqi ground forces and was turning to an effort to wreck the regime's command structure. Unfortunately, the hit on the Al Firdos bunker would end that second effort; as for the first, there was nothing the Iraqis could do to prevent Coalition air from wrecking the morale and much of the equipment of their ground forces deployed in the KTO.

5

Diminished Attack on the Center

During the war's last two weeks, Coalition air forces sent more than 90 percent of their strike sorties against the Iraqi army in the KTO. One night, even F-117s, which had become accustomed to working in and around Baghdad, headed into Kuwait. There they raided pumping stations that were to feed oil trenches whose flames were to thwart Coalition ground attacks. F-117s, however, did not join CENTAF's other precision bombers, F-111Fs and F-15Es, in daily attacks against tanks and other equipment of the enemy's ground forces. Schwarzkopf recognized that enough unfinished business remained in Iraq to require attention from F-117s, but the stealth bomber received little help with its precision bombing there.[1]

British Buccaneers did laser designation for Tornados dropping guided bombs in central Iraq as well as the KTO. In addition, several Tornados also carried the new Thermal Imaging and Laser Designation (TIALD) system. RAF Tornados had dropped unguided bombs in the campaign's first two weeks; in the second two weeks, they began dropping guided bombs; in the last two weeks of the war, they dropped nothing but laser-guided bombs. Their guided bombs, however, weighed only a thousand pounds each and lacked penetrating warheads which enabled American two-thousand-pound bombs to break through the reinforced concrete of Iraqi bunkers. U.S. Navy A-6s and FA-18s, flying from carriers in the Red Sea, dropped a few laser-guided bombs in central Iraq, but those Navy laser-guided bombs also lacked penetrating warheads. Navy aircraft on the Persian Gulf carriers expended all their

[1](S) On Schwarzkopf's priorities for bombing in Iraq, see msg, CINCCENT to COMUS CENTAF, subj: 72-Hour Pre-Cease-Fire Campaign guidance, 130850Z Feb 1991, GWAPS BH Deptula 19A, which is discussed later in this chapter. The F-117 raid on the oil trench system occurred on the night of 15-16 Feb 1991; see (S) Contingency Hist Rpt, 37 FW(P), 10-16 Feb 1991, AFHRA.

bombs in the KTO, and even the Red Sea force did much of its bombing there.[2]

The remaining forces available to bomb central and northern Iraq lacked precision-bombing capability. Air Force F-111Es and F-16s in Turkey had remained north of the thirty-fifth parallel during the early weeks of the war, but in the final two weeks they came south, almost reaching Baghdad. Air Force B-52s from England bombed only in northern Iraq, while B-52s based in Saudi Arabia, Diego Garcia, and Spain concentrated on the KTO with occasional runs into central Iraq. None of these forces, however, could do the precision, bunker-busting work of F-117s. As for F-117s, CENTAF could no longer send them anywhere it pleased–Baghdad targets now required approval from the theater commander and above.

Constraints and Competitive Objectives

On 13 February, a few hours after F-117s had gutted Baghdad's Al Firdos bunker, Schwarzkopf recognized that the Coalition had major press and political problems. If he had any reluctance to recognize these problems, the JCS Chairman, General Powell, called to underline both. Cable News Network television cameras had recorded Iraqi officials removing the bodies of dead women and children. The Bush administration did affirm the legitimacy of the target publicly, but there were fears that such pictures might turn many Americans against the war. Convinced that the bunker had become a communications center for an intelligence organization bombed out of its original headquarters, air planners were dismayed to learn that Iraqi families had been using the upper floor as a bomb shelter. Speculation within the American intelligence community that someone of importance in Saddam's regime may have died in the bunker did mollify unhappiness about the bunker's adverse publicity to some degree. Nevertheless, Schwarzkopf told Horner and the Black Hole that henceforth CENTAF could no longer attack targets

[2](S) Rpt, Frank Schwamb, et al., *Desert Storm Reconstruction Report, Vol II: Strike Warfare* (Washington: Center for Naval Analyses, 1991), GWAPS NA 368; (S) note for record, G. J. Onslow, RAF Strike Cmd, Op Res Br, Analysis of Attack and Reconnaissance Operations from Operation Granby, Jul 1991, GWAPS NA 515E.

in Baghdad without his approval. The Black Hole was under the impression that Schwarzkopf soon was checking all such targets with Powell.[3]

Curtailment of the air assault on Baghdad had begun in early February, when the Navy stopped launching Tomahawk cruise missiles against the capital. Since Tomahawks alone had been attacking Baghdad in daylight, their absence meant that city residents no longer had to fear attacks during normal working hours. At night their homes remained free of attack, because F-117s attacked only office buildings and bunkers. Under the circumstances of this new form of air war, the most foolish thing any Iraqi could do was leave his own house in favor of the shelter offered by a bunker. Most residents of Baghdad did not have to ponder this question, since there were only enough bunkers to house the families of the regime's elite.[4]

The Navy had used less than three hundred of approximately five hundred Tomahawks available. For the remainder of the war, Navy and Air Force planners proposed new Tomahawk missions, but Schwarzkopf refused approval for such attacks. Either January's television pictures of Tomahawks sailing through downtown Baghdad at midday had bothered someone in Washington, or their great cost and relatively small warhead made CENTCOM deem them too expensive for further use.[5]

Early in February, television cameras also publicized a British daylight strike against the bridge at Nasiriyah on the Euphrates, 150 miles southeast of Baghdad. Civilian deaths at that site may have increased Powell's reaction to F-117 night strikes against bridges in downtown Baghdad. Since communications cables ran under some of Baghdad's six bridges, air planners hoped to make communications in the capital yet more difficult by telephone as well as by car. But after strikes against

---

[3](S) Intvw, Wayne Thompson, GWAPS, with Lt Col David A. Deptula, Pentagon, 26 Aug 1991; (S) Intvw, Richard G. Davis, Perry Jamison and Barry Barlow, AF Hist Program, with Lt Gen Charles A. Horner, Shaw AFB, South Carolina, 4 Mar 1992; Schwarzkopf, *Hero*, p 435; (S) Intvw, Wayne Thompson with Lt Col David A. Deptula, Pentagon, 26 Aug 1991.

[4](S) Rpt, Frank Schwamb, et al, *Desert Storm Reconstruction Report, Vol II: Strike Warfare* (Washington, 1991), esp Chapter 8, GWAPS NA 368.

[5](S) *Ibid.*

four bridges during early February, Schwarzkopf told the Black Hole there would be no more bombing of Baghdad's bridges. In this context, the Al Firdos bunker strike made all targets in the capital suspect. While restrictions on some targets loosened at the end of the war, potential bomb shelters and bridges in Baghdad remained forbidden.[6]

If the Al Firdos and bridge affairs pushed F-117s out of Baghdad, there were other forces also pulling them to targets outside the capital. Realization in early February that F-111Fs and F-15Es could "plink" tanks with guided bombs sucked those precision bombers into the KTO. Precision-bombing everywhere else in Iraq now was the mission of F-117s almost alone. F-111Fs bombed outside Kuwait and southeastern Iraq on only a dozen occasions in the last two weeks of the war–about seventy-five sorties flew those missions. The largest F-111F package going north in this period consisted of twenty aircraft scheduled to bomb the conventional arms plant at Al Iskandariyah (thirty miles south of Baghdad) on the last night of the war. Bad weather kept all but one from dropping bombs, and those bombs did not guide. But a smaller package of twelve F-111Fs had enjoyed better luck against this target on 17 February, as had six B-52s on 14 February, and five F-117s on 23 February.[7]

The most important targets outside both Baghdad and the KTO were those relating to Iraq's development of nuclear, biological, and chemical (NBC) weapons. The administration in Washington wanted Iraq to emerge from the war without NBC weapons–or the capability to produce them. By mid-February, however, the Black Hole had become more interested in bombing leadership targets in Baghdad than NBC targets elsewhere. Since this renewed focus on leadership followed the weeks when aircraft shelters had been the prime target, more than a dozen suspected chemical and biological weapons storage bunkers remained to be bombed.[8]

---

[6](S) Notes, Wayne Thompson, Checkmate mtg, 9 Feb 1991, GWAPS Historical Advisor's Files. According to the RAF database sent to GWAPS, the RAF attacked the bridge at Nasiriyah on 4 Feb first with guided bombs and then seconds later with unguided bombs. While visiting GWAPS in December 1992, however, researchers from the UK Ministry of Defence said that only guided bombs were used against the bridge. In any case, most of the casualties at Nasiriyah were caused by accurate bombs which struck the bridge and the people crossing it. See the sortie data attached to (S) ltr, Air Vice Marshal P.T. Squires, HQ RAF Strike Command, to E. Cohen, 22 Sep 1992, GWAPS NA 515.

[7] (S) GWAPS Database; Cont Hist Rpts, 37 FW(P), 10-16 Feb 1991 and 17-23 Feb 1991, AFHRA.

[8]The focus on leadership dated from the earliest Instant Thunder planning. The

When CENTAF intelligence's chief of targets, Lt. Col. F. L. Talbot, brought this situation to Glosson's attention on 13 February, the latter exploded: "If this is an indication that 'stress' is getting to you . . . and a break is needed–I can arrange."[9] Glosson indicated that he did not think Talbot's assessment was accurate. If it were "and you have waited until now to tell me–your departure is imminent."[10] Stress may have momentarily affected Glosson on the day his aircraft had struck the Al Firdos bunker. On that same day, Schwarzkopf announced not only that targets in Baghdad would require his approval but also that he wanted CENTAF to ensure that it had destroyed all NBC targets before the end of the war. Talbot's warning on the remaining bunkers may have seemed like piling on, and Glosson's steadily deteriorating relationship with CENTAF intelligence suffered another jolt. But in this case, Talbot had provided accurate information, as timely as it was uncomfortable. Although the Black Hole believed that Coalition aircraft had destroyed two targets on Talbot's list, Glosson's planners eventually included his other targets on a priority list for Schwarzkopf.[11]

Schwarzkopf directed Horner to plan a seventy-two-hour bombing effort against remaining NBC targets "in the event a cease-fire is declared and only seventy-two hours remain prior to implementation."[12] Since late January, Checkmate had also developed a war termination list of NBC targets and pressed their importance on Cheney as well as on the Black Hole. The Black Hole's first draft of a seventy-two-hour list included leadership targets in Baghdad, but Schwarzkopf's directive ignored that category in favor of NBC targets and other offensive capabilities such as Scuds. Although integrating Talbot's list of NBC targets, the Black Hole gave priority to research and production facilities instead of storage bunkers. While Talbot had more concern about weapons that Iraq could use against Coalition forces in this war, Schwarzkopf also wanted to eliminate Iraq's capabilities for making war in the future with such weapons.

---

renewal of this focus in mid-February 1991 can be followed in the Black Hole's daily master attack plans, GWAPS BH 1-25 through 1-32.

[9]Brig Gen Glosson's handwritten comments on memo, Lt Col F. L. Talbot, CENTAF Chief of Targets, subj: ATO Daily Prioritized Target Nominations, 13 Feb 1991.

[10]*Ibid.*

[11]The development of this list is discussed below. See also Lt Col Deptula's file on the "72 Hour Target List" in GWAPS BH Deptula 19A.

[12](S) Msg, CINCCENT to COMUSCENTAF, subj: 72-Hour Pre-Cease Fire Campaign guidance, 130850Z Feb 1991, GWAPS BH Deptula 19A.

When Bush declared a cease-fire on 27 February, he gave Coalition forces only a few hours notice. But the rapid progress of the ground offensive launched on 24 February had already given CENTAF ample warning that the war would soon end. By then, F-117s had hit NBC targets on a continually updated seventy-two-hour list for two weeks. They struck some in the final seventy-two hours, but bad weather made a surge impossible. In any case, Schwarzkopf at the end finally approved a few leadership targets in Baghdad; CENTAF grasped eagerly at an opportunity denied since Al Firdos had put much of downtown Baghdad off limits.[13]

Bad weather and continuing restrictions muffled the return to Baghdad. The war ended with Saddam's regime in control of Baghdad and Sunni-dominated central Iraq, if not the northern Kurdish and southern Shi^c^te regions. Whether bombing more office buildings or command bunkers would have made a major difference can not be known. Nor can we calculate whether more extensive bombing of NBC targets in the war's last two weeks made much difference in Iraq's long-term offensive capabilities. As usual, one of the constraints on air leaders and planners was the necessity of working within the bounds of imperfect intelligence about the enemy.

Attacking Nuclear, Biological, and Chemical Capabilities

The Black Hole headed its seventy-two-hour target list with the same target that had seemed the most important NBC target in Iraq since the onset of the crisis in August. The Baghdad Nuclear Research Center at Tuwaitha had been familiar to Americans at least since Israeli F-16s had attacked it in 1981. American F-16s struck it during the first week of the air campaign and F-117s visited it often. With approximately one hundred structures in the compound, the target warranted repeated visits. F-117s returned to this favorite target on February 18th, 19th, and 23rd. While closer to Baghdad than most NBC targets, Tuwaitha was ten miles south of the city–outside the area over which Schwarzkopf controlled target selection. Weather was a problem on the 18th and only four of ten F-117s dropped on the target, most of the others diverting to alternates; the next night four of six sorties scored hits. Shortly after midnight on

[13]See the section on attacking Saddam's regime in this chapter.

the 23rd, thirteen F-117s bombed Tuwaitha in good weather. At least eighteen of twenty-six bombs hit structures in the compound on the last raid against Iraq's premier nuclear target.[14]

By the end of the Gulf War, American intelligence had only begun to realize the extent of Iraq's nuclear weapons development beyond Tuwaitha. The Black Hole's final seventy-two-hour list on 28 February included seven more targets suspected of having a nuclear role. Although U.N. inspection teams eventually found three times that many nuclear facilities after the war, American intelligence had learned enough about several of the most important in time to subject them to bombing.[15]

One of the suspected nuclear facilities was just south of Baghdad, two miles closer to the city than Tuwaitha. The Black Hole raised this facility to number two on its priority list, right after Tuwaitha. On 22 February, five F-117s put all ten bombs on target. Perfect accuracy was unusual even for F-117s, and in northern Iraq aircraft lacking precision-bombing systems attempted to attack similar targets.[16]

Suspected nuclear targets in northern Iraq were within reach of Proven Force's F-111Es and F-16s in Turkey. Indeed the most frequently bombed target in all of northern Iraq was a suspected nuclear production facility twenty-five miles northwest of Mosul; after the war this site became known to U.N. inspectors as Al Jesira. Proven Force flew no less than twenty-five strikes against Jesira, two-thirds in the war's last two weeks. Usually four F-111Es hit the facility at night, or four F-16s in daytime. F-111Es each carried four 2,000-pound bombs or fourteen 500-pound bombs, while F-16s usually carried two 2,000-pound bombs or six 500-pound bombs. The cumulative weight of strikes against Jesira was considerable and damage to the facility was severe. But since Proven Force bombs remained unguided throughout the war, ten F-117s flew into northern Iraq on the night of 15-16 February and bombed several facilities, including Jesira; of five guided bombs which fell on Jesira, however, only two hit their targets.[17]

---

[14](S) Cont Hist Rpt, 37 FW(P), 17-23 Feb 1991, AFHRA.

[15]Rpts, UN Inspection Teams, GWAPS NA 2; (S) target list, CENTAF 72-hour, 28 Feb 1991, GWAPS BH 4-72.

[16](S) Cont Hist Rpts, 37 FW(P), 17-23 Feb 1991, AFHRA.

[17](S) Rpt, USEUCOM Bomb Damage Database, GWAPS CHST 54-1; (S) Cont Hist Rpt, 37 FW(P), 10-16 Feb 1991, AFHRA.

When a pair of F-117s returned to Mosul on 22 February, their luck was even worse. They dropped four laser-guided bombs on a suspected underground nuclear facility thirty miles north of Mosul, but all four missed. That was the only strike on this facility, because Proven Force lacked laser-guided bombs with penetrating warheads. At the war's end, the suspected underground facility ranked second on CENTAF's priority list possibly requiring a strike. However, since Black Hole planners had not yet received adequate bomb-damage assessment for the 22 February strike, they did not recommend a restrike.[18]

Six F-117s had better luck in western Iraq on 20 February; they attacked the Al Qaim uranium extraction facility near the Euphrates, where it crosses from Syria. The attacking aircraft dropped ten bombs with only two missing. This was the major F-117 mission to Qaim, and Proven Force's F-111Es and F-16s never attacked this target. But the F-111Fs of the 48th Fighter Wing continued to visit. Indeed, Qaim was the only target outside the KTO which F-111Fs attacked with any regularity during the last two weeks of the war; they conducted five separate precision strikes on Qaim, totalling twenty-three sorties. Other frequent visitors were Navy A-6s and FA-18s, which attacked Qaim from the Red Sea.[19]

Three nuclear facilities attacked during Desert Storm came to the attention of the Black Hole as rocket or missile development centers. Well before the end of the war, American intelligence revealed that the rocket facility at Tarmiya, twenty-five miles north of Baghdad, also probably performed nuclear work. A similar facility at Ash Sharqat, half way between Tikrit and Mosul, remained merely a rocket facility in American eyes; admittedly, the Iraqis may not have used it to perform the nuclear functions for which it had been designed. With less than a week left in the war, the Black Hole learned that structures adjacent to the rocket engine test facility at Musayyib, thirty-five miles southwest of

---

[18](S) Target list, CENTAF 72-hour, 28 Feb 1991, GWAPS BH 4-72.

[19](S) GWAPS Database; Cont Hist Rpt, 37 FW(P), 17-23 Feb 1991, AFHRA; (S) rpt, Frank Schwamb, et al., *Desert Storm Reconstruction Report, Vol II: Strike Warfare* (Washington: Center for Naval Analyses, 1991), App C, GWAPS NA 368.

Baghdad, might also be conducting nuclear work. Only after the war would the U.N. teams learn that the Iraqis had designated this facility, known as Al Atheer, to be the place where they would create their first nuclear bomb; in spring 1990, important parts of the Iraqi nuclear program had begun the move from Tuwaitha to Al Atheer.[20]

Coalition aircraft bombed the three rocket-nuclear facilities as rocket facilities before their nuclear connection was suspected. Proven Force F-16s and F-111Es ran a series of six raids on Ash Sharqat in mid-February, culminating with a strike by four F-117s on 16 February. Because the attack achieved a high level of damage and because intelligence did not suspect Ash Sharqat of nuclear activities, neither Proven Force nor the F-117s troubled it again. They paid subsequent visits to Tarmiya, however. When F-117s and B-52s bombed Tarmiya on 15 February, Coalition intelligence still regarded it as a rocket facility. But when F-117s returned on 23 February, it had been upgraded to a possible nuclear facility. On the latter occasion, two of four F-117s could not bomb Tarmiya due to bad weather. The weather continued to be a problem on 25 February, when less than half of sixteen Proven Force F-16s dropped their bombs. That night Proven Force intended to make up the difference by sending a flight of four F-111Es, but again weather caused trouble; this time the entire mission was scrubbed. Tarmiya ended the war as the top target on the Black Hole's priority list.[21]

The Black Hole found the bombing of Al Atheer more satisfactory. After learning about Al Atheer's nuclear role, CENTAF had only a few days to attack it before the war ended; unfortunately, during most of that time the weather was bad. But on 25 February two F-117s put three of

---

[20](S) Intvw, Wayne Thompson, GWAPS, with Lt Col David A. Deptula, Pentagon, 13 Nov 1992; rpt, International Atomic Energy Agency, Seventh Inspection in Iraq under UN Security Council Resolution 687, 14 Nov 1991, GWAPS NA 3. A target photo transmitted to the Black Hole by CENTCOM intelligence on 23 February 1991 indicated the suspected nuclear activity of the facility (later known to the UN inspection teams as Al Atheer) adjacent to the Musayyib rocket motor test facility.

[21](S) Target list, CENTAF 72-hour, 28 Feb 1991, GWAPS BH 4-72; GWAPS Database; (S) rpt, HQ USEUCOM. Proven Force BDA Database, GWAPS CHST 54-1; (S) Cont Hist Rpts, 37 FW(P), 10-16 Feb 1991, 17-23 Feb 1991, 24 Feb-2 Mar 1991, AFHRA.

four bombs on the facility. Just as the war was ending the weather cleared over Musayyib, and not long after midnight on 28 February, nine F-117s attacked the rocket engine test facility and the adjacent Al Atheer nuclear facility–which the Black Hole still referred to as the Musayyib missile development facility. At least seven bombs appear to have hit Al Atheer targets, and the Black Hole judged its bombing objectives achieved for the entire Musayyib-Al Atheer complex. Had the Black Hole known more about Al Atheer's central importance in Iraq's nuclear weapons development program, the planners might not have been so comfortable with the level of damage.[22]

American intelligence's picture of the enemy's development of chemical and biological weapons was somewhat clearer (if no more certain) than the nuclear picture. Intelligence reported that the principal research and production facility for biological weapons was at Salman Pak on the Tigris, a dozen miles southeast of Baghdad. Three other biological production facilities were in the Baghdad area–two at Abu Ghurayb west of the city and one at Taji north of the city. In February, intelligence found evidence of another biological production facility at Latifiya, fifteen miles south of the capital. While it was possible that Salman Pak might also be producing chemical weapons, the principal center for that business was at Samarra, on the Tigris fifty miles north of Baghdad. Three facilities near Habbaniya (thirty-five miles west of Baghdad) provided precursor chemicals used by Samarra to produce weapons.[23]

Coalition aircraft had attacked all known biological and chemical production facilities by mid-February with considerable success. After two strikes on the suspected biological facility at Latifiya, intelligence that the Iraqis were removing crates from the ruins prompted a third strike. On 19 February, a pair of F-117s bombed this facility as part of a larger attack on the neighboring solid propellant factory; other nearby factories produced liquid propellant, Scuds, and explosives. Two of four bombs guided to the biological target, and the Black Hole crossed the site off their list together with the solid propellant plant, which absorbed fourteen hits.[24]

---

[22](S) Intvw, Thompson with Deptula, 13 Nov 1992; (S) Cont Hist Rpt, 37 FW(P), 24 Feb-2 Mar 1991, AFHRA; IAEA rpt, 14 Nov 1991, GWAPS NA 3.

[23]For two HQ USAF Checkmate files on chemical and biological weapons in Iraq, see GWAPS CHSH 100 and CHST 18.

[24](S) Memo, Rear Adm McConnell, DIA, to Brig Gen Leide, CENTCOM, subj: BW Activity, 20 Feb 1991, GWAPS BH Deptula 19b; (S) Cont Hist Rpt, 37 FW(P), 17-23 Feb 1991, AFHRA.

Whether any biological weapons had actually been in the bombed facilities is not known. The only indication that such might have been the case was an article in the Egyptian press in early February. According to this article, which stimulated a subsequent article in the Soviet press, an attack on a biological weapons facility near Baghdad had led to the death of fifty guards from a rapidly progressing disease that spread to Baghdad. No more, however, has been heard of this case.[25]

There was always the possibility that Iraqis would move biological and chemical weapons development and storage to other locations. CENTAF did a thorough job on the designated targets, with the major exception of eight chemical storage bunkers at Samarra.[26] To some degree this omission was a consequence of the focus on production facilities. When F-117s attacked Samarra for the last two times on 23 and 24 February, they again struck the production buildings and left storage bunkers untouched.[27]

Nevertheless, CENTAF had made a successful effort to eliminate the other suspected chemical and biological bunkers. Of thirty suspected chemical storage bunkers, air attacks hit twenty-three and destroyed seventeen. Of twenty-one suspected biological bunkers, bombers destroyed nineteen; intelligence discovered the remaining two too late to bomb. The slightly better record against biological bunkers perhaps reflected greater concern over biological weapons. There was also more reason to believe that bunkers labeled biological might actually contain most of Iraq's biological weapons.[28] The problem with trying to identify facilities housing chemical weapons was that the Iraqis could keep such weapons in "virtually any secure building or bunker."[29] According to experts, there were more than three thousand storage structures in Iraq and even if one limited the target set to bunkers, that left approximately eight hundred targets.[30]

---

[25]Msg, FBIS London to FBIS Reston, subj: Fifty Die After Air Raid, 101738Z Feb 1991, GWAPS CHST 18-10.

[26]Seven of these remained intact at the end of the war.

[27](S) Rpt, DIA Final BDA Status, 14 Mar 1991, GWAPS CHST 49-1.

[28](S) *Ibid.*

[29](S) *Ibid.*

[30](S) Imagery Analysis Rpt, GWAPS CHSH 100-3.

While intelligence believed that only one bunker in northern Iraq held biological weapons, the Iraqis had located eight chemical bunkers (of the thirty suspected) near the cities of Kirkuk and Qayyara. Since American planes based in Turkey lacked precision-bombing capability, they could do little more from medium altitude than limit access by scattering mines around the bunkers. Ten F-117s came north to destroy most of those bunkers on 11 February, the very day that dedication of the F-111Fs to "tank plinking" created a demand for Proven Force's F-111Es and F-16s to fly further south and help F-117s in central Iraq.[31]

Joint Task Force "Proven Force" and B-52s

F-117s attacked northern Iraq only occasionally. Most bombing in that region came from air force aircraft based in Turkey and England. Not surprisingly, American strike aircraft north and west of Iraq bombed targets in northern Iraq. In the case of Proven Force's eighteen F-111Es and thirty-six F-16s, located at Incirlik air base in Turkey, range limitations discouraged any inclination to use those aircraft in the KTO. Eight B-52s at RAF Fairford in England could not receive air tasking orders from Riyadh via the Computer Assisted Force Management System (CAFMS). Consequently, folding those B-52s into Saudi-based packages was too cumbersome.[32]

When Moron Air Base, Spain, got CAFMS in mid-February, the twenty-two B-52s there were able to bomb Iraqi ground forces in the KTO for the first time in the war. During the early weeks of the war Moron had only ten B-52s, all restricted to missions in northern Iraq. At the same time that Moron got CAFMS and more bombers, the eight B-52s newly arrived at RAF Fairford in Great Britain took over Moron's old task of bombing northern Iraq. Like Moron's B-52s, the Fairford "Buffs" looked to Proven Force for targets and support packages.[33]

---

[31](S) Cont Hist Rpt, 37 FW(P), 10-16 Feb 1991, AFHRA.

[32](S) Hist, SAC, 1990, AFHRA.

[33](S) *Ibid.*

In addition to F-111E and F-16 strike aircraft, Proven Force had "Wild Weasels" (F-4Gs and F-16s) for SAM suppression; EF-111s for radar jamming and Compass Call EC-130s for communications jamming; RC-135s (based in Greece) for electronic intelligence; E-3s and F-15Cs for protection against Iraqi fighters; KC-135s for refueling; and helicopters to rescue downed aircrew. This composite force built its own strike packages without assistance from CENTAF. Fairford B-52s were scheduled to hit targets in northern Iraq when Proven Force's support aircraft were available. Usually a cell of four B-52s would share the support package built for nightly strikes by F-111Es. Proven Force also ran several F-16 strikes during each period of daylight, with the bigger ones employing as many as twenty F-16s.[34]

The independence of Proven Force's operations reminded some older airmen of arrangements used in attacking North Vietnam two decades earlier, when Air Force and Navy had divided the enemy's country into seven route packages–each bombed by one service or the other. Such a compromise had never satisfied believers in unity of command, including Horner and Glosson who had flown fighter bombers into North Vietnam. The single air tasking order (ATO) had aimed to avoid route packages, but CENTAF made an exception in the case of Proven Force, which belonged to United States Air Forces in Europe (USAFE). Although Proven Force aircraft came under Horner's operational control, geography dictated a de facto route package that would have been needlessly doctrinaire to oppose.[35]

While its sorties were in CENTAF's daily Master Attack Plan, Proven Force built support packages without formal coordination and issued its own ATO. Underlying this informality were frequent communications between the composite wing commander, Brig. Gen. Lee A. Downer, and two of CENTAF's air division commanders, Glosson and Profitt; the latter had been a major proponent of Proven Force before leaving Germany in December 1990 to replace Henry as Horner's electronic combat commander. So long as Proven Force stayed north of the 35th parallel, there was little need to coordinate with anyone other than the Fairford B-52s–except when F-117s attacked targets in the north.[36]

---

[34](S) Hist, Joint Task Force Proven Force, by CMSgt Jerome L. Schroeder, and SMSgt Thomas L. Raab, HQ USAFE, Dec 1991, AFHRA.

[35](S) Intvws, Center for Air Force History, with Lt Gen Horner, 4 Mar 1992, and Maj Gen Glosson, 12 Dec 1991.

[36](S) Intvw, GWAPS with Brig Gen Downer, Ramstein AB, Germany, 30 Apr 1992. For the Black Hole's role in Proven force targeting, see (S) planning binder, "Northern Iraqi Target Base," GWAPS BH 7-95.

The Black Hole assigned targets to Proven Force (often targets recommended by Proven Force itself), but the latter decided when to attack and with which aircraft. These local decisions, based partly on intelligence from USAFE headquarters at Ramstein Air Base in Germany, went into CENTAF's Master Attack Plans. Since targets in northern Iraq received lower priority for imagery than those in the KTO or central Iraq, Proven Force depended heavily on its own reconnaissance aircraft for target photography. Six RF-4Cs had arrived at Incirlik on 3 February; by the end of the war, they had flown more than a hundred sorties in northern Iraq.[37]

Maj. Gen. James L. Jamerson, who commanded Proven Force, adopted an air campaign plan with phases different from those used by CENTCOM. He broke the first CENTCOM phase in two and replaced phases two and three with a phase dedicated to interdiction. Jamerson's first phase was an attack on command, control, and communications nodes. His second phase involved targeting weapons production and storage, electricity, oil, airfields, and aircraft. Jamerson never got to execute his third phase, interdiction of enemy bridges and troops in northern Iraq. Horner did not want to expend much effort interdicting those Iraqi forces unless they started to move south. The Iraqis stayed put, and consequently even the Republican Guards in northern Iraq passed through the air campaign mostly unscathed. Those forces then supported Saddam against civil unrest following the Gulf War.[38]

As with CENTCOM's first three overlapping phases, Proven Force's first two phases merged. There was, however, something of a north to south progression in the bombing. The final southward push was in response to CENTAF's call in mid-February for help in attacking targets below the thirty-fifth parallel. Before that, however, Proven Force's lack of stealth and precision had caused Jamerson to think in terms of rolling back Iraqi defenses from north to south rather than paralyzing the enemy's defenses at the outset. For some air defense targets, like the sector operations center at Kirkuk, he needed help from CENTAF's F-117s.[39]

---

[37](S) Hist, Joint Task Force Proven Force, AFHRA.

[38](S) Intvw, GWAPS with Brig Gen Downer, Ramstein AB, 30 Apr 1992; (S) Hist, Joint Task Force Proven Force, AFHRA.

[39](S) Rpt, 12 TFS, "Daylight Tactical Air Combat Operations in Northern Iraq," 1 Jun 1991, GWAPS NA 516; (S) intvw, CMSgt Jerome E. Schroeder with Maj Gen James L. Jamerson, Incirlik AB, Turkey, 27 Mar 1991.

Proven Force's lack of precision flowed from deployment of all available precision attack aircraft in Europe to Saudi Arabia before establishment of Proven Force at the beginning of the air campaign. Although such a force had been under consideration for months, few had believed that Turkey would permit the use of Incirlik to launch air raids against Iraq. There were limits to Turkey's cooperation, but they mostly affected special operations forces under Jamerson's command; the Turks would not let him insert such forces into Iraq except to rescue downed aircrew. As a consequence, special operations forces could not provide laser designation from the ground, which in some cases would have enabled Jamerson's aircraft to drop laser-guided bombs. Jamerson did request F-4E aircraft with laser designation pods from Clark Air Base in the Philippines, but while the planes arrived before the end of the war, the pods did not.[40]

Jamerson and Downer made a number of other attempts to improve the precision of Proven Force bombing. Like CENTAF, they did not risk going to low altitude for better accuracy. But three of Downer's F-111Es used Global Positioning System receivers to improve navigation and to act as pathfinders for other F-111Es. Downer commented after the war that this increased accuracy by "a hundred per cent."[41] Still, Proven Force's only precision weapons were HARMs, Shrikes, and Mavericks carried by "Wild Weasel" F-4Gs and F-16s. Despite their small warhead designed for use against tanks, Mavericks were useful against other targets besides SAM sites, including an electric power plant and an aircraft on the ground. Such targets were unusual, however, and Proven Force expended only fifty-five Mavericks.[42]

A major focus of Proven Force attacks during much of the war was the military research and development complex located near the Tigris north of Mosul. In addition to suspected nuclear production facilities already discussed, there was a missile plant, another development facility whose purpose had yet to be discovered, a SAM support facility, and a signals intercept station. Day after day, Proven Force attacked these targets around the clock in an area that pilots took to calling "Happy Valley," where unusually heavy air defenses sparkled harmlessly below them. On 13 February, for example, four F-16s dropped a total of twenty-four 500-pound bombs on the signals intercept station with four

---

[40](S) Hist, Joint Task Force Proven Force, AFHRA.

[41](S) Intvw, GWAPS with Brig Gen Downer, Ramstein AB, 30 Apr 1992.

[42](S) Hist, Joint Task Force Proven Force, AFHRA.

hits on the main building and several secondary explosions. Meanwhile, four other F-16s attacked the nuclear production facility with eight 2,000-pound bombs, three of which hit one building; this attack was unusually accurate. The next day, Proven Force sent eight F-16s against the nuclear production facility, followed by four F-111Es that night. Another four F-111Es led four B-52s in a raid on the missile production facility to conclude two typical days of air campaigning in "Happy Valley."[43]

While giving "Happy Valley" more attention, Proven Force got more satisfaction from its single raid on Iraq's biggest oil refinery at Bayji on the Tigris 100 miles south of Mosul. Proven Force's strike did not occur until after other Coalition planes had already raided the target. Six Tomahawk cruise missiles hit Bayji on 22 January. Two weeks later, on 7, 8, and 9 February, a total of twenty-four British Tornados came just north of the thirty-fifth parallel with a hundred 1,000-pound unguided bombs and eight laser-guided bombs. On 8 February, six B-52s joined the attack and dropped nearly three hundred 750-pound bombs.[44]

Jamerson then gave the go ahead for Proven Force aircraft to join in bombing Bayji. Although previous attacks had left at least a dozen storage tanks already destroyed or burning, not to mention many pipeline cuts, Proven Force sent most of its fighters. Twenty F-16s hit the refinery on the morning of 9 February, followed by sixteen F-16s in the afternoon, and six F-111Es in the evening. They dropped nearly a hundred 2,000 pound bombs with spectacular results. A big black mushroom cloud rose over burning oil tanks, and weeks passed before the smoke cleared. In addition to destroying approximately forty storage tanks, Proven Force severely damaged two cracking towers. Ever since Checkmate's original Instant Thunder plan, cracking towers had been off limits, because their destruction would make refinery repair after the war more difficult. As Downer later recalled, CENTAF told Proven Force to "knock it off" and Proven Force ceased to bomb oil targets.[45]

---

[43](S) Rpt, HQ USEUCOM, Proven Force BDA, 4 Apr 1991, GWAPS CHST 54; (S) rpt, 612 TFSq, "Daylight Tactical Air Combat Operations in Northern Iraq," Jun 1991, GWAPS NA 516.

[44](S)Rpt, RAF sortie data, GWAPS NA 515; (S) intvw, CMsgt Jerome E. Schroeder with Maj Gen James Jamerson, Ramstein AB, 27 Mar 1991; (S) intvw, GWAPS with Brig Gen Downer, Ramstein AB, 30 Apr 1992.

[45](S) Intvw, GWAPS with Brig Gen Downer, Ramstein AB, 30 Apr 1992. See also (S)rpt, HQ USEUCOM, Proven Force BDA, 4 Apr 1991, GWAPS CHST 54.

CENTAF's reaction could not dim Proven Force's pride in so smokey a triumph, but this kind of dramatic result was both rare and deceptive. It was likely that Iraq had enough surviving fuel and lubricants in the KTO to render Bayji unimportant for months to come. On the other hand, the suspected research and development facilities in "Happy Valley" might really have held keys to Iraq's development of special weapons, including nuclear ones. Nevertheless, it was the Bayji raids that aircrews remembered with greatest pleasure.

The Bayji raids brought Proven Force to the thirty-fifth parallel, the southern edge of its route package. A few days later, CENTAF told the Incirlik F-111Es and F-16s to attack further south to help F-117s bomb central Iraq. The principal target area that the Black Hole had in mind was the Taji military complex; that facility surrounded an airfield on the northern outskirts of Baghdad, approximately fifteen miles north of the downtown area. On the first night of the campaign, an F-117 had struck the Taji air defense sector operations center there, but the number of targets there far exceeded available F-117 sorties. Hundreds of machine shops, bunkers, warehouses, and sheds were packed with military equipment in storage or under repair. Taji's components included air and ammunition depots; missile, tank, artillery, and aircraft engine repair facilities; as well as barracks for three brigades. There was also a steel fabrication plant whose products intelligence believed included items used in making nuclear weapons.[46]

CENTAF's guidance for Proven Force attacks on Taji was even more basic than usual. Glosson told Downer to leave nothing at Taji standing "taller than a taxi light."[47] During the last two weeks of the war, thirteen Proven Force strike packages–totalling approximately 140 F-111E and F-16 sorties–struck these facilities. While the mission was straightforward, Proven Force now had to submit its aircraft to more detailed control by CENTAF. Not only were they operating in the middle of CENTAF's territory, but they were using CENTAF support packages. Since Proven Force could not cross Syria, their missions against targets in central Iraq were a third longer than necessary. But at less than 700 miles each way, Proven Force had less distance to cover than F-117s coming from the southern end of Saudi Arabia.[48]

---

[46](S) Planning binder, "Taji Military Complex," GWAPS BH 7-92.

[47](S) Downer's recollection in intvw with GWAPS, Ramstein AB, 30 Apr 1992.

[48](S) Hist, Joint Task Force Proven Force, AFHRA; (S) rpt, HQ USEUCOM, Proven Force BDA, 4 Apr 1991, GWAPS CHST 54.

Fairford B-52s could not follow Proven Force to Taji, because Fairford lacked the computer link of the Computer Aided Force Management System to the ATO system. Instead, bombing Taji became the favorite recreation for B-52s whose normal targets were Iraqi positions in the KTO. The theater-based B-52s took the lead in forming packages with their more distant partners in Spain (nearly three thousand miles away) and Diego Garcia (more than three thousand miles away). About seventy B-52 sorties struck Taji (as many as a dozen at a time) and dropped more than 3,000 bombs. Taji was the sort of complex for which area bombing seemed particularly well suited, and while no towering cloud of black smoke rewarded the attackers, there was much destruction.[49]

Attacking Saddam's Regime

Approximately twenty miles separated North Taji from Taji. Except for their military affiliation, the two places were very different and posed dissimilar targeting problems. Instead of hundreds of warehouses, North Taji had two big, tough bunkers. These command bunkers were so hard that they had thus far thwarted the F-117's best penetrating bomb, the 2,000-pound GBU-27. Even when Schwarzkopf kept F-117s from attacking leadership targets in downtown Baghdad, the North Taji bunkers remained fair game. But CENTAF did not have a weapon that could do the job.[50]

Tactical Air Command and the air staff wrestled with this problem throughout the air campaign. Possible solutions included dropping a series of as many as four 2000-pound bombs in quick succession on the same aimpoint to dig through perhaps thirty feet of concrete slabs, crushed rock,and soil. This idea was never tried, but CENTAF did request immediate development of a new bomb, utilizing off-the-shelf technology. Normally a new bomb would have taken years to develop. Under the pressure of war, the U.S. weapons development community produced four GBU-28s in a month. Their bodies were at one time artillery gun barrels, and each weighed nearly 5,000 pounds. They went to Nevada for testing. The first GBU-28 missed a concrete slab but penetrated deeply into the soil. The second penetrated concrete without breaking up. The remaining two GBU-28s were flown to Taif, Saudi Arabia, and on the last night of the war a pair of F-111Fs dropped them on one of the bunkers at North Taji. GBU-28 number three buried itself harmlessly in the desert, but the fourth penetrated the bunker.[51]

---

[49](S) Hist, SAC, 1990, AFHRA; (S) rpt, HQ SAC Plans and Resources, *B-52 Desert Storm Bombing Survey*, 15 Dec 1991.

[50](S) Planning binder, "Taji Military Complex," GWAPS BH 7-92.

[51](S) Background paper, Capt Bernier, TAC, 9 May 1991; (S) msg, Vice Cmdr TAC to SAF/AQ, subj: Desert Storm Deep Hardened Target Penetration Test, 191803Z, Feb 1991, both in GWAPS NA 334. See also (S) rpt, SAF/AQ, Deep Penetration Munitions Study, 29 Jan 1991, GWAPS CHST 16-1.

More GBU-28s were in production when time ran out in Iraq. Except for the other bunker at North Taji, one at Abu Ghurayb west of Baghdad, and possibly one downtown, no Iraqi bunker was so strong that only a GBU-28 (and not a GBU-27) could penetrate it.[52] During the last week, the Abu Ghurayb bunker once again proved impervious to a GBU-27. Given the strength of these bunkers, the Black Hole had reason to think that they might hold senior Iraqi leaders, even Saddam. Although Saddam's death was a bonus hoped for rather than a necessity planned, Coalition aircraft attacked targets associated with him from the beginning to the end of the campaign.[53]

Most leadership targets were in Baghdad and off limits for at least a week after Al Firdos, but several like the bunkers at North Taji and Abu Ghurayb were outside the city. While intelligence had pinpointed a large residence at Abu Ghurayb as Saddam's, CENTAF bombed other residences whose connection with Saddam was only suspected. Late in the war, for example, F-117s bombed a suspected residence across the Tigris from the Taji complex; early in the war they bombed another one at Abu Al Jahish farther up the Tigris, five miles north of the Bayji refinery.[54]

Even more numerous and elusive than Saddam's fixed residences were his conference vehicles. In the 1980s Iraq had purchased twenty-four motor homes (or "recreational vehicles") from an American company, the Bluebird Wanderlodge Company. On at least one occasion he had put his staff on board this fleet and taken them into the desert for a conference away from normal distractions. One week into the air campaign, Saddam appeared on American television from inside one of the conference vehicles. Toward the end of the war, American intelligence discovered a Bluebird Wanderlodge at a motor pool near Qaim in western Iraq. Before dawn on 22 February, a pair of F-111Fs fresh from

---

[54](S) The possible exception in Baghdad was the bunker under the New Presidential Palace. Steel beams in the roof of the building could knock a GBU-27 off course before it could reach the bunker, but a bomb entering through a side portico might penetrate. See memo, Checkmate to CENTAF/XX (Black Hole), subj: Baghdad New Presidential Palace, 242300Z Feb 1991, GWAPS CHST 14-35.

[55]On the relationship between CENTAF planning and the possible death of Saddam, see the GWAPS Planning report.

[56](S) Cont His Rpts, 37 FW(P), AFHRA.

"plinking" tanks in the KTO, flew north to Qaim and used 500-pound laser-guided bombs to plink the Bluebird (which the Americans usually referred to as a command "Winnebago," the name of a more famous recreational vehicle). Meanwhile, another pair of F-111Fs with 2,000-pound laser-guided bombs attacked a nearby command bunker.[55]

Whatever damage these scattered attacks on places associated with Saddam achieved, his survival as well as the survival of his regime put a premium on severing communications between the regime and its forces–particularly ground forces in the KTO and mobile Scud launchers. CENTAF planners assumed that Saddam and his senior subordinates spent most of their time in Baghdad; possibly they moved from house to house in residential neighborhoods where American bombs never fell. Although CENTAF bombed key nodes in the national telephone system at the outset of the war, the fact that the Iraqis made little use of radio communications indicated that they were probably still using land lines, however cumbersome the switching and routing of calls.[56]

Bombing the Rasheed Hotel remained out of the question, but the Black Hole continued to hope for permission to bomb other Baghdad targets. For about a week after Al Firdos, Schwarzkopf made it plain that he would not (or could not) approve most targets in downtown Baghdad. Except for a couple of strikes on the city's military airfields, F-117 attacks stayed outside the city limits. Black Hole planners even quit asking for permission to bomb downtown targets, while their Checkmate allies did what they could.[57]

---

[55](S) Msgs, 48 TFW to CENTAF, subj: Misrep, mission 3467-68A, 220645Z,Feb 1991; mission 3461-62A, 220650Z,Feb 1991, both in GWAPS Database. See also (S/NF) memo, James K. Swanson, Defense Technology Security Administration, to Deputy Under Secretary of Defense for Trade Security Policy, 29 Jan 1991, GWAPS CHST 15-17; (S/NF) msg, SSO Robins to SSO DIA, subj: Possible Use of US Built Motorhome by Saddam Hussein and Iraqi General Staff, 270456Z, Jan 1991, GWAPS CHST 15-28; (S) notes, TSgt Scott Saluda, CENTAF TACC, 22 Feb 1991, AFHRA.

[56]Such a supposition proved correct, because as soon as the war against the Coalition was over the Iraqis extensively used their radios in putting down the Shiʿte and Kurdish rebellions.

[57](S) Intvw, Wayne Thompson, GWAPS, with Lt Col David A. Deptula, Pentagon, 26 Aug 1991.

On the morning of 15 February, when Warden learned that no F-117s would attack Baghdad that night for the first time since the beginning of the war, he took his objections to Secretary of the Air Force Donald Rice; Warden also sent a subordinate to convey his complaint to Cheney's staff. Four days later, Rice brought Cheney into Checkmate for the third time since the beginning of the air campaign. Warden argued in favor of striking internal security facilities in Baghdad with F-117s and Tomahawk cruise missiles.[58]

Deptula then drafted a request for permission to attack six targets in Baghdad: the regional headquarters of the Iraqi Intelligence Service (possibly the new national headquarters of this service, the regime's principal agency for controlling its dissidents through informants, surveillance, and torture), the headquarters of the Special Security Service (the guardians of Iraq's leaders), that of the Ministry of Strategic Industry and Planning (responsible for nuclear, biological, and chemical weapons development), the suspected new operating location of the Ministry of Defense in a building adjacent to the Ministry of Petroleum, the Republican Guard headquarters, and the headquarters of the Ministry of Military Industry. Deptula argued that destruction of these targets might "further cripple the Saddam regime such that even with cessation of hostilities he may become impotent and subject to replacement."[59]

Schwarzkopf approved the first two targets on CENTAF's list and for a time approved the Republican Guard headquarters as well. The Black Hole made the most of this opportunity by scheduling relatively heavy F-117 raids against the available targets. The Special Security Service and the Iraqi Intelligence Service regional headquarters would suffer more than the one or two bombs dropped in earlier raids. Only after the war would the U.S. learn that Iraq kept its American prisoners in the Intelligence Service's regional headquarters; fortunately, none were hurt in the attack. Schwarzkopf canceled a strike on Republican Guard headquarters after a squabble within the American intelligence community

---

[58] (S) Thompson notes, 15, 19 and 21 Feb 1991.

[59] Draft memo, Lt Col Deptula for Lt Gen Horner to Gen Schwarzkopf, subj: Air Strategy, 21 Feb 1991, GWAPS BH Deptula 19C.

about whether that headquarters had moved or whether it had already been bombed.[60]

In the face of these objections to target nominations of 21 February, the Black Hole took a different approach. Instead of placing priority on the regime itself, the Black Hole recommended bombing three notorious symbols of the regime: Ba'th Party Headquarters, an enormous statue of Saddam more than 60 feet tall, and an even more enormous pair of victory arches commemorating the Iran-Iraq War; the last were massive bronze magnifications of Saddam's forearms, holding swords which cross some 150 feet above a broad avenue. Schwarzkopf liked all three targets, and he was especially enthusiastic about bombing Saddam's statue. But targeting the statue and the arches ran into objections from army lawyers both in Riyadh and in Washington.[61]

Military lawyers performed two important services for the air campaign: they helped the campaign to conform with international law and they helped to prevent excessive restrictions based upon misreadings of international law. But when Black Hole planners had proposed an attack on Saddam's monuments earlier in Desert Storm, an Air Force lawyer at Tactical Air Command headquarters had objected to bombing such targets as cultural monuments. Throughout the war, CENTAF had scrupulously avoided genuine cultural monuments like the ziggurat at Ur–even when the Iraqis parked fighter aircraft nearby to gain protection. But to regard Saddam's propaganda symbols as "cultural monuments"

---

[60](S) Thompson notes, 22-24 Feb 1991; (S) Cont Hist Rpts, 37 FW(P), 17-23 Feb 1991, 24 Feb - 2 Mar 1991, AFHRA; memo, Lt Cmdr Gonzalez to Brig Gen Glosson, subj: TLAM Tasking Against Ministry of Petroleum, 25 Feb 1991, GWAPS BH Deptula 19C.

[61]The Black Hole's target recommendations to Schwarzkopf for this period are in GWAPS BH Deptula 19C. On Schwarzkopf's views, see his *Hero*, esp pp 457 and 468. On the statue, see the Checkmate target file, GWAPS CIT 390. On the victory arches, see Samir al-Khalil, *The Monument: Art, Vulgarity and Responsibility in Iraq* (Berkeley, 1991).

was akin to regarding Hitler's Nuremberg parade grounds in a similar light. CENTAF was certainly correct to believe that Saddam's propaganda symbols were legitimate targets.[62]

Military lawyers felt Saddam's propaganda symbols were protected by international law as "cultural monuments."

While Tactical Air Command's legal advice was simply wrong on this matter, Army lawyers confused matters by raising objections which had little to do with the legality of targets. They wished to minimize bombing in Baghdad to avoid further incidents like Al Firdos. They argued that a psychological target like Saddam's statue might have contributed to the Coalition air campaign early in the war, but with the conflict nearly over such attacks carried unnecessary risks. Whatever the merits of the lawyers' arguments, their special position gave legal weight to their views. When military lawyers advise against action for whatever reason, politicians and generals tend to think in terms of legality. On 25 February, after approving raids on the statue and arches, Powell asked

[62](S) Thompson notes, 9 Feb 1991.

Schwarzkopf to hold up on the strikes; they were never again approved as targets.[63] After the war, Horner remained under the misconception that the strike on Saddam's statue had been prohibited by international law.[64]

An Air Force lawyer in Washington suggested that CENTAF's recommendation of Saddam's statue as a target demonstrated the need for more thorough legal screening of targets.[65] Such conclusions condoned rather than corrected the air campaign's failure to conduct psychological operations against Baghdad. While dropping leaflets in the KTO had stimulated desertions, Schwarzkopf's staff vetoed dropping leaflets on Baghdad–where they might encourage rebellion against Saddam's regime. CENTCOM's rationale was a mixture of deference to perceived Saudi uneasiness about seeking democratic upheaval in the Arab world along with the notion that encouraging the collapse of an enemy government at war was somehow illegal.[66]

CENTAF's three symbolic targets in Baghdad boiled down to one, Ba^cth Party Headquarters, only lightly damaged by Tomahawk warheads on the campaign's first night and hit again by F-117s in mid-February. The Black Hole planned the biggest F-117 raid of the war against this single target, thirty-two F-117s over the night of 25-26 February. But the weather again failed to cooperate. For the first time in the war, it kept the F-117s from bombing anything for an entire night and reduced their effort on the following evening to dropping a few bombs outside Baghdad.[67]

Bad weather interfered just as the F-117 wing was transitioning into its surge schedule. In place of a normal schedule of three nighttime waves of ten sorties each, the wing had aimed to send two waves of

---

[63]Schwarzkopf, *Hero*, pp 457 and 468.

[64]*Air Force Times*, 8 Mar 1991.

[65]Suggestion, JULLS 21335-07500 (00006), HQ USAF/JACM.

[66](S) Thompson notes, 24 Feb 1991.

[67](S) Cont Hist Rpt, 37 FW(P), 24 Feb - 2 Mar 1991, AFHRA.

thirty-two sorties each. That meant F-117s must fly two long six-hour sorties in a single night. The first wave had to finish its work around midnight so that the wing could turn the aircraft and send them back for a strike before dawn. In the end, it managed to fly only one of these two-wave nights before weather ended the surge.[68]

F-117s finally returned to Baghdad on the night of 27-28 February. By then the ground war's rapid progress signaled that a cease-fire could come at any time. The F-117 wing flew a three-wave schedule, with a beefed-up first wave of twenty aircraft; after announcement of the impending cease-fire, the third wave was cancelled. The Black Hole reduced the size of the raid on Baᶜth Party Headquarters to conform to this schedule and to make F-117 sorties available for other pressing targets, including the suspected nuclear facility at Al Musayyib (Al Atheer) and two transport aircraft at Baghdad's Muthena Airfield (planners suspected that Saddam might try to leave Baghdad). Still, CENTAF sent sixteen F-117s which did considerable damage to the Baᶜth Party Headquarters. This attack also demolished a statue in front of the building - a statue possibly of Saddam, but probably of a Baᶜth Party founder. By this time, CENTAF planners were happy just to eliminate any symbol of the regime.[69]

Conclusion

The air campaign had begun only six weeks earlier in front of a worldwide television audience fascinated by the bombing of Baghdad. When the last bombs fell on one of the original Baghdad targets, the television audience had moved on to the ground war in Kuwait and southern Iraq. Coalition air forces had long since led the shift in focus to the KTO, but continued efforts in central and northern Iraq by a few aircraft, including the exceptionally capable F-117s, testified that the Coalition wanted to do more than evict Iraqi forces from Kuwait. If the attacks on Saddam's regime and its weapons of mass destruction did not achieve complete success, they at least worked toward a worthy end–an Iraq less threatening to its neighbors and the world's oil supply.

---

[68] (S) Cont Hist Rpts, 37 FW(P), 17-23 Feb 1991, 24 Feb - 2 Mar 1991, AFHRA.

[69] The Black Hole planning sheets for the Baᶜth Party Headquarters raid are in GWAPS BH Deptula 21D. Bomb-damage photos are in GWAPS CIT 291.

6

Air Against Iraq's Ground Forces

The most opaque and controversial portion of the air campaign against Iraq was the effort against the enemy's ground forces. That effort began on day one and continued to the end of the war. On it rested Coalition hopes that a ground campaign, if necessary, would result in few casualties. In fact, the eventual ground war resulted in Coalition casualties far below the most optimistic prewar estimates. But the question remains as to the effectiveness of air attacks against Iraqi ground forces throughout the KTO. This chapter will evaluate the conduct of Coalition air operations focused against Iraq's field army in the KTO before the hopefully will contribute to an understanding of the larger picture.

In the past, air forces have contributed significantly to destruction of enemy ground forces and to ground campaigns.[1] But never has an air force found itself in the position of "preparing the battlefield" to the extent that ground commanders counted on air power being able to achieve a 50-percent level of destruction of the enemy's equipment. What is remarkable about the prewar period is the alacrity with which senior army commanders, including Schwarzkopf, assigned air power the mission of taking Iraqi military forces down by half; what is perhaps even more surprising was the willingness of air commanders to accept this charge.

[1]The application of Allied air power against German ground forces in Normandy is a case in point. From the opening of that campaign with Allied attempts to isolate the battlefield in northwestern France by attacks on the French railroad system to the devastating attacks on German panzer and infantry forces as they escaped the Faliase pocket, air power played a crucial role in the Battle of France in summer 1944. Yet, whatever the similarities between 1944 and 1991, there is no comparison between the sustained weight of effort involved in the two campaigns; Desert Storm represented a quantum leap in technological sophistication and capability in comparison to any previous air campaign against enemy ground forces.

In the end, much of the air effort centered on attacking the equipment of the Iraqi military in the KTO. Air attacks aimed at destroying or damaging measurable, quantifiable percentages of the Iraqi Army's tanks, armored personnel carriers, and artillery pieces. Ironically, however, when the war was over, many POWs would suggest that the B-52s, the most inaccurate and least precise platform in the Coalition inventory, had had the greatest impact on their morale.[2]

The Iraqi Army: Dispositions and Strategy in the KTO

Earlier, this study suggested the general framework of Iraq's strategy and Saddam's assessment of his opponents.[3] For our purposes, we need to recall that framework to understand Iraqi intentions in deploying their ground forces in the KTO. The Iraqis had followed their invasion of Kuwait with a move of their Republican Guard formations up to the frontier into Saudi Arabia.[4] When this attempt to intimidate the Saudis failed, they then moved to a defensive strategy. The Republican Guard now moved back to form a theater-level reserve, and a flood of reserve infantry divisions deployed along the Kuwait-Saudi frontier.[5] The Iraqis established a three-tiered defense, similar to Soviet doctrinal conceptions and in line with their experiences in the Iran-Iraw war. Across the Kuwaiti-Saudi frontier and along the Gulf coast they deployed reserve infantry divisions dug into extensive defensive positions consisting of deep trench lines, mine fields, barbed wire, and even ditches to be fired with petroleum. [For the disposition of Iraqi forces in the KTO see Map 32.] Behind these positions lay artillery set to fire at predetermined ranges. The initial defensive forces were to tie up and attrite attacking allied forces, so that Iraqi reserves could mass for major counterattacks.[6]

Immediately behind the infantry divisions were armored and mechanized divisions of the regular army. Their mission was to launch immediate counterattacks on any breakthroughs by Coalition forces. Finally, if the Coalition ground troops did claw their way through defenses and counterattacks, the Republican Guard, positioned on the Iraqi side

---

[2]See among many others (S/REL UK) Department of the Army, 513th Military Intelligence Brigade, Joint Debriefing Center, "The Gulf War: An Iraqi General Officer's Perspective," JDC Rpt #0052, 11 March 1991.

[3]See Chapter 3.

[4]Gen H. Norman Schwarzkopf, *It Doesn't Take a Hero*, with Peter Petre (New York, 1992), p 229.

[5]*Ibid*, p 346.

[6](S) CIA Brfg, GWAPS, 25 Jun 1992.

of Kuwait's northwestern bulge, would launch a devastating counterattack. With the exception of frontline divisions, the Iraqis spread armored and mechanized counterattack forces over a wide area to make them less vulnerable to air attack; once the ground campaign began, they believed that they would have sufficient time to concentrate for the "Mother of all Battles."

Map 32

Disposition of Iraqi forces in the KTO

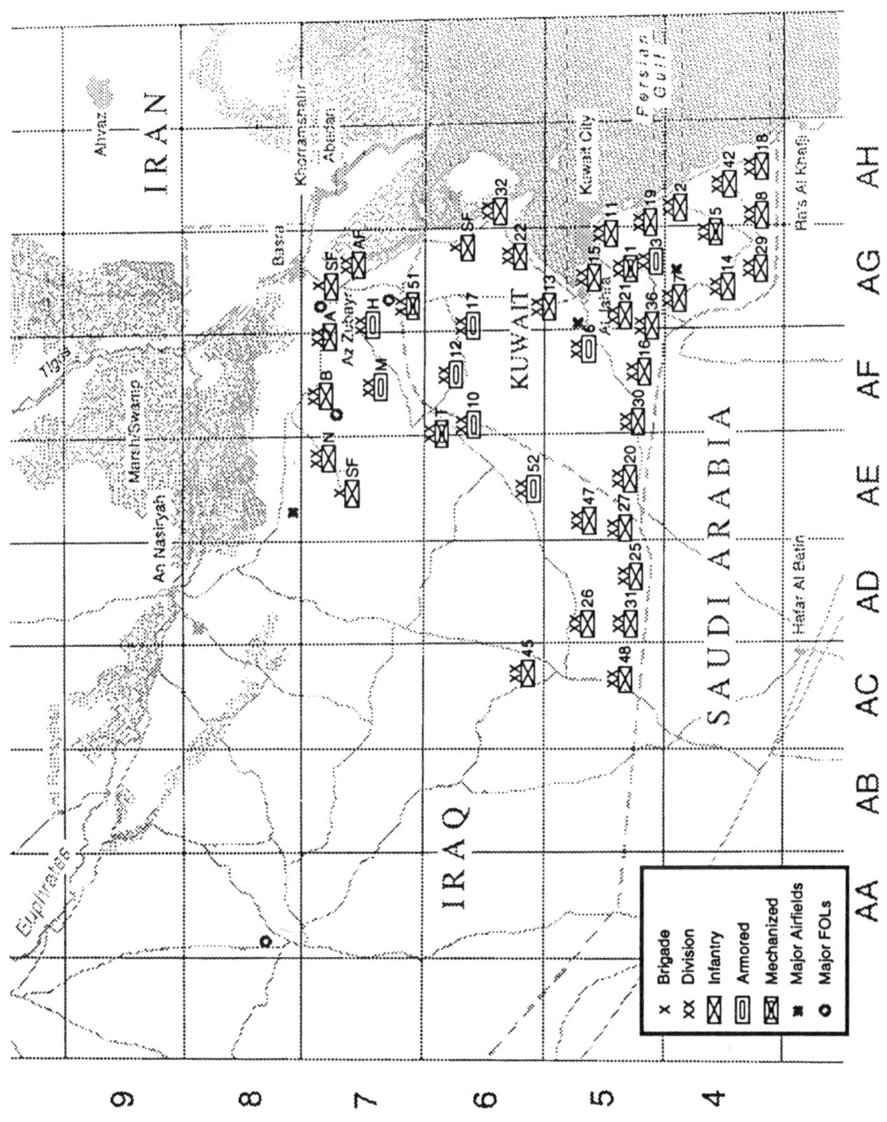

In assessing the operational picture, the Iraqis calculated that Coalition commanders had only three options: an amphibious landing by the Marines, a drive up to the Gulf coast, or an offensive from western Kuwait by the Wadi al-Batin. But they excluded a wider encircling hook from the west for a variety of apparently sensible reasons. First, they recognized the thoroughly inhospitable nature of the desert and assumed that their opponents would be equally loath to move through western Iraq. Secondly, they saw no preparations for such a move before 17 January; after that date they had other things on their mind.

Finally, there was one other major deficiency in the Iraqi deployments. The forces in the KTO were under Baghdad's direct control and Saddam's deadening hand. Above corps level, there was no army command charged with defense of Kuwait. Hence, General Headquarters in Baghdad–firmly under Saddam's thumb–made virtually all operational decisions. Consequently, even under the best of circumstances, there would be substantial delays in transmitting orders out to the field. Needless to say, the air campaign insured that these were not the best of circumstances.

It still remains unclear how much force the Iraqis deployed into the KTO. The paper strength of the Iraqi Army in the region was indeed impressive. In the KTO the Iraqis emplaced thirty-one infantry divisions, eight armored, and three mechanized divisions. Based on TO&Es (Tables of Organization and Equipment), U.S. intelligence assessed Iraqi strength at approximately 540,000 troops, 4,280 tanks, 2,870 armored personnel carriers, and 3,110 artillery tubes.[7]

In fact, Iraqi forces in the KTO were far weaker than these intelligence estimates. First, the reserve divisions called up in the summer never received a full complement of manpower or equipment.

---

[7] Even a year after the war the Department of Defense's estimates were still in this range: Department of Defense, *Conduct of the Persian Gulf War, Final Report to Congress* (Washington, 1992), pp 113, 356.

The situation got steadily worse as the conflict approached. Average frontline and second echelon divisions deployed severely underpowered between then and the outbreak of the ground war they lost more manpower to "desertions, AWOL, and casualties." The Effectiveness study in the Gulf War Air Power Survey estimates that the Iraqi Army in the KTO probably numbered on more than 336,000 when the war began; after the sustained bombardment of the air campaign that number appears to have declined to approximately 220,000 due to casualties and desertions.[8]

The equipment situation was hardly more impressive. In contrast to the intelligence estimates quoted above, the Iraqis possessed approximately 3,475 tanks, 3,080 armored personnel carriers and 2,475 artillery pieces in early December.[9] Most Iraqi units that deployed to the KTO were short of what their TO&E called for Consequently, Iraqi ground forces represented a less formidable opponent than intelligence assessments indicated. Luckily, the Iraqis themselves appear to have been equally deceived by their underserved reputation for military competence and power.

Planning the Air War in the KTO

How to attack the concentration of Iraqi military power in the KTO was the fundamental strategic and operational problem confronting the Coalition's high command. In the beginning, air staff planners argued

---

[8] (S) Effectiveness report, Chapters 4 and 5.

[9] This information is based on U-2 photography, 1 December 1990 through 1 March 1991 [(S) CIA Brfg, GWAPS, 25 Jun 1992]. No evidence exists that any substantial increments of equipment arrived in the theater after the beginning of the air campaign.

that a strategic air campaign could mitigate the need for and/or the course of ground operations against Iraq. Instant Thunder plans stressed air power's ability to attack enemy centers of gravity and its potential to break the enemy's will without prolonged ground operations.

Nevertheless, with the exception of a few on the air staff, senior military and political leaders in Washington concluded that there was a strong likelihood of a ground campaign, if war were to occur. Even more so, those in Saudi Arabia confronting Iraqi troops deployed in jump off positions recognized that enemy ground forces represented an intractable and dangerous problem. Horner and Henry had initially focused on the defensive problem of using air power to attack a major Iraqi incursion into Saudi Arabia. Both recognized that the crucial warning of an invasion would be deployment of the SA-6s from Kuwait City. Coalition air would first destroy the Kuwaiti Sector Operations Center, then the missiles, and then the armored spearheads.[10] One senses that here there would have been no effort to fly above enemy antiaircraft; instead A-10s and F-16s would have gone to low levels to attack enemy armored forces as well as their soft-skinned logistical support. Air losses would have been much heavier than in Desert Storm, but Iraqi armored forces bunched in combat array would indeed have made an inviting target.

By mid-October, the air staff was itself looking closely at Phase III, preparing the battlefield.[11] Checkmate's early studies predicted that Coalition air forces could destroy 50 percent of Iraqi tanks, artillery, trucks, and troops in the KTO in twenty-three days of good weather.[12] As hostilities loomed, the ground support portion of air plans continued its growth. While some retained considerable hope that "strategic" bombing might persuade Iraq to retreat from Kuwait, a firm understanding also existed that air operations would move fairly quickly from strategic targets to Iraqi ground forces if war occurred.

With Phase I now listing the Republican Guard as a strategic target, and with Phase III, defined as "shaping the battlefield," with 600 sorties a day to the KTO–not counting A-10s, AV-8s, and B-52s–the assumption

---

[10] Intvw, Maj Gen Larry Henry with GWAPS personnel, 28 Aug 1992.

[11] See the notes by Lt Col Harvey, 16 Oct 1991, GWAPS, CHP 10.

[12] Checkmate Briefings reporting the results of its computer modeling in GWAPS, CHSH 6 and 8.

was that air power could greatly reduce the combat power of the Iraqi Army, if not destroy it. Even postulating that a quarter of the planned sorties might not find their targets, CENTAF's air planners calculated that four to five days of air attacks would suffice to destroy 50 percent of the Republican Guard's armor, with 80-100 percent attrition by day nine. They applied the same criteria to attacking Iraq's regular army; ten to twelve days of air attacks would, they believed, produce 50 percent attrition. Eighteen days of air attacks would take out 80 to 100 percent of enemy forces. Consequently, concentrated, focused air power would wreck Iraqi forces in the KTO. Unfortunately, such assessments were dangerously optimistic; as we will discuss below, a number of factors combined to lower the effectiveness of air strikes against Iraqi ground forces.

By early September, with the balance between Coalition and Iraqi ground forces more favorable, Schwarzkopf turned to offensive options. By mid-month a team of SAMS (School of Advanced Military Studies, at Fort Leavenworth) graduates was in Saudi Arabia and examining ground war options.[13] Given the forces in theater, they did not have much with which to play. Their most obvious move was a combination turning movement and envelopment against the enemy's right flank that floated exposed out to the west in the desert. But even with surprise, the balance of forces would result in unacceptable risks. A relatively weak strike into the Iraqi rear with available forces might not achieve decisive victory; if it were to become hung up in the Iraqi rear, it would inevitably lose the ensuing battle of attrition. Without sustained, heavy combat power, a Coalition envelopment faced the prospect of being destroyed in detail. In the end, Army planners did move to such a scheme, but only after the President added a reinforced, heavy corps to the order of battle.[14]

Given available forces, CENTCOM planners advocated a smaller, one-corps attack; they suggested an attack straight up the middle, at mid-point along the Kuwaiti-Saudi frontier. Coalition ground forces would drive to the main road junctions north of Kuwait City. There, hopefully, they would entrap many of Iraq's infantry divisions. Nevertheless, such

---

[13]Schwarzkopf, *Hero*, p 354.

[14]Details of the work of the SAMS team and the development of the ground plan are in the (S) CENTCOM J-5 After-Action Report, 21 Mar 1991, GWAPS, NA 259. See also Schwarzkopf, *Hero*, Chapter 9 for discussion of the development of the ground plan.

an offensive would attack into the heart of Iraqi defenses and face counterattacks from enemy armored formations.[15] Such an operation risked heavy casualties, as well as the threat that Iraq would emerge with much of its army intact and its prestige enhanced.

The final melding of air and ground into a campaign plan for the KTO resulted from briefings in October. On 6 October, CENTCOM planners presented their plan to Schwarzkopf: a one-corps operation with the main emphasis west of Kuwait's southern "elbow." Later that week, Glosson and Maj. Gen. Johnston briefed the entire plan, all four phases, air as well as ground, in Washington. While U.S. leaders expressed confidence in air phases, Phase IV, built around a direct assault on Iraqi positions in Kuwait,provoked grave concerns. Again on 22-23 October, Powell and Schwarzkopf reviewed options; the CINC detailed the two-corps envelopment plan that his staff had examined. Powell raised some logistic doubts, but Vietnam was clearly on his mind.[16] He did promise Schwarzkopf that if it proved necessary to fight, "tell me what you need to do this. The U.S. military is available to support this operation."[17]

With such support, Schwarzkopf had his planners explore in detail other alternatives; they focused on the two-corps envelopment. On 6 November, they briefed the proposed operation to Schwarzkopf; he reiterated his belief that the Republican Guard was a major target. He told his planners that the offensive must cut off and destroy them.[18] On 15 November, Glosson briefed the CENTCOM staff on air portions of the coming war (Phases I-III). Some Army officers apparently raised concerns that CENTAF had put the plan together without ground inputs, but Glosson noted that the air plan had met Schwarzkopf's guidance. He added that he would solicit Army input for Phase IV.[19]

---

[15]Schwarzkopf, *Hero* pp 356-57.

[16]*Ibid*, p 366.

[17](S) CENTCOM J-5, After Action Report, 21 Mar 1991, GWAPS, NA 259.

[18](S) *Ibid*.

[19](S) *Ibid*. See below for a discussion on the difficulties that Schwarzkopf's peculiar organization of ground forces in CENTCOM would impose on army-air force relations in the coming campaign.

Planners continued their work throughout December, and new concerns surfaced. Chief among them was the process of tying the air campaign to ground operations; there were also worries about bomb-damage assessment: could CENTCOM's intelligence evaluate the combat status of Iraqi units in Kuwait? Some fixes were easy. When Army planners calculated that ground forces would need two weeks for redeployment to the west, air and ground planners quickly agreed that the air campaign would aim at cloaking this massive flank march.[20] Other problems, like bomb-damage assessment, offered no easy solutions. Schwarzkopf himself could only caution against "over-reliance on force correlations." He noted that prudent military judgment must be the final arbiter.[21]

Organizational and Employment Problems

On the organizational side of CENTCOM's preparations, there were factors that influenced the air campaign in the KTO; these remained beyond the control of Horner and his air planners. The most important may have been Schwarzkopf's decision not to name a ground component commander. There was, admittedly, an Army component commander (Lt. Gen. John Yeosock) and a Marine component commander (Lt. Gen. Walter Boomer), but no senior officer represented the ground forces in discussions between Schwarzkopf and Horner. Schwarzkopf apparently aimed at running the ground war himself, in effect becoming the ground component commander.[22]

---

[20](S) *Ibid.*

[21](S) *Ibid.* In this Schwarzkopf was entirely correct.

[22]In many respects, Desert Storm presents a picture analogous to the Normandy invasion in terms of the enormous forces deployed, the complex inter-allied relations, the vast number of joint capabilities deployed and interfacing, and the political problems that had to be negotiated between the CINC and the various capitals of members of the Coalition. In 1944, Gen Eisenhower was the Supreme Allied Commander; given the complexities of his many duties and responsibilities, he appointed a ground component commander, Field Marshal Bernard Montgomery, even though that involved placing Bradley's army directly under Montgomery's command for the first two months of the invasion.

Schwarzkopf's decision had important consequences in the Army's attitude toward the conduct of the air campaign.[32] For justifiable reasons and with his authority as CINC, Schwarzkopf determined that the air effort in the KTO would emphasize the destruction of the Republican Guard.[24] Unfortunately, he never appears to have communicated his priorities for the air campaign to field commanders. As a result, they watched the air force seemingly ignore their target nominations.[25] Moreover, for most of the war Schwarzkopf short-circuited his targeting board's recommendations, while telling Horner and Glosson directly what they should strike in the KTO. The result, unfortunately, was considerable, and needless, misunderstanding between Army and Air Force.

There were also organizational weaknesses within the planning system. Up to December, the Black Hole had concentrated on taking Iraq apart at the highest level and at removing the Iraqi threat to peace and stability in the Middle East. The focus of that planning effort was, thus, almost exclusively on the first phase of the air campaign. In December, in his reorganization of CENTAF, Horner folded the planning group responsible for the daily flying training ATO and defensive plans to meet an Iraqi invasion into the Black Hole. This new group, mostly drawn from the Ninth Air Force staff, became responsible for the air war against the KTO.

In no sense was this new section in the Black Hole prepared to tackle the problems involved in using air power to degrade and destroy an enemy's ground forces. In fairness, few others in the Air Force were any better prepared. Without a conceptual framework, the planners in the Black Hole's KTO cell fell back on racking up targets and reliance on numerical indices–all unclear from the evidence (BDA)–to determine the

---

[23]It is worth noting that the author's discussions in early September 1991 with a number of senior officers in XVIII Airborne Corps made clear that most of those on that staff felt that Schwarzkopf's failure to name a ground component commander had had a number of serious consequences beyond Air Force Army cooperation. Some went so far as to argue that the failure to close off the exits to the KTO reflected Schwarzkopf's incapacity to run the war from so far in the rear end with so many distractions.

[24]Schwarzkopf's continuing and consistent emphasis on the Republican Guard as the *primary target* for the air campaign in the KTO appears across virtually all of the GWAPS interviews with the senior planners of the air war. It is also in the TACC Logs and in all of the Master Attack Plans for the war.

[25]This affected the Marines less, since they had direct access to their own air resources.

progress of the air campaign. Without any conception of using air power as an operational instrument–the only possible employment became that of a sledge hammer. In the end, Horner was indeed correct to characterize the air effort in the KTO as "pounding a tethered goat."

Two other factors conspired to make the air assault in the KTO more difficult. The first was the decision to move the attack levels of Coalition aircraft to altitudes above enemy antiaircraft artillery (AAA) defenses. By so doing, especially after allied SEAD attacks gutted Iraq's SAM defenses, the Coalition could continue its air campaign with minimal losses. The political and morale gain to the Allied forces was enormous.

On the other hand, bombing above AAA had a substantial negative impact on employment of most conventional nonprecision weapons. For A-10s, the higher altitude made the 30-mm Gatling gun, a most effective anti-tank weapon–firing depleted uranium rounds–considerably less effective. Even more serious was the loss of accuracy that bombing at medium-level altitudes with nonprecision weapons caused a number of sophisticated platforms. Unfortunately, because of this altitude change, the nonprecision munitions expended by F-16s and F/A-18s were incapable of hitting individual pieces of equipment. Weather exacerbated the difficulty of using "dumb" bombs from medium altitudes. The percent of targets obscured by clouds increased from 1 to 2 percent to 33 percent, a more than fifteen-to-one increase.[26] When weather was bad, these aircraft had to bomb by radar. In addition, winds at altitude–sometimes in excess of 100 knots–further degraded bombing accuracy.

There was also a substantial problem in how air force planners in the Pentagon and theater had estimated air power's effectiveness in attacking Iraqi ground forces. Numerous estimates and briefings throughout the prewar period on how air power could destroy the Iraqi Army assumed that F-16s would use Maverick, anti-tank missiles, or CBU-89s against tanks and other equipment. CENTAF's mid-November "Theater Air Campaign," for example, had calculated that a four-ship of F-16s, carrying eight Mavericks or sixteen CBU-89s,would destroy three tanks.[27]

---

[26]GWAPS Space report Chapter 7, p 25.

[27](S) CENTAF, "Theater Air Campaign," Brfg, Nov 1990, GWAPS, CHC 19-17.

Unfortunately, the Maverick has never been the weapon of choice by the F-16 community; few of its pilots had trained with or used the weapon in peacetime training, while cockpit instrumentation was far from optimal for the utilization of the weapon. Consequently, hardly any F-16 sorties against the Republican Guard or Iraqi Army units used the missile. During the war, some 8,700 F-16 sorties dropped dumb bombs; fewer than 130 expended Mavericks. F-16s did deliver large numbers of CBUs and Rockeyes–some 12,500 and 3,600 respectively.[28] But the release altitudes used were typically so high–8,000-12,000 feet above the ground–that most of these munitions were not effective. For example, the canister and fuse combinations for the CBU-2/58/57 "performed poorly throughout the war with excessively high dud rates."[29] Particularly against dug-in Iraqi armor, the preferred F-16 munition was the CBU-87 combined-effects munition (CEM). But CENTAF's restrictions on the use of this munition in the middle of the war–a sensible decision in view of the heavy fighting that might have occurred during the ground war–limited its employment as well. As a result, for much of the air campaign F-16s were attacking Iraqi armor and artillery in the KTO with dumb bombs from altitudes at which they had little hope of hitting their targets–a situation not foreseen by air planners in either Washington or Riyadh.

Counting and Miscounting the Results

CENTCOM'S commanders, air as well as ground, saw attrition of this force as a prerequisite for a successful ground campaign. Knocking out tanks, however, represented only one criterion. As suggested above, there were disconnects between Schwarzkopf and his ground commanders as to what they wanted air power to do. Finally, there was soon to be an almost endless argument about bomb-damage assessment-the counting of destroyed tanks, armored personnel carriers, and artillery. The result was a confusing, contentious, and seemingly unending argument over the performance of air power in, to use the Army term, "preparing the battlefield."

What did Schwarzkopf expect air power to accomplish? Here the 50 percent attrition goal set for air power in operational plans raises its

---

[28] GWAPS Missions Database, Apr 1993.

[29] Tactical Analysis Bulletin, 91-2, Jul 1991, p 4-13.

head. How Coalition air power would achieve the "fifty percent solution" or even what it meant, became issues still exercising inter-service relations. It is still not clear, for example, how Schwarzkopf himself evaluated the battle damage assessments he received. From 16 January (D-1), ARCENT's J-2 briefed the CENTCOM staff on estimates of tanks, armored personnel carriers, and artillery pieces remaining in theater. One observer noted that Schwarzkopf had elected to focus on using air power to inflict around 50 percent equipment attrition (armor, artillery, etc.) as early as August 1990; he did not concern himself with more esoteric, aggregate measures such as combat power or potential.[30] Horner, on the other hand, has stated that neither he nor Schwarzkopf placed much faith in battle damage reports of such attrition once the war started. Rather he suggests the CINC brought his own estimate of the situation to bear in calculating enemy potential; and Schwarzkopf's estimate generally placed more reliance on the *number* of air strikes against Iraqi units as the primary indicator of enemy effectiveness rather than the damage reported. For his part, Horner resolved to stay out of bomb-damage assessment (BDA) fights altogether. Since BDA against the Iraqi field army was an Army concern, he expected the Army to address the problem.[31]

But the lack of agreement on how to calculate BDA caused endless problems, not the least of which was the divergence between Air Force targeting and Army BDA. Many Coalition sorties attacked truck convoys, ammunition dumps, and other targets in the enemy's supply network. How should one evaluate such sorties? What did their BDA mean in terms of a future ground war? These were vexing problems with which commanders had to wrestle but could never fully solve. Ultimately, it was the assessments imposed by Schwarzkopf that ended much of the argument on BDA.

Throughout the air campaign, the Republican Guard and its attrition remained central in Schwarzkopf's thinking. As the air war unfolded and Coalition air forces expended increasing ordnance on these divisions, BDA estimates caused increasing controversy within CENTCOM. On 29 January, Schwarzkopf noted a lack of BDA regarding these formations; he was apparently concerned that such stringent reporting criteria existed that

---

[30]Col Gary Ware, GWAPS intvw (by telephone), 26 Feb 1992.

[31](S) Intvw, Perry Jamison, Rich Davis, and Barry Barlow with Lt Gen Charles E. Horner, 4 Mar 1992, Shaw Air Force Base, GWAPS, NA 322.

only vehicles on their backs like "dead cockroaches" would count as kills.[32] Two days later, in reply to this rebuke, Yeosock confirmed in a briefing to the CENTCOM staff that the Republican Guard divisions remained at 99 percent strength.[33]

The Army estimate, however, did not go unchallenged, since well over 300 sorties by F-16s and twenty-four B-52 sorties alone had attacked these units per day in the war's first two weeks.[34] CENTAF soon discovered that Yeosock's staff had only counted A-10 mission reports in calculating bomb-damage assessment. Again this reliance on hard numbers caused problems for CENTAF planners; the targeting strategy did, after all, aim at degrading enemy unit effectiveness, without necessarily always destroying enemy assets physically. Horner's air interdiction instructions, for example, issued each day as part of the "Air Guidance Letter," called on friendly forces to "delay and attrit Iraqi forces (focusing on the Republican Guard) by concentrating . . . attacks against POL supply vehicles, water supply vehicles, and other portions or other logistics supporting Iraqi forces."[35] ARCENT's system and methodology were neither prepared nor interested in evaluating the results of such sorties.

With ARCENT's numbers under close scrutiny, estimates by the national intelligence agencies complicated the situation. CIA and DIA, working independently as well as together, produced assessments differing markedly from CENTCOM's. Working strictly from national collection systems (often degraded by weather conditions in the theater and without access to video BDA films), they consistently credited Iraqi forces with greater strength and Coalition air power with less effectiveness than did estimates on the scene. Their estimates raised fears that, as in past wars, inflated BDA claims would lead to substantial miscalculations of the enemy's strength. On 12 February for example, CENTCOM reported 25

[32]Lt Col Lewis, HQ/USAFE/XPPF, Notes: "Close Air Support in Desert Storm."

[33]*Ibid.*

[34]*Ibid.* Lewis confirmed to Lt Col Rich King via telephone that the original version of this background paper had omitted the words "per day."

[35](S) COMUSCENTAF, Air Guidance Letter, filed in "Daily Planning Materials," Box 3, Folder 3, in Black Hole materials, GWAPS.

percent of Iraq's in-theater armor as destroyed; DIA's estimate stood at 10 percent.[36]

Yet, in the final analysis, much of the bean counting entirely missed the point. The number of tanks, vehicles, trucks, and artillery pieces destroyed did *not* determine whether the Iraqi Army would fight or even how well it would fight. Its battlefield effectiveness would depend on the state of mind of Iraqi soldiers and their officers. Consequently, the impact of the air war depended, to a great extent, on psychological imponderables, and such uncertainties are not congenial to staff officers or to those statistical managers that have so bedeviled American military and intelligence agencies over the past twenty years.

Air Operations in the KTO Before the Ground War

With the onset of the air campaign, Coalition air forces also embarked on their great effort to "prepare the battlefield." Their contribution would be both direct and indirect. Schwarzkopf had forbidden any moves that might give away the deployment of Coalition ground forces out into the western deserts in preparation of what he later termed the "Hail Mary Plan."[37] The move to the west now began on 17 January. It succeeded without the Iraqis ever picking up the slightest hint of what was unfolding. Of all the air campaign's contributions to the allied victory on the ground, this was one of the most important. When the ground offensive broke on the Iraqis, it caught them completely by surprise as to direction and intent.[38]

The second major contribution was that of tactical airlift in the redeployment of XVIII Airborne Corps and VII Corps to the west. The

---

[36] GWAPS Working Paper by Thomas Keaney, "Study of Two Target Sets."

[37] Generals are of course prone to overstatement, and in this case Schwarzkopf indulged himself. The movement to the west, followed by the sweeping envelopment of Iraqi forces, reflected the strengths of US and Coalition military forces: their logistical sophistication–consistently derided by the military reformers in the 1980s, their capacity to maneuver, their flexibility, and above all the advantage that air power provided, namely the ability to operate in an environment in which they never came under the observation of their opponent, much less his attack.

[38] This was due to the fact that Coalition dispositions before the war confirmed Iraqi conceptions that an allied attack would come from the directions suggested above. After 17 January they saw nothing.

work horse in this was the C-130, performing in much the same fashion as it had in Vietnam.[39] C-130s flew most of the personnel of XVIII Airborne Corps from King Fahd to Rafha, a distance of more than 400 miles. The flow into Rafha averaged one landing every seven minutes for the first thirteen days of the move. After closing XVIII Airborne Corps, C-130s turned to building up logistic bases and hauling fuel, food, water, parts/supplies, and ammunition to places such as "Log Base Charlie," a highway strip along the Transarabian pipeline near Rafha.[40]

Similarly, C-130s played a crucial role in helping VII Corps and the Marines shuffle personnel in their redeployments after the beginning of the air campaign. Moreover, C-130s were a crucial link in the ground forces' logistic system; they moved critical parts and items out to the troops in the desert on demand. Much of the high operationally ready rates that ground forces enjoyed throughout the period of Desert Shield/Desert Storm rested on that timely delivery of parts by these transports. Finally, the C-130s moved approximately 600,000 gallons of fuel to Air Force forward operating locations and isolated army logistic bases.[41]

As suggested in Chapter 3, Schwarzkopf began exerting considerable pressure as early as the second week to move the air campaign's emphasis from the strategic offensive to the KTO. There was some redundancy in this pressure because Horner was already pushing air assets into striking ground force targets. On the first days of the air war, Air Force aircraft had flown 381 interdiction/battlefield air interdiction sorties, and seventy "close air support strikes" (CAS); Marine air units added an additional forty-six interdiction sorties and twenty-eight "CAS" sorties as well.[42] Perhaps more importantly, the Master Attack Plan had targeted

---

[39]The bulk of these C-130s came from Air Force regular, reserve, and national guard units, but it is worthy of note that some Navy, Marine, RAF, and even Korean C-130s participated in airlift operations within the theater.

[40]Brig Gen Edwin E. Tenoso, "A COMALF Perspective," Speech at Air Force Association Session VII, St. Louis, Missouri, 2 Aug 1991.

[41]For a more detailed look at the tactical airlift within the theater see Appendix 4A of the GWAPS Logistics report.

[42]GWAPS Database. The sorties that were reported as CAS during this period were so only in the definitional sense of proximity to the Iraqi-Saudi border; they did not support coalition ground forces engaged with Iraqi units.

Iraq's strategic reserve, the Republican Guard Divisions for heavy strikes. Throughout the first three days of the air war, these Republican Guard divisions, deployed primarily inside Iraq between Jaliba Air Base and the point where the Iraqi-Kuwaiti border turns south, felt the weight of Coalition air power. [See Map 32 for depiction of the deployment of Iraqi ground forces in the KTO.]

Throughout the air war against the Iraqi ground forces, the KTO cell in the Black Hole tasked allied aircraft to attack targets in "kill boxes." These boxes were in fact nothing more than grid references on maps. Each kill box was thirty miles on a side, and was divided into four quadrants, each fifteen miles on a side. To find the appropriate kill box, one need only to refer the various maps in this chapter that deal with the KTO, and then the appropriate quadrant by alphabetical designation. One would find quadrant AF6NE by looking first at the top reference grid and finding AF; then look down the side of the page for 6. Having found the kill box, NE would then designate the north east quadrant. The need for kill boxes reflected the fact that there were few, if any, visual points of reference in the desert. Without physical features, planners had to devise a method to control and focus air attacks on specific geographic areas, where intelligence had located Iraqi units. Each one of these kill boxes represents a considerable amount of real estate.[43] Map 33 indicates a kill box superimposed on a map of New York City. The extent of a kill box is 900 square miles; each quadrant 225 square miles. Unfortunately, the Iraqi Army had more than five months to dig in and camouflage its forces; on the basis of experiences in the Iran-Iraq War, it made good use of that time. The extent of the theater and the dispersal of Iraqi forces within kill boxes proved a major problem for aircraft tasked to attack targets in the KTO.

---

[43] De Saint Exupèry noted in his classic: "One fact the enemy grasped and exploited–that men fill small space in the earth's immensity." De Saint Exupèry, *Flight to Arras*, p 56.

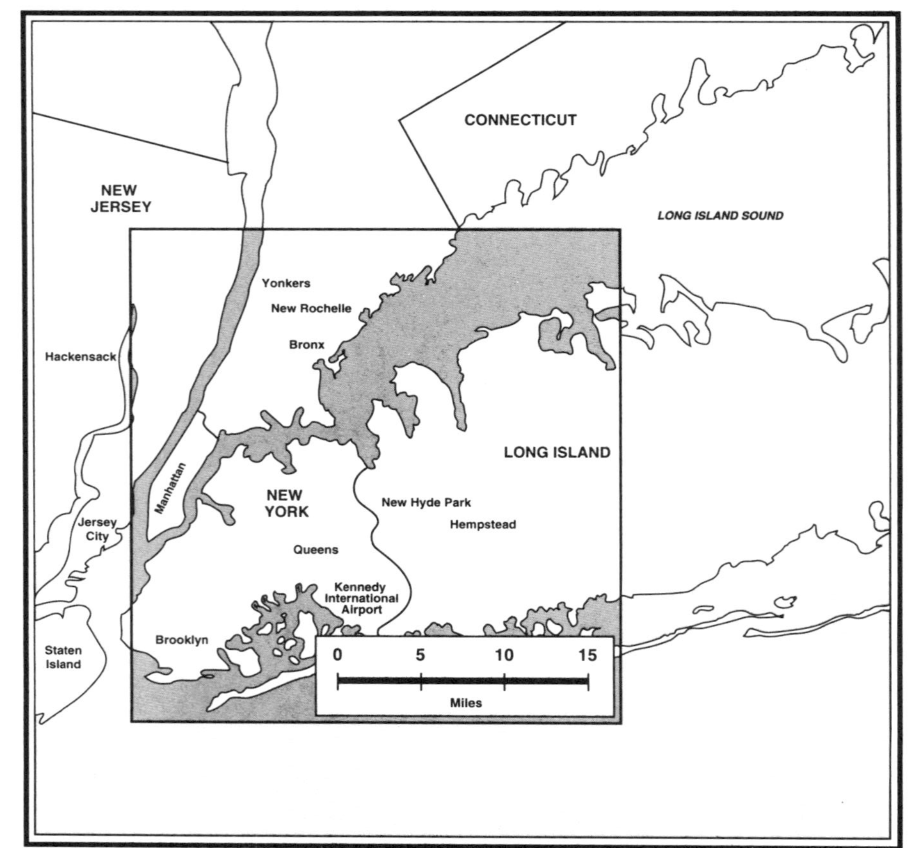

Map 33
Kill Box Comparison in Relation to New York City
Kill Box is 900 square miles

Although bad weather and the hunt for Scuds delayed Coalition air strikes on strategic targets, Schwarzkopf remained unswerving in his insistence that the Republican Guard receive a top priority. Observers in the Tactical Air Control Center record that as early as 23 January, Horner, undoubtedly reflecting CINC guidance, stressed the Republican Guard as a crucial target set.[44]

Even with the Scud hunt in full cry, Horner proclaimed "days" in "honor" of the Republican Guard Divisions: 27 January, for example, was "Hammurabi Day." In post-briefing comments on that day, Horner emphasized Schwarzkopf's resolve to destroy Saddam's elite units and repeated the CINC's intention to destroy Iraqi morale by physically annihilating one of the Republican Guard divisions.[45] According to Horner, Schwarzkopf still hoped to get Iraqi forces in Kuwait to surrender–Coalition aircraft had dropped more than one million leaflets suggesting such a course on the KTO on 19 January. But the Republican Guards were the exception: they were to die![46] Even as the Battle for Khafji was about to unfold, Horner warned his subordinates not to allow that battle to divert them from the main effort, the Republican Guard.[47]

Over the course of the first week, nearly 750 Coalition air sorties went into the KTO to attack Iraqi ground forces.[48] The major attention focused on three kill boxes close up on the Iraqi-Kuwaiti frontier. [See Map 34 for a depiction of the air effort during the first week in the KTO

---

[44] Historians' Logs, TACC Notes, 23 Jan 1991, GWAPS.

[45] *Ibid*, 27 Jan 1991.

[46] *Ibid*, 27 Jan 1991. For a summary of the Leaflet drops, see USAF, "Persian Gulf War: An Air Staff Chronology," p 224. The crucial point here is that *despite the emphasis* on the Republican Guard, air attacks failed to attrit these units as heavily as was the case with those units of the Iraqi Army closer to the frontier into Saudi Arabia.

[47] *Ibid*, 27 Jan 1991.

[48] These figures are from the GWAPS Database and are based on mission reports (misreps) of sorties flown into the KTO.

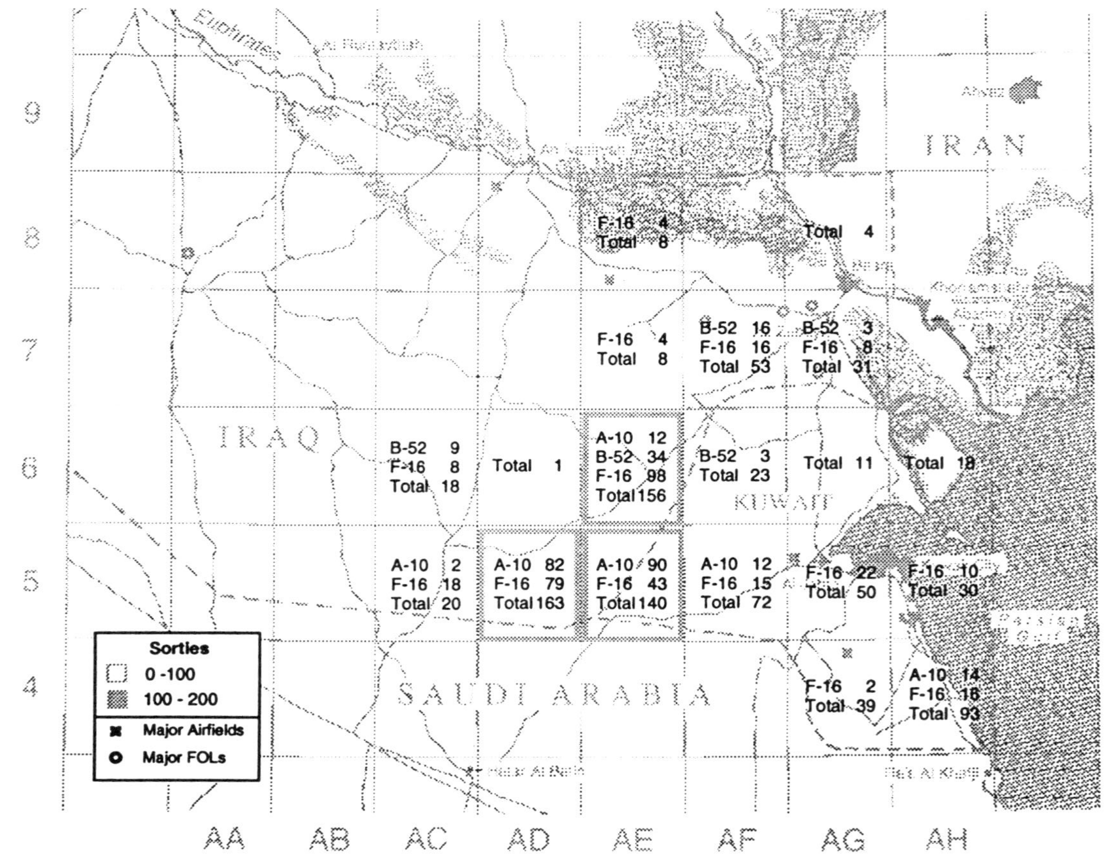

Map 34
Week I
Strikes in KTO
938 Total Sorties

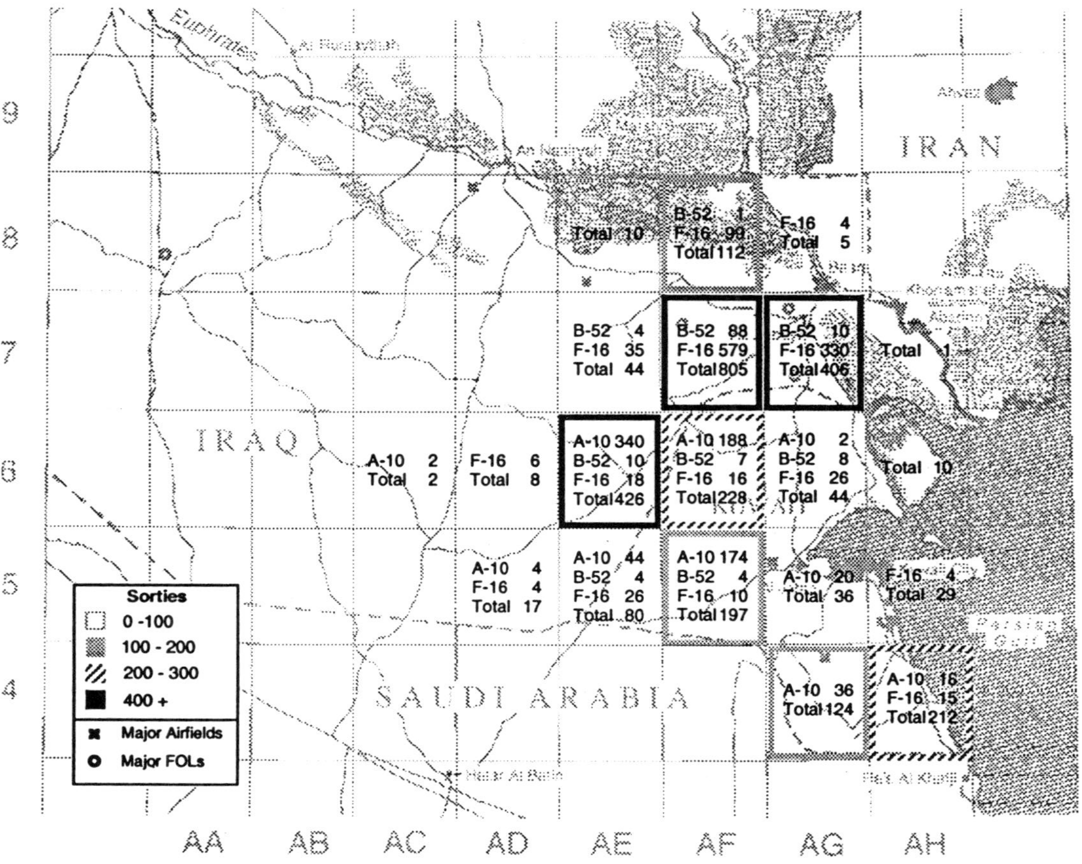

Map 35
Week II
Strikes in KTO
2796 Total Sorties

and Map 35 for the second week.] In the second week, there was a general sharpening of the intensity of attacks–nearly 2,800 sorties attacked the KTO–as well as a refocusing of the effort.[49] During Week Two, there was a clear emphasis on the Republican Guard: kill box AF7 containing the Madinah and part of the Hammurabi heavy divisions received no less than eighty-eight B-52 attacks and 579 F-16 strikes.[50]

How much physical damage these attacks imposed on the enemy is questionable. The majority of F-16 sorties appear to have destroyed little of the Iraqis' dug-in armor and artillery. But the real significance of such attacks, particularly B-52 strikes, was that they began a period during which the Iraqi Army *knew* that it was under sustained, unremitting attack, and that it had neither the defenses nor means of retaliation against its tormentors. Later, when F-111Fs began using GBU-12 500-pound laser-guided bombs to attack Iraqi armor, especially in Republican Guard units, the sudden vulnerability of even T-82s forced Iraqi crews to cease living in their vehicles, which meant that the readiness for battle of both crews and equipment inevitably began to break down. Combined with the psychological pressure from attacks by less accurate aircraft like F-16s and B-52s, the combat capability of even the better Iraqi units began to decline, although precisely how much was never quantified, either during or after the war.

Mounting pressure from Coalition air power on the Iraqi field army in the KTO provoked the Iraqis to respond, however, even before the so-called "tank plinking" began in early February. The Iraqis' initial response became known as the battle of Khafji. To understand this battle, one needs to estimate what was occurring "on the other side of the hill."[51] Saddam and his senior advisers appear to have believed that operationally and tactically, their forces would and could absorb a three-to-seven day air offensive, and then the ground war would begin.[52] Beginning with

---

[49] GWAPS Database.

[50] GWAPS Database. See Map 38.

[51] Unfortunately, one of the great differences between the *Gulf War Air Power Survey* and the *U.S. Strategic Bombing Survey* is the lack of access that the former has had to the enemy's documents. Thus, any assessment for the foreseeable future will lack the assurance that historians could offer in evaluating Luftwaffe responses, for example, to Allied air power–at least until Iraqi documents become open.

[52] (S) CIA Brfg, GWAPS, 25 Jun 1992.

D-Day those expectations began to fail. The first several days of the air campaign did not appear to inflict irremediable harm on either Iraq or its forces in the KTO. In effect, the minimization of collateral damage by precision-guided munitions may well have misled Saddam as to what was occurring. Nevertheless, some dangerous warning signs were appearing by the second week; the first was the shelter-busting attacks on the Iraqi Air Force. Secondly, by week two it was apparent that the Scud offensive had not had the desired impact; the Israelis had stayed out of the conflict and the Coalition had hung together.[53]

The third shock, and perhaps the most devastating from an Iraqi perspective, was an emerging recognition that the Coalition air offensive was not the prelude to an immediate ground attack, but rather that it would continue for an indefinite period of time.[54] Comments by CENTCOM briefers at the end of January, as well as CNN broadcasts to the world, underlined that the air campaign would continue for the foreseeable future. There was little pressure on Coalition commanders to begin the ground offensive. That news may finally have awakened Saddam to the fact that the air offensive could be of interminable length.[55]

Moreover, by the second week, the darkness that the Coalition's air offensive had thrown over movements on its side of the frontier was also apparent to the Iraqis. In response, they now moved on the ground. Their operation had two probable aims. At a minimum, Saddam hoped that the attack would display Iraq's willingness to fight.[56] The Iraqis also probably hoped that by inflicting significant losses and/or by achieving a ground victory they would gain a significant propaganda coup. But their primary aim was to force the Coalition to initiate ground operations that would turn the war to what they believed were Iraq's greatest strengths.[57]

---

[53] See Chapter 4 of this report for an analysis of the Scud attacks and their impact on the Coalition.

[54] (S) CIA Brfg, GWAPS, 25 Jun 1992.

[55] (S) *Ibid.*

[56] General Sir Peter De La Billiere, *Storm Command, A Personal Account of the Gulf War* (London, 1992), p 252.

[57] (S) CIA Brfg, GWAPS, 25 Jun 1992.

In general, the Iraqi attack on Khafji was a botched operation from beginning to end. The Division in the front line was to make the breakthrough, while another then exploited whatever advantage initial patrols gained.[58] Three Iraqi probes that the 5th Mechanized Division moved out to make contact with their enemy; all three probes apparently got lost, but one found its way into Khafji, where Coalition forces eventually destroyed it.[59] The morale of none of the attackers was particularly high.[60]

The Coalition initially failed to pick up the significance of the probe at Khafji; the Saudis had abandoned the town at Schwarzkopf's urging because it lay within range of Iraqi artillery. The fact that it was unoccupied may explain the initial hesitation by allied commanders to the Iraqi move.[61] But the Coalition possessed such abundant air resources that continuing the "strategic" campaign, albeit on a reduced scale, hunting for Scuds, and pounding the Republican Guard left Horner with sufficient sorties to deal with this first, and as it turned out, only Iraqi attack of the war.

The Tactical Air Control Center (TACC) did not react to the first warning signs that the Iraqis were moving. That lasted only until Horner arrived on the scene. Over the night of 30 January, the TACC retasked more than 140 U.S. tactical aircraft to conduct repeated strikes against the Iraqis. Air Force and Marine aircraft pounded the Iraqi probes throughout the day and night; where they caught the enemy concentrated, these strikes were particularly effective.

One of the 5th Mechanized Division's subordinate units, a Tank Brigade, was especially hard hit; it was traversing its own mine field when

---

[58]The 5th Mechanized Infantry Division was considered to be one of the better ones in the Iraqi Army. It had gained an excellent reputation during the Iran-Iraq War.

[59](S) CIA Brfg, GWAPS, 25 Jun 1992. Reasons for the Khafji Failure.

[60]Plan to Attack Khafji Possibly Unknown to Iraqi Troop Participants.

[61]Schwarzkopf, *Hero*, p 424.

Coalition air attacks disabled the lead tank, and thereby stalled the entire unit, strung out in column. When the slaughter was over, little remained of the brigade. One survivor, a veteran of the Iran-Iraq War, claimed that all that the brigade had endured in the ten years of the war with Iran did not equal what had happened to the unit in a quarter of an hour in the desert north of Khafji.[62] The 3d Armored Division never had a chance to concentrate, so intense were the attacks over its area of responsibility.[63] Altogether, the Iraqis appear to have lost substantial number of tanks, armored personnel carriers, and soldiers in the operation.[64]

Khafji did set up jitters on both sides of the line. Many in the TACC believed that the attack represented a feint–the prelude to larger strikes that would occur further west.[65] The Army, not surprisingly, felt that such attacks would come down the Wadi Al Batin in its area of responsibility, while the Marines were sure that it would come along the Kuwaiti-Saudi elbow.[66] But in fact, the Iraqis had received such devastating blows from the air around Khafji that they had no intention of moving again; nor did they for the rest of the air war.

At the same time that the attack occurred against Khafji, the Iraqi navy came out. Using TNC 45s armed with Exocet missiles and Soviet Osas armed with Styx missiles, the Iraqis may have had some illusions of supporting the raid on Khafji.[67] It is also possible that Iraqi naval

---

[62](S) CIA Brfg, GWAPS, 25 Jun 1992.

[63]Source Debriefing.

[64](S/NF) *Air Staff Chronology*, p 281; and DOD, *Report to Ccngress*, vol. II, VI-125-126.

[65]There was considerable interest in the TACC Log as to whether the Republican Guard was in the process of concentrating or moving south. The most likely place for it to attack would be out of western Kuwait–hence the Army worries. Several Air Force pilots reported seeing just such movement; their vision was undoubtedly helped by the request that they had received to look for a movement of the Republican Guard.

[66]The Marines went to a high state of alert as did the Iraqi 1st Mechanized across from them, both sides seeing the increasing alert status on the other side as a sign of impending attack. For the fears over a major Iraqi attack occurring elsewhere see the TACC log for the period 30 January - 1 February.

[67]The study on Gulf war naval activity performed by the Center for Naval Analyses suggests that the Iraqis were attempting to flee to Iran. Given what they were also doing with their air force that was a distinct possibility. (S) Jeffrey Lutz, et al, "Desert Storm,

forces, like their air force, were running for Iran. Whatever the case, Royal Navy Lynx helicopters refueling and rearming off two destroyers in the northern waters of the Gulf fired twenty-five Sea Skua missiles–of which apparently eighteen hit.[68] Not surprisingly, the United States Navy also engaged; A-6Es first picked up the movement into the Gulf. Using laser-guided bombs, the A-6s disabled three boats; throughout the day A-6s and F/A-18s struck the Iraqi boats with laser-guided bombs, cannon, and Rockeye cluster munitions. In the end, Coalition air attacks damaged eleven Iraqi vessels, two of which managed to reach Iran.[69]

In a less paranoid state than Iraq, the devastating defeat at Khafji, largely at the hands of Coalition air power, destruction of a quarter of its navy, and the continuing hammering that Iraq and its military organizations were suffering would have set off alarm bells. Certainly it should have suggested that all of Iraq's strategic and political assumptions were invalid. But in the world of Iraqi politics, one can wonder whether Saddam ever received a complete account of what was transpiring. Here, as throughout the crisis and the ensuing war, the nature of the Iraqi regime ("the Republic of Fear") made it impossible for the regime and its military commanders to recognize their strategic and operational position.

Week three of the air campaign again saw a significant jump in the number of sorties attacking the KTO–to more than 3,500.[70] [For the distribution of those sorties by kill box see Map 36.] The Republican Guard positions up along the Iraqi-Kuwaiti border continued to receive substantial attention. Significantly, however, the intensity of Coalition attacks along the immediate border areas had moved up several notches. Part of this was undoubtedly the direct result of Khafji, and part resulted from jitters that the Iraqis might launch a bigger offensive while allied forces were in the middle of their deployment out to the western desert. But the weight of air effort against the KTO continued to climb as Horner shifted his resources away from the strategic campaign in central Iraq.

Reconstruction Report, Vol. VI: Antisurface Warfare," Center for Naval Analyses, Alexandria, VA, p 4-6.

[68] De La Billiere, *Storm Command*, p 254.

[69] (S) Lutz, "Desert Storm Reconstruction Report, Vol. VI," p 4-13.

[70] GWAPS Database.

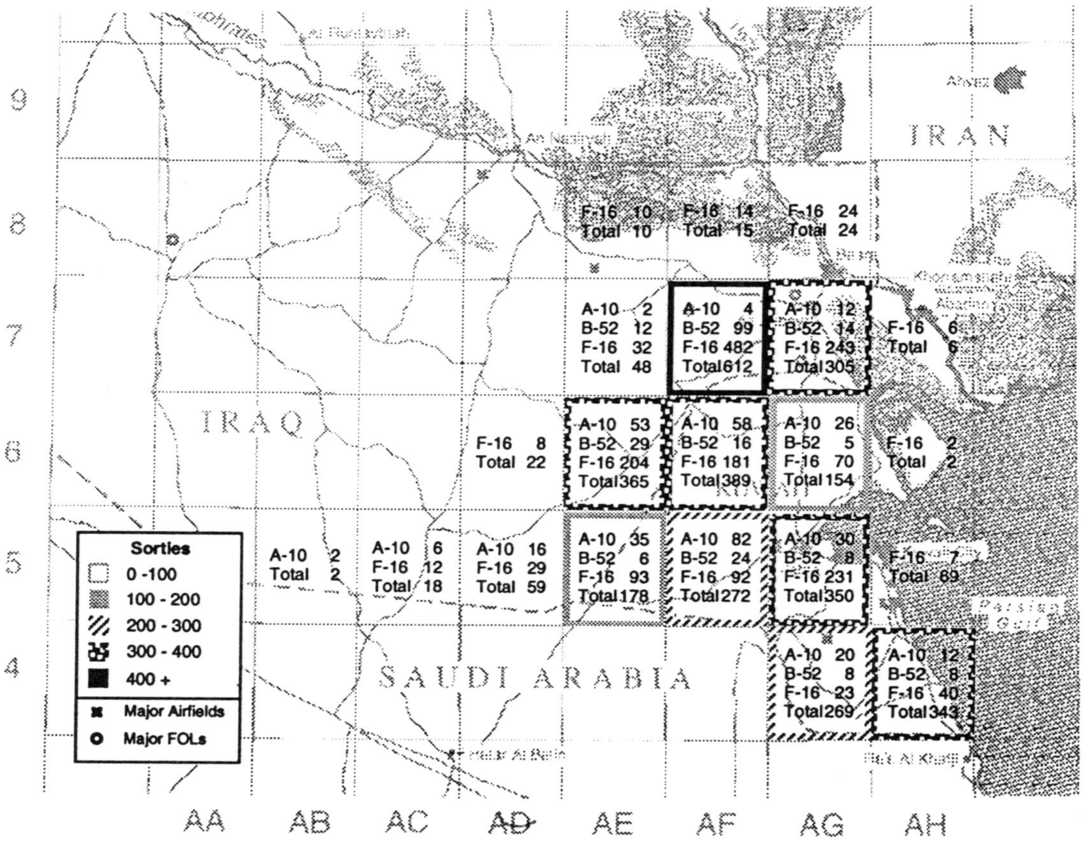

Map 36
Week III
Strikes in KTO
3512 Total Sorties

The period of early February saw considerable adaptation to the KTO's changing tactical environment. Difficulties in target recognition in the faceless desert, even within the kill box system, led to reintroduction of "fast" forward air controllers (FACs) for F-16s, although this time called "Killer Scouts." The ATO now deployed flights into each box at designated times; upon arrival, strikers checked in with the GPS-equipped F-16 "Pointer" scouts, who worked geographic areas over time and therefore could identify targets more readily.[71] Helping the accuracy of such strikes was the fact that the decreasing effectiveness of Iraqi antiaircraft artillery allowed aircraft like the F-16s and A-10s to attack from lower altitudes.

But the crucial development in early February came with the introduction of precision-guided munition capabilities into the KTO. We have already quoted Horner's enthusiastic response after viewing the video of Pave Tack-equipped F-111Fs "plinking" tanks.[72] Allocation of one of the most capable bombing platforms in CENTAF was a surprising and innovative decision. It reflected the high priority that Horner was giving the "preparation of the battlefield" phase. Admittedly, the decision to use the entire F-111F fleet for virtually all the rest of the war to attack enemy armor and artillery removed a crucial platform from the strategic campaign. The debate may well continue between some in the Air Force and the Army about the wisdom of this decision, but it revolves around judgments as to just what were Iraq's centers of gravity. This author's opinion is that the Republican Guard represented a crucial element of support–both in political and military terms–for Saddam's regime. In that context, allocation of critical "strategic" capabilities made sense, particularly viewed within the context of the necessity for a ground war.[73]

The increasingly effective air campaign into the KTO continued apace in the fourth week of operations. [See Map 37 for depiction of

---

[71]Lt Col Mack A. Welsh, "Day of the Killer Scouts," *Air Force Magazine*, Apr 1993, pp 68-69. The killer-scout F-16s from the 388th Fighter Wing operated under the call sign "Pointer," which reflected their primary task: pointing ground-attack fighters to the best targets.

[72]See above Chapter 4. See also TACC, CC/DO Current Ops Log, 7 Feb 1991, GWAPS, NA 215.

[73]See above Chapter 2.

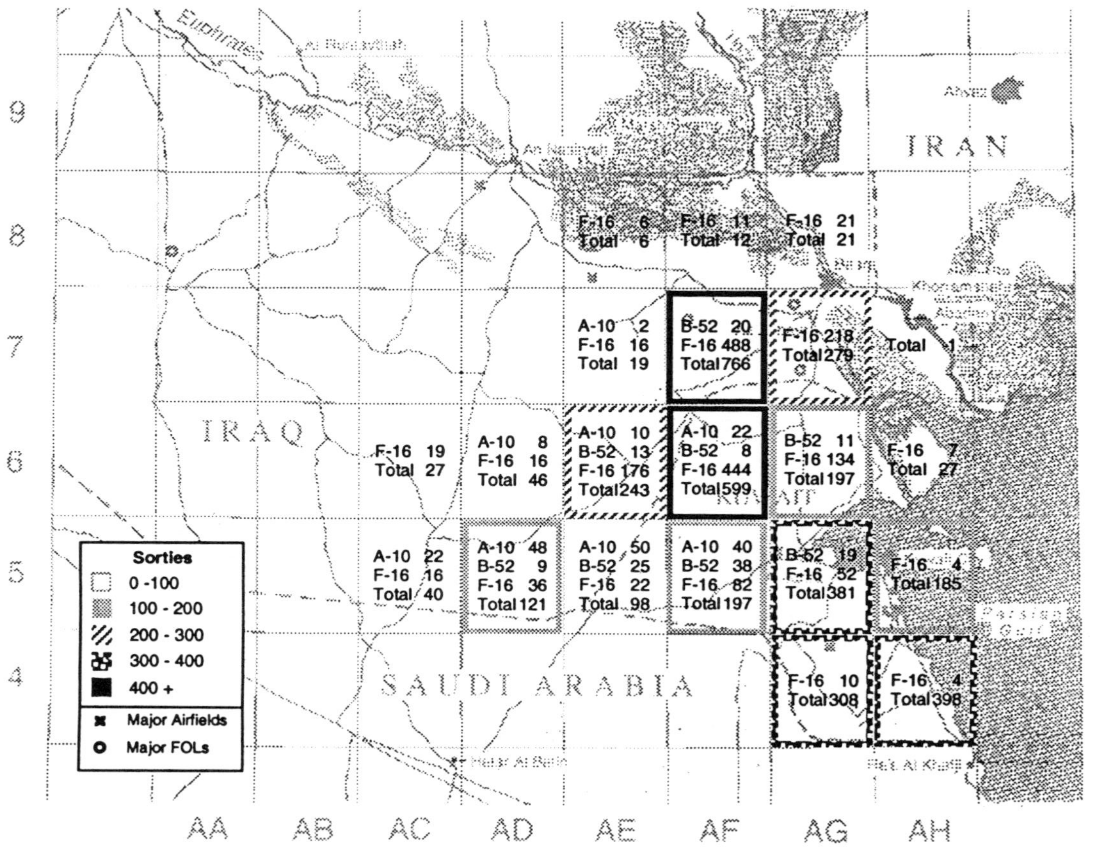

Map 37
Week IV
Strikes in KTO
3972 Total Sorties

where the sorties went in the KTO.] Nearly 500 sorties more than the previous week went into the theater. More than 360 of those were F-111Fs delivering 500-lb. laser-guided bombs against Iraqi armor.[74] During this week, there was less emphasis on border areas where the Army was deploying than had been the case the week before; this may have represented an effort at deception. The kill boxes close to the Marines continued to attract heavy attention from Marine air, while the Republican Guard received its usual drubbing, including attention from F-111Fs. In the southern portion of Kuwait, special operations MC-130s dropped 15,000-lb. BLU-82 fuel/air bombs on Iraqi positions to help lower the morale of enemy troops.[75]

At the end of the fourth week, Horner and his planners had confronted the crucial decision of what to do with the deep strike mission of the A-10s. By this point in the war, the "Warthogs" were operating over the Republican Guard kill boxes as well as over the areas immediately adjacent to the Saudi frontier. Late on the morning of 15 February, the TACC log recorded that an A-10, badly damaged by a near miss from an Iraqi SAM, had recovered despite the fact that the missile had blown the right elevator off, bowed in the right rudder, and perforated the entire tail area aft of the engines. The fact that the pilot was the commander of the 354 TFW(P) added special emphasis to the notation in the log.[76] Before the day was out, CENTAF would lose two more A-10s, this time shot down by Iraqi missiles.[77] Horner's reaction was immediate; within two hours of learning that a second A-10 had probably gone down, he restricted the Warthogs to within twenty nautical miles of the frontier.[78]

On the next day, Col. David Sawyer, Commander of the 354th and survivor of the previous day's incident, wrote a detailed summary of the A-10s travails to that point in the war. For the first two weeks in the war, his A-10s had operated at medium-level altitudes in an effort to minimize potential losses. But even using binoculars, such attack altitudes made it difficult for pilots to identify the targets which they were

---

[74]GWAPS Database.

[75]USCINCENT to AIG 904, subj: Sitrep, 082115Z Feb 91, GWAPS, CSS #29.

[76](S) TACC Log, 15 Feb 1991, 0820Z.

[77](S) *Ibid*, notation 1323Z and 1500Z, 15 Feb 1991.

[78](S) *Ibid*, notation 1720Z, 15 Feb 1991.

attacking. On 31 January, Glosson (as 14th Air Division Commander) had ordered the Warthogs to move down to 4-7,000 feet unless the ground threats dictated otherwise. From that point, the success rate for A-10s climbed significantly, but so did their exposure to enemy antiaircraft defenses. In the two weeks before 31 January, A-10 squadrons had suffered damage to three of their aircraft; in the two weeks thereafter, they had six more aircraft damaged and one shot down.[79]

Such losses did not seem insupportable compared with the Vietnam war or earlier conflicts. But on the 15th, after laying low for a considerable period of time, the Iraqis fired no less than eight infrared SAMs at their A-10 tormentors. On returning to Coalition lines with his damaged aircraft, Sawyer noted a flight of F-16s working over Iraqi positions just north of the frontier. As he commented to Horner, "A-10s over the Republican Guards and F-16s in the southern KTO doesn't compute."[80]

From the point of view of aircraft performance and survivability, Colonel Sawyer had a point. But from the point of view of hitting targets on the ground, the use of A-10s against the Republican Guard had made sense. However, the use of infrared surface-to-air missiles and the ensuing losses had caused Horner to rethink this approach. Henceforth, A-10s would only fly along the border. There was some considerable loss in daytime capabilities, since the F-16s were not capable of hitting Iraqi ground targets with the accuracy of the A-10s and their Mavericks. But at this point in the war, with F-111Fs attacking the Republican Guard, it no longer seemed worth the risk to expose A-10s and their aircrew to sophisticated enemy air defenses and missiles.

The fifth week–the last without ground combat–saw a continued upswing of air force and other sorties attacking KTO targets. In fact, the sortie total reached the highest number flown in the KTO during the entire war–4,048.[81] [For the distribution of Coalition sorties over the course of the fifth week see Map 38.] The Republican Guard was again the major interest of Coalition air power, but Iraqi positions opposite the Marines

---

[79](S) Letter from Col David A. Sawyer to Lt Gen Charles A. Horner, 16 Feb 1991, Ref. 1519302 Msg, "Aircraft Losses."

[80](S) *Ibid.*

[81]GWAPS Database.

also received much attention. What appears to have been a relative paucity in the number of sorties delivered against kill boxes in the west, probably reflects Coalition deception efforts and fewer enemy targets.

Air operations during these two weeks represented an intensive effort to pound the Iraqi Army into the ground. However, there is no consistent pattern in the Master Attack Plans beyond geographic distribution and tank "plinking" efforts of F-111Fs. As suggested above, the impression is of a great effort to bludgeon the enemy into collapse. These air attacks were already destroying much Iraqi equipment, but it is impossible on the basis of the video tapes to determine whether the destruction was of tanks, armored personnel carriers, trucks, or artillery pieces. Many enemy supply dumps went up in smoke under B-52 or other attacks.[82] In fact one B-52 strike hit the Adnan Division's logistic site near Basra with such effect that the secondary explosion was seen and reported by Space Command.[83] Both the Soviets and Israelis appear to have initially estimated that someone had fired a nuclear weapon in the theater; the resulting cloud reached 25,000 feet.

Much of the daytime truck traffic had ceased soon after the beginning of the war, but there was no coherent or consistent effort to close down nighttime traffic. JSTARS reported major enemy movements, and Coalition aircraft, if available, would strike such targets. Overall, the interdiction effort was not high on most priority lists.[84] By early February, most of the bridges into the theater had been cut as a result of Coali-

---

[82] Personal testimony of Lt Col Clint Ancker to the author. Col Ancker was the XO of the 2d Armored Division's Brigade Forward that filled out 1st Infantry Division in place of its reserve roundout brigade.

[83] TACC, CC/DO, Current Ops Log, 28 Jan, GWAPS, NA 215.

[84] There was some effort to cut down the Iraqi capacity to move in and out of the theater, but Coalition commanders estimated that with five months to get ready the Iraqis had stockpiled more than enough ammunition and supplies in the theater to last a considerable period of time. They were right.

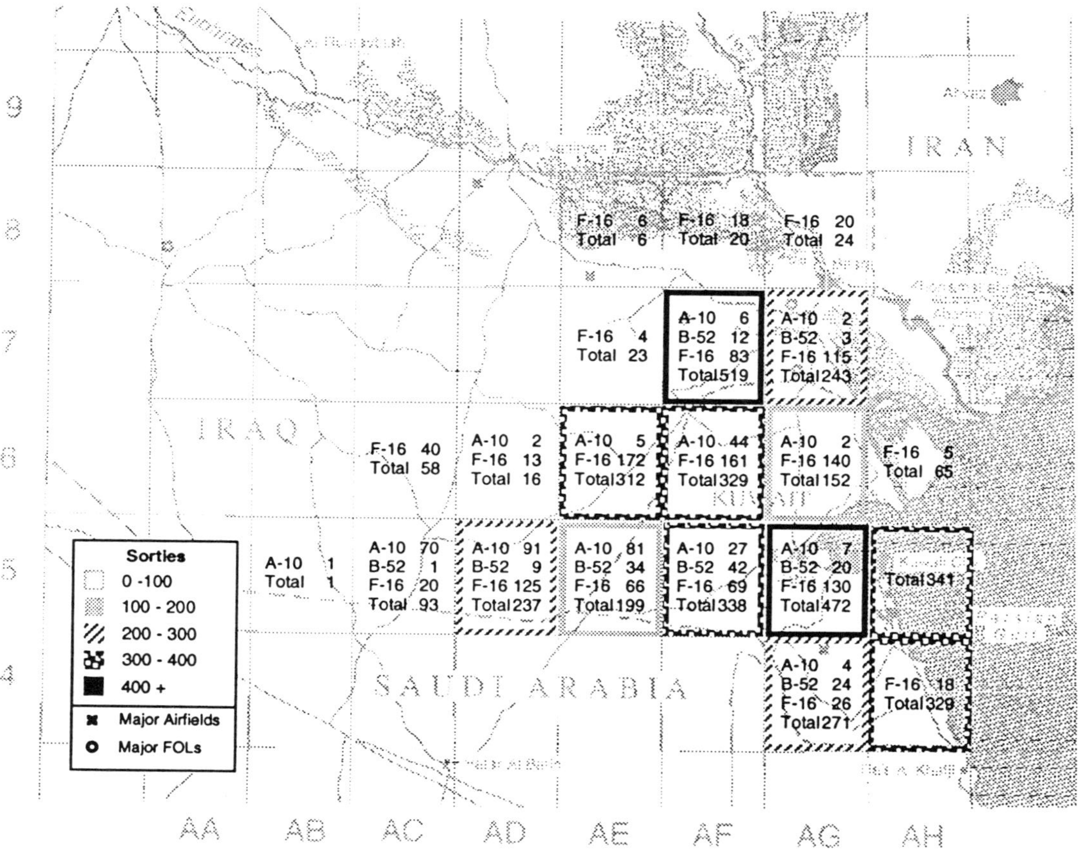

Map 38
Week V
Strikes in KTO
4048 Total Sorties

tion air attacks.[85] But the Iraqis proved most resourceful, constructing pontoon bridges and filling in where possible with earth-moving equipment the damage caused by air attacks.

Still, by 11 February ARCENT showed enemy frontline divisions below 50 percent; operational reserves at 71 percent; and theater reserves, the Republican Guard at 82 percent.[86] However, on the 15th, DIA reassessed the Tawakalna division at 74 percent; CENTCOM's estimate had put the unit at 48 percent. With the ground war looming, and largely dependent–at least in terms of casualties–on the success of the air campaign, this higher assessment was deeply disturbing. Not surprisingly, it prompted further controversy. Just prior to the onset of the ground war, the CIA, skeptical of CENTCOM's claims of 1,700 tanks, 900 armored personnel carriers, and 1,400 artillery kills took its concerns, which had been communicated previously to CENTCOM, to the President. The agency could validate only about 500 kills and felt it had no choice but to surface its concerns prior to G-Day. However, Secretary of Defense Cheney, having seen the video films of F-111F strikes, backed CENTCOM's estimates and it is likely that his influence was decisive with the President to push forward with the offensive.[87]

In the end, Schwarzkopf played a crucial role in the assessment process. While he did not fully agree with all of CENTAF's claims, by and large he came down on their side. Ultimately, it was not the amount of damage to Iraqi military equipment that mattered, but rather the damage done to the minds of the Iraqi soldiers. And so Schwarzkopf determined how CENTCOM would assess the strength of each individual Iraqi unit; his criteria were as much subjective as objective. However, as the ground war would prove, his estimates were closer to the mark in estimating Iraqi fighting power than were those based on various "objective" measures.

---

[85] GWAPS Chronology, *The War*, Vol. II, p 31

[86] Lt Col Lewis, "Close Air Support in Desert Storm."

[87] Lewis, "Close Air Support in Desert Storm."

Final Arguments with the Corps Commanders

Between 20 February and D-Day (24 February) there was another and mercifully final controversy over the employment of air in preparing the battlefield. Army corps commanders complained as before, but more urgently, that insufficient sorties were attacking Iraqi frontline divisions. With the so-called "breaching operations"–breaking through Iraqi mine fields and defensive positions while under fire–soon to occur, ground commanders wanted maximum firepower concentrated on targets immediately next to them. Schwarzkopf, on the other hand, was still directing Horner to attack the Republican Guard. Since few ground commanders were privy to the CINC's guidance, ground commanders blamed the air force for failing to strike their target nominations. To make matters thoroughly testy, CENTAF planners often found Army target nominations out of date or of low priority. The result was that Coalition air power often failed to strike targets nominated by ground commanders: after the war, corps commanders criticized the Air Force by claiming that the ground forces had nominated more than 2,000 targets, and air had attacked only 300 (15 percent).[88]

Throughout February, battlefield preparation was the principal mission of Coalition air forces. By 20 February, when corps commanders became most concerned, the air effort was pouring into the KTO, primarily against armor, artillery, and armored personnel carriers. On 23 February, the ATO tasked 89 percent of all sorties against the Iraqi Army and Republican Guard. BDA calculations, while not matching earlier predictions of annihilation, or even reaching 50 percent criterion, were nonetheless impressive. By 22 February, Checkmate reported twenty-two of Iraq's forty-three divisions at less than 75 percent; of these, eleven were less than 50 percent effective, including Iraqi frontline divisions closest to VII Corps' area of operation.[89] Of the Republican Guard divisions, only two, in Baghdad, were fully intact; the rest varied in effectiveness between 55 and 88 percent.[90]

Whatever the actual effectiveness of the Iraqi Army on G-day, Coalition ground forces did not suffer from lack of air support. As G-day

---

[88] *Ibid.*

[89] Point Paper: Checkmate Strategic Assessment, 22 Feb; Checkmate File CC-35.

[90] *Ibid.*

approached, Horner ordered his aircrews to press attacks home at lower altitudes, even with an accompanying higher risk. The cumulative effects of the bombing reduced the food, water, and ammunition distributed to enemy frontline forces; most POWs asked for food from their captors.[104] [For the total strikes and the total strikes by selected airframes, see Maps 39, 40, 41, 42, and 43.] The air campaign planners termed the result not "battlefield preparation, but battlefield destruction."[91] But at CENTCOM disagreement continued over how to shape the target list and score (BDA again) what had been attacked.

One such misunderstanding occurred regarding targeting. Both Lt. Gen. Walter Boomer of the Marines, and Lt. Gen. Frederick Franks of the Army, noted after the war that it was artillery pieces they needed air power to destroy, not tanks.[92] Marine ground commanders in particular feared Iraqi artillery, because it outranged Coalition guns and threatened breaching operations. Just prior to G-day, however, VII Corps requested that two Iraqi divisions credited with greater than 50 percent effectiveness, the 47th and 26th Infantry Divisions, receive additional air strikes. The 47th was a particularly urgent target, as it apparently possessed more than 200 artillery pieces in its divisional park–the standard Iraqi division had seventy-two–and was in a position to fire against either the Egyptians or VII Corps. Over the night of 22 February, CENTAF diverted the F-111Fs from the Republican Guard, to the 47th. The F-111Fs claimed more than 100 artillery pieces destroyed, yet ARCENT had not credited the kills by the start of the ground war.[93] Thirty-six

[91]"Planning and Executing the Air Campaign against Iraq: An Interview with Brig Gen Buster Glosson," 6 Mar 1991. On 29 Jan, Col Deptula had posted a sign in the Black Hole which read, "We are not preparing the battlefield, we are destroying it!" Richard P. Hallion, *Storm Over Iraq, Air Power And The Gulf War* (Washington, 1992), p 209.

[92]Intvw, Lt Gen Walter Boomer with GWAPS personnel (Thomas Keaney, Wayne Thompson, and Eliot Cohen), 18 Feb 1992.

[93]Lewis, "Close Air Support in Desert Storm."

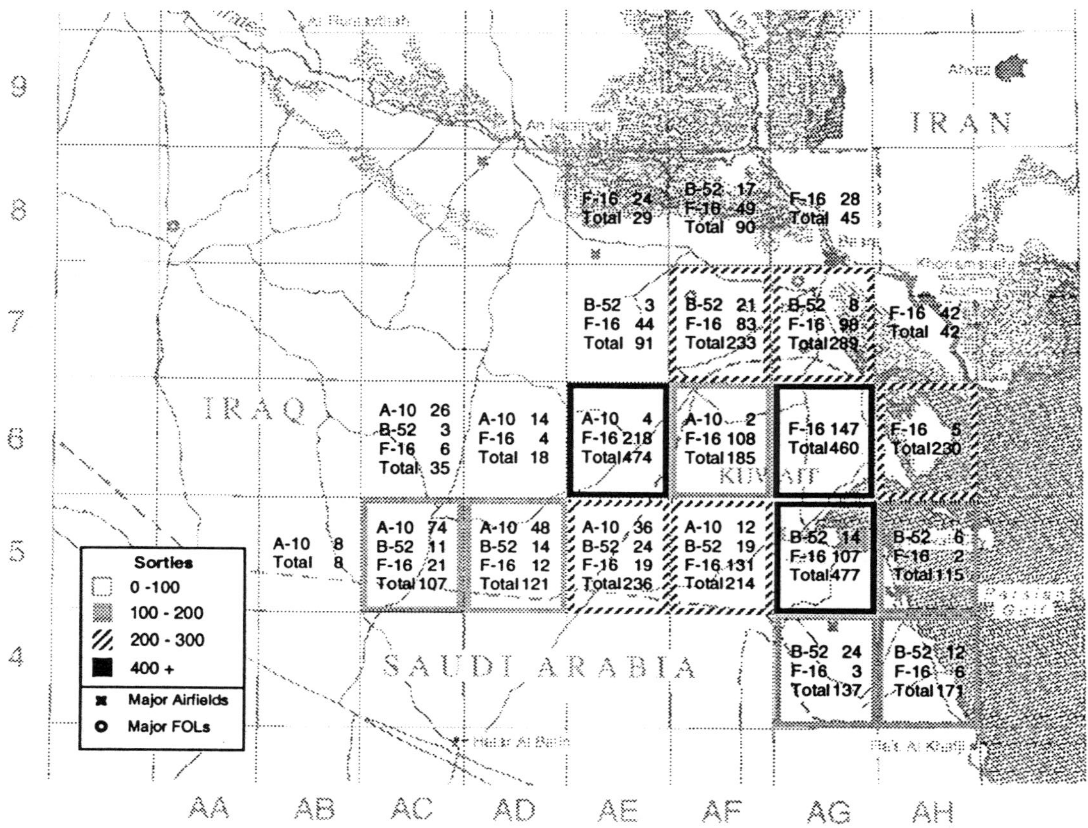

Map 39
Week VI
Strikes in KTO
3807 Total Sorties

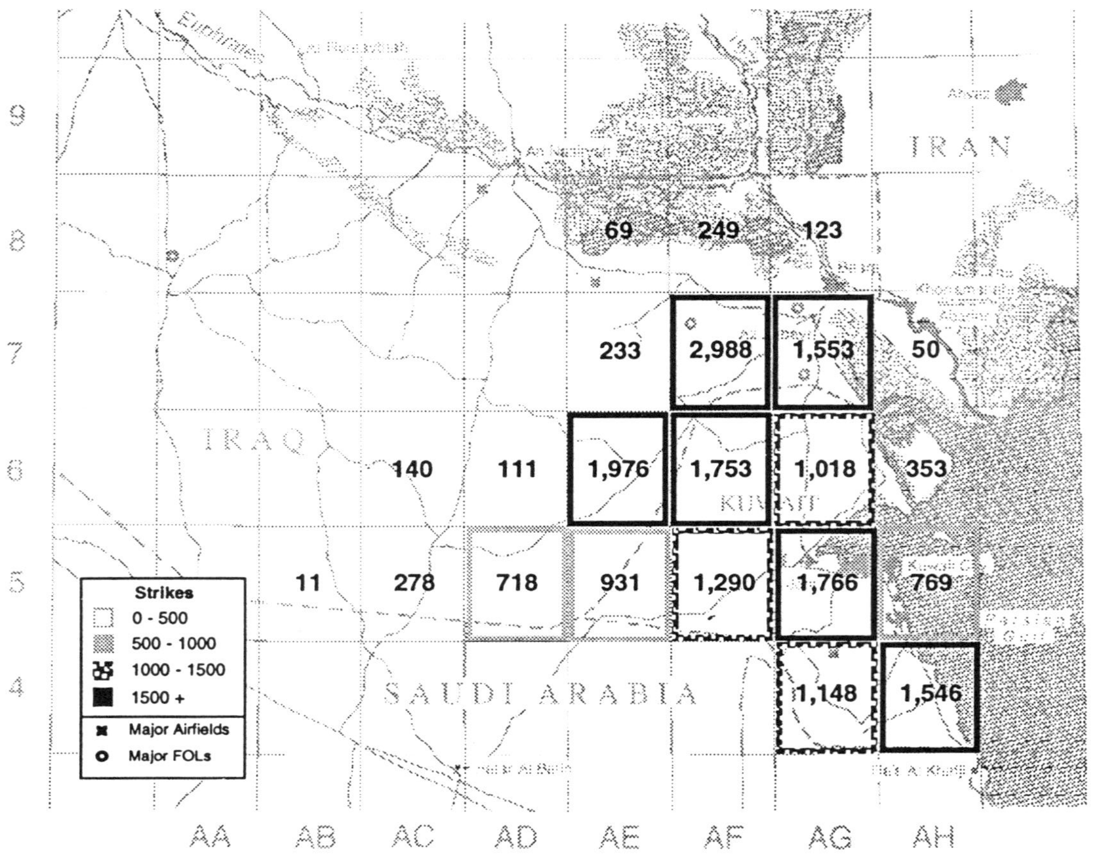

Map 40
Total Strikes Against Kill Boxes in the KTO

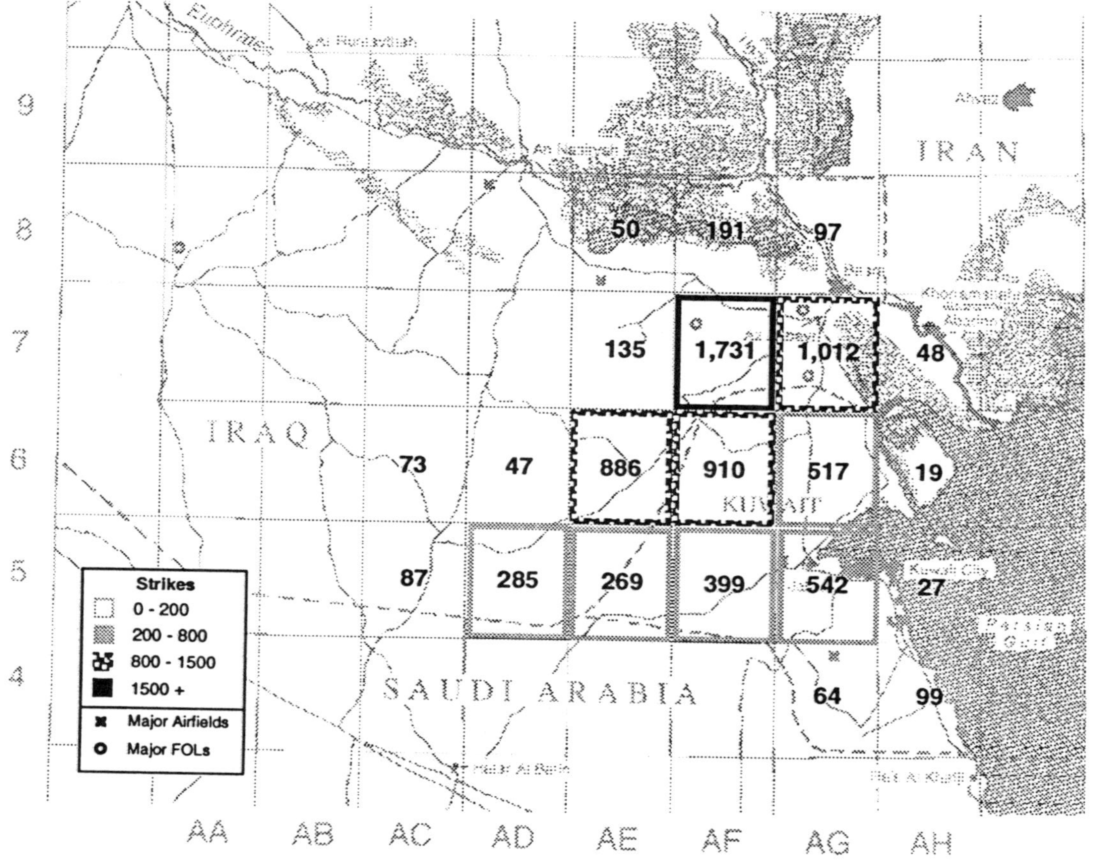

Map 41
Total F-16 Strikes Against Kill Boxes in the KTO

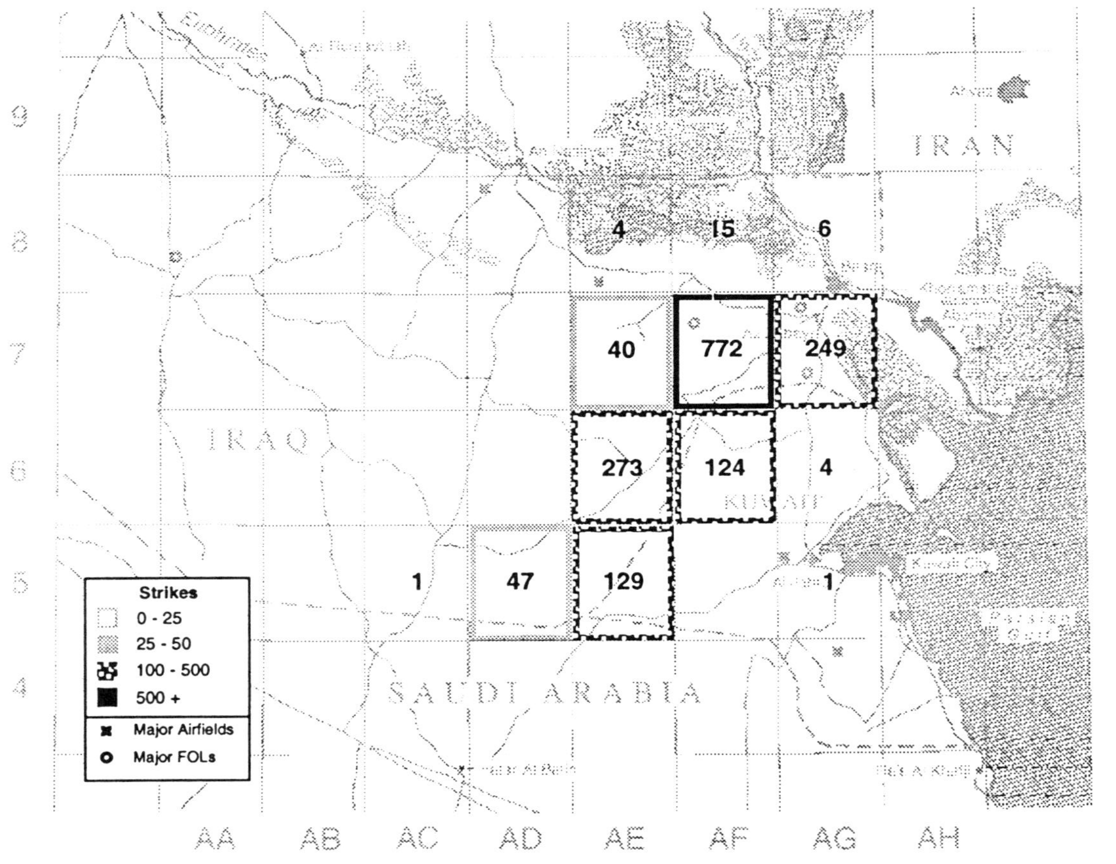

Map 42
Total F-111 Strikes Against Kill Boxes in the KTO

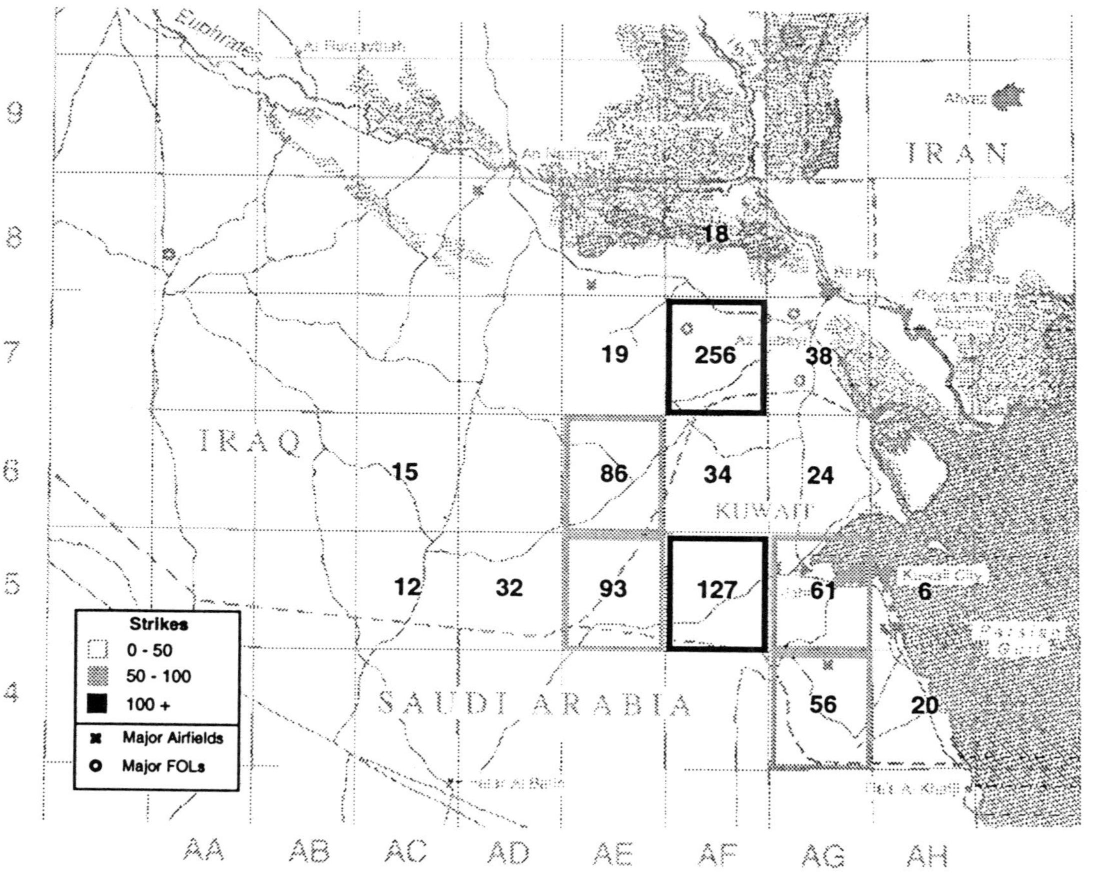

Map 43
Total B-52 Strikes Against Kill Boxes in the KTO

hours later, however, as VII Corps undertook its breaching operation, an operation designed to allow its armor to drive into the flank and rear of Iraqi forces, enemy artillery remained silent.[94]

In the last days before the ground war, Checkmate planners urged CENTAF to reexamine the allocation of air effort between the strategic portion of the air campaign and the KTO. Warden argued that the strategic bombing campaign should be intensified to avoid a ground war entirely.[95] But this was not to be, and Horner's focus was on doing everything possible to ensure that Coalition casualties during the ground campaign would be minimal. Any serious "diversion" from this tasking was unthinkable and would have intensified an already difficult situation between Horner and ARCENT's subordinate commanders.

Conclusion

By 24 February, as the diplomatic *pas de deux* between Iraq and the powers ended, the air campaign had focused on the Iraqi Army for most of the campaign and with increasing intensity over the past four weeks. The campaign was an odd mixture of the scientific and the primordial: from F-111Fs, precisely "plinking" tanks and other Iraqi military equipment, to B-52s, spreading fear and demoralization from high altitude. The result was a campaign that is difficult to measure. Neither Air Force nor Army had developed a methodology for attacking ground forces from the air, and once this task was undertaken, both discovered that they lacked the systems or the concepts to evaluate, except in the loosest fashion, how the campaign was going. It was ironic that Horner felt compelled to take some of his most accurate bombing platforms and task them to attack tanks in order to satisfy stringent BDA criteria for an overall goal that was itself exceptionally high; at the same time, ground commanders were clamoring for B-52 strikes, which, because of their bombing parameters and weaponry, provided sorties with no quantifiable BDA.

As the ground war began, then, one could find reason for optimism, for pessimism, certainly for skepticism, regarding the conduct of air

---

[94]"Conduct of the Persian Gulf War," Vol. II, p VII-187.

[95]Msgs: Checkmate to CENTAF/XX, 18-24 Feb 1991, GWAPS, Checkmate Box 3, folder 6.

operations thus far in the war, and what the ground war would bring. Certainly there were positive signs, from increasing numbers of deserters to the continuing air supremacy enjoyed by the Coalition. Still there were questions: how effectively had air power attrited the enemy? What was the psychological state of Iraqi soldiers after the sustained pounding from the air? How at risk would Coalition ground forces be in their "assault columns," as they breached Iraqi front lines? Would the anticipated allied victory be decisive? And most importantly and ominously of all: what would it cost?

An Iraqi POW is being inprocessed into the 101st MP co. POW camp 80 miles inside Iraq.

7

The 100-Hour Ground War

Planning for the ground war had begun in earnest in September, 1990.[1] To destroy what many in the intelligence community regarded as the "battle hardened," highly sophisticated Iraqi ground forces,[2] the Army brought together a team of graduates from its Command and General School for Advanced Military Studies. Over succeeding months, that team played a crucial role in putting together CENTCOM's plans to destroy Iraqi ground forces in the KTO.

Two assumptions formed the core of their eventual plan; both rested on the success of the air campaign. The first was that air power would allow a massive redeployment of Coalition forces to the west and shield that movement entirely from Iraqi intelligence. The creation of a secure zone over U.S. ground forces has been a basic task of American air power since the earliest days of World War II–one that Air Force, Navy, and Marine aircraft have accomplished over every battlefield on which American ground forces have fought, since spring 1943 in North Africa.

Still, the hundreds of thousands of troops moving west with tens of thousands of vehicles and the great supply dumps provided an enormously lucrative target. As one of the several U.S. Army histories of the war points out:

> If an Iraqi pilot had managed to penetrate the airspace over the border area during the great shift west, he would have been stunned by the panorama below. It was "mile after mile of tank transporters, gasoline tankers, troop and ammunition carriers," while "overhead was the continuous clatter of C-130 transport planes and cargo helicopters.". . . If

---

[1]Frank N. Schubert and Theresa L. Kraus, eds, *The Whirlwind War, The United States Army in Operations Desert Shield and Desert Storm*, draft manuscript, Center for Military History, United States Army, p 174.

[2]See in particular: US Army Intelligence and Threat Analysis Center, "How They Fight: Desert Shield Order of Battle Handbook," AIA-DS-2-90, Sep 1990.

any proof of Allied air supremacy were necessary, this was it: "I shudder to think," an American observer wrote, "what a couple of Iraqi planes could have done to that column on a strafing and bombing run." Fortunately, as the phrase went, Saddam Hussein had been "deaired."[3]

But equally important, the Iraqis had not picked up the slightest hint as to what was occurring on their western flank. The blow from that direction would come as a complete surprise to Iraqi commanders at every level.[4]

The second assumption on which Army planning rested was that an air campaign could reduce the enemy's fighting power by 50 percent.[5] As suggested in previous chapters, it was remarkable that Army planners believed that air power could achieve such effectiveness, as well as that the Air Force would sign up to the task. By 24 February air attacks had in fact reduced enemy combat effectiveness in many units in the KTO below that 50-percent criteria. On this bewildered and battered force the Coalition ground offensive fell.

With defeat at Khafji, Iraq had the choice of either quitting or hunkering down and hoping that its ground forces could withstand the pressure until the beginning of the ground campaign. By mid-February, however, the destruction of Iraqi units in the KTO finally worked its way into the consciousness of the Iraqi senior leadership. They seem finally to have recognized that not only might they lose Kuwait, but that they might also suffer the loss of their entire army in the process. Such a result would have completely destabilized the Ba^cth regime; the threat created a situation where Saddam finally acted to end the war.[6]

---

[3]Schubert and Kraus, *The Whirlwind War,* p 265.

[5]It is worth noting that had the Iraqis possessed a few RPVs (remotely piloted vehicles) they could have picked up at least some of this movement at no cost to themselves. What they could have done with this knowledge is, of course, another question.

[5]Schubert and Kraus, *The Whirlwind War,* p 179.

[6](S) CIA Briefing to GWAPS, 25 Jun 1992.

But still, even at that late date, he believed he had cards to play. On 15 February, the Iraqis offered to withdraw from Kuwait; the offer's conditions, however, made it easy for the Coalition to reject. Among other things, Iraq demanded the Western Powers withdraw their military forces from the Middle East and persuade Israel to leave the occupied territories, while the Gulf states and Saudi Arabia paid off Iraq's war debts.[7] The scornful response underlined the Coalition's determination to finish the war.

Thereafter, the Iraqis came up with more proposals, none of which, however, had much relationship to actual conditions. Only at the last moment, on 21 February, did they finally make a more serious effort to escape their hopeless position; Soviet diplomats, with Iraqi concurrence, proposed an immediate ceasefire in return for an unconditional Iraqi withdrawal from Kuwait.[8] It was all too late. Nevertheless, these diplomatic moves underlined Iraq's desperation to escape with some shred of reputation, as well as Saddam's continuing disbelief that the U.S. would actually risk a ground war against his army.[9]

The U.S. plan on which ground operations rested had evolved into a highly sophisticated plan based on deception and rapid movement–maneuver warfare in its classic and best sense. Far to the west, XVIII Airborne Corps was to strike at the Euphrates Valley in a move that the Iraqis might well interpret as the first stage of an assault on Baghdad. The primary purpose of XVIII Airborne Corps' move, however, was to establish a blocking position and to protect the flank of the main drive by VII Corps. That corps would also swing in from the west to attack the Republican Guard and the heart of the Iraqi Army.

Further east, 1st Cavalry Division would make a major demonstration up the Wadi al Batin at the onset of ground operations to confirm Iraqi assumptions that a major attack might develop from that direction.

---

[7]Schubert and Kraus, *The Whirlwind War*, p 282.

[8]*U.S. News and World Report, Triumph without Victory, The Unreported History of the Persian Gulf War* (New York, 1992), p 279.

[9](S) CIA Brfg, GWAPS, 25 Jun 1992.

Finally, two Marine divisions, reinforced by the Army's "Tiger" Brigade with M1A1s, would push almost due north from Saudi Arabia towards Kuwait City, while an amphibious task force demonstrated off the coast. The intention of these various moves was to overload the enemy's command structure by confirming previous assumptions, along with moves that seemed almost impossible in terms of Iraqi doctrine and experience. All these drives, except for the main attack by Frank's VII Corps,would begin on D-Day. Here the intention was to force the Iraqis to commit their operational reserves before the main blow occurred.

CENTCOM plans expected the support of considerable air assets for the ground offensive: interdiction and deep strikes to prevent the Iraqis from concentrating their forces for counterattacks and close air support strikes to smooth the Coalition advance. They were not wrong in expecting that the air forces under Horner would give extensive cooperation. The CENTAF Commander made clear at his evening briefing on 24 February the level of support he expected air units to provide soldiers and marines on the ground:

> There are people's lives depending on our ability to help them, if help is required. So I want a push put on. I want people feeling compulsion to hit the target. I do not want fratricide. . . .But up over the battlefield, it's time to go to work. Because other people's lives depend on ours. It's no longer a case of the air just risking their own lives[;] other lives have to be considered.[10]

On a number of other occasions Horner had emphasized his worries about fratricide; he expected his pilots to return with their munition loads still

---

[10](S) Daily Comments of Gen Horner, 1700 Brief, 24 Feb 1991, HQCENTAF, Office of History, 20 Mar 1991. Horner had told his morning briefing, "The pressure today is for us to provide support for the maneuvering forces on the ground. So be alert and aggressive. I want the close air support to be flown. I'm not particularly concerned about the weather. The interdiction targets should be flown as possible. . . .I think the ground forces will do just exactly what they want to do, and they'll execute superbly. So make sure that the air is there where they need it, when they need it–that's your job. No excuses. I don't want to have any weather abort or any of that crap. Get up there and do the job the best you can." (S) Daily Comments of Gen Horner, 0900 Brief, 24 Feb 1991, HQCENTAF, Office of History, 20 Mar 1991.

onboard their aircraft rather than drop on targets that might harm friendly troops.[11] Once G-Day arrived, Horner kept this admonition in place, but ordered his pilots to take greater risks to support Coalition ground forces.

At 0100 on 24 February the Coalition ground offensive officially began.[12] [For the movement of Coalition ground forces up to 0800 hrs, 25 February, see Map 44.] French scouts probed the desert before the main attack by their 6th Light Armored Division rolled towards the Iraqi forward-operating air base at As Salman. On the way, the French ran into a portion of the Iraqi 45th Infantry Division–assessed at 50 percent effective as a result of air attacks. Gazelle helicopters prepped the Iraqis and the ensuing battle cost the French two dead and twenty-five wounded. They captured 2,500 prisoners and left an unknown number of enemy dead on the battlefield.[13]

Shortly after the French, the 101st Airborne launched its helicopters to seize forward operating base "Cobra," 110 miles deep in Iraq. Apache helicopters took the unfortunate Iraqis in the vicinity under fire; then a mission coordinated through the air liaison officer brought A-10s to pound Iraqi opposition further. In the end, 340 Iraqis surrendered.[14] Shortly after 1030, the forward base was ready to support the 101st's Apache helicopters in further attacks to the north.[15] Meanwhile, a massive supply convoy drove forward to establish the logistic infrastructure

---

[11](S) *Ibid*, Brfg on 23 Feb 1991. Horner commented: "The point we must remember is that our weapons are far more lethal than anything the Iraqi has in his inventory. Therefore we must be absolutely sure where we put our munitions, whatever role you play in putting munitions onto a target, that it is in fact an enemy target. Because we're better off if we don't drop and let an Iraqi escape by mistake than if we make a mistake the other way and kill a lot of Coalition forces on the ground."

[12]The Coalition ground forces had already started to mount cross border raids for intelligence purposes well before G-Day on 24 February.

[13]Schubert and Kraus, *The Whirlwind War*, p 290.

[14]Brig Gen Robert H. Scales, Jr, *Certain Victory: The U.S. Army in the Gulf War*, draft manuscript, Chapter 5, p 5.

[15]101st Airborne Division (Air Assault), "After Action Report Operation Desert Shield/Desert Storm," Command Report, 13 Jun 1991, pp 45-7.

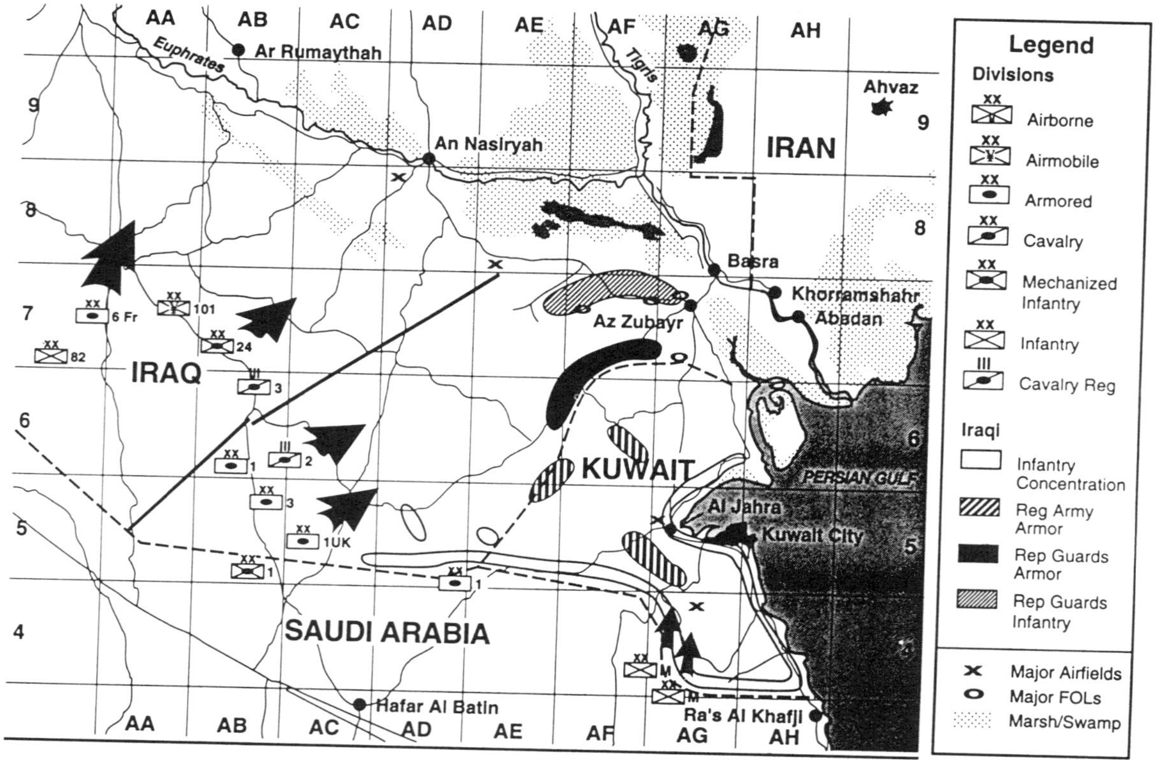

Map 44
Ground Forces
25 February
0800 hours

required for the next move. By noon, 25 February, the 101st was within forty kilometers of the Euphrates; by late afternoon its Blackhawk helicopters had put troops down on Highway 8, a major highway along the Euphrates River Valley.

The third and most powerful prong of XVIII Airborne Corps, the 24th Infantry Division, moved out last. By midnight on the 24th/25th, it had reached seventy-five miles into Iraq. Its mission was perhaps the most complex of any confronting divisional size units among Coalition ground forces. First, it had to form a blocking force to protect full deployment of VII Corps; then it had to catch up with and shield the advance of that neighboring corps and, finally, it would form the last gate slammed shut on Iraqi forces in the KTO.

Further east, 1st Cavalry Division launched a series of limited probes near Wadi al Batin to pin down Iraqi forces and persuade the enemy that the main offensive would occur in this area. So successful was it in this mission that in the first two days of the war–before it pulled out to support VII Corps' drive directly–it destroyed elements from five separate enemy divisions.[16]

The Marines in the east, directly opposite Kuwait, had the shortest distance to go, but were supposed to face the most significant defensive obstacles and defenses. Yet, from the first, the Marine advance, in Schwarzkopf's words, "encountered no impassable mine fields, no wall of flame, no murderous gas barrage, and very little resistance."[17] While its advance did not reach as far as Army units on the first day,2d Marine Division had captured the enemy's 9th Tank Battalion intact with its thirty-five T-55s, along with 5,000 men in the first twenty-four hours. Also, by the end of day one, the 1st Marine Division attacked and captured Al Jaber airfield, while it destroyed twenty-one tanks and captured 3,000 Iraqis.[18]

These first advances of XVIII Airborne Corps and the Marines underlined that Iraqi resistance would crumble at the first push; to wait until D + 1 to launch the main attack of VII Corps was to risk the possi-

---

[16]Schubert and Kraus, *The Whirlwind War*, p 297.

[17]Schwarzkopf, *It Doesn't Take a Hero*, pp 452-53.

[18]*Ibid*, p 300.

bility that the Marines might push the Iraqis out of Kuwait before the sledgehammer blow from the west slammed the door shut.[19] As a result, Schwarzkopf ordered VII Corps to begin its advance on mid-afternoon, 24 February.[20] Unfortunately, the ensuing advance was more cautious than that of the neighboring corps; Franks' troops only reached approximately fifteen miles into Iraq before going into a laager for the night.[21]

The enemy displayed little capacity to react to these unexpected blows. "Tactical armored reserves, crippled by air attack, failed to counterattack in any coherent fashion. Saddam's infantry collapsed into disorganized rabble."[22] The Iraqis had believed that the coming ground battle would quickly degenerate into a static meat grinder battle with heavy attrition on both sides. They had positioned frontline units to provide warning and begin the process of attrition; extensive mine fields and burning oil trenches were to increase that attrition of Coalition forces and gain time. Behind frontline divisions, four armored divisions of the regular army were then to launch local counterattacks to seal off penetrations. Behind these divisions, two maneuver corps would launch heavier counterattacks; finally Republican Guard divisions were to provide the *coup de gras* by launching an operational level counterattack. Crucial to their conceptions was the assumption that Iraqi troops would have time to concentrate and counterattack at each stage in the battle.[23]

None of the Iraqi assumptions held. The infantry immediately collapsed, largely as a result of the air campaign. Rear area reserves then confronted Coalition forces moving faster and deeper than the Iraqi high command had calculated. Coalition deception plans had reinforced Iraqi

---

[19]It is worth noting that the whole idea of holding up VII Corps attack for a day assumed that the enemy high command possessed the communications, sophistication, and intelligence to recognize and react to the opening moves in the first twenty-four hours.

[20]Schwarzkopf, *Hero*, p 453 and Scales, *Certain Victory*, Chapter 5.

[21]*Ibid*, p 455. In fairness to VII Corps one must note that 1st Infantry Division and the British 1st Armored Division were about to do a passage of lines after the former had breached Iraqi defenses, and a passage of lines by division-sized formations under the conditions of combat is no easy task.

[22]Scales, *Certain Victory*, Chapter 5.

[23]See the numerous EPW (enemy prisoner of war) reports from which this study has drawn much of its picture of the Iraqi Army in the KTO.

beliefs that the attack would come from the south or the Persian Gulf; blinded by Coalition air power, the Iraqis only recognized the blow coming from the west at the last moment when it was far too late.

Not only was the speed and flexibility of the Coalition advance beyond enemy comprehension, but delaying tactics (such as setting fire to oil trenches to create impenetrable walls of fire in front of defenses) no longer functioned because of air attacks. Even F-117s had participated in that effort; but most of the task of destroying the oil trench systems had fallen to work horses of the ground support war, A-10s, AV-8Bs, and F/A-18s.[24]

Throughout the daylight period of the ground war, Air Force, Navy, and Marine fighter units expended a maximum effort to ease the way for ground forces. Much of that effort occurred beyond the Fire Support Coordination Line (FSCL)–the line within which ground force commanders directly controlled delivery of ordnance to minimize the possibility of fratricide. Within this area between FSCL and the front lines, aircraft sorties rendered close air support and remained under rigid control from ground units. Because of problems in identifying targets from the air as well as the need for greater accuracy, altitude restrictions no longer applied.

The provision of close air support was a "push CAS" system in which aircraft launched into particular areas at set intervals–in some cases

---

[24] On the night of 15-16 February a substantial F-117 raid–for the only time into the KTO–had taken out most of the oil trench system by destroying its tanks and distribution system [Contingency History Report, 37 FW(P), 10-16 Feb 1991, AFHRA]. As late as 22 February, however, the A-10s had nearly lost an aircraft on such a mission: "Capt Rich Biley, 76th TFS, returned with yet another badly damaged A-10. He had undertaken a mission to set fire to the oil trenches in southern Kuwait in preparation for the ground war. While undertaking a firing pass with white phosphorous rockets, his aircraft's tail was struck by a SAM (in very favorable visual conditions for an optically-guided missile). Captain Biley lost complete hydraulic power, and recovered only through the use of manual reversion and throttle manipulation." Combat Chronology, 23/354 TFW(P), 17 Jan-28 Feb 1991.

as rapidly as seven-minute intervals, if an area possessed particularly heavy concentrations of Iraqi forces. If ground forces did not need that close air support, these aircraft then moved on to strike predetermined targets that lay deeper on the battlefield; new aircraft arriving on station would then replace those that departed; as a result ground forces would always have close air support aircraft available for unforeseen situations. For the most part, the system worked relatively well. Nevertheless, such an operational approach depended on the fact that there was a surplus of air power available within the theater. On 24 February, planners provided no less than 600 Air Force and Marine close air support sorties–A-10s, AV-8Bs, and F/A-18s.[25] The major problem for all aircraft operating in the KTO was that of visibility. Not only was the weather bad through most of the ground war, but dense smoke rose from oil well fires set by Saddam's troops.

The initial Coalition moves on the first day of the ground campaign succeeded beyond CENTCOM expectations.[26] For the Iraqis the picture remained unclear. Something completely unforeseen was occurring along the Euphrates west of An-Nasiriyah; moreover, U.S. Marines were making such good progress towards Kuwait City that they were approaching a position that threatened to cut off troops in the Kuwaiti capital as well as Iraqi forces in southeastern Kuwait.

On day two, the offensive gathered steam; 101st Airborne Division completed its task of establishing blocking positions along the Euphrates west of An-Nasiriyah; its troopers thereby cut Highway 8. [For the movement of ground forces up to 25 February, 2400 hrs., see Map 45.] Their movement up on the Euphrates would receive considerable help from C-130s which dropped over 100 tons of food and water to replace the supplies that the large number of prisoners taken thus far in the war

---

[25] USCINCCENT Sitreps, 23-28 Feb 1991; also see the (S) Master Attack Plan for 24 Feb and the GWAPS Database.

[26] Schwarzkopf records in his memoir the call from Lt Gen Gary Luck, commander of XVIII Airborne Corps on the morning of the second day to report that his units had already captured all of the objectives for the first two days and that the casualties thus far in the war for US units in his corps *amounted to one wounded man*. Schwarzkopf, *Hero*, p 456.

had substantially depleted.[27] To its east, 24th Infantry Division closed on its first objectives and would soon be in the position to cover VII Corps' flank. Unfortunately, the division ran into difficult terrain where the desert transitioned into the Euphrates River Valley; heavy rains made much of the terrain impassable even to light vehicles; the division spent much of 25 February looking for the few passable routes through the quagmire.[28] Nevertheless, XVIII Airborne Corps had achieved its three objectives in a day and a half.

Meanwhile, VII Corps moved forward to contact. First and 3d Armored Divisions, screened by 2d Armored Cavalry Regiment, rolled north to form the corps' left wing, while the British completed passage through 1st Infantry Division's breach.[29] Seventh Corps met only scattered resistance during the day. First Armored Division began prepping areas of enemy resistance thirty-five to forty miles away with massive doses of A-10s as it moved forward. Then, as it closed on the enemy, it plastered the area with artillery and rocket fire; in its only significant engagement of the day, one brigade destroyed an enemy counterattack of forty to fifty tanks in ten minutes.[30] By evening deployment of VII Corps was nearly complete with 1st and 3d Armored on line and beginning to turn east.[31] Further south, the British 1st Armored Division was also turning east in preparation for its coming destruction of the Iraqi 52d Armored Division.

The Marine drive was also gathering steam. The Iraqis made some attempt to interfere with the advance by launching a series of

---

[27]GWAPS Logistics report, Chapter 4.

[28]Scales, *Certain Victory*, Chapter 5.

[29]In expanding their breech, units of the 1st Infantry captured the command post of the Iraqi 26th Infantry Division and its entire staff. Schubert and Kraus, *The Whirlwind War*, p 304.

[30]*Ibid*, p 304.

[31]The advance of the 2d Armored Cavalry Regiment to and through "Objective MERREL" was helped considerably by what one of its officers termed the "incessant attacks by A-10s." 1st Lt John Hillen, "Desert Storm, 2d Armored Cavalry: The Campaign to Liberate Kuwait," *Armor*, Jul-Aug 1991, p 9.

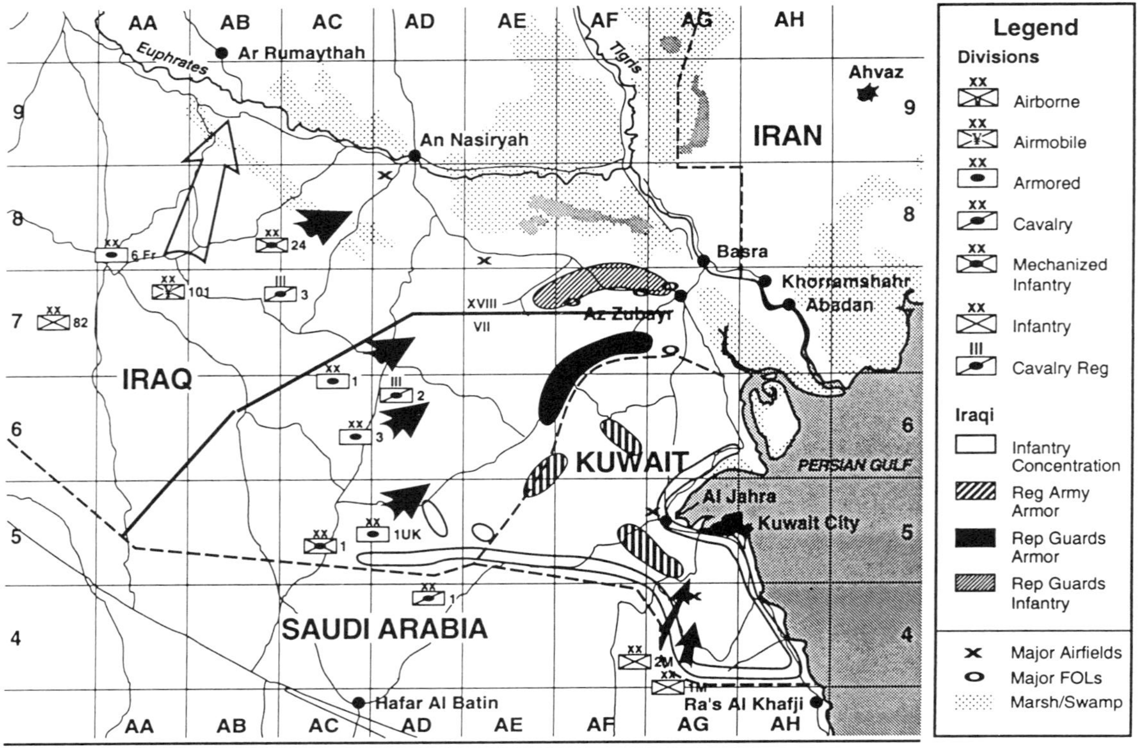

Map 45
Ground Forces
25 February
2400 hours

counterattacks.[32] After fighting off these attacks, with minimal loss, the Marine divisions and the Army's "Tiger" Brigade continued their advance to the north. If their move forward was slower than in other areas, there were good reasons; enemy defenses were stronger and it paid to be cautious to keep American casualties down. Equally important was the fact that too rapid an advance might push the Iraqis out of the sack before the advance from the west closed in. This advance towards Kuwait City involved considerable use of close air support throughout the ground war. Particularly on 25 February, AV-8Bs, and at times A-10s and F/A-18s, worked in the difficult conditions to provide ground forces with air support.[33]

Twenty-five February was one of the better times in the war for those who flew in the KTO. A message from the A-10 wing to CENTAF ended with the comment: "Having a wonderful day."[34] Despite the fact that weather conditions were less than optimal, with cloud cover, thunderstorms, and even dust storms throughout the region, air operations went forward with a vengeance.[35] Horner commented after his morning briefing:

> Of course, the real tragedy of all this is what he [Saddam] is doing to Kuwait on the way out. There is no excuse for that–and it should not be forgotten. In war there [are] a lot of horrible things that go on but they're understandable in light of the people protecting their own lives and fighting for their country. But to desecrate a country because you're losing, there is no excuse for that and no forgiveness. So I hope we're just as tough, mean, and vicious as we possibly can be in these last two days and get it over with.[36]

---

[32] Their attack was, of course, in line with their (and Soviet) doctrine of counterattacking enemy breakthroughs and sealing up any breaches that the enemy made. But the Iraqis possessed neither the weapons nor training to be effective against American forces. The pounding that they took from Marine close air support reinforced their dismal showing.

[33] "Testimony of Maj Gen James M. Myatt, 8 May 1991," Hearings before the Committee on Armed Services, United States Senate (Washington, DC, 1991), pp 60-2.

[34] (S) Combat Chronology, 23/354 TFW(P), 17 Jan 1991-28 Feb 1991, entry for 25 Feb 1991.

[35] Kenneth R. Walters, Sr, et al, "Gulf War Weather," USAF Environmental Technical Applications Center, Mar 1992, pp 3-90 to 3-91.

[36] (S) Daily Comments of Gen Horner, 25 Feb, 0930 Brfg, HQCENTAF, Office of History, 20 Mar 1991.

As the A-10 wing chronology noted, the "Warthog" was in its element. "As the ground battle swept away fixed AAA and SAM sites, the A-10 roamed the battlefield with near total impunity. The only problem was actually employing weapons, as many aircraft were in the queue." Consequently, of 239 sorties launched, eighty-nine were "ineffective."[37] Flying at lower altitudes, A-10s could use their 30-mm Gatling guns armed with depleted uranium slugs with deadly effect. Two pilots, Capt. Eric Salmonson and 1st Lt. John Marks, received credit for destroying twenty-three tanks by ground forward air controllers. In another case, Iraqi soldiers surrendered themselves and their tanks at the first appearance of A-10s overhead.[38]

On the 25th, the Iraqis finally appear to have woken to the extent of the looming battlefield catastrophe. Saddam announced a general withdrawal from Kuwait.[39] The Iraqi high command undertook to get as much of its army out of Kuwait as it could. While ill-prepared Iraqi forces scrambled to escape, the Iraqis attempted to establish two screens to cover the retreat. In the west, the Republican Guard was to gain time against the Coalition drive from the west; regular armored divisions further east were to screen the retreat from Kuwait City. Both moves resulted in Iraqi forces having to fight in positions not of their own choosing. The Iraqi high command also undertook another redeployment that had considerable political consequences after the war. It moved units of the Republican Guard that were outside the theater to occupy Baghdad and Basra. When the war was over, that deployment allowed the regime to maintain its hold over the center and southern portions of Iraq despite the political ramifications of its disastrous military defeats.[40]

---

[37] Marine AV-8Bs seem to have had the same problem as A-10s–out of 274 close air support missions, 143 resulted in no drop. The record for the A-10s was 316 no-drop sorties out of 909 launches. These high totals reflected a number of causes: 1) the Iraqis did not fight with anything like the intensity expected; consequently there were less targets to strike; 2) the bad weather undoubtedly interfered with air operation and coordination with ground forces; and 3) there were often too many sorties in the air and available for the number of targets. "Marine Corps Reconstruction Report," Vol IV, p 77.

[38] (S) Combat Chronology, 23/354 TFW(P), 17 Jan 1991-28 Feb 1991.

[39] Undoubtedly a political smoke screen to cover the regime from the political fall out of having its army thrown out of Kuwait.

[40] The US and British advance from the west, of course, would have forced the Iraqis to fight under such circumstances.

By midday 26 February, 24th Infantry Division had completed its move into the Euphrates River Valley. Its advance on this day established a second powerful block on Highway 8 and involved its units in heavy fighting to overrun the airfields of Tallil and Jaliba. The attack on Tallil received considerable support from preparatory A-10 strikes.[41] By evening 26 February both fields were in American hands and 24th Infantry Division could advance down the Euphrates to cover the VII Corps' flank and destroy whatever Iraqi units got in its way.

By this point, VII Corps completed its combat deployment to the north; it was ready to move east to sweep up Iraq's ground forces. From north to south, VII Corps deployed four divisions and one armored cavalry regiment: 1st Armored Division, 3d Armored Division, 2d Armored Cavalry Regiment, 1st Infantry Division–which ironically, given its name, possessed more tanks than any other U.S. division in the theater–and the British 1st Armored Division. To the south, ARCENT released 1st Cavalry Division–which had formed the theater reserve and had launched the demonstration attack on the Wadi Al-Batin–to VII Corps.

Wretched weather, including rain showers, thunderstorms, and dust storms, accompanied VII Corps' advance during the night of 25/26 February.[42] In this situation there was little that air units could do to support the advance directly; their contribution to the ensuing ground battles depended on the effectiveness of their efforts in the KTO since 17 January. Beginning in late afternoon, the wedge of VII Corps chewed through enemy formations. The Iraqis were in considerable disarray; units supposedly in blocking positions had not yet arrived when Coalition forces attacked them; Saddam's retreat order added to the confusion; and as always, air attacks throughout the KTO created further disorder.[43] What occurred over the night of the 26th/27th was the wholesale destruction of Iraqi ground forces in their blocking positions. [For the ground situation as of 26 February, see Map 46.] The attacking forces of VII Corps destroyed 12th and 52d Armored Divisions, much of the Tawakalna Republican Guard Division, and the 48th Infantry Division with minimal loss to U.S. units.

---

[41] Scales, *Certain Victory*, Chapter 5.

[42] Walters, et al, "Gulf War Weather," pp 3-94 to 3-95.

[43] For a reconstruction of the difficulties encountered by the 50th Armored Brigade see Scales, *Certain Victory*, Chapter 5.

By 26 February the Marine advance had broken up whatever cohesion remained in Iraqi defenses south of Kuwait City. Saddam's retreat order completed the disarray, as desperate Iraqis, civilian administrators as well as soldiers, desperately sought to flee. By early afternoon "Tiger" Brigade had reached the main highway running out of Kuwait City to Basra. Air Force, Navy, and Marine strikes had already bottled up a flood of fleeing military and civilian vehicles. With the head of the pass blocked by vehicles destroyed by air attacks, a gigantic traffic jam formed–one that Army and Marine units pounded along with aircraft in the area. Most Iraqis had sense enough to abandon their vehicles and walk out; the "Highway of Death," a name popularized by the press, was in fact largely a highway of dead vehicles, but the name certainly conveyed the extent of the Iraqi defeat.[44] While the advance to the "Highway of Death" occurred, other Marine units reached Kuwait International Airport south of the capital. Here the Iraqis put up stiff resistance. The Marines found close air support of direct utility; their own AV-8Bs and F/A-18s provided considerable preparatory support for their mechanized units to finish off Iraqi resistance in front of Kuwait City.[45]

The ground advance on the final day involved cleaning up the wreckage of fleeing enemy units. [For the ground situation of 28 February, 1400 hrs, see Map 47.] All pretense by the Iraqis of forming a coherent defense ended as they desperately attempted to extricate what was left in the theater. Many surviving units, including those from the Republican Guard, managed to reach Basra. In that position, they were exposed to a thrust by 24th Infantry Division, supported by 1st Cavalry and 1st Armored Divisions. But at the time, it appeared wiser to cease military operations and grant the Iraqis an armistice.

Coalition air power rendered useful support to ground forces in flying close air support missions. There were some striking differences in how such missions were flown. Seventh Corps utilized its air power assets in accordance with the army's "air-land battle" doctrine–as a tool to fight the deep battle.[46] The lack of coherent or effective Iraqi ground

---

[44] Schubert and Kraus, *The Whirlwind War*, pp 311-13.

[45] "Testimony of Maj Gen James M. Myatt, 8 May 1991," Hearings before the Committee on Armed Services, United States Senate (Washington, DC, 1991), pp 60-62.

[46] Intvw, Gen Frederick Franks with GWAPS personnel (Thomas Keaney), 2 Sep 1992.

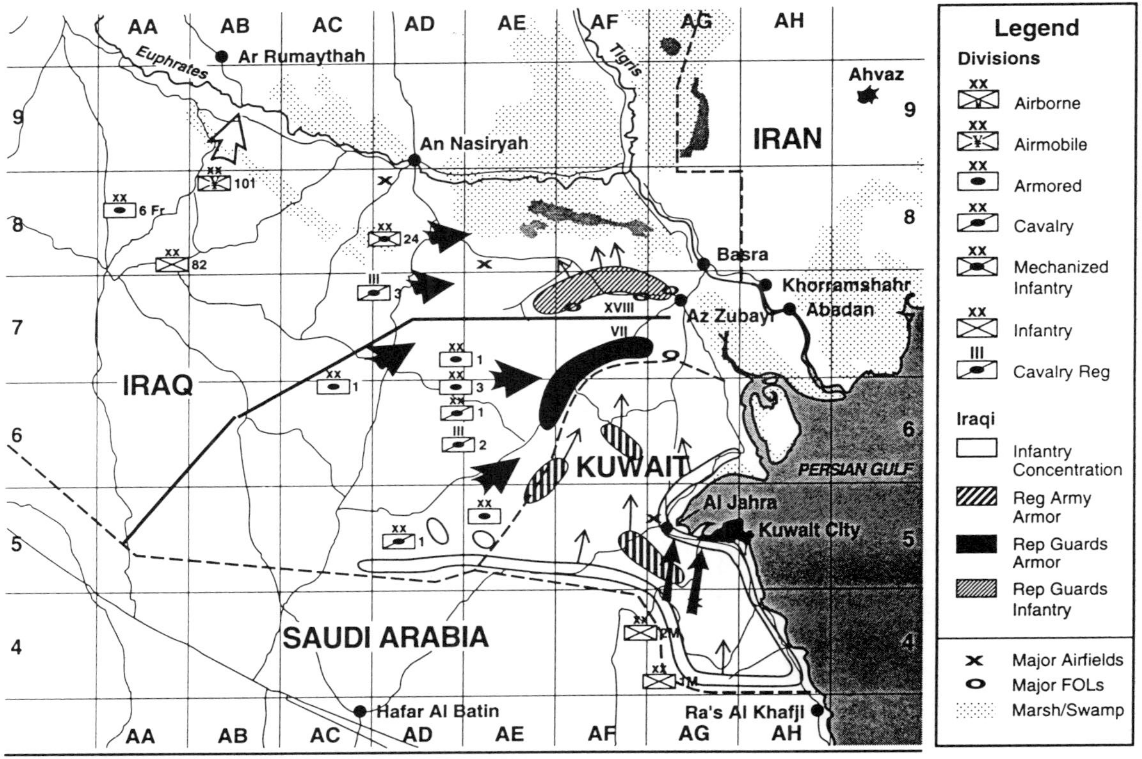

Map 46
Ground Forces
26 February
2400 hours

resistance aided that conception. On the other hand, the Marines with less organic firepower in their ground units depended more on close air support. Never, however, in either case,did the Iraqis put up effective enough resistance to test the system fully.

The bulk of Coalition sorties in the KTO during the ground war flew against interdiction targets. While bad weather made the task of providing close air support almost impossible at times, it was not much kinder to aircraft flying interdiction missions. In terms of the state as well as capabilities of Iraqi ground forces after the air campaign, one can agree that close air support was never essential to accomplishment of the ground mission.[47] But on the interdiction side of the ledger with the Iraqis concentrating to meet the ground offensive, air power was in a position to strike lucrative targets. Unfortunately, bad weather prevented Coalition aircraft from taking advantage of this situation to the fullest extent.

Air interdiction involved two distinct periods during the ground war: in the first, Coalition air power aimed to destroy, disrupt, and delay the enemy's ability to launch effective counterattacks against Coalition ground forces. However, once it became clear on 25 February that the Iraqis were fleeing Kuwait as quickly as possible, the interdiction focus shifted to attacks on a fleeing enemy.[48]

The interdiction effort against fleeing targets was not as successful as air commanders expected. There were a number of reasons why this was the case. The weather was a major factor. Both the Iraqi concentrations and retreat from the theater took place under conditions adverse to the employment of air power. The choke point north of Kuwait City involved mostly civilian vehicles commandeered by fleeing Iraqi soldiers. There was the possibility of a second choke point west of Basra, where Coalition air attacks had destroyed most of the bridges over

---

[47]The case is somewhat different with regards to the Marines. The Army has always invested heavily in artillery support for frontline units; the Marines on the other hand have put its resources into support for their own air component. Consequently, particularly in the Kuwait theater they had to have close air support at times, while Army units could rely on artillery fire to fight the close in battle.

[48]For a more detailed discussion of the interdiction effort, see The Effectiveness report, *Gulf War Air Power Survey*, Chapter 5.

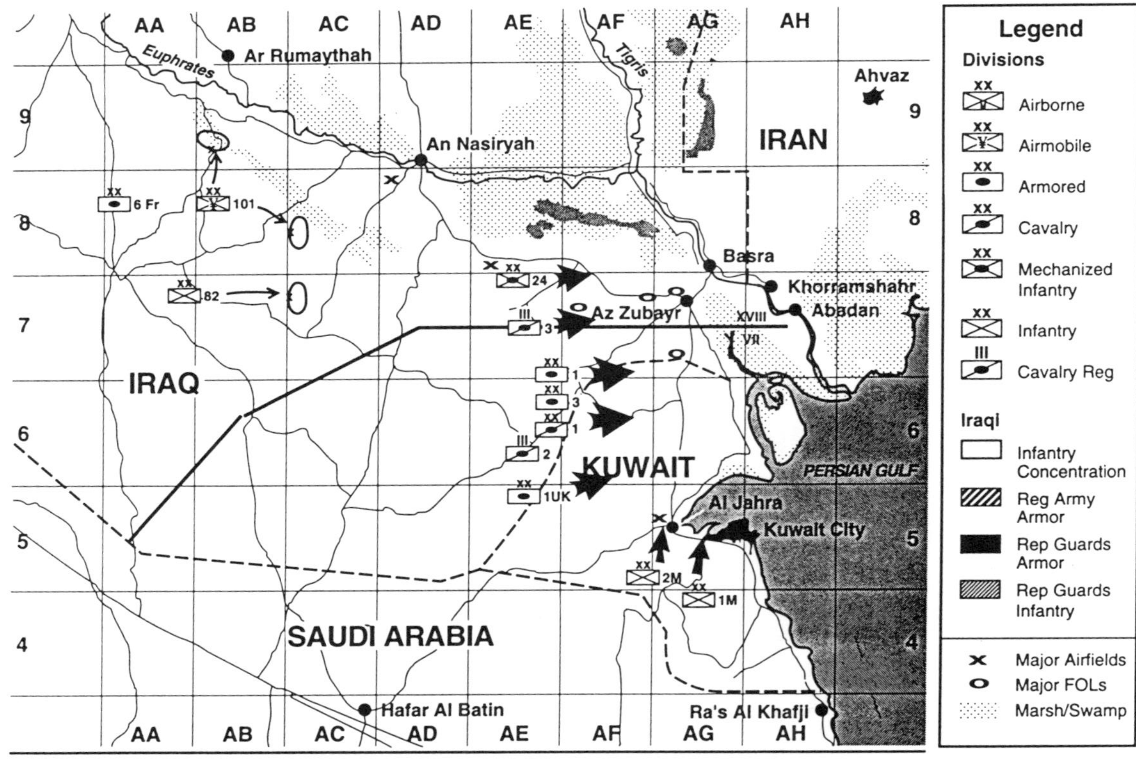

Map 47
Ground Forces
28 February
1400 hours

the canals. However, a final reckoning from the air did not occur. For one thing, bad weather with low ceilings forced attacking aircraft to bomb through clouds on radar. Moreover, Schwarzkopf's fears about a possible incident with Iran led him to put the area near the Iranian frontier off limits to air attacks.[49]

During the last forty-eight hours, a serious dispute arose between Army and Air Force over placement of the fire support coordination line (FSCL)–a dispute which shows neither service in the best of lights. The FSCL represents an essential element in inter-service cooperation to limit fratricide. Between front line and FSCL all aircraft sorties remain under the positive control of ground forces or airborne forward air controllers in communication with those on the ground; beyond the FSCL, attack aircraft have *carte blanche* to attack any targets they believe to be enemy.

This is not an arcane doctrinal issue; aircraft not under positive control and attacking targets in the vicinity of friendly ground forces–particularly in a war of rapid movement–may either bomb their own troops or themselves fly into artillery or rocket barrages. Consequently, within the FSCL all Coalition aircraft remained under the positive control of forward air controllers. AWACS and ABCCC generally coordinated the flow of information from JSTARS, but crucial to the information flow to the forward air controllers were the corps' Air Support Operations Centers (ASOC). That direct link provided immediate confirmation as to whether units seen moving on the ground were hostile or friendly. In one case, an F-16 "Killer Scout" reported to XVIII Airborne Corp's ASOC a major armored formation near the Iraqi airfield of Jaliba; the Corp's ASOC identified the armored formation as a brigade of the 24th Infantry Division. Consequently, despite considerable enthusiasm by aircraft arriving on station to attack "the mother lode just northeast of Jaliba,"[50] the "Killer Scout" warned the aircraft off what appeared to be a wonderful target, but which in fact were friendly troops.

---

[49](S) "TSgt Barton's Notes from the TACC," 1020 25 Feb 1991, GWAPS, NA 200; and TACC Log, entries for 27 Feb 1991, GWAPS, NA 215.

[50]Capt Rob Hartberg, "Beyond The Fire Support Coordination Line (FSCL): Contact The Killer Scouts," *USAF Fighter Weapons Review*, Spring 1992, p 12.

There were, of course, a number of fratricide incidents. Because of the low casualty rates, the Army was able to examine in great detail nearly every incident in the war involving the loss or injury of its troops. The dark side of the Coalition victory was the significant percentage of Coalition casualties inflicted by "friendly fire." In recognizing that considerable percentage, however, one needs to keep in mind the extraordinary rapidity of the ground force's advance. Considering that speed and the conditions of the battlefield–much bad weather and the smoke from Kuwait's oil fields–it is perhaps surprising that there were so few incidents. One might have lowered the level of fratricide by slower and more methodical movements. Such an approach would have allowed greater ground-air coordination, but that in turn might well have raised the gross number of casualties by allowing the Iraqis greater time to recover their equilibrium.

However, there were problems with the fire support coordination line (FSCL). Late in the ground war, army commanders, without reference to their air counterparts, moved the FSCL, in one case north of the Euphrates, and in another close to Basra. The first case is the most interesting and deals with XVIII Airborne Corps. On 27 February, XVIII Airborne Corps wanted to use its helicopters against enemy targets on the causeway at Hawr al Hammar; consequently, it moved the FSCL forward to accommodate such strikes. By moving the line forward, the airborne corps staff avoided having to put its helicopters under Air Force control. That decision, however, had unforeseen consequences; XVIII Airborne Corps had created a situation that severely limited the potential of the Coalition's available air power. Despite the fact that no U.S. ground troops were north of the Euphrates–nor were there plans for such a movement–navy and air force aircraft now could only attack the causeway and highways north of the Euphrates under direct control of forward air controllers (FACs). But virtually all the FACs were concentrated in supporting troops in combat further south in Kuwait. Moreover, conditions were not favorable to the employment of FACs even if they had been available.[51]

---

[51](S) Intvw, Maj Gen John A. Corder with GWAPS, 18 May 1992; TACC log, entries of 27 Feb 1991, GWAPS, NA 215; TACC Historian Transcripts, "TSgt Scott A. Saluda's Notes," GWAPS, NA 200.

In the end, the TACC appealed to Schwarzkopf to move the FSCL back to the Euphrates so that air strikes could hit both the causeway and the roads north of the river. Unfortunately, it took *fifteen* hours to resolve the dispute–a period during which there were only sporadic helicopter attacks on fleeing Iraqis, while the bulk of Coalition air power remained on the sidelines.[52] In the end, the argument may not have played a decisive role in the enemy's escape. The weather was such that it is improbable that Coalition air power could have prevented the retreat of most of those Iraqi forces, given the difficulty in employing precision-guided munitions in bad weather. Nevertheless, the incident does suggest a parochialism that for the most part was not prevalent during the war. Fortunately such incidents rarely occurred during the conflict.

The Impact of Air Power on Ground Forces

There is no exact fashion in which one can measure the impact of the air campaign on Iraqi ground forces. After the war, there was no way to calculate the contributions that air attacks had made in preparing the battlefields on which Coalition ground forces fought. Even officers in senior positions serving in the same brigade with previous combat experience were unable to agree on what air power had done. Lt. Col. John Brown, battalion commander in the 2d Armored Division's Brigade forward–part of 1st Infantry Division–noted to this author that the battlefield crossed by his unit suggested that air attacks had not destroyed much Iraqi armor or artillery; nevertheless, he believed that those air attacks had savaged the enemy's transport with innumerable truck wrecks as witness.[53] On the other hand, the G-3 of that same brigade, Lt. Col. Clint Ancker, noted that from his vantage point air attacks had destroyed much Iraqi armor.[54] Ancker noted a number of tank wrecks and cold T-72s that the Iraqis had abandoned either because of crew desertions or supply difficulties resulting from the air campaign. Brown and Ancker transited Iraqi territory within approximately a kilometer of each other; yet their impressions were considerably different. Admittedly, their units were trying to move rapidly to the east, were involved in "heavy" fighting, and were often enshrouded in miserable weather.

---

[52](S) *Ibid.*

[53]Intvw, Lt Col John Brown with GWAPS personnel (Williamson Murray), Naval War College, May 1992.

[54]Intvw, Lt Col Clint Ancker with GWAPS personnel (Williamson Murray), Naval War College, May 1992.

Their differences encapsulate the difficulties confronting the historian in estimating the effects of the air campaign against Iraqi ground forces. Had U.S. authorities undertaken a systematic survey of the battlefield after hostilities, we might possess a more coherent picture on which to estimate the direct results of the air campaign–at least against equipment. But neither Air Force nor Army displayed much interest; therefore the data available comes from aerial surveys–which do not indicate what destroyed Iraqi equipment–or individual surveys undertaken by the units themselves.[55]

The GWAPS Effectiveness report has examined the question of the equipment air attacks destroyed or damaged in detail.[56] It is, however, useful for our purposes to recapitulate its main argument. Destruction of Iraqi equipment depended on the air campaign's focus in the KTO as well as its form. The destruction wrought by Coalition air and ground campaigns against Iraq's forces are indeed impressive. Of approximately 3,475 tanks in theater on 15 January, the Iraqis possessed only 842 on 1 March; the artillery losses were even heavier: of 2,475 tubes on 15 January, only 279 remained at the beginning of March.[57] Of course, the ground war did destroy much of that equipment.

---

[55] In this case the 2d Armored Division's Brigade (forward) did send a team under Col. Ancker to survey the area through which it moved during the fighting. But while that team made a complete survey of all damaged and destroyed equipment, it did not have the technical expertise to determine what weapons systems had achieved the destruction. The largest official effort to survey damaged Iraqi military equipment, the Joint Intelligence Survey Team, only examined a sample of 163 tanks out of the 2,633 tanks that were destroyed during the war. This team examined 145 hits on 85 tanks (78 of the 163 were not hit) and found that 28 had been hit by air-dropped or fired munitions. The fact that 78 tanks had been abandoned does suggest an indirect impact of air attacks, but the sample size is too small and isolated in its geographic area to reach any firm conclusions. Memorandum and attached briefing viewgraphs (S), Foreign Science and Technology Center, "Joint Intelligence Survey Team Report," 14 Jan 1992, GWAPS, NA 167. See also Marine Corps Research Center, "Armor/Antiarmor Operations in Southwest Asia," Research Paper #92-0002, US Marine Corps, Quantico, VA, Jul 1991.

[56] (S) Effectiveness report, *Gulf War Air Power Survey*, Chapter 4.

[57] 1 Mar 1991 equipment totals derived from U-2 Imagery of the same date. Data provided in the CIA Briefing to GWAPS, 25 Jun 1992.

Much destruction centered on units of Iraq's army; despite heavy attacks on the Republican Guard, those units suffered less heavily. Undoubtedly, that fact reflected the heavy engineering preparations undertaken by the enemy to protect these elite troops, as well as the wide area over which the Republican Guard had dispersed.[61] But even among regular army units, there were disparities in losses that units suffered. Again the determining feature appears to have been the degree to which units were removed from Coalition air attacks and the extent of defensive preparations.[58]

In retrospect, the most effective weapons against Iraqi equipment were the laser-guided bombs. Here again, it was the degree to which the Iraqis protected their equipment that was critical in weapon effectiveness. The analysis suggests that ARCENT assessments that laser guided bomb hits against enemy equipment in revetted positions should count as a 50 per cent kill were close to the mark.[59]

Maverick missiles (over 5,000 expended by air force aircraft) also made a major contribution to destruction of Iraqi armor; there is no reason to disbelieve the one third credit that ARCENT gave to Maverick claims. However, the combination of laser-guided bomb and Maverick successes suggests that aircraft dropping free-fall bombs–B-52s, F-16s, F/A-18s, and AV-8Bs–achieved relatively little against enemy equipment despite considerable efforts. At the beginning of the ground war on 23 February, CENTCOM's reported attrition of Iraqi equipment had reached the following totals: 1,688 armored fighting vehicles (39 percent), 929 armored personnel carriers (32 percent), and 1,452 artillery pieces (47 percent).[60] Again, as the Effectiveness report suggests:

> The best approximation, and that is all it can be, is that while the *numbers* claimed by Central Command on 23 February were high, the *percentages* were probably not (given that there were fewer tanks and artillery pieces in the theater than believed). In other words, the counts of tanks and artillery pieces destroyed by air prior to the ground war are each too high by around 300 pieces of equipment.[61]

---

[58] Since they were far removed from the front lines the Iraqis felt that they could disperse more widely and that they would then have sufficient time to concentrate when warning came that the Coalition ground offensive had begun.

[59] A 50% success rate is still an impressive rate of success by anyone's criteria.

[60] Viewgraph contained in "J2 BDA Briefing to the President," GWAPS, NA 353 has the JCS/CENTCOM figures.

[61] Effectiveness report, *Gulf War Air Power Survey*, Chapter 4.

The disquieting aspect of any analysis of the air campaign against enemy ground forces is the fact that the Republican Guard, which received a disproportionately heavy emphasis in CENTAF's targeting, suffered less damage than the other units of the Iraqi Army. Moreover, it also seems to have kept it morale in better shape throughout the attacks. Undoubtedly, the fact that it were dispersed over wider areas and possessed substantially better engineer support in laying out defensive revetments contributed to its ability to withstand the air bombardment.

The beginning of F-111F attacks with precision-guided munition capabilities in early February caused a significant rise in Republican Guard losses, but such losses never caught up with the level of damage that Coalition aircraft had inflicted on other Iraqi formations. Moreover, CENTAF pulled the A-10s, the other precision-guided munition-capable aircraft, out of Republican Guard areas in mid-February because of the missile threat.[62] Unfortunately, those aircraft that dropped "dumb" bombs contributed little to the direct attrition of equipment possessed by the regime's elite divisions. Consequently, despite heavy commitments of F-16s and B-52s against the Republican Guard these elite troops, crucial to the regime's political survival, suffered less than their army counterparts.

But the air campaign's true impact should not be measured on the basis of indices that calculate only the amounts of equipment destroyed by air attack. The issues on which one needs to judge the air campaign's effectiveness are the degrees to which air attacks impeded or prevented enemy military action to protect his forces and to which air attacks reduced the willingness of Iraqi soldiers to fight.[63] The problem with estimating the indirect effects of air attacks on Iraqi ground forces has

---

[62]As discussed above, on 15 February the A-10s lost two of their aircraft with one damaged. "Operation 'Desert Storm' A-10 Combat Recap," GWAPS, NA 292.

[63]On the basis of the EPW interviews, the morale of Iraqi forces was not high even before the air campaign began. As one of the comprehensive intelligence debriefs suggested: "There is little doubt that there were many thousands of veterans of the Iranian war in the army Saddam Hussein rushed to the south. However, the evidence is convincing that most Iraqi soldiers, both officers and enlisted, did not believe in the cause." Department of the Army, 513th Military Intelligence Brigade, Joint Debriefing Center, "Analysis of Source Debriefings," JDC Rpt #065, 15 Mar 1991. See also (S) IIR 6-072-0037-91.

much to do with the nature of evidence. The low casualty rates suffered by Coalition forces are the best indicators of the air campaign's contribution to the ground war, but here one deals entirely with intangibles. There is no way of estimating casualty levels that would have occurred had there been no air campaign.[64] And we have suggested, little documentation outside of POW (prisoner of war) reports exists on the Iraqi Army before or during the ground war.[65]

Consequently, interrogations of Iraqi POWs provide the best evidence on the indirect impact of the air campaign. Even here there are ambiguities. The greatest number of the POWs came from Iraqi units deployed furthest forward; Coalition ground forces captured and interrogated significant numbers of senior officers from these infantry divisions defending the Saudi border. Unfortunately, only a few Republican Guard officers fell into Coalition hands. As a result, the picture of the air campaign's impact is much clearer for regular army units than for those of the Republican Guard.

Nevertheless, one can make interesting judgments. It did not take the Iraqis long to recognize that Coalition aircraft were targeting equipment; as soon as precision-guided munitions impacted on equipment near their positions, Iraqi troops moved away from the danger area. As one Iraqi noted to his captors after the war, "The love affair between tank and tankers ended."[66] The result was a direct decrease in maintenance and preparation of equipment for combat. Moreover, precision-guided munition attacks reinforced Iraqi perceptions of an overwhelming American technological superiority. POW reports do provide evidence that CENTCOM analyses of enemy equipment losses were close to the mark.

---

[64] One of the Army veterans from "Desert Storm" who talked to GWAPS commented that the air attacks had broken most of the Iraqi Army before the ground war began. He had no doubt that Coalition ground forces could have beaten the Iraqis without an air campaign, but noted that Coalition ground casualties would have increased *significantly.* Oral presentation, Lt Col Clint Ancker to GWAPS, 19 Oct 1992.

[65] Given the nature of the Iraqi regime and Saddam's ability to remain in power whatever the level of disaster for which he is responsible, it is unlikely that we will ever get a clear picture of what happened within the Iraqi military as the air campaign unfolded. What makes the future picture even darker is that considering the nature of the Ba'th tyranny, it is doubtful whether the Iraqis themselves could construct an accurate picture of what happened in the Gulf War.

[66] Department of the Army, 513th Military Intelligence Brigade, Joint Debriefing Center, "Analysis of Source Debriefings," JDC Rpt #065, 15 Mar 1991.

During the five months before 17 January the Iraqis had stockpiled large amounts of ammunition, fuel, and rations. They had done this not because of expectations that the air campaign would last a long time, but rather because they believed the ground war, if it occurred, would become a long slogging match similar to the war against Iran. Since the enemy had such large stockpiles, Coalition planners dealing with the KTO never attempted a coherent campaign to interdict the flow of supplies into the theater; but air attacks did knock out the railroad running from Baghdad to Basra, while other attacks took out most of the bridges along the Euphrates. In the latter case, the aim was as much to prevent the escape of the Republican Guard as the movement of supplies into the theater.

> Equipment attrition due to the air campaign appears to have been extremely heavy, with all sources reporting that tanks, trucks, water and fuel tankers, armored personnel carriers and anything else that moved were systematically targeted by Coalition aircraft with great success.[67]

Air attacks also imposed a significant level of interdiction on the flow of supplies within the KTO. Ironically, that effect was an indirect result of Coalition air attacks; there is no evidence that planners in the "Black Hole" aimed at interdicting the resupply of Iraqi forces from supply bunkers to defending units.[68] During the day, Coalition aircraft, when weather permitted, did a thorough job of shutting down movement of Iraqi vehicles; during the night, however, a different situation obtained and the Iraqis could move some needed supplies from depots to units.

Nevertheless, there were serious problems for the Iraqis. For one thing, few supply vehicles were bunkered; they were therefore more vulnerable to air attacks. One Iraqi indicated that he had felt that the Coalition had waged a systematic campaign against the logistic system. Another Iraqi indicated that whereas supply runs had occurred before

---

[67] Department of the Army, 513th Military Intelligence Brigade, Joint Debriefing Center, "The Gulf War: An Iraqi General Officer's Perspective," JDC Rpt #0052, 11 Mar 1991.

[68] GWAPS discussions with those running the JSTARS effort suggest no consistent effort to shut down the movement of Iraqi vehicular traffic at night, unless it involved the movement of large convoys. Most Iraqi resupply took place with small groups or single trucks distributing supplies to the units. See the oral interview, Brig Gen George K. Muellner with GWAPS personnel (Thomas C. Hone, Anne Leary, Mark Mandeles), 16 Apr 1992.

the war in daylight, "supply runs now were made at night with the runs routes varied for safety reasons. As the air war progressed, these became harder to make as more trucks were damaged and the fuel became scarcer."

The Iraqi Army was not in danger of starving to death. But the collapse of its logistics, occurring in a number of divisions, resulted in pervasive problems in supplying frontline units with anything more than bare necessities. As early as Khafji, this state of affairs was clear in looking a POWs. Intelligence reports at the time indicated that Iraqi POWs were in wretched health and malnourished, but wearing new boots and new uniforms. As the Effectiveness report suggests: "The one pattern that emerges from the evidence is not of a starving army, but of the signs evident in a country in which the distribution system has ceased to function–illogical distributions, goods absent, being hoarded, or lying unused."[69] By the beginning of the ground campaign much of the Iraqi Army was in serious trouble with a collapsing logistical system. Several POWs went so far as to state that the ground campaign was unnecessary, and had the air campaign continued two or three weeks longer, the Iraqi Army would have been forced to withdraw due to logistical strangulation.[70]

POW reports on their logistics suggest that a more methodical campaign against the enemy's distribution at night as well as by day might have brought Iraqi forces to the brink of collapse.[71] As it was, the effects of air operations on the enemy supplies caused serious difficulties to Iraqi troops. These difficulties, however, represented only a portion of what was occurring to the enemy's army.

The breakdown of consistent and coherent supply also had a direct impact on Iraqi morale. But the steady pounding of the Coalition air campaign had the greatest impact on the enemy. Again to quote from the Effectiveness report:

---

[69] Effectiveness report, *Gulf War Air Power Survey*, Chapter 4.

[70] Department of the Army, 513th Military Intelligence Brigade, Joint Debriefing Center," The Gulf War: An Iraqi General Officer's Perspective," JDC Rpt #0052, 11 Mar 1991.

[71] Such a campaign might have been waged by using JSTARS, but it is clear that there was no clearly thought-through plan for using this new technological intelligence system

> The pervasive impression left by the interrogation reports of prisoners who deserted or who were captured was the sense of futility felt by the Iraqis after weeks of extensive bombing. When the bombing started, their ground transportation began to crumble. They ran short of water, food, fuel, and all spare parts. Some units had their supply stocks destroyed. Training in the units ceased. Soldiers moved apart from their equipment because they well understood what the targets were. Many captured Iraqis stated they thought the air campaign would last several days to a week at most. When it did not end, the sense of futility and inevitability of the outcome became more apparent.[72]

Here the question is not one of equipment destruction, but rather the impact that ceaseless air attacks had on the minds of enemy soldiers. No Iraqi could know whether B-52 raids attacking neighboring divisions were hitting their targets or not; the sounds and trembling in the ground told him all he needed to know.

In the meantime, Coalition psyops leaflets assured him that soon he and his unit would also fall under the B-52's terrible wrath. If that were not enough, day-to-day living conditions worsened with the incessant appearances of A-10s and F-16s. Here again the issue is not one of accuracy. Iraqi soldiers had no idea of whether bombs impacting down the road were hitting targets or not; psychologically, the air attacks added to the sense of an endless terror–a situation moreover, where the Iraqis could undertake no action to retaliate for the punishment that Coalition aircraft inflicted on them.

As suggested above, Iraqi ground forces were already in bad shape before the air campaign began. But air bombardment placed extraordinary pressures on vulnerable military forces. It took a weak reed and smashed it into the ground.

---

in such a role. Rather than as a guide to funneling real-time intelligence into air operations (with the possible exception of the battle of Khafji), JSTARS seems to have played a role as a glorified ABCCC and allocated sorties among different sets of targets drawn up by competing authorities on the ground (The Battlefield Control Element, CENTCOM, ARCENT, MARCENT, and even VII Corps). JSTARS also participated in the hunt for Scuds. But the evidence does not suggest that those in JSTARS or those who attempted to utilize it ever conceived of it as having a mission to participate in the closing down and interdiction of the Iraqi supply system within the theater. See in particular: Oral intvw, Brig Gen George K. Muellner with GWAPS personnel (Thomas C. Hone, Anne Leary, and Mark Mandeles) 16 Apr 1992.

[72] (S) Effectiveness Report, Gulf War Air Power Survey, Chapter 4

The POW reports underline the terrible effects that unceasing air attacks had on Iraqi troops. Most felt no shame for having surrendered because they were overwhelmed by the Allied air campaign and that resistance was futile." High desertion rates suggest the general breakdown of enemy ground forces as they awaited the start of the "Mother of all Battles." More over, one must place such desertion rates, reaching 50 percent, within the context of Iraqi political life: anyone who crossed the regime risk ed paying a heavy price not only in terms of his own survival, but for that of his family as well.

As the pounding continued, the Iraqi high command displayed some sense of what was happening in the KTO. It ordered commanders to undertake summary executions of deserters.

From the Iraqi perspective, there were several factors that resulted in the collapse of morale. The length of the air offensive as well as its intensity played a major role in undermining morale. Soldiers recognized that they were helpless. Their equipment steadily disappeared in explosions and smoke; trucks on which resupply depended disappeared fastest of all; but as day-to-day living conditions deteriorated, all feared that aircraft attacking their comrades would soon come after them.

One comes away from extensive readings in the POW reports that whatever will existed in the Iraqi Army to see another war through to the end that might have existed on 17 January, had vanished by the beginning of the ground campaign. Some units did admittedly fight, but for the most part, the structure collapsed as its most basic building block, the common soldier surrendered, in great numbers and after minimal resistance.

Conclusion

The 100-hour ground war to a great extent represented the achievement of air power. By creating the conditions under which CENTCOM could redeploy its forces and by executing an almost ceaseless campaign against enemy forces in the KTO, air power established the conditions under which Coalition ground forces could catch enemy forces by surprise. By hammering Iraqi forces in the KTO from the beginning of the war, Coalition air power destroyed whatever willingness most might have had to fight the ground battle with the kind of tenacity that they had displayed during the Iran-Iraq War. One of course will never know how well the Iraqi Army might have fought without an air campaign. But the extraordinarily low level of casualties in the ground war is a fitting tribute to the efforts and success of those airmen who flew in the KTO.

8

Conclusion

At the beginning of this report, we recorded Gen. Bernard Trainor's observation that the Gulf War represented the first conflict in which a ground campaign had supported an air campaign. In this sense, the war against Iraq represented air power's coming of age; for the first time in history, air power had reached the expectations of its proponents.

Any critical examination of American performance in the war may seem like quibbling with what was an enormous success story. One could also argue that the U.S. brought such power and superiority to the Gulf that victory was a foregone conclusion. Yet such a conclusion would be misleading. It was not inevitable that Coalition forces would break Iraqi air defenses at such low cost or with such devastating ease. Given the often vast gap between "real war" and "war on paper," the American military did perform in a highly competent fashion. Admittedly, there were weaknesses and areas that deserve attention. But Coalition forces consistently placed their strengths against Iraqi weakness.

Moreover, any serious analysis of the results in the Gulf during Desert Storm must recognize the imponderables. It was not inevitable that Saddam Hussein would allow the Coalition time to gather, organize, and deploy its forces to the Gulf. It was not inevitable that the Iraqis would deploy so much of their ground forces in the desert areas of Kuwait and southeastern Iraq–a region that minimized their strengths and maximized their weaknesses. The Coalition did reap full advantage from the mistaken decisions and misapprehensions of Iraqi leaders before the war. Again, this was not inevitable.

Yet this study of the Gulf War also suggests that the air campaign operated, as have all previous campaigns, within the realm of friction and ambiguity. Historians may never be able to unravel some of the effects of the air campaign against Iraq and its forces–the impact of bombing on the morale of Iraq's soldiers is a particularly good example. Allied air commanders and planners, however, had to operate in their real world of incomplete information and uncertainty; their decisions consequently reflected the situation as they saw it and external pressures–political as well as military–all worked on their judgements of the situation. It is in that light that one must assess the operational conduct of the air war against Iraq and its military forces.

We might begin our conclusion by examining the larger question of what the air campaign achieved in the political realm. The saga of Saddam's success in maintaining his hold on power and his defiance of those who have brought his regime to its current state have suggested to many that the war against Iraq failed. After all, it did not remove the dictator from power. With two years of hindsight and Iraqi intransigence, it is thus easy to argue that Coalition failed to achieve its goals. But in the political conditions of the time, the maximum goals that the Coalition could pursue were the liberation of Kuwait, the destruction of Iraq's armed forces to the greatest extent possible, and the debilitation of Saddam's efforts to construct weapons of mass destruction. The pursuit of more ambitious goals than these might well have led to the collapse of the Coalition; it certainly would have resulted in serious troubles within the Arab world.[1] Within the political and international context of the 1990/1991 period, President Bush staked out a maximalist position for the Coalition in the confrontation with Iraq.

The best way to judge the Coalition's strategic and political achievements in the air campaign is to estimate what might have happened had the United States and its allies *not* embarked on war in January 1991. At this time there were substantial numbers in Congress and the media who argued that a continued embargo would resolve the crisis and force the Iraqis to disgorge Kuwait. The intransigent and often effective campaign that Saddam has waged *since* Iraq's military defeat to undermine, mitigate, or ignore the UN Security Council underlines what Iraq's behavior would have been had there been no air and ground campaign to

---

[1]As stated in Chapter 1 of this study, the Coalition's objectives as stated in the last operations plan before the onset of the war were: 1) destroy Iraq's military capability to wage war; 2) gain and maintain air superiority; 3) cut Iraqi supply lines to the KTO; 4) destroy Iraq's chemical, biological, and nuclear capabilities; 5) destroy the capabilities of the Republican Guard; and 6) liberate Kuwait City. (S) HQUSCENTCOM, Combined OPLAN for Offensive Operations to Eject Iraqi Forces from Kuwait, 17 Jan 1991, pp 2-4.

limit its options.[2] Under such circumstances it is unlikely that the Coalition could have held for a substantial period of time, or whether the United States, Great Britain, and France could have maintained those forces deployed before November 1990 for an indeterminate period. Moreover, an unwillingness to take on Iraq's military forces would have had a disastrous impact on political attitudes within the Arab world; the actions of the Palestinians and troubles in Morocco, Algeria, and Egypt during the crisis suggest that any perception in the Arab world that Saddam had successfully defied the west would have had a disastrous impact on moderate regimes in the Arab world. Finally, without the war, Saddam might well have had nuclear weapons as early as 1995; one can scarcely imagine a more destabilizing factor in the Middle Eastern balance.

Beyond the air campaign, one must note that it was essential for the Coalition to conduct a ground campaign to lay out the impact of the air campaign on Iraqi ground forces. Through mid-February, Saddam retained the option of abandoning Kuwait and thereafter claiming that his ground forces had remained unbeaten in the field, too powerful and tough for soft Americans to attack.[3] But Saddam seems to have calculated that the Coalition would not attack on the ground, or he may have thought that his forces would be able to turn a Coalition offensive into a bloody meat grinder. In the end, his miscalculation was disastrous; the resulting Allied success in the ground war and the concurrent collapse of Iraqi forces largely rested on the effects of the Coalition's air campaign.

If the Coalition achieved its strategic goals, how did the air campaign fit within this strategic and political framework? Here one might contrast the air war in the Gulf with the air campaign against North

---

[2]One can also gain insight into Iraq's capacity to defy the United Nations and "world public opinion" by noting the effective campaign of defiance and ruthless military action that little Serbia has pursued against its neighbors. An Iraq emboldened by a refusal of the Coalition to take action is not a pretty picture to consider.

[3]This is of course what happened in World War I, when a German Army, completely beaten on the Western Front, was allowed to retreat to the Fatherland rather than surrender in place. Within a matter of months, the German military and right-wing political leaders were claiming that the army had stood unbeaten in the field, only to be stabbed in the back by traitors, communist In the case of Iraq, it is worth noting that within a year after military defeat in Kuwait, Saddam was holding great celebrations and parades to honor the heroes in his armed forces on their "victorious" effort against the Coalition.

Vietnam from 1965 through 1968. In Vietnam, American airmen argued at the outset of Rolling Thunder that they should wage a campaign aimed at breaking the will of Ho Chi Minh's regime to continue the war in South Vietnam.[4] The strategic assumption on which such a campaign rested was that the North Vietnamese regime represented a relatively easy political target for air power–properly employed of course–to force the North Vietnamese to the peace table. Moreover, airmen did not estimate the enemy's operational and tactical capabilities to defend himself at a high level.[5] In both respects, events proved their calculations over-optimistic, but the dramatic air campaign recommended by the airmen was not permitted by the politicians.

In the conflict against Iraq, Coalition air commanders and planners did *not* underestimate enemy operational capabilities. If anything they overestimated those capabilities.[6] But on the strategic and political levels, Coalition air plans did underestimate the political stability of the Ba^cthist regime, as their predecessors had done with the North Vietnamese. The calculations on which Instant Thunder rested were indeed dangerously optimistic. Six days of strategic bombardment in anything other than a nuclear context–which of course was completely unthinkable–had little chance of persuading Iraq to do the Coalition's bidding. The political strength of Saddam's regime was such that only a campaign aimed at breaking Iraq and probably involving tens of thousands of casualties

---

[4]Department of Defense, *United States–Vietnam Relations, 1945–1965* (Washington, 1971), Book 4, Part IV.C.3, pp 71-72. Even after the war was over, airmen continued to argue that "dramatic, forceful, and *consistent* application of air power" would have achieved US political objectives. Adm U.S.G. Sharp, *Strategy for Defeat, Vietnam in Retrospect* (Novato, CA, 1978), p 268.

[5]For the best study thus far on the nature of the air war against North Vietnam and the weaknesses within which airmen cast their approach see: Mark Clodfelter, *The Limits of Air Power.*

[6]As we have argued in Chapters 2 and 3, the US planners recognized substantial weaknesses within the Iraqi military organizations. Nevertheless, Horner, Glosson, and the planners in the Black Hole did expect some substantial losses, especially in the opening days of the air offensive; moreover, the meticulous planning that went into the opening moves of the war indicate a healthy respect for the enemy's defenses. In the end, the airmen may have overestimated the enemy's capabilities, but that overestimation and the careful planning that resulted from that overestimation only magnified the success. Only if overestimation had led to a Coalition refusal to undertake military action would such an assessment have resulted in serious consequences.

could have toppled the dictator. Such an approach was also clearly unthinkable within the context of American politics.

Basic to the U.S. approach was a belief that the weak link in Iraq's armor was its political stability: a major setback would lead to a collapse of the regime either through political action or military coup.[7] As suggested in Chapter Two, such an assessment had the situation in Iraq reversed. In fact, it was the military who were the weak link, while the political regime displayed an impressive capacity to absorb punishment and retain its hold on power.[8] In the end, this miscalculation did not interfere with the Coalition's successful prosecution of the war or the achievement of political goals, as they existed in January, 1991. But airmen would do well to remember that even direct attacks on centers of enemy military power from the Second World War to the present have had little effect on the *political* stability of regimes under attack. In this sense, despite the introduction of new weapons possessing vast technological capabilities, the results were similar to those obtained in the strategic bombing campaign against Germany: whatever impact bombing might have had on popular morale, neither campaign resulted in the overthrow of the tyrant.

On the operational side of the air campaign, there are a number of significant points. To begin with, the success of the opening two days of the air campaign represent the operational high point of the conflict. Air attacks fully achieved their immediate objectives in deconstructing the Iraqi air defense system and laying open Iraq and its military forces to a

---

[7]It is worth noting that a belief in the political vulnerability of regimes to the political impact that strategic bombing would have on the will of the people to continue a conflict has been an article of faith among airmen since the first prophets of air power began writing. It was central to the arguments of Trenchard and Douhet and implicit in the writings of Mitchell and the teachings at the Air Corps Tactical School in the 1930s.

[8]The misassessment flowed as much from the peculiar political misconceptions and misunderstandings of Americans in general as from the errors that US military or intelligence organizations made during the crisis. The latter of course reflect the cultural attitudes and misperceptions of American society, and Americans, at least in the 20th Century, have had a difficult time in recognizing or understanding the importance of ideology to other peoples or cultures in the world. The attention of the reader is once again drawn to Samir Al-Khalil's *Republic of Fear, The Politics of Modern Iraq* (Berkeley, CA, 1989) as a book that should have disabused most military planners and commanders of the notion that military pressure, no matter how successfully applied, would quickly lead to Saddam's replacement by a more acceptable leadership in Baghdad.

sustained air campaign. Moreover, these strikes obtained their objectives at an astonishingly low cost in aircraft and aircrews lost.

Indeed this is the first case in military history in which commanders and planners were able to use air power directly, as an operational tool, to achieve immediate results. In February 1944, during World War II, Eighth Air Force had attacked the Luftwaffe's production facilities to prevent German industry from producing the single-engine fighters that were the backbone of its air force. "Big Week" did in fact damage the German aircraft industry, but it could not stop aircraft production; ironically over the course of 1944 enemy fighter production increased dramatically.[9]

Nor did air battles at the end of February 1944 break the Luftwaffe as a fighting force. Instead a great three-month battle of attrition occurred that finally destroyed the effectiveness of the Luftwaffe's fighter pilot force. The results of the focused attempts to destroy the Luftwaffe by destroying its production base were thus indirect. Similarly, attacks on German oil production which began in May 1944 were also indirect in their impact on the *Wehrmacht*'s ability to continue to prosecute the war. Whatever the aims, the achievements of strategic bombing in World War II remained indirect in their impact on the course of the conflict.

In the case of the war against Iraq, however, the air planners sought to attack the center of Iraq's military power in order to break up the capacity of its air defense system to mount effective resistance. By a skillful use of deception, drones, ECM capabilities, F-117s and Tomahawk missiles, preemptive fighter sweeps, and a carefully crafted plan that launched a massive SEAD package disguised to look like the great air attack on downtown Baghdad, the planners succeeded in sowing doubt, confusion, and disruption–rather than destruction–throughout the whole of the enemy's system.

---

[9]However, it is worth noting that while German fighter production increased 55% over the course of 1944, the weight of airframes produced by German industry only increased 22% in comparison to the previous years production. The Germans were able to get such an increase only by halting the production of every other type of aircraft, including bombers. Moreover, the quality of the fighters that German industry produced in 1944 also showed a significant decrease. See Williamson Murray, "Reconsidering the Combined Bomber Offensive," *Militärgeschichtliche Mitteilungen*, Heft 1, 1992.

Moreover, unlike the envelopment of Iraq's army that took place at the end of February, Coalition air attacks against the Iraqi air defense system–and other targets–occurred in the teeth of enemy defenses as yet undamaged and fully expecting an allied air attack. The fact that F-117s flew into the heart of enemy defenses without any support at the onset of the war suggests the extraordinary capabilities that Coalition air forces brought to the job. But it was *how* planners and commanders utilized those capabilities that represented the significant innovation of the Gulf War.

Given the disparity between contending forces in the Gulf, it is impossible to see how Coalition armed forces could have lost the war–except perhaps in the political sense. Yet there were other approaches to air war that would have carried with them less effective uses of resources as well as the possibility of considerably higher losses. In the mid-1980s there had been opposition from the Navy and Marines even to the concept of a joint forces air component commander (JFACC). It was certainly not incumbent on Schwarzkopf that he appoint Horner as the JFACC with the powers to control and coordinate.[10]

Without a JFACC, Schwarzkopf would have had to assign the different air forces separate areas in which to operate: the Navy would most probably have gotten much of western Iraq and a slice of eastern Iraq where Iraq's naval forces lay. The Air Force, probably supported by the Coalition air forces, would have gotten the central section, especially the area around Baghdad.

Such an air campaign would not have had a coherent focus. Given the problems that occurred in providing battle damage assessment to a centralized command structure in the war, it is difficult to see how Coalition commanders in a route package system could have gained any clear idea of what levels of damage their attacks had achieved. Much like the air campaign in the KTO, such an air war against Iraq–one could hardly have spoken of a campaign–would have degenerated into racking up sorties, generally attacking targets rather than target sets, and pursuing a number of uncoordinated aims.

---

[10]Schwarzkopf was probably driven to assigning Horner so much power to conduct the air campaign, because it was the only obvious way that they could control the air resources available.

A route package war would also have carried with it the danger that the operational coordination between Coalition air forces would have run into substantially greater problems. Certainly, coordinating tankers and SEAD packages would have been more difficult, and such difficulties would have resulted in the cancellation of sorties beyond those lost for coordination breakdowns.[11]

Moreover, such an operational approach would have created fault lines between these separate air wars. Even within the JFACC system, there were problems between conflicting jurisdictions. On 25 January the Iraqis were able to get two Mirages out into the Gulf within range of Coalition ships, largely because their flight path followed a gray area between Coalition air defense areas of responsibility. Since the USS *Roosevelt* had just arrived, it was not familiar with the procedures in the theater; its F-14s on Combat Air Patrol (CAP) over the Gulf thus did not have the frequencies on which AWACS was operating–nor for that matter did the USS *Worden* that was controlling the CAP station. Consequently, the Navy did not pick up AWACS warnings. A Saudi F-15 who was monitoring the calls from AWACS eventually splashed the Iraqis.[12]

The point here is not to find fault with the Navy, but rather to underline that even within the JFACC system, coordination problems could occur. Within the context of an air war where there were competing commands with little coordination, the potential for such incidents would have been greater. Whether the Iraqis would have utilized such opportunities is open to question. But the possibility would have been there, and any Iraqi successes would have had considerable political and strategic consequences.[13]

---

[11]This certainly occurred in the week after the first two days and reflected the considerable problems of coordination even when there was a central directing authority and process.

[12](S/NF) Charles E. Chambers, *Desert Storm Reconstruction Report, Vol III: Antiair Warfare*, Center for Naval Analyses, 1991.

[13]The crucial point here is not whether the Iraqis might or might not have taken advantage of such a situation. A route package approach to attacking Iraq would have inevitably led to a roll back campaign against the enemy air force; the Iraqis in turn would have possessed air options that were not open to them as a result of the focused campaign that began on 17 January. And with such options available to attack the Coalition forces,the Iraqi,could have launched their aircraft against an air defense system with competing authorities, unclear jurisdictions, and gray areas between areas of responsibility.

Whatever the possibilities that a splintered air war would have offered the Iraqis, there would certainly have been increased chances of blue-on-blue engagements resulting in aircraft losses. The fact that there were no such losses is indeed high tribute to the professionalism of the aircrews flying in the Gulf. It is also a tribute to the organizational framework and operational control within which this campaign functioned. But an operational framework that depended on a number of independent air authorities would have invited trouble. It certainly would have added to the inherent frictions involved in the complex tactical and operational environment of the Coalition's air campaign.

In the end, any reasonable examination of the issue suggests that there were no alternatives to the air campaign that would have much improved its conduct; and most alternatives, in all likelihood, would have been less effective.[14] Admittedly, the air tasking order (ATO) process was cumbersome and awkward in planning and processing the thousands of sorties that made up each day's effort against Iraq. Nevertheless, it achieved considerable success and made possible an operational employment of air power. Undoubtedly, the Air Force and the Navy will improve the *process* of putting together an effective ATO.

But improvements in the process only beg larger issues raised by the conflict. Shortly after the war was over, a senior naval officer wrote a perceptive critique of naval operations in the Gulf; his criticisms of certain areas of Navy preparations for the war are worth quoting in detail, not because of what they say about Navy leadership, but because they apply equally to the senior leadership of the Air Force–and the other services as well:

---

[14]As one Navy commentator on the war noted: "During my trip [to the Persian Gulf], several senior officers expressed reservations about the Navy's involvement in an air campaign directed by a Joint Force Air Component Commander (JFACC), a function performed in Desert Storm by the Air Force Component Commander. They were concerned that independent naval operations were threatened by that participation because the carriers' missions were tasked by the JFACC using the . . . ATO system. But the Navy has no alternative to the ATO system. Without it, the campaign would have been planned and directed manually. Sortie rates would have been far lower and strike deconfliction much less certain." Letter from Captain Steven U. Ramsdell to Director, Naval Historical Center, Subject: Trip Report, 14 May 1991.

> Lacking any system to plan and direct air campaigns, the Navy has no policy or official view of them. . . .[The Navy's alternative to the fashion in which the air campaign was conducted–by route packs] is the epitome of operations designed to facilitate tactics, not to achieve strategic [or operational] objectives. . . .The source of the trouble is that the concept of conducting campaigns and the process of implementing an approach to war in which tactical decisions are driven primarily by strategic objectives have not been within the field of view of our leaders in the fleet. . . .In my opinion, the Navy paid a significant price during Desert Storm in the areas of campaigning and jointness for its neglect of the non-technical education of its senior officers. . . .The real barrier that must be broken is the pervasive belief that war fighting is mostly a matter of technology and logistics and that, consequently, there is little to be gained from time spent studying other subjects. In fact, the most decisive factors in war above the tactical level are intellectual, not technical or material.[15]

No more than the Navy did the Air Force prepare its leaders to wage an air *campaign* that aimed at achieving operational-level objectives. Throughout the 1980s, the Air Force had set about to remove the *tactical* weaknesses that had shown up during the course of Vietnam. It succeeded admirably in that effort. But it did not aim at creating an officer corps that understood the wider application of air power or which could address the substantial problems raised by the use of air power on the operational level of war.

How then to explain CENTAF's success in developing a focused, operational-level air campaign?[16] Much of the credit rests on idiosyncratic factors that placed individuals in control of CENTAF and within its planning process who either intuitively understood or who were willing to be educated in the possibilities that such an operational-level air campaign could offer.[17]

---

[15]*Ibid.*

[16]Cynically one might suggest that 1) the disparity of power between Iraq's air power and that of the Coalition was so great that the result was completely inevitable, and 2) with five months to prepare to launch the knock out blow it would have been almost impossible to design a faulty plan. Such explanations, however, largely beg any close look at how the air campaign was planned and was executed.

[17]It is worth noting for those who believe that chance plays little role in war that the two greatest commentators on this aspect of human nature, Thucydides and Clausewitz, place chance at the heart of any understanding of war. According to Clausewitz: "If we

That is not, however, to suggest that planning and execution occurred flawlessly or that there were not substantial problems. The first two days' success suggests the strengths of the plan and its execution. By providing the Iraqis with what appeared to coincide with their expectations, Coalition air power deconstructed the enemy's defensive *system* and prevented any coherent defense of Iraqi air space during the entire war.

In effect, Coalition attacks over the course of the first two days maximized frictions within enemy forces. Air attacks destroyed, damaged, or impaired many targets crucial to the effective running of his air defenses. But the crucial element both in the planning and in the results was not the number of targets destroyed or damaged; rather it lay in the overall effectiveness of what those attacks achieved. The KARI computer system no longer functioned as an integrated air defense system. We cannot identify the exact point at which this event occurred–nor quite probably could the Iraqis who survived the collapse of the system. But sometime during the first six hours the system died.[18]

Admittedly, pieces of the system did put up resistance. But those pieces functioned in fitful fashion. This was particularly the case with portions of the Baghdad defenses, as the fate of Package Q demonstrated on the afternoon of the third day. The initial wave of attacks on the first night only damaged sector and intercept operations centers (SOCs and IOCs); many SAM sites remained untouched. But the psychological impact of the first two days' attacks suppressed the effectiveness of what had survived. Enemy communication systems no longer functioned effectively; radar operators were unwilling to turn their radars on for sustained periods of time; SAM sites fired their missiles ballistically. And the continuing pressure of Coalition SEAD aircraft thoroughly intimidated

---

now consider briefly the *subjective nature* of war–the means by which war has to be fought–it will look more than ever like a gamble. . . .In short, absolute, so-called mathematical factors never find a firm basis in military calculations. From the very start, there is an interplay of possibilities, probabilities, good luck and bad that weaves its way through the length and breadth of the tapestry. In the whole range of human activities, war most closely resembles the game of cards." Clausewitz, *On War*, pp 85-86. In this case chance determined that the commanders and planners at the highest levels of the air campaign would be more than adequate.

[18]Various pieces of evidence that were available to GWAPS–enemy radar emissions, communications between parts of the defensive system, as well as the responses that the Iraqis were able to make to the attacks–suggest to those involved in the Operations and the Effectiveness reports of The Gulf War Air Power Survey that the system ceased to function during that period of time.

the defenders. A SAM site whose commander was afraid to turn on his system was as good as destroyed, at least for the purpose of attacking Coalition aircraft.

In effect, Coalition air attacks significantly increased the enemy's level of friction both relatively and absolutely. Consequently, the Iraqis confronted not only the normal frictions that occur during war, but a host of additional frictions that air attacks had imposed on their systems and combat organizations. In no fashion, especially in view of the political framework within which they operated, could the Iraqis deal with such a state of affairs. One suspects that Saddam never fully came to grips with how extensive was the damage that Coalition air attacks had achieved in their attacks on the air defense system and then on the whole military structure.

If planning and conduct of the air war in the first two days underlines the possibilities open to a coherent, operational focus, then the remainder of the war suggests some of the limitations as well as the difficulties involved in such an endeavor. The enemy, no matter how badly damaged, was able to impose frictions on the Coalition's campaign. The Scud campaign was a sure indication that no matter how well things might go, the enemy may possess unpleasant operational capabilities of his own.[19] In this case, a considerable portion of the Coalition's precision-bombing platforms pursued the will-o'-wisp of mobile Scud launchers with little evidence to suggest success.

One of the Coalition's planning assumptions had been that once air attacks had wrecked the KARI system, CENTAF could send large formations of F-16s downtown to accomplish two objectives. The first was that, even considering the inaccuracy of the F-16 bomb platform–using conventional unguided munitions from medium altitudes–such attacks could destroy large industrial targets in and around Baghdad. This would allow precision F-117s to concentrate on targets that demanded greater accuracy. Similarly, they also believed that large packages of F-16s flying downtown on a regular basis would have a significant effect on Iraqi morale. While the F-117s flew only at night, F-16s could bolster

[19] It is well to remember the extraordinary inaccuracy of the missiles. Had the Iraqi Scuds had even slightly greater accuracy, their military and political impact would clearly have increased enormously.

and prolong the daylight attack begun by the Navy's Tomahawk cruise missiles.

Unfortunately, Package Q underlined that such assumptions were dangerously flawed. Enemy air defenses in the Baghdad area *were* able significantly to threaten such attacks.[20] Then too, if one placed F-16s over densely populated areas and exposed them to the threat of SAMs, one risked the possibility that the fighter bombers, to evade SAMs, might jettison their bombs. The risk of the resulting civilian casualties was one that Coalition air commanders did not want to take. What is significant here, however, is not that Coalition commanders and planners held faulty assumptions; the crucial point is that they readily adapted to the situation as it actually was: F-16s were no longer tasked to go to downtown Baghdad.

At this point in the war, the mere presence of the Iraqi Air Force, lamed, blind, and inert in its hardened aircraft shelters, represented a sufficiently powerful threat to refocus Coalition air attacks on the shelter-busting effort. Whatever the success of that campaign in destroying hardened shelters, the number of precision weapons expended would undoubtedly have done much damage to other target sets in the strategic campaign. Considering the poor showing that the Iraqi Air Force had made in both the Iran-Iraq War and in the Gulf War, one can question whether it represented much of a threat to anyone in the Middle East. But perhaps the political value of an air fleet "in being" was such that air leaders felt constrained to eliminate the enemy's force before moving on to other targets. Here the dark memory of the Tet offensive during the Vietnam War raised fears in the minds of U.S. commanders that the Iraqis might launch a sudden, massive, and suicidal air attack that could turn the war against the Coalition–at least in a psychological sense.

As the Iraqi shelters disappeared in clouds of smoke and debris, Schwarzkopf and the looming ground campaign forced the shifting of F-111Fs to a campaign against Iraqi ground forces in the KTO. There was, in fact, no other choice, given the poor performance of nonprecision munition platforms against targets in the KTO. Since political necessity

---

[20] Although in fairness, one should note that larger SEAD support packages would probably have been able to suppress the threat of enemy SAMs. The next day, for example, a package of F-16s would reach within the environs of the Baghdad air defense system and not suffer any losses.

dictated an absolute requirement for a ground war, Coalition air power had to achieve significant reductions on the enemy ground forces before the ground war could begin. This again had an effect on the forces available to attack strategic targets with precision weapons.

But there were options beyond limiting the strategic campaign to only F-117s at this point in the war. One of the few oversights in the conduct of the air campaign was the failure to provide lasing capability to F-111Es operating from Incirlik. Only at the end of the war did F-4s from Clark Air Base arrive, but their designator pods did not reach the theater until after the war. Such a capability in Turkey would have accelerated destruction of strategic target sets.

Still the Black Hole retained considerable assets in the F-117s. Even here, friction interfered with hopes of decapitating the Iraqi leadership by sustained attacks on headquarters and command and control centers within Baghdad. The night of 12/13 February was the first of a number of nights in which planners hoped that air attacks would accomplish this objective. The Al Firdos incident, however, ended this effort before it had barely begun.

An examination of air attacks against central Baghdad suggests the parameters within which strategic attacks on the enemy's heart occurred. Over the first twenty-four hours F-117s dropped only fourteen bombs against nine targets in downtown Baghdad; thirty-nine cruise missiles were launched against six other targets.[21] Over the course of the next twenty-four hours, F-117s managed to drop only one bomb there, while the Navy launched eighteen Tomahawks against three targets. The major F-117 attack of the war against Baghdad occurred over the night of 12/13 February; F-117s struck fifteen targets with thirty-four bombs.[22] As a result of Al Firdos, there were no bombs dropped on the capital for a week.

Then, with the end of the war rapidly approaching, F-117s were to strike a few carefully selected targets in central Baghdad. While the F-117s dropped eighty-five bombs on Baghdad over the last week, they attacked only five targets, and one of those targets was Muthena airfield,

---

[21]GWAPS Database.

[22]*Ibid.*

which drew nearly one-third of their effort.[23] One senses that attacks on Muthena (and Rasheed airfield in the city's outskirts) represented an effort to keep the psychological pressure on the capital and Iraqi leadership. But the record suggests that there was no sustained attack on Baghdad as an operational focus of the campaign. There was an effort made throughout much of the war to lead the capital's population to believe that they were under siege. Nevertheless, as a coherent focus for the air effort, Baghdad faded in and out of the Coalition campaign. One must recognize that a more sustained effort against the headquarters structure of the regime might well have resulted in an Al-Firdos-like incident earlier in the war.

The Effectiveness study examines in greater detail the effects and effectiveness of Coalition air power against various targets sets, including the nuclear, chemical, and biological programs of the Iraqi regime. What assessments in that report emphasize is the fundamental uncertainties that underlay much of the conduct of the air campaign against such special targets. To begin with, intelligence was generally unclear as to the extent of Iraqi programs in these areas. Furthermore, the operators failed to query their intelligence about likely enemy countermeasures and reactions to affect or ameliorate Coalition air power. Granted, even the best intelligence in the real world would have confronted difficulties in answering what the Iraqis had done, were doing, and might do in dispersing programs in such a fashion as to make them largely invulnerable to Coalition air attacks. But the fact remains that neither intelligence nor operators made much of an effort to address, much less resolve, such questions.

Once the air campaign began, problems arose in achieving satisfactory feedback from intelligence to those who were responsible for planning the conduct of operations. It is not the responsibility of this report to assign blame; neither operations nor intelligence appears in a particularly favorable light. That problems should arise in this area is not surprising, especially considering the divorce between operations and

---

[23] *Ibid.*

intelligence that has occurred–and not just in the Air Force but in the other services as well.[24]

The air campaign against the KTO stands in stark contrast to the strategic campaign against the Iraqi heartland. Whatever difficulties and frictions arose in the conduct of the latter, there was a recognizable effort to conceptualize the operational-level employment of air power against the enemy. Throughout this report, we have catalogued efforts to focus air power to achieve larger effects in the attacks on Iraq beyond a mere racking up of targets hits. Whatever the difficulties of waging such a campaign, and they were considerable, there was an *overarching* conception.

None of the documents dealing with the air war against the KTO, however, suggest such an effort to conceptualize an operational-level air campaign against Iraqi ground forces. The planners in the Black Hole responsible for the KTO simply threw air power up against an enemy sheltered in well-dug-in positions. Every day large numbers of aircraft flew into kill boxes where the Iraqi Army had hunkered down; some dropped precision-guided munitions; others spread their loads of bombs and cluster bomb units over the landscape, in hope that if they did not hit anything then at least they would damage Iraqi morale. Whatever focus the campaign against Iraqi ground forces possessed only existed in numerical indices of aircraft committed to particular kill boxes.

In effect, the air campaign in the KTO represented a massive hammer that aimed to bludgeon enemy ground forces and combat potential into dust. In the end, the campaign was relatively successful, but only because the time and air assets that were available to attack those enemy forces were almost limitless and because Coalition commanders had so much surplus air power available to pursue their goals.

---

[24]Here it is worth noting the one intelligence organization that functioned in an exemplary fashion throughout the period leading up to the war and during the course of the war as well: namely the Navy's SPEAR. The reason for the success of that organization appears to have been the Navy's willingness to fashion SPEAR in such a fashion that both operators and intelligence officers worked together to impart the wisdom of their separate worlds to each other. Moreover, SPEAR had a clearly understood mission to serve the tactical and operational employment of naval and naval air power in combat situations.

Moreover, there was a substantial disconnect between the assumptions of those who planned and estimated the effects of an air campaign against Iraqi ground forces, and the units who actually executed the plans. In particular, Checkmate's estimates had calculated the effectiveness of a campaign against Iraqi ground forces on the basis that F-16s would use Mavericks against enemy equipment. But the F-16 community had not prepared itself in peacetime to employ that anti-tank missile and so it could not utilize that weapon in the ground war.

In the end, these difficulties with conceptualization and employment of air power in the KTO did *not* matter. The sheer magnitude of the air campaign against the Iraqi ground forces in the KTO achieved reasonable levels of destruction against the enemy's equipment in the theater. Also, the shift of the F-111Fs to "plinking" tanks finally began to deliver on the promise that air power could substantially attrit the enemy's equipment. Even more to the point was the effectiveness of the attacks in damaging the morale of the Iraqi soldier.[25] By the end of the campaign against the Iraqi ground forces in the KTO, air power had achieved much the same effect that it had achieved against Iraq's air defenses; it had broken the enemy force into its component parts and those parts could no longer put up a coherent or effective resistance.

All the squabbling about numbers of tanks and artillery pieces destroyed that occurred during the war, and which even two years later remain as a bones of contention, however, miss the point. It was not the numbers of tanks or artillery pieces destroyed, or the number of Iraqi soldiers killed that mattered. It was the effectiveness of the air campaign in breaking apart the organizational structure and cohesion of enemy military forces and in reaching the *mind* of the Iraqi soldier that counted.

---

[25]There is some irony in a comparison of the casualties caused by air attacks against Baghdad and those caused in the KTO. In the case of the former, those who were killed and wounded in the Al Firdos bunker were the family members of the elite of the Baʿthist regime (the regime did not make shelters for the general population of Baghdad–only for those with connections to the powerful); the casualties at the bunker were intimately tied to the elite who had imposed such misery not only on their own population, but those of Iran and Kuwait as well. On the other hand, most of the soldiers that Iraq deployed to Kuwait, certainly in the regular army, were conscripts who had not wanted the war, had little desire to fight, and for the most part despised the regime. The sympathy that the Al Firdos victims received does stand in some ironic contrast to the lack of sympathy that the Iraqi soldier received.

There is a larger issue here: to believe that levels of destruction of certain items of equipment guarantees success misses the nature of military organizations. Military forces reflect their human creators. The death of such an organization occurs in a biological fashion. For example, in a heart attack, death occurs not at some precisely calculable point when 30 or 40 or 50 percent of the heart muscles, heart nerves, or heart valves lose their ability to function, but rather at some inexplicable threshold when the degrading synergies between the damage to different, interrelated systems cause the general and complete collapse of the whole. For military organizations, the French author Antoine de Saint Exupèry caught this phenomenon best in his book on the 1940 campaign in France:

> In every region through which [the German *Panzers*] have made their lightning sweep, a French army, even though it seems to be virtually intact, has ceased to be an army. It has been transformed into clotted segments. It has, so to say, coagulated. The armored divisions play the part of a chemical agent precipitating a colloidal solution. Where once an organism existed they leave a mere sum of organs whose unity has been destroyed. Between the clots–however combative the clots may have remained–the enemy moves at will. An army, if it is to be effective, must be something other than a numerical sum of its soldiers.[26]

De Saint Exupèry's description of the death of French armies in 1940, although written over a half century ago, applies even more vividly to the death of Iraq's air defense system as well as the death of the Iraqi Army in the KTO.

---

[26]Antoine de Saint Exupèry, *Flight to Arras*, translated by Lewis Galantière (New York, 1942), p 56.

Appendix

Disposition of U.S. Aircraft

Airfield	Aircraft	1-Sep-90	1-Oct-90	1-Nov-90	1-Dec-90	1-Jan-91	1-Feb-91
USAF							
Abu Dhabi	KC-135	-	-	-	-	-	10
Al Ain	C-130	15	31	32	32	32	40
Al Dhafra	F-16C	46	48	48	48	72	72
	KC-135R	5	7	7	7	7	7
	RF-4C	6	6	6	6	0	18
Al Kharj	C-130	-	-	-	-	8	16
	F-15C	-	-	-	-	24	24
	F-15E	-	-	-	-	48	48
	F-16A	-	-	-	-	22	24
	F/A-16A	-	-	-	-	-	18
Al Minhad	F-16C	36	48	48	48	48	74
Bateen	C-130	16	16	16	16	16	16
	C-29	-	-	1	1	-	-
	EC-130(CC)	5	-	5	5	5	6
	EC-130H	2	5	5	5	5	8
Cairo West	KC-135E	-	-	-	-	15	15
	KC-135R	-	2	3	3	3	-
Dhahran	F-15C	48	48	48	48	48	48
Diego Garcia	B-52G	20	20	20	20	20	19
	KC-10	-	2	2	2	2	7
	KC-135R	8	6	7	5	5	5
Doha	F-16C	24	24	24	24	24	25
Dubai	KC-135	-	-	-	-	-	10
Jeddah	KC-10	-	2	2	2	2	13
	KC-135	-	-	-	-	-	66
	KC-135A/Q	-	-	-	-	20	-
	KC-135E	18	18	20	20	25	-
	KC-135R	10	20	20	20	20	-
King Fahd	A-10	72	96	96	96	114	131
	AC-130	-	5	5	4	4	3
	C-130	-	-	-	-	-	16
	C-130	-	-	-	-	-	3
	EC-130(VS)	2	2	2	2	2	2
	HC-130	4	4	4	4	4	4
	MC-130	4	4	4	4	4	4
	MH-53	4	8	8	8	-	-
	MH-60	-	8	8	8	8	-
	OA-10	-	-	-	-	6	12
King Khalid	KC-135L	-	-	-	-	-	2
	KC-135	-	-	-	-	-	46
	KC-135A	-	-	5	27	20	-
	KC-135Q	-	-	3	8	7	-
	KC-135A/Q			20	40	20	-
	KC-135R	20	20	20	5	25	-

Disposition of Aircraft (cont'd)

Airfield	Aircraft	1-Sep-90	1-Oct-90	1-Nov-90	1-Dec-90	1-Jan-91	1-Feb-91
Masirah	C-130	16	16	16	16	16	16
	F-15C	-	-	4	5	-	-
	KC-135R	-	-	2	2	10	10
Moron	B-52	-	-	-	-	-	10
Riyadh	C-20	1	1	1	1	1	-
	C-21	4	8	8	8	8	8
	E-3	6	6	6	6	7	11
	E-8	-	-	-	-	-	2
	EC-130E	3	-	6	6	4	7
	KC-135Q	10	10	10	10	10	10
	RC-135	4	4	4	4	4	7
Seeb	KC-10	-	2	2	2	2	10
	KC-135R	10	10	8	10	10	15
Shaikhisa	F-4G	24	36	36	36	48	49
	RF-4C	-	-	-	-	6	18
Sharjah	C-130	3	16	16	16	16	16
	EC-130E	6	6	-	-	-	-
Tabuk	F-15C	22	24	24	24	24	24
Taif	EF-111	10	14	14	14	18	18
	F-111F	18	32	32	52	64	64
Thumrait	C-130	16	16	16	16	16	24
	F-15E	24	24	24	24	26	48
Proven Force							
Hellenikon	RC-135	-	-	-	-	-	2
	KC-135	-	-	-	-	-	7
Incirlik	E-3A	-	-	-	-	-	3
	EC-130	-	-	-	-	-	3
	EF-111A	-	-	-	-	-	6
	F-111E	-	22	22	22	22	26
	F-15C	-	-	-	-	24	29
	F-16C	-	-	-	-	-	24
	F-16WW	-	-	-	-	-	12
	F-4G	-	-	-	-	-	13
	F-4E	-	-	-	-	-	4
	RF-4C	-	-	-	-	-	6
	C-130H	-	-	-	-	-	11
	C-130E	-	-	-	-	-	8
	EP-3	-	-	-	-	-	2
	KC-135A	-	-	-	-	-	15
Malpensa	KC-10	-	-	-	-	-	7
Zaragoza	KC-10	-	-	-	-	-	7
	KC-135	-	-	-	-	-	1
Mont de Marsen	KC-135	-	-	-	-	-	9
Mildenhall	KC-135	-	-	-	-	-	9
Andravida	KC-135	-	-	-	-	-	1

Disposition of Aircraft (cont'd)

Airfield	Aircraft	1-Sep-90	1-Oct-90	1-Nov-90	1-Dec-90	1-Jan-91	1-Feb-91
Souda Bay	RC-135	-	-	-	-	-	2
	HC-130	-	-	-	-	-	4
	MC-130	-	-	-	-	-	3
	MH-53J	-	-	-	-	-	5
USN							
America	A-6E	-	-	-	-	-	12
	E-2C	-	-	-	-	-	5
	EA-6B	-	-	-	-	-	4
	F-14	-	-	-	-	-	20
	F/A-18	-	-	-	-	-	20
	KA-6D	-	-	-	-	-	4
	S-3B	-	-	-	-	-	8
	SH-3	-	-	-	-	-	6
Independence	A-6E	13	13	13	-	-	-
	C-2A	1	1	1	-	-	-
	E-2C	4	4	4	-	-	-
	EA-6B	4	4	4	-	-	-
	F-14	18	18	18	-	-	-
	F/A-18	18	18	18	-	-	-
	S-3B	7	7	7	-	-	-
	SH-3	6	6	6	-	-	-
Kennedy	A-7	-	24	24	24	24	24
	A-6E	-	13	13	13	13	13
	E-2C	-	4	4	4	4	4
	EA-6B	-	5	5	5	5	5
	F-14	-	20	20	20	20	20
	KA-6D	-	4	4	4	4	4
	S-3B	-	8	8	8	8	8
	SH-3	-	5	5	5	5	5
Midway	A-6E	-	-	-	-	-	14
	C-2A	-	-	-	-	-	1
	E-2C	-	-	-	-	-	4
	EA-6B	-	-	-	-	-	4
	F/A-18	-	-	-	-	-	30
	KA-6D	-	-	-	-	-	4
	SH-3	-	-	-	-	-	6
Ranger	A-6E	-	-	-	-	-	24
	C-2A	-	-	-	-	-	1
	E-2C	-	-	-	-	-	4
	EA-6B	-	-	-	-	-	4
	F-14	-	-	-	-	-	22
	S-3B	-	-	-	-	-	7
	SH-3	-	-	-	-	-	6

Disposition of Aircraft (cont'd)

Airfield	Aircraft	1-Sep-90	1-Oct-90	1-Nov-90	1-Dec-90	1-Jan-91	1-Feb-91
Roosevelt	A-6E	-	-	-	-	-	18
	C-2A	-	-	-	-	-	10
	EA-6B	-	-	-	-	-	5
	F-14	-	-	-	-	-	18
	F/A-18	-	-	-	-	-	20
	S-3B	-	-	-	-	-	4
	SH-3	-	-	-	-	-	6
Saratoga	A-6E	-	-	-	14	14	14
	E-2C	-	-	-	4	4	4
	EA-6B	-	-	-	4	4	4
	F-14	-	-	-	19	19	19
	F/A-18	-	-	-	18	18	18
	KA-6D	-	-	-	4	4	4
	S-3B	-	-	-	10	10	10
	SH-3	-	-	-	6	6	6
***USMC**							
King Abdul Aziz	AV-8B	40	40	40	40	60	59
	OV-10A/D	-	8	8	8	8	19
Sheik Isa	A-6E	9	10	10	10	20	20
	EA-6B	12	12	12	12	12	12
	F/A-18A/C	48	48	48	48	72	72
	F/A-18D	-	-	-	-	-	6
	KC-130	6	8	8	8	12	15
Al Jabail	AH-1T/W/J	34	39	40	28	28	39
	CH-46E	15	24	24	24	24	60
	CH-53D	12	20	20	20	20	29
	CH-53E	8	15	15	15	15	24
	UH-1N	18	18	18	18	18	30
Afloat	AH-1T/W/J	-	6	7	15	15	36
	AV-8B	-	20	20	20	21	25
	CH-46E	-	36	36	24	48	60
	CH-53E	-	20	20	14	18	24
	UH-1N	-	10	8	6	18	20
USA							
Unknown	AH-1S	4	48	82	84	112	141
	AH-64	46	108	144	146	189	245
	CH-47	-	49	84	84	99	127
	OH-58C	40	119	175	178	257	324
	OH-58D	21	43	56	59	79	97
	UH-1H	4	50	127	127	169	202
	UH-60	52	152	205	206	279	303

Source: "Desert Shield CSAF Briefings," GWAPS Folders #32-#35; USCINCCENT SITREPS; USCINCENTAF SITREPS; CMSgt J.E. Schroeder, USAF, "History of Joint Task Force Proven Force (U), 27 Dec-7 Jan 91, Vol I – Narrative," HQ USAFE/HO, Ramstein AB, Germany.

*HQMC Monthly Operations Summaries (S).